OPERATION WORLD

A Handbook for World Intercession

P. J. Johnstone

STL PUBLICATIONS
P.O. Box 48
Bromley, Kent, England

© 1978, Dorothea Mission, 179 Coldharbour Rd., Bristol BS6 7SX
All rights reserved.
1st British edition 1978
2nd. British edition 1979

Published by Send The Light Trust,
P.O. Box 48,
Bromley, Kent BR1 1BY, England

ISBN's 0 903843 08 0 (paperback)
      0 903843 09 9 (hardback)

Printed in Great Britain by
Lowe & Brydone Printers Limited
Thetford, Norfolk

CONTENTS

ALPHABETICAL INDEX OF COUNTRIES

There are about 223 separate states or territories in the world. We have omitted those with insignificant populations. We have included 190 in this survey. This list is therefore not complete. We mention also a number of better known names of territories that are obsolete, or have been incorporated into larger states; this being indicated by the name being indented. Those in small type no longer exist as a separate political entity. The new name, or state into which the territory is incorporated, follows in brackets.

Page No.   *Page No.*

FOREWORD

He who reads this book with real application of heart and mind to its contents will find that he cannot remain indifferent to the great task of proclaiming the Gospel in the world. He will be stirred to pray and spurred to action. The thrust of the book can be found in the words on page 27:

"This is certainly not the time to give up, but to mobilise the believers of the world to finish the task."

On nearly every page facts and figures will be found that bear this out.

Reading a survey like this, a believer is caught up in a new way in the excitement of the love of God moving out to a lost world. He understands more of the tremendous battle taking place between the forces of light and darkness in this very decade. What an impact the Gospel is making! He finds his heart moving out in sympathy for a world in the travail of tremendous political and spiritual upheavals. He cannot help but adore the power of Him who first sent out a small band of apostles from a small country and whose Name became a worldwide and eternal blessing to millions. He senses how far we have moved forward in the march of the ages towards the return of the Lord Jesus Christ in glory.

The favourable reaction we have received from many parts of the world to the first edition of the book has greatly encouraged us. It has proved to be a book with an impact.

One of the reasons for this is that the writer himself is caught up as a missionary in the fulfilling of the last command of our great Lord and King: "Go ye therefore . . ." As in the case of the first edition, one is impressed by the proficient way in which Mr. Patrick Johnstone has gathered together a mass of information and ordered and spiritually evaluated all the different facts.

This foreword is also an appropriate place for the Dorothea Mission to thank him for his dedicated work, which has the glory of God and the extension of His Kingdom as its aim.

We lay down this book at the feet of Him who hears and answers prayer and to whom all flesh shall come (Ps. 65:2) for His blessing upon it so that it may become a blessing to the world.

Hans von Staden
(Director, Dorothea Mission)

PREFACE

Why Operation World?

The Dorothea Mission evangelistic teams in various African countries have, since 1943, sought to bring lost sinners to a saving knowledge of Jesus Christ as their Saviour and Lord, and to then link them up with fellowships of believers. Then God began to show us with greater clarity that no evangelistic campaign however successful, and no army of preachers however fervent could gain spiritual victories on the vast scale needed in today's darkening world. Only prayer could possibly achieve this – the powerful united prayers of believing people all over the world.

The Lord then led the Director of our Mission, Hans von Staden, to initiate *Weeks of Prayer for the World* to which believers could come with the one aim of taking time to meet together in intercession for the countries of the world and the extending of the Kingdom of God. Over the years, an increasing number of these Weeks of Prayer have been held in different countries of Africa and Europe. With these came an increased demand for adequate information to stimulate intelligent and directed prayer. The years of information gathering eventually led to the compiling of the first edition of *Operation World* and its printing on our Mission press in 1974.

This limited first edition, with all its faults, seems to have helped to fill an unmet need for simplified information for the ordinary believer on the state of the missionary cause all over the world. After we received requests from Christian organisations in a number of countries for a reprinting of *Operation World*, I felt it essential that the old edition be completely revised. It is now probable that this second edition will be printed in a number of languages and lands.

This book has been completely rewritten, and we send it out with the fervent prayer that the Lord Jesus Christ may be glorified and the evangelisation of the world furthered thereby.

The Coverage of Operation World

I have sought to give background information and basic prayer needs on every country of the world. This book has to be brief, but is already longer than intended. I have therefore cut out all details and personalities that do not emphasise the major overall needs. There are inevitably two dangers in any such work:
1) The increasingly rapid changes in the modern world quickly date the information. However I trust that this book will be of value for most countries for the next few years.
2) The condensation of information is such that distortions, sweeping statements and omissions are inevitable, and errors and uncharitable comments likely. For every mistake I ask your forgiveness. Please feel free to correct any such that you may find, and I will gladly make the necessary changes in any future edition should the Lord so lead.

Acknowledgements

It is manifestly impossible to quote all sources of information in a book of this size. I have used thousands of prayer circulars and missionary magazines sent out by the Missions and Agencies listed on subsequent pages. To all these worthy organisations I express my deep gratitude.

I have also written personal letters to Christian workers in many lands, and from them received information of inestimable value. I thank you all for sparing your valuable time for this ministry.

I have also used many books, but only a few of these can I acknowledge in our Introduction. My prayer is that all who have assisted in this project with advice, information and criticism may find their ministries enriched through the prayers stimulated by this book that they have helped to make a reality.

Finally, I give thanks again to the Lord for His undertaking and grace in bringing this work to completion.

Patrick J. St.G. Johnstone
Dorothea Mission
179 Coldharbour Rd.,
Bristol BS6 7SX.

INTRODUCTION

The Spiritual Nature of our Warfare

There are many facts in the pages that follow. Some tell of encouraging advances, and others of great hindrances in the LORD'S WORK. So it is good that we remind ourselves that we must not look at these things from a human standpoint, but a heavenly one.
FOR THOUGH WE LIVE IN THE WORLD, WE ARE NOT CARRYING ON A WORLDLY WAR, FOR THE WEAPONS OF OUR WARFARE ARE NOT WORLDLY BUT HAVE DIVINE POWER TO DESTROY STRONGHOLDS . . . 2 Cor. 3, 4.
FOR WE ARE NOT CONTENDING AGAINST FLESH AND BLOOD, BUT AGAINST THE PRINCIPALITIES, AGAINST THE POWERS, AGAINST THE WORLD RULERS OF THIS PRESENT DARKNESS, AGAINST THE SPIRITUAL HOSTS OF WICKEDNESS IN THE HEAVENLY PLACES . . . Eph. 6:12.
There is a war in the spiritual realm, but it is a war already won by the Lord Jesus on Calvary. This victory is only applied to the present world need as we perseveringly and believingly pray. As we pray, we stand on victory ground, and can shout the Hallelujah of victory whatever seeming setbacks and trials come upon the work of God. We are therefore optimists because:

1. It is based on the FACT that God is in control. All history is His story. Even the nations are, to Him, as a drop in the bucket and even the wrath of man praises Him. God has worked in power in the past, and we know that He will continue to do so, for He is unchanging (Is. 40:15; Ps. 76:10; Heb. 13:8).

2. It is based on the PROMISES OF GOD IN THE BIBLE. He promises us the ministry of the Holy Spirit in prayer and service. He promises that there will be representatives of every race and tribe and tongue before His throne to praise Him. He promises that prayer is effectual. His promises cannot be broken. (Lk. 24:49; Rom. 8:26–27; Rev. 7:9–10: Jas. 5:16).

3. It is based on the COMMAND OF JESUS HIMSELF. He commanded us to preach the Gospel to every creature in every nation. This commandment must be a possibility for us as we are moved by the Holy Spirit in obedience to His will. (Matt. 28:18–20; Mark 16:15).

4. It is based on the imminent RETURN OF THE LORD JESUS IN GLORY. He promises revival in the last days. Although much of nominal and organised Christianity may be dead in that day, Jesus is coming to take a mighty, powerful, revived Church to be with Him in Heaven for evermore (Joel 2:28–29; Eph. 5:27; I John 3:2–4).

Prayer is a mystery. God is all powerful, yet He desires our prayers to accomplish His work in the world. A prayer inspired by the Holy Spirit has a part in forming the eternal decrees of God. Prayer unites puny man to Almighty God in a miraculous partnership. Prayer moves the Hand that made and upholds the Universe. It is the most noble and most essential ministry God gives to His children – but is the most neglected. May God make us real intercessors as we turn to the world in its great need.

How to Use This Book

It is intended that this book should give sufficient background information to enable you to pray intelligently about that which you read in newspapers, missionary prayer circulars and magazines. We pray that this information may fill this gap, and also challenge you with the great need for prayer for the world.

This information can help in both private and corporate prayer, but was originally gathered to provide prayer fuel for **Weeks of Prayer for the World**. We therefore add a few hints and also warnings to those who may be called on to provide information for a prayer group.

1. **Be brief** – the people are gathered to PRAY, and not to be impressed by the amount of information presented! Only a quarter to one third of the time should be set aside for reporting on the need.

2. **Be personal** – we have deliberately refrained from mentioning individuals, but rather to give the overall situation in a given country. Personal information on individual workers, etc. can be added by the leader.

3. **Be selective** – Too many facts will not be retained unless they are written down. Rather select those items for prayer that will challenge and burden believers long after the meeting.

4. **Beware of statistics.** Too many figures make any report very dull! Only choose those statistics that specifically apply to the prayer items you mention. The many figures are given so that you may have the facts available.

5. **Be dependent** – on the leading of the Holy Spirit. Only the burdens imparted by Him will inspire others to pray in the Spirit, and then move them into God's will for their lives – in intercession, giving and even going to that area or people as a missionary.

How to obtain more prayer information

This book is only intended to be a catalyst to link you with the world that needs Jesus. Please seek out more prayer information – through reading missionary books, and writing to organisations and missions mentioned below for regular prayer circulars and magazines. This book goes out with the prayer that many all over the world may get involved in the missionary task. So please avail yourself of some of the addresses below as the Lord leads you.

General Prayer Information covering the whole world and many missions:

1. **Evangelical Missionary Alliance Information Service,** 19 Draycott Place, London SW3 2SJ., England.
2. **"LOOK"** and **"KOINONIA"** edited by L. Brierley of Worldwide Evangelisation Crusade, Bulstrode, Gerrards Cross, Bucks SL9 8S7, England.
3. **MISSIONARY MANDATE** (6 times a year) under auspices of the E.M.A. Lancing Tabernacle, 1 Grand Ave., Lancing, Sussex, England.
4. **WORLD VISION MAGAZINE** (monthly), 919 West Huntingdon Dr., Monrovia, CA 91016, U.S.A.
5. **Evangelical Missions Information Service**, Box 794, Wheaton, IL 60187, U.S.A.

Prayer Information given by some more significant Evangelical Missions
It is quite impossible to mention all the worthy missions and denominations that have contributed so much to the evangelisation of the world. I have therefore rarely mentioned the names of specific denominations unless their contribution has been very great. In the selected list that follows I have not mentioned the addresses of denominational missions, since interest in their work will largely be confined to members of that group, and they are well able to obtain the information for prayer from their own mission boards.

Further, I have chosen around 60 significant interdenominational missions and agencies for specific mention in this book and in the accounts of the different countries that follow. In these missions serve about 30% of all Protestant missionaries. Please forgive me if some groups worthy of mention have been excluded. I believe that all these missions value prayer support more than anything else, so do not hesitate to contact them.

There are about 1,100 Protestant missionary or aid sending agencies in the world. About 150 have sending bases in Great Britain, and 620 in the U.S.A.

The Missionary Societies Mentioned in this book:

The agencies with a sending base in Britain are written in BOLD TYPE.

The abbreviations for each mission are used throughout the book.

The penultimate column of figures gives the approximate number of missionaries from Britain serving overseas, or in a cross cultural ministry from home base.

The final column of figures gives the approximate number of missionaries from all over the world serving with these organisations.

		U.K. miss.	World miss.
ABC	**Afghan Border Crusade** 36 Brookwell Close, Chippenham, Wilts. SN15 1PJ	4	9
AE	**Africa Enterprise** P.O. Box 988, Pasadena, CA 91102, U.S.A.	–	16
AEF	**Africa Evangelical Fellowship** 30 Lingfield Rd., London SW19 4PU	38	339
AEM	**Andes Evangelical Mission** 41 Boulton Rd., Reading, Berks RG2 0NT	13	85
AIM	**Africa Inland Mission** 43 Blackstock Rd., Finsbury Park, London N4 2JH	77	491
AO	**Asian Outreach** P.O. Box, 13448, Hong Kong	–	10
BEM	**Belgian Evangelical Mission** P.O. Box 101, Worthing, West Sussex BN11 1AA	15	104
BMMF	**Bible and Medical Missionary Fellowship** 352 Kennington Rd., London SE11 4LF	125	300
CAM	**Central American Mission** 8625 La Prada Drive, Dallas, TX 75228, U.S.A.	–	252
CCC	**Campus Crusade for Christ** 105 London Rd., Reading, Berks., RG1 5BY	66	217
CEF	**Child Evangelism Fellowship** Barkers Chambers, Barker St., Shrewsbury, Salop SY1 1SB	7	146
CFC	**Cambodia For Christ** 19 Edale Moor, Liden, Swindon, Wilts SN3 6LT		
CLC	**Christian Literature Crusade** The Dean, Alresford, Hampshire SO24 9BJ	103	103+
CMA	**Christian and Missionary Alliance** 27 Wilfred Gardens, Ashby-de-la-Zouche, Leics., LE6 5GX	3	920
CMCW	**Christian Mission to the Communist World** P.O. Box 19, Bromley, Kent BR1 1DJ	–	–
DM	**Dorothea Mission** 179 Coldharbour Rd., Bristol BS6 7SX	15	108
ECF	**Evangelize China Fellowship** 3 The Brae, Groomsport, Bangor, Co. Down BT19 2JG	–	10
ECM	**European Christian Mission** Heightside, Newchurch Rd., Rossendale, Lancs BB4 9HQ	?	125
EUSA	**Evangelical Union of South America** 6 Novar Rd., London SE9 2DW	79	80+
FEBA	**Far East Broadcasting Association** 45 High St., Addlestone, Weybridge, Surrey KT15 1TU	34	60
FFM	**Fellowship of Faith for the Muslims** 13 Stemmels Rd., Halesowen, West Midlands B62 8QJ	–	–

		U.K. miss.	World miss.
GEM	**Greater Europe Mission** 1516 East Roosevelt, Wheaton IL 60187, U.S.A.	–	172
GMU	**Gospel Missionary Union** Drawer C., Smithville, MO 64089, U.S.A.	–	450
GRF	**Gospel Recordings Fellowship** Block 12E, Gloucester Trading Estate, Hucclecote, Glos., GL3 4AA	8	110
ICF	**International Christian Fellowship** 20 Vicarage Farm Rd., Hounslow, Middlesex TW3 4NW	38	100
IEM	**Indian Evangelical Mission** 4 Kingston Rd., Bangalore 560025, India	–	65
IM	**International Missions** 61 Bath St., Leicester LE4 7QE	10	200
IMF	**Indonesian Missionary Fellowship** Institut Injil Indonesia, Batu, Malang, E. Java, Indonesia		60?
INF	**International Nepal Fellowship** 25 Upper High St., Epsom, Surrey KT18 5AQ	41	57
IVF	**Intervarsity Fellowship** (affiliated to International Fell. of Evangelical Students **IFES**). Now known as **UCCF** (Universities and Colleges Chr. Fell. of Evang. Unions), 38 de Montfort St., Leicester LE1 7GP	3	40
JEB	**Japan Evangelistic Band** 26 Woodside Park Rd., London N12 8RR	13	54
JOMA	**Japanese Overseas Missionary Association**	–	40
JM	**Japan Mission** (for Hospital Evangelism) 44 Weald Rd., Brentwood, Essex, CM14 4TH	2	57
LAM	**Latin American Mission** P.O. Box 341368, Coral Gables FL 33134, U.S.A.	–	160
LM	**Leprosy Mission** 50 Portland Place, London WIN 3DG	?	100
MAF	**Missionary Aviation Fellowship** 3 Beechcroft Rd., South Woodford, London E18 1BJ	27	173
MECO	**Middle East Christian Outreach** (LEM, MEGM, ALM union) 22 Culverdon Park Rd., Tunbridge Wells, TN4 9RA	22	35
NAM	**North Africa Mission** 12 Devonshire Square, Loughborough, Leics., LE11 3DW	32	107
NTM	**New Tribes Mission** 3 Tudor Drive, Belfast BT6 9LS, Northern Ireland	?	1,150
OD	**Open Doors** with Brother Andrew P.O. Box 6, Standlake, Witney, Oxon OX8 7SP	–	–
OM	**Operation Mobilisation** 142 Dantzic St., Manchester M4 4DN	200	1,040
OMF	**Overseas Missionary Fellowship** (+ **Borneo Evang. Mission**) Belmont, The Vine, Sevenoaks, Kent TN13 3TZ	316	950
OMS	**OMS International** 1 Sandileigh Ave., Didsbury, Manchester M20 9LN	29	450

		U.K. miss.	World miss.
QIM	**Qua Iboe Mission**		
	Room 317, 7 Donegall Square West, Belfast BT1 6JE	29	29
RBMU	**Regions Beyond Missionary Union**		
	Harley House, 99 Thurleigh Rd., London SW12 8TY	46	174
RSMT	**Red Sea Mission Team**		
	33–35 The Grove, Finchley, London N3 1QU	28	60
SGM	**Scripture Gift Mission**		
	Radstock House, 3 Eccleston St., London SW1W 9LZ	–	–
SIM	**Sudan Interior Mission**		
	84 Beulah Hill, Upper Norwood, London SE19 3EP	95	1,180
SU	**Scripture Union**		
	47 Marylebone Lane, London WIM 6AX	13	200
SUM	**Sudan United Mission**		
	75 Granville Rd., Sidcup, Kent DA14 4BU	143	520
TEAM	**The Evangelical Alliance Mission**		
	400 South Main Place, Carol Stream, IL 60187, U.S.A.	–	1,005
TEAR	**Fund, The Evangelical Alliance Relief Fund**		
	1 Bridgeman Rd., Teddington, Middlesex TW11 9AJ	124	124
TWR	**Trans World Radio**		
	175 Tower Bridge Rd., London SE1 2AS	12	329
UE	**Underground Evangelism**		
	16 Morden Rd., London SW19 3BJ	–	–
UFM	**Unevangelised Fields Mission**		
	9 Gunnersby Ave., London W5 3NL	83	529
WBT	**Wycliffe Bible Translators**		
	Horsleys Green, Stokenchurch, High Wycombe, Bucks	119	3,823
WEC	**Worldwide Evangelisation Crusade**		
	Bulstrode, Gerrards Cross, Bucks., SL9 8SZ	305	955
WIM	**West Indies Mission**		
	P.O. Box 343038, Coral Gables, FL 33134, U.S.A.	–	307
WRMF	**World Radio Missionary Fellowship**		
	63a Main St., Bingley, West Yorkshire BD16 2HZ	9	325
WV	**World Vision International**		
	919 West Huntingdon Drive, Monrovia, CA 91016, U.S.A.	–	21
YWAM	**Youth With a Mission**		
	P.O. Box 44, Crawley, West Sussex RH10 4ES	?	1,190
		2,956	19,686

These 19,686 missionaries represent 34% of the world total.

The 2,956 British missionaries represent 50% of all British missionaries serving overseas.

Defining our Terms
Abbreviations

Apart from the abbreviations used for missions mentioned on the previous page, there are the following:

*	See **Unreached Peoples** (page 20)	
BCC	**Bible Correspondence Courses** See page 30.	
EiD	**Evangelism in Depth** }	Both being forms of Saturation Evangelism (page 32)
NLFA	**New Life For All** }	

NT   **New Testament**

TEE   **Theological Education by Extension** (page 32)

There are several much misunderstood words that we must seek to define, for they are often used in this book.

Revival

Revival is not an evangelistic campaign. It is the restoring to life of believers and churches that have previously experienced the life of God in being born again of the Spirit, but who have become cold, worldly and ineffective. It is the greatest need of the Church of the Lord Jesus Christ. Revival will later affect the unbelievers. Revival cannot be organised, for it is given by our Sovereign God when He sees fit and in answer to prayer.

Awakening or Outpouring of the Spirit

The moving of the Spirit of God on a whole area or nation on both believers and unbelievers.

People Movement

A mass movement of a non-Christian group, tribe or nation into the churches. This is often a group decision. It is a wonderful opportunity to win and disciple many for the Lord if there are sufficient believers to lead them to a personal experience of the new birth, and teach them how to go on in the Lord. It can also be a great danger, for failure to adequately disciple them can rapidly lead to a nominal and syncretic church.

Church

Church with a capital "C" is used for the whole company of believers in the world or particular area, and also for the names of specific denominations.

Church with a small "c" is used for a local fellowship of believers. Where the name of a church is followed by initials in brackets, this indicates the parent mission.

Evangelism

The preaching of the Gospel to the unconverted in such a way that they are clearly and understandably presented with its message so that they have the opportunity to accept or reject the Lord Jesus Christ as their Saviour and Lord. The work of an evangelist is not complete until those evangelised are so discipled as to become, in turn, evangelists (compare 2 Tim. 2:1-2 with 2 Tim. 4:5).

Missionary

One who is sent with a message; having the same root meaning as the word "apostle" in the N.T. The missionary is one commissioned by a local church to evangelise, plant churches and disciple people away from his home area and often among people of a different race, culture or language.

Present usage is rather different. We now use this term solely for those who cross a cultural, linguistic or national boundary in order to evangelise and disciple people.

Yet in these days all our definitions are inadequate, and statistical numbers of missionaries misleading! Many who are classified as missionaries are technically not missionaries – administrators or involved in purely philanthropic work. Then others, again, are not classified as missionaries, yet from within a "tentmaking" ministry, are able to do a better job of evangelising and discipling than those who are!

Unreached Peoples

Definable units of society with common characteristics (geographical, tribal, social, etc.) that **either:**

Have not heard sufficient of the message of the Gospel within their own culture, and in their own language so as to make Christianity a meaningful alternative to their present religion and life style.

or: Have not responded to the Gospel message because of lack of opportunity, or because of rejection of the message to the extent that there is no significant group of believers effectively communicating the message to their own people. (Derived from MARC (**WV**)'s **Unreached Peoples Directory** which lists 413 such unreached peoples. Of these, 200 are described in **Unreached Peoples Folders**. Those referred to in this book are marked by *). Please write to WV for such, should you desire this information.

The Statistics Presented Here

I have sought to obtain, as far as possible, consistent and accurate figures for populations, religions and for the Christian Church. There are many points at which care is necessary – at the source, varying dates of publication and in the final editing and compilation. Likewise care is necessary by those who subsequently use the figures. I trust that the figures here presented will give a balanced picture of the world and its spiritual need.

Unexpanded statistics often obscure the real issues. For example, to quote a single example: thus to say that Denmark is 96% Protestant may be true, but one also needs to add that only a very small percentage of this number are born-again believers. In order to give a better gauge of the spiritual life of a nation and of the Protestant Church, we have made an estimate of the size of the Evangelical community in each country (see below for our methodology). This will help Evangelical Christians to gain a clearer picture of the unfinished task of winning the world. These figures form the basis of many of the conclusions drawn in this book, and also for the shading used in the area maps.

Major Statistical Sources

Primary Source -- numerous letters, communications, interviews and other documents from individual Christian workers and mission societies.

Secondary Sources – we have consulted the following:

a) **General Statistics**
   1976 "World Population Data Sheet" (Population Reference Bureau, Washington, U.S.A.)
   1975/6 **Statesman's Year Book**, edited by J. Paxton (MacMillan, U.K.).
   1976 **Book of the World** (Tandem, U.K.).

b) **Christian Statistics**
   1968 **World Christian Handbook**
   1974 **Country Profiles** (1974 International Congress on World Evangelism, Lausanne).
   Africa: **Frontier Situations for Evangelisation in Africa 1972** – David Barrett.
   Latin America: **Latin American Church Growth** by Read, Monterroso & Johnson (Eerdmans 1969).
   Asia: **The Church in Asia**, edited by D. Hoke (Moody 1975).

c) **Christian Missions**
   A Global View of Missions by J. H. Kane (Baker U.S.A., 1971).
   1973 **U.K. Protestant Missions Handbook**, edited by P. W. Brierley (E.M.A., U.K.).
   1976 **North American Protestant Ministries Overseas**, edited by E. R. Dayton (MARC).

We must now define the different terms we use for Christians in this book:

1. **Protestant percentages** – These are usually obtained from government sources. This represents the total of those who claim to be adherents of one or another Protestant denomination. This is usually higher than the figure for the Protestant community except in lands where persecution is severe.

2. **Protestant community** – This is the approximate number of people given by the various denominations for those affiliated to them. This includes the children of believers and those who regularly attend church. This figure is necessary to make a fair comparison between churches that baptise children, and those who do not. This is usually 2-3 times that of the Protestant adult membership.

3. **Protestant membership** – This refers to those who are full adult members of the various denominations. We have only sparingly used this figure, because it often gives a distorted picture. Some churches constantly revise their lists of members, while others retain names of backsliders for years. In some lands full membership is much higher than the average Sunday attendance, and in others less.

4. **Evangelical community** – This survey includes, for the first time, estimates of the total strengths of the Evangelical community within Protestantism in each country. We define **Evangelicals** as those Protestants and Anglicans who hold a conservative evangelical view of the Bible and who emphasise commitment to personal faith, conversion and evangelism. Our figure for Evangelicals in each country includes the following categories:

a) The entire community of Christians, consisting of church members and their children, of all denominations that are conservative evangelical in doctrine and emphasis.

b) The proportion of the total community of all other Protestant denominations and Anglican dioceses who individually are Evangelicals even though their denomination is not.

c) The proportion of the total community of denominations in the Third World (where doctrinal positions are less well defined) that would be regarded as Evangelicals by those in the above categories.

Our method should not be construed as implying that all who claim that they are Evangelicals are born again, nor does it mean that all born-again people are included in this figure, for an increasing number of Christians in non-Protestant churches are testifying to the evangelical experience of the new birth. Our method does, however, give a reasonably objective measure of the size of the Evangelical community in relation to other branches of the Christian Church. It also illustrates that there are considerably more Evangelicals than has hitherto been realised.

The statistics of Evangelicals in this book were calculated by myself together with David Barrett, editor of the **World Christian Encyclopedia** (Oxford University Press: forthcoming), using our joint mass of data on the subject. Some of the documentation behind these figures is given here in **Operation World**, and also, in more detail together with exact methodology and the data for every denomination on which our figures were based, in the Encyclopedia. The figures I give will differ slightly in places from those in the Encyclopedia because of a number of small differences of definition; for example, my figures of Evangelicals include Anglicans and some indigenous churches holding Evangelical views on the Scriptures; in the Encyclopedia these are enumerated separately.

I. THE WORLD

BACKGROUND

Area: 143 million sq. km. (including Antarctica).

Population: 4,019 million in 1976. It was about 1,590 million in 1900, and will be 6,214 million in 2000 A.D. if the present 1.8% annual rate of increase continues. Yet it seems as if the population growth rate is slowing. Average number of people per sq. km. – 30. Every year there are 121 million born.

Peoples: There are about 223 states and territories in the world, and about 5,770 different languages spoken.

Urbanisation:23% – 163 cities of over one million inhabitants in which live 9% of the world's population. The urban population is growing rapidly and is strategic for the spread of the Gospel. Proportionately, too little evangelical missionary work has been directed to the cities in the past.

Economy: The most rapid rate of population growth is in the poor and hungry "Third World" of Asia, Africa and South America. The future there is generally bleak, with large scale famines imminent in some areas. The richer nations become richer and the poorer ones more poor. The world economy still continues to reel under the devastating impact of the Oil Crisis with its fourfold increase in the price of crude oil in 1974 and massive redistribution of the world's wealth. The economic future is not bright.

Politics: Post-war nationalisms have helped to break up old empires and nations. The spread of two brands of Communism that differ only in methods for world subversion and conquest have conversely speeded the formation of vast new political power blocs. The widespread and indiscriminate distribution of terrifying weapons of war have greatly increased the number of violent conflicts and local wars. The world is "shrinking" through satellite television, air travel, rising literacy and the intercontinental migrations of peoples. An event in one part of the world can quickly affect every continent. We truly live in serious days – yet God has put us here for such a time as this – for there are unparalleled opportunities to witness.

Religion: These figures below are an approximate indication only!

Secularists, Atheists, etc. 24% – largely in the Communist countries, but also an increasing number in the Western World.

Animists 3.4% – largely in Africa with pockets in Asia and Latin America. Yet possibly 40% of the world's population are influenced by animism (ancestor worship, appeasement of spirits and witchcraft). Animism underlies the basic belief of most Hindus, the ancient religions of China, etc., and there is hardly a major religion in the world untainted by it – Buddhism in Asia, Islam in Indonesia, etc., Roman Catholicism in Latin America, Protestantism in Africa. There is a great upsurge of witchcraft and demonism in Europe and North America.

Hindus 13% – the majority religion of three nations.

Buddhists 8% – 7 nations in S.E. Asia recognise this as the state religion. The rise of nationalism has revitalised Buddhism, and several forms of Buddhism are now actively propagated in the West.

Jews 0.44% – totalling 18 million. 58% of these are in the Western World, 22% in Communist lands and only 11.7% in their national homeland, Israel.

Muslims 17% – totalling 700,000,000 – most living in the great belt of land stretching from the Atlantic coast of North Africa to deep in central Asia and the South Pacific. It is the majority religion of 35 countries. Through the centuries Islam has been Christianity's greatest and most successful opponent and also the hardest field for the Christian missionary.

Christians 33%. It is reckoned that in 1900, 29% of the world was nominally Christian. There has been a decline in absolute percentages in the Western World, but an increase elsewhere. Christianity is the major religion of 5 of the 8 areas into which we have divided the world. Christianity has truly become a world religion! Though only a small proportion of these could possibly be classified as born again Christians.

Christianity is subdivided into:—

Roman Catholics 19% or 765 million, and numerically strong in Europe, Latin America, parts of Africa and the Philippines in Asia. Roman Catholic growth has been greater in many lands due to the huge investment of money and missionary manpower, but this has been at the expense of quality – with much superficiality among their converts. Internal tensions plus the erosion of papal authority and credibility spell future trials for this body. The charismatic movement has profoundly affected the R.C. Church, with now possibly two million charismatics in the R.C. Church. The liberalising Vatican II Council has radically altered the course of the Church. It is difficult to predict how this will affect Roman Catholicism.

Orthodox Churches 4% or 155 million. Strong in Eastern Europe and remnants in the Muslim Middle East.

Independent Churches 0.6–1.0% – a growing phenomenon in the Third World, where churches are springing up totally independently of the Western missionary movement. Largely in Africa.

Protestants 9.5% or 380 million (including the 68 million Anglicans). Strongest in North America, Northern Europe, parts of Africa and also the Pacific. Growth of the Protestant Church in the Third World has often been dramatic, though nominalism in the areas earlier evangelised is a serious problem. A significant part of Protestantism are the Evangelicals.

Evangelicals 3.6% or 160 million adherents of churches and denominations within Protestantism. Just under half of this number would be communicant members of these churches.

Distibution of Evangelicals:—

		Percentage of area's population	
Western World	49 %	13 %
Africa	17 %	,, ,,	8 %
Latin America	12 %	,, ,,	6 %
Communist Bloc	9 %	,, ,,	1.1%
Asia	9 %	,, ,,	1.1%
The Pacific	2.3%	,, ,,	17 %
The Caribbean	1.2%	,, ,,	6 %
The Middle East	0.3%	,, ,,	0.2%

The Worldwide Spread of the Gospel

Protestants 200 years ago were confined to Northern Europe and the Atlantic seaboard of North America, with a few outposts in the Caribbean, South Africa, Dutch East Indies (Indonesia) and India (see map). Then came the Moravian and Methodist Revivals that gave birth to the modern missionary movement. The amazing failure of earlier Protestants to obey the command of the Lord Jesus in Matt. 28:18-20 has been counterbalanced by the astonishing success of subsequent missionaries to take the Gospel to every part of the known world. The missionary vision began in the Western lands, but is now being taken up by the daughter churches in the other continents.

The initial missionary outreach had its fervour blunted during the 19th Century by the deadening effects of humanistic ideas and liberal theology. Later missionaries were often not evangelical. God then raised up many new interdenominational missions to take the

THE WORLD 1978

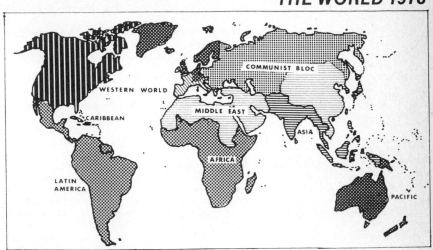

Evangelical Community as percentage of population

20 – 25	10 – 19	5 – 9	2 – 5	1 – 2
0·5 – 0·9	0·2 – 0·5	0·1 – 0·2	0 – 0·1	

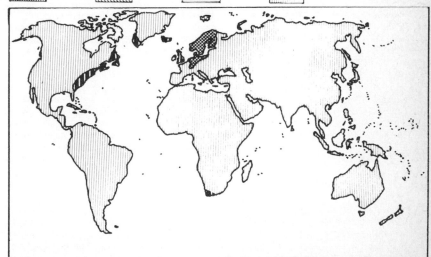

THE WORLD 1778

Gospel to the world to supplement the earlier work of the pioneering missions. As a result, churches have been planted all over the world; some are weak and introspective, while others are spiritually strong and growing fast. In the churches in Asia, Africa and South America there is often more love for the Lord, more sacrificial giving and service, and more effective outreach than in those of the Western World.

The success of this outreach can be seen in the above figures

1) There are now more evangelical Christians outside the lands of the West than in them, yet 200 years ago virtually all the world's evangelical believers were to be found in the West. Please study the maps on page 25.
2) The growth of Evangelicalism in Africa, Latin America and parts of Asia continues at a rate far higher than the population growth.
3) Africa is rapidly becoming, nominally, a Christian continent – more than half of Black Africa now claims to be Christian.
4) The continued survival and rapid growth of the churches in nearly all Communist lands is miraculous.

The pessimism of many Christians in the West about the decline of Christianity is not based on reality, though there is a great declension visible in the Western World.

The Mission Field Today

The **World** is the mission field (Matt. 13:38). Too long we have divided the world into mission sending lands and mission receiving lands. The Scriptural picture is for **churches** to send missionaries, and for the **world** to receive them! ALL the churches in the world have a responsibility for evangelising ALL the world. Asians and Africans have just as much a responsibility to evangelise the needy areas of Europe as vice versa. Praise God, that this is what is happening. Just as the centre of gravity of Evangelical Christianity has now shifted from the lands of the West to the Third and Communist Worlds, so also is the proportion of missionaries being sent out by these areas steadily increasing. This vision must grow so that all Christians all over the world see and understand that they have a part to play in the fulfilling of the Great Commission. This is the reason for this book. The approximate numbers of missionaries sent out by churches in the 8 major regions of the world are given below, though the figures for the Third World are very difficult to obtain, and may be too conservative.

Missionaries from the Western World			Missionaries from the Third World		
North America	30,300	(53.8%)	Asia	2,200	(3.9%)
Europe	14,700	(26.1%)	Africa	1,830	(3.2%)
Australasia	3,700	(6.5%)	S. America	960	(1.7%)
Southern Africa	1,600	(2.8%)	Oceania	620	(1.1%)
			Middle East	130	(0.2%)
	50,300	(89.9%)		5,840	(10.1%)

There are therefore about 56,140 Protestant missionaries who have left their homes to serve the Lord in peoples or nations not their own. Of these 10% are from the Third World. Note that these figures do not include the army of temporary missionaries, the short termers, who may number, worldwide, between 10,000 and 15,000. Nor does this figure include missionary workers at home bases. There are now around 200 missionary sending agencies in the Third World.

The Unfinished Task

We have spoken of the successes of the modern missionary movement, but we must not be blind to the fact that the world has not been fully evangelised. There are yet many areas and peoples that remain unreached or resistant to the message of the Gospel. These must be effectively given the Gospel in order for the condition of the Lord Jesus in Matthew 24:14 to be fulfilled so that He may return. Pray especially for the following:–

1) **Islam.** Probably no more than 300,000 have been converted out of Islam in this century, and most of these have been from one nation – Indonesia. Five of the six nations that are closed to the Gospel and have no known national believers are Muslim. A mighty army of importunate prayer warriors and intrepid evangelists are needed that the Lordship of Christ be recognised in the Muslim world. The approximate 3,000 missionaries working among Muslims together with the thousands of expatriate Christians in secular employment need prayer.
2) **Hinduism.** It is reckoned that only 1% of the Christians now in the churches in India have been converted out of Hinduism – this means that there are only about 200,000

converts out of Hinduism in India living today. The Gospel is not yet making a decisive impact on the Hindu population.

3) **The Buddhists** have proved a hard field and converts few and hand picked. After all the years of effort in Sri Lanka, nominal Christians are reverting to Buddhism. In Thailand, Burma and Indo-China the converts out of Buddhism number only a few thousand. Most of the converts come from despised or rejected elements of society.

4) **Lands with no known national believers and closed to the Gospel:-** Pray these doors open: – Libya, Maldive Islands, Mauritania, Saudi Arabia, Qatar (all Muslim), Mongolia (Communist). Also the Muslim Malays in Malaysia.

5) **Lands closed** but in which only a handful of believers are known: – Albania, Iraq, North Korea, South Yemen, Zanzibar.

6) **Lands open or partially open for the Gospel, but in which there are very few believers:** – Djibouti, Comoros, Afghanistan, Turkey, Morocco, Algeria, Arabian Gulf States, Iran, etc. – though one must hasten to add that the degree of openness in some of these is so small as to almost constitute a closed door!

7) **Unreached peoples** number many thousands all over the world. MARC (WV) is engaged in a big operation to gather information about all these groups and inform the believers of that need. You may obtain a folder from them about some of these peoples. These folders are available for all the tribes and peoples in the ensuing pages that are followed by*.

8) **It is reckoned that** 80% of the 3,000 million unreached people of the world can only be reached by cross-cultural missionary effort. **This is not the time to give up, but to mobilise the churches of the whole world to finish the task!**

There is a trend in many lands to limit the number and type of missionaries that are allowed. Some doors are closing to expatriate missionaries, yet on the other hand, others are opening (e.g. the Comoros, Djibouti, former Portuguese Timor, Sudan, etc.). The age of missions is NOT passing. The only orders for missionary withdrawal or a moratorium on missions will not come from the World Council of Churches but from the Lord Jesus Christ when He comes in the clouds to call all believers to be with Him for ever (Matt. 24:14). It is the Lord Jesus who opens and shuts doors of service, and He alone! (Rev. 3:7-8). Therefore we are not to be discouraged by the closure of some lands – for there are still far more open doors that have not been entered. This is the time for us, as believers, to go up and possess the lands for our Lord Jesus Christ.

The challenge to believers all over the world has never been greater. We have more information on the need than ever before. Great Congresses on Evangelism in every continent have helped Christian leaders to plan and mobilise the churches for the last great thrust for evangelising the world before the Lord returns. The 1974 World Congress of Evangelism in Lausanne has stimulated an enormous burst of activity all over the world. Pray that believers may heed God's call, and complete the task according to His will and in the strength of the Spirit of God.

The World – General Prayer Targets

The whole strategy of world evangelisation, the sending of missionaries, and the theology of the meaning of the Church and its mission is now being re-thought. All is changing. We cannot discuss this here. Here we give just a few prayer guidelines for Christian bodies and ministries that are frequently, but briefly, referred to later in the book.

1. The Church

All over the world are congregations of believers. In some lands these churches are few, in others there are thousands. These are imperfect reflections and manifestations of the true and invisible Church of the Lord Jesus Christ. Each church must grow and become a centre for missionary outreach. If it does not do so, it is failing in the very reason for its existence. Here are a few prayer points:–

a) **Leadership** is the key. Pastors and ministers need much prayer. There is a world-wide lack of men truly called of God and who are willing to suffer scorn, poverty and the shame of the Cross for the sake of their Saviour. There are too few teachers and expounders of the Scriptures. Without men with the right spiritual gifts, and a close walk with God, the churches will never grow and never be mobilised to win the lost.

b) **Spiritual depth** is rare in the churches. Superficiality, inadequate devotional life and worldliness are common. This highlights the need for the teaching of the content, doctrines and applicability to life and witness of the Word of God in the mother tongue.

c) **Victorious optimism** is rare in chuches where evangelical believers are a small and despised minority. These believers are often introspective and timid, and hardly a mighty power for the pulling down of the fortifications of the devil. Believers need prayer that they may witness boldly and effectively.

d) **Purity of Doctrine.** Too often believers' thoughts, prejudices and fears are more moulded by the prevailing philosophies, superstitions and religions of the society around them than by the Bible. Humanism in the West, Hinduism in India, etc. are examples. All such rob Christians of their assurance, power and joy in the face of a hostile world, and sidetrack believers into secondary or irrelevant issues.

e) **Young people** in this modern age are often lost to the world after a Christian upbringing because of a growing generation gap. Every new generation needs to be evangelised afresh, or the churches soon become nominal. Young people need prayer as never before.

f) **The missionary vision.** Believers need to see that missions are not just a minor department of the church (if there *is* a missions department!), but its reason for existing. Pray for a real interest and concern for the world. Pray also for the calling of people into full time service. Pray for continued concern for missionaries in the churches from which they are sent out.

g) **Revival** – the constant need of the churches all over the world.

2. Missions

a) **Pray for the right strategy** in these days of explosive change. Some missions cannot adapt to new circumstances or make use of new opportunities because of too little flexibility in methods. Many missions have outlived their usefulness. Mission leaders need the wisdom of God in these days of stress.

b) **Leadership of missions** – wisdom in setting clear goals for the work, guidance in selection of candidates, placing of workers, personality problems, dealing with sensitive governments, and home base and field churches, etc.

c) **The wisest use of resources.** The place of institutional work and social aid is more and more called to question as to whether it has really helped in the planting of strong churches. Guidance is needed for the wisest use of such tools where necessary. In some lands, institutional work is the only legal means of witness; in others, it is no longer necessary or helpful.

d) **Relationships with home and daughter churches** – one of the most tricky problems with which many missions are struggling in these days of sensitive nationalisms and serious misgivings about the very purpose of missions.

3. The Missionary

The old colonial type of missionary is no longer acceptable. Much of the glamour of being a pioneer missionary has gone. The modern missionary must be a spiritual giant – humble and self-effacing, willing to work under nationals less able to do some jobs than he, and to work without any praise (and often with no gratitude!). For this, a close walk with God is necessary. Pray for:–

a) **His health** – in a climate possibly very different to his homeland. Sickness has shortened the careers of many missionaries.

b) **The protection of his mind** – the devil uses discouragement, loneliness, lack of fruit, and evil thoughts to make him useless for the Lord's work.

c) **Protection from Satan's attacks** – the powers of darkness are very real. Pray for authority to resist the devil, and to spoil his goods.

d) **Culture shock** – over one quarter of all missionaries who return prematurely from the field do so because they could not adapt to new languages, foods and customs. Humility is needed to adapt to and respect the cultures of those to whom the Lord has sent them.

e) **Failures in personal relationships** between missionaries and nationals are the cause of many missionary casualties. The grace of God is needed to live in harmony and close spiritual fellowship with other workers.

f) **Lack of personal discipline** – in having a Quiet Time, in the use of time, overworking, etc., causes many missionaries to fail on the field. Pray for the effective and wise use of time.

g) **The Love of God for sinners** –– human pity and love are insufficient; only the constraining love of Christ can help a missionary to love the unlovely.

h) **Brokenness** – in dealing with national believers, fellow workers, difficult orders from those in authority, and also "impossible" home conditions. Pray that all these trials may drive him to a dependence on Jesus alone.

i) **The anointing of God** in his ministry, and also the constant knowledge of God's will in the big and small events of his life.

j) **His family.** There is often an inadequate family life with many separations. The wife is often alone with insufficient money and few amenities. The children are often separated from their parents for long periods, and can become rebellious and resentful in their teens. Pray that missionary families may be an effective witness of all that a Christian family ought to be, for believers saved out of a heathen background often have low standards for marriage.

k) **His financial need** – many live poorly and sacrificially by the standards of their homeland, but magnificently in the eyes of the local people. Pray for a right balance in the use of money and possessions, and the supply of all his needs.

l) **Furloughs** are longed for, but are often a great disappointment – lack of interest from believers, re-adaptation to a changed homeland, etc.

m) **Priorities in service** – he needs clear objectives in his ministry, and the time to attain them. Interruptions and trivialities are common! He needs a sense of urgency, for his time on the field can suddenly be terminated.

4. Bible Translation

An essential ministry if strong, Bible reading churches are to be planted.

a) **Languages yet to be translated** – 257 have the whole Bible and 368 just have the New Testament. Only 1,600 of the world's 5,700 languages have a portion of God's Word. The remaining 3,100 are spoken by only 3% of the world's population, but they need to have a fair chance to hear the Gospel in their own language. Most of these languages are in Asia, Africa and the Pacific.

b) **Translators need prayer.** Pray for the calling of more missionaries, and especially nationals for this ministry, and for their adequate training. This is a long and slow work – to reduce languages to writing, to learn to speak it fluently, as well as to later be able to translate the Scriptures both accurately and understandably.

c) **Wycliffe Bible Translators** – a mission wholly committed to Bible translation with 3,720 workers translating in 600 languages around the world. They pray for a staff of 8,000 in order to translate the Bible into languages known to need such. Many other missions are also involved in the translation ministry. There are about 900 languages in the world in which translation work is in progress.

d) **Literacy work** is an essential minisry. Illiterate people would otherwise not be able to read the Scriptures once they are translated.

e) **Revisions and common language translations** are multiplying. Pray for all involved in this ministry.

5. The Bible Societies

They perform a valuable task in advising translators, and printing and distributing Bibles cheaply. There are national Bible Societies in most countries of the world. The Evangelical Trinitarian Bible Society and the **Scripture Gift Mission** have a valuable ministry in distributing Bibles, portions of Scripture, etc. In 1973, 249 million pieces of Scripture were distributed worldwide.

a) Pray for the personnel and their walk with God in their varied ministries.

b) Pray for the large sums of money needed for the printing of Scriptures.

c) Pray for Bible distribution – especially in lands where this is difficult – such as the Communist and Muslim lands.

6. Christian Literature

More than half the born again Christians in the world testify that literature played a part in their conversion. Its role in strengthening Christians is incalculable. The Communists appreciate the importance of literature and spent over 5,000 million dollars (US) on propaganda in 1973. The astonishing impact of Mao Tse Tung's little Red Book of quotations is well known – 740,000,000 were produced between 1966 and 1968. Someone made the jibe "The missionaries taught the people to read and the Communists supply their reading material". Here are some prayer points:–

a) **Crash literacy programmes** in many parts of the world create an immense desire for ANY literature by newly literates. Pray for a greater interest among churches in this ministry. Pray for more and better Christian literature.

b) **Very few languages have an adequate range of Christian Literature.** Literature translated out of English can be good, but can never be a substitute for that written by nationals. Yet there is a critical lack of spiritual and mature Christian writers in nearly every language.

c) **The rapidly increasing costs of printing** and the poverty of the people most needing the literature hinder this ministry. Pray for needed funds to launch programmes. Pray that profitable areas for selling Christian literature may be used to finance production in poorer areas and where there are few Christians.

d) **There is a worldwide shortage of Christian printers.** Pray for all engaged in printing, and also for the smooth running of expensive machinery – breakdowns in underdeveloped lands can be disastrous.

e) **Literature missionaries are too few.** Pray for the calling of those with the right qualities and qualifications for this ministry – in journalism, printing, publishing, writing, distribution, etc. Few Bible Schools give adequate attention to the training of literature missionaries.

f) **Distribution** – Christian bookstores, colportage, Bible vans, etc. – pray for those serving in such. Pray for opportunities for personal witnessing and counselling in this distribution work. Pray for fruit from the literature sold or handed out. One mission especially worthy of prayer is the **CLC** – with 99 Christian bookstores in 42 countries. CLC urgently needs 200 more workers. . . !

g) **Christian magazines** have had a valuable ministry in many parts of the world – both evangelistic, and in helping Christians. Production costs now harm sales, and threaten their viability. Pray for guidance for those who have to make difficult decisions. Pray also for spiritual fruit from this ministry.

h) **Gospel broadsheets** have had an amazing growth since God called **WEC** to this ministry. These "SOON" broadsheets are produced bi-monthly in English, French, Portuguese, Arabic, Urdu, Thai, Hindi, Bengali, etc., and distributed free by hand and post. The testimonies, short articles and offers of BCCs have brought a dramatic response. Over one and a half million copies are printed every issue.

i) **Gospel ships** – The vision of **OM** in using passenger ships for literature distribution, encouragement of believers, evangelism and leadership training has proved a great boon for Christian work in many difficult parts of the world. Pray for this ministry, and for its enlargement. Pray for all involved in the complex organisation it requires.

7. Bible Correspondence Courses

This ministry is only about 35 years old, but has grown to be one of the most effective means for following up contacts from literature distribution and Christian radio programmes. The relative ease in using the post in sensitive areas of the world and the emphasis on studying the Word of God has had a great impact on BCC students – some being converted, and others being strengthened in their Christian life. This has proved the best single means of winning Muslims.

a) There are reckoned to be over 300 centres sending out evangelical BCCs. **Pray for the workers involved in preparation of materials,** and helping the students through the post.

b) **Pray for the publicising of BCCs** in lands where there are few believers, and closed doors to missionaries – often through tracts, radio programmes or other students.

c) **Pray for the effective personal follow-up of students** by local Christians and for their integration into Christian fellowships.

8. Gospel Records

The ministry of **Gospel Recordings** in producing simple messages on gramophone records has helped in the evangelising of small tribes and inaccessible peoples, for among such they are often the ONLY means available to preach to them. These records can be played over and over again on cheap battery or hand winding record players.

  a) **GR have now produced records** in 3,900 of the world's 5,700 languages. Fifty skilled recordists are needed to complete recordings for the remaining 1,800 languages – mainly in Russia, China, Indonesia, India, Mozambique, Nepal and the Pacific.
  b) **Pray for the field recordists** – often working in dangerous and inaccessible regions. Pray for the right language informants, preparation of texts, recording and production of the records. Pray for the good working of delicate equipment under difficult conditions.
  c) **Pray for the distribution of the records.** Importation into many lands is difficult due to import restrictions, prohibitions, high customs dues, etc. Pray for wise distribution by Christian workers.
  d) **Pray for fruit** – even in areas closed to the Gospel proclaimed by other means. The response is very good in Mexico and Brazil at present.

9. Cassette Tape Ministry

The arrival of cheap cassette tape recorders has made it possible to distribute tapes with Christian messages fairly cheaply to believers with little access to a good teaching ministry, and where there is much illiteracy. The recent development of a hand wound recorder promises a greater impact in poorer lands.

  a) **Pray for skilled labourers** – to produce tapes, handle equipment, maintain tape recorders and distribute tapes.
  b) **Pray for the best use of Bible tapes** – many languages are now on tape. This is particularly valuable for getting the Word of God to illiterate people and to those for whom there is yet no written Scriptures, and where there is a real threat that political events may prevent their printing and distribution – such as in Ethiopia today.
  c) **Pray for the evangelistic and teaching ministries of these tapes,** and their effective use by believers as a means of church growth.

10. Christian Radio and Television

This is one of the most useful, yet costly, aids for the evangelisation of the world. There are now over 65 Christian Radio stations in the world, and many other Christian programmes being broadcast over national and commercial stations. There are estimated to be over 600 million radios and 250 million television sets in the world, and relatively few people do not have access to a radio set.

  a) **Funds are needed.** The huge expenses involved in buying equipment, erecting buildings and aerials, broadcasting and maintaining large staffs are justified by the results. Pray for the provision of all needs.
  b) **Christian Radio** is the only direct means of preaching the Gospel in 44 lands and 1,700,000,000 people (one third of mankind) – especially in Communist and Muslim lands. The message still penetrates the Iron and Bamboo Curtains despite Communist attempts to jam them. Many churches have been planted as a result of this ministry, and there are possibly one million believers in Russia converted through such broadcasts. Pray for the raising up of national believers originally from closed lands who may be able to prepare and broadcast programmes to them.
  c) **Programme production** – pray for Spirit filled messages and music that will challenge and inspire, and meet the needs of the hearers. Pray for all involved in the producing of programmes – pastors, churches, programmers and technical staff. Competition on the radio waves is intense, and the casual listener will only be gripped by good programmes.
  d) **Pray for Missions specialising in this ministry.** Most notable are:–
  the pioneers of this ministry, the **World Radio Missionary Fellowship** in Ecuador, **ELWA (SIM)** in Liberia, **TWR** in Monaco, Netherlands Antilles, Swaziland and Sri Lanka, **FEBA** in Seychelles, **FEBC** in the Philippines. The latter produces about 1,000 hours of programmes every week. Christian broadcasters put out more hours of broadcasting than Communist propaganda stations.

e) **Pray for the staffs of these Christian stations.** Many have to work in difficult climates and conditions. Pray for growth in their spiritual lives, and maintenance of their vision for the salvation of the lost in the midst of all their technical and administrative tasks. Pray for the calling of the skilled workers needed.

f) **Pray for good reception in target areas** – wave bands are increasingly crowded, and more and more powerful transmitters are needed to "shout down" other stations. Pray also for good publicity for programmes in lands closed to the Gospel.

g) **Pray for spiritual fruit in saved souls and blessed Christians.**

h) **Pray for follow-up work** – many stations have a large staff to cope with the flood of correspondence from all over the world. Pray for the personal letters, literature and BCCs sent out. Pray for the linking up of contact with local believers. Pray that this may result in the planting and growth of churches.

11. Theological Education by Extension (TEE)

This is one of the exciting new tools in the hands of the Church for the training of church leaders. For years the churches of the West have used Seminaries and Bible Colleges for the training of full time workers, but in the rest of the world this system has its weaknesses – too few of the right candidates, lack of funds, the poverty of the students, and those trained are often not the actual leaders in the churches. The rate of multiplication of churches in many parts of the world is so great that no residential training scheme could ever provide the workers needed. TEE is a system of training the actual leaders as they lead their congregations by helping them to study in their homes using specially prepared teaching materials (programmed instruction) and frequent contacts with travelling lecturers. TEE is cheap, practical, adaptable, and can be tailored to fit the individual student and his needs. TEE has spread to every continent. There are now at least 250 evangelical centres with over 27,000 students all over the world. Pray for: –

a) **Trained workers** for preparing teaching materials and maintaining contact with the students. Preparing the literature is a skilled task, needing prayer.

b) **The students** – often studying under difficult conditions in simple homes, and in the midst of a very busy life.

c) **The enrichment of the churches** through a better teaching and pastoral ministry.

12. Saturation Evangelism

Saturation evangelism is the total mobilisation of the active membership of a church, group of churches, or believers, to cover an entire area with the Gospel. This was pioneered successfully by **LAM** in Latin America under the title **Evangelism in Depth** (EID), and later it spread to many other lands under different titles, such as **New Life For All** in Africa. The effects were good, with much church growth in a few areas where the churches were young and evangelical (such as parts of Latin America and central Nigeria). Elsewhere, results were less satisfactory. In large and nominal Protestant communities with many large denominations it degenerated into converting dead church members at the best. Here are a few points for prayer: –

a) **Pray for a continued development of the Scriptural principles of S.E.** The ideal is correct, but many mistakes have been made in the past – too grandiose schemes, involvement of the unconverted in trying to win the unconverted, too hasty a preparation time, lack of spiritual local leaders to mobilise the ordinary believers, etc.

b) **Many local churches are now adapting the principles** for individual congregations with much prayer backing and careful spiritual preparation of the believers with very beneficial results. This is the most efficient method of believer mobilisation. Pray for this to become the basic life pattern of churches all over the world, and not just a once-for-all effort.

13. Student work

Often one of the most neglected, yet strategic fields of Christian witness (there are about 20 million university students in the world). A number of interdenominational organisations have been raised up by God to fill this need – to mention a few worthy of much prayer: –

a) **Scripture Union** in secondary schools round the world – with remarkable fruit among the educated young people in Africa, Europe and parts of Asia. SU is working in 67 countries of the world.

b) **Campus Crusade for Christ** with a vigorous ministry in North America and then fanning out all over the world and now working in 70 countries. CCC emphasises mass evangelism by mobilisation of believers and discipleship training, largely among university students.

c) **Inter-Varsity Fellowship** (International Fellowship of Evangelical Students) **IVF (IFES)** has spread to universities around the world with an emphasis on evangelism, Bible study groups, literature and missions. This vital field needs much prayer: – 1. **for the extension of the evangelical witness to universities without one.** Areas of need – Latin America, Muslim world, French speaking Africa. 2. **for the right leadership** in the rapidly changing population of the student world – for adult advisers, travelling secretaries and student leaders. 3. **for outreach** – students are often the most open and enquiring section of society. The winning of these potential national leaders is strategic. Pray for all forms of evangelism used. Pray also for the witness to overseas or foreign students – often from lands closed to the Gospel. 4. **for the students in Communist lands** -- that Christians may be able to stand for Christ and win others for the Lord. There is one IFES staff worker in Communist Eastern Europe. 5. **for the Christian students and their growth in the Lord,** and that from their number, some may go into full time service for the Lord.

14. Christians in Service Overseas (CSOs)

God has raised up an army of believers of every nationality who have left their homelands so that they may serve the Lord in another land as teachers, university lecturers, doctors, agriculturalists, aid experts, technicians, etc., They often go unlinked to any evangelical mission, and are able to enter lands or strata of society that are closed to the professional missionary. There are known to be about 15,000 British Christians serving in this way. This type of ministry can often achieve as much in terms of fruit as any full time ministry for the Lord. There are over 50 countries of the world in which this type of ministry is very valuable, and a further 28 in which it is the ONLY way that Christians may enter and witness (often very tactfully!). Such need prayer: –

a) **For the right use of time** – to do the secular job in a way that Christ is glorified, yet also so that adequate time can be given to various forms of witness.

b) **Wisdom and tact** in lands where all witnessing is illegal, and yet that they may be used of God to win some. They need divine protection as they challenge the powers of darkness in these lands.

c) **The conversion of prominent citizens** of these countries through their witness. Such could totally change the attitudes of governments and open the doors for other Christian workers.

d) **For God's call to many others to serve Him in this way.** These "tentmaking" missionaries will probably become more important as governments continue to increase restrictions on the entry of professional missionaries.

15. Missionary Aviation

This has become an essential help ministry for missionaries working in areas difficult of access by transporting personnel, patients and supplies. Many missions have their own pilots and planes, but special mention must be made of **MAF**. Over 160 families of **MAF** operate 103 aircraft in 24 countries – North American **MAF** in 13 lands, British **MAF** in 4, Australian **MAF** in 5 and South African **MAF** in 2. Pray for: –

a) **Safety** – most pilots have to operate from primitive airstrips, in wild terrain and difficult climatic conditions. There have been some tragic accidents in recent years, but the safety record has been astonishingly good.

b) **Spiritual effectiveness of the staff** – with their many unusual opportunities to witness for the Lord.

c) **The supply of all needs** – aircraft, spares and fuel are expensive; and doubly so in some of the lands from which **MAF** operates; also the supply of the skilled manpower to maintain equipment and pilot the planes.

16. Medical Mission Work

This ministry has been one of the major Christian ministries on the mission field for many years. The appalling suffering and need, and the total lack of any medical attention in many fields impelled the pioneer missionaries to expend much labour and money in developing clinics, hospitals, leprosaria, etc. It is estimated that today there are about 12,000 medical missionaries in the world. This ministry needs prayer in these days of change, for: –

a) **Adaptability**. Governments demand higher standards, and in some lands, are taking over all non-government health services. Medical missionary work must constantly be assessed as to its usefulness in changing circumstances. The present trend is for fewer but better equipped and staffed mission hospitals, and an emphasis on preventative medicine.

b) **Supply of needs in funds and personnel** – that mission boards and national churches responsible may know how best to apportion them in accordance with the spiritual benefits to be reaped. Such programmes can often become the master rather than the servant!

c) **Usefulness in winning people to the Lord and for the churches.** The primary aim of medical missionary work can sometimes be forgotten in the busyness of a large institution. Yet many can be won by this means and are. Pray for fruitfulness.

d) **To open doors for the Gospel.** In many lands this is the only form of missionary work permitted – such as Yemen, Arabian Gulf States, Afghanistan, Nepal, Bhutan, etc. Pray that the witness of these medical missionaries, albeit tactful, may lead to the conversion of some, and the planting of churches.

e) **Leprosy work** will probably long remain a ministry for which Christians will be largely responsible, for the disease is unpleasant, the cure long, and the psychological and social problems many. There are over 18,000,000 leprosy sufferers in the world, but only 20% are receiving treatment. Pray for the work of the **Leprosy Mission** and others in seeking to alleviate the sufferings of these unfortunate people, and win them to the Lord in leprosaria around the world. Pray for the conversion of some, and also for their re-integration into their communities as witnessing Christians and foci of new churches. There has been a great increase in the incidence of this disease over the last 15 years.

17. The Evangelising and Discipling of Medical Workers
Because more people pass through the hospitals of the world than through its churches, the **IHCF** seeks to win for Christ and train medical personnel – doctors, dentists, nurses, para-medicals, etc. – to share their faith with those whom they serve medically. Pray for: –

a) The conversion to Christ of many members of the healing team.
b) The witness of Christians in the healing team to be both wise and bold to both patients and colleagues.
c) Communist takeovers mean the closing of churches, but not of hospitals – hence the strategic value of this work. Pray for Christian medical workers serving in hazardous circumstances.
d) Pray for IHCF staff workers round the world. Pray for additional staff. Pray also for the IHCF Staff Training Centre in the Netherlands, the HEART magazine that circulates in 100 lands, and for the radio ministry through **TWR.**

18. Short Term Workers
More and more young people (and some older too!) have been serving the Lord in a cross-cultural situation for a short period of a few weeks to three years. This is a significant world-wide development. It is impossible to reckon the numbers of believers all over the world who give some or all of their time during one year to missionary work, for, including the Third World, this may equal the entire world's missionary force! In 1975 there were over 5,764 North American short termers. Many thousands of young people in Europe, Africa and Asia move out every year with such groups as **YWAM, CCC** and **OM** as short term literature missionaries, evangelists, etc. Others serve the Lord for special projects with missionary societies. Pray for: –

a) **Usefulness** in these short spells of service. Such short "blitzes" can do much to revolutionise the spiritual situation in a hard field.
b) **Avoidance of blunders** – through inexperience, lack of understanding of a different culture and languages, etc.
c) **The calling of the right short termers** – unsuitable ones can cause havoc in teams in difficult circumstances.

d) **The challenging of short termers** to a more holy and earnest living for God when their term is ended. Pray for the calling of some into full time service.

19. Relief and Aid Ministries

An increasing amount of money is being contributed by churches to help poorer nations in specific social aid programmes.

a) Pray for missions and agencies involved in such ministries. Pray especially for such evangelical groups as **WV, TEAR Fund,** etc.

b) Pray that all such aid may contribute to the opening of hearts to the Gospel and the strengthening of national churches.

II. THE WESTERN WORLD

NORTH AMERICA 1978

Evangelical Community
as percentage of
total population

over 20%	
10 – 20	
5 – 9	
2 – 5	
1 – 2	
0·5 – 0·9	

BACKGROUND

For this survey we define the Western World as the non-Latin countries of North America and the non-Communist lands of Europe. For map on Europe see page 43.

Area: North America 20,185,000 sq. km. (14.1% of land surface of the world). Western Europe 3,590,000 sq. km. (2.0% of land surface of the world).

Population: 583,100,000. This is 14.5% of the world's population.

Peoples: **Europeans** 93%, living in 29 countries and speaking 33 languages.
African Origin 4.5% – 24,000,000 in North America, 2,600,000 in Europe.
Asian Origin 1.3%; **Others** 1.2%
Migrant Labour – the industrial West attracts many from the less developed parts of the world – often to these lands' detriment. Latin American and

Caribbean peoples to North America; S. Europeans, N. Africans and Middle East peoples (12,000,000) to Northern Europe.
Urbanisation:71%; 48 of the 163 cities of world with over 1 million people in West.
Religion: **Christians 92% Jews 1.8% Muslims 0.7%**
          Orthodox Churches 3.3% – largely Greece and N. America.
          Roman Catholics 50% – in N. America it is 37%, Western Europe 58%.
          Protestants 39% – in N. America it is 52%, Western Europe 29%.Evangelicals
          13% – in N. America it is 25%, Western Europe 5%.
          Breaking down this figure for Europe: –
          Predominantly Protestant lands of W. Europe – 11% Evangelical. Predominantly R.C. and Orthodox lands – 0.5% Evangelical.
          Missionaries from West 46,092 (as reported from the fields)
          Missionaries serving in West 3,223 (in Europe)

The Importance of the West in the World

The nations of the West have dominated the political, cultural and economic life of the world for 500 years. The West's political dominance rapidly came to an end in the 25 years that followed World War II, with the rise to power of the Communist Bloc and the coming of independence to the Third World from colonial rule. The last 5 years have also seen the erosion of the economic dominance of the West due to internal weaknesses in many nations and also the 1974 Oil Crisis. Nevertheless the enormous economic power and cultural influence of the West continues to deeply affect every country of the world. A spiritual awakening in the West would affect the whole world more quickly and deeply than any similar movement of the Spirit of God in the past.

The West and the Spread of the Gospel

After the Muslim invasions of the 8th Century, Christianity was virtually wiped out in the lands of the Middle East where the early Church first took root. For nearly 1,000 years the countries of the West became the only refuge for Christianity, for the encircling Muslim lands effectively prevented any missionary outreach to Africa and the lands of Asia. It was not until the Reformation that the decadent Christianity in these lands became a vital force for the evangelisation of the world. Over the last 250 years a growing stream of Roman Catholic and Protestant missionaries have reached out to virtually every country to make Christianity the first really worldwide religion.

The Spiritual Decline of the Western Lands

Yet even while this spreading of Christianity was taking place, a deadening anti-Christian humanism was spreading through the West. This philosophy has corrupted every part of its culture – art, music, social values, morality and theology It has also spawned Communism; a system determined to eradicate Christianity. The resulting moral collapse of the West has brought these lands into their tragic, spiritually bankrupt state in the face of the most determined opposition it has ever had to face. People now speak of the dying civilisation of the West, the de-Christianising of Europe or even the post-Christian era.

The Shadow of Communism

The Communist leaders are dedicated to the strategic aim of gaining Western Europe and the world while political and religious leaders in the West complacently or even wilfully ignore the notable advances of Communism. The lands of the West are being infiltrated by those dedicated to their overthrow – trade unions, political parties and churches being objects of this infiltration. Military blackmail is increasingly used to cow non-Communist lands, yet Communism seeks to put on a mask of peace with the smile of a Trojan Horse type of Euro-Communism. The believers need to be aroused to prayer and also to a zeal and dedication that far exceeds that of the Communists, to win the lost and evangelise the world.

The Spiritual Need of the West

The decline of Christianity in the West has been in contrast to the dramatic growth in many other parts of the world. There are almost as many evangelical believers in Africa now as in all of Western Europe. For evangelical believers, the Roman Catholic lands of Europe rank as the second most needy mission field in the world after the Muslim Middle East. Even some parts of Protestant Europe such as Denmark, Iceland and part of Germany have so few Evangelicals that these must also be seen as a mission field. We mention several areas that we must classify as unreached: –

a) Lands with no known permanent evangelical witness: – **Andorra, Liechtenstein.**

b) Lands with a very small evangelical witness: – **Spain, Greece, Luxembourg, Cyprus** and **Malta.**

c) The Immigrant communities:

Turks – about 1,200,000 in Northern Europe

Spanish and **Portuguese** in France and Germany

Yugoslavs and **Albanians** in Germany, Austria, etc.

Muslim North Africans in France and the Low Countries

Indians and **Pakistanis** in Britain

Overseas Students – especially in U.S.A., Canada, France and Britain – they number over 500,000 at any one time and come from many lands all over the world, some from lands closed to all open evangelisation.

May many believers be burdened by the Lord for these and other needs that will be mentioned in the following pages.

Encouraging Signs of the Working of the Holy Spirit in Europe and North America

The decline in overall church attendances and memberships of many denominations is partly due to the non-Biblical theologies propagated by many preachers, but does not tell the whole story. There is much to encourage. We name a few: –

a) The number of evangelical believers is steadily rising – especially in the largely non-evangelical denominations.

b) The evangelical voice in North America, Britain and Germany has gained a new authority and commands more respect than at any time in this century.

c) The concern and hunger for revival in the hearts of many Christians is increasing. There have been touches of revival in parts of Canada, U.S.A. and Finland.

d) The rapid rise of many strong youth movements in all countries with a great emphasis on evangelism and missionary work – especially noticeable in the U.S.A., Finland and Germany.

Pray that the Western lands may yet be a great blessing to the world.

e) The remarkable people movements among the Gypsy people all over Europe with many being converted in Spain, France and Romania.

A. North America

<u>CANADA</u>

BACKGROUND

Area:	9,980,000 sq. km. The world's second largest country, but much is cold arctic tundra and forest and is very sparsely populated.
Population:	23,100,000 Growth 1.3% (nearly half growth through immigration). Two thirds of population within 150 Km of the 7,000 Km U.S. Border. 2 people per sq. km.
Peoples:	**British** 42%. **French** 28%, **German** 6%, **Italians** 4%, **Ukrainians** 3.5%, **Dutch** 2.5%, **Polish** 2.5%, also there are **Chinese** 120,000 plus **Indians** 52,000. The French have lived for centuries in Quebec Province where most still live today. The French resent the cultural and linguistic domination of the English speaking majority in a theoretically bilingual country according equal rights to both. **Amerindians** 300,000, **Eskimos** (in the Arctic) 18,000.
Capital:	Ottawa 622,000. Major cities – Montreal 2,750,000, Toronto 2,600,000, Vancouver 1,180,000. Urbanisation 76%.
Economy:	Seeking to be a national unit independent of U.S. domination.
Politics:	Continual attempts to prevent cultural and political absorption by the much larger neighbour to the south (U.S.A.). This fact and the restless French community help to determine Canada's independent line in foreign affairs.
Religion:	**Roman Catholics** 47%. Almost the entire French and Italian communities are R.C. **Greek Orthodox** 2%. **Jews** 1.2%. **Protestants** 44%, Community 6,600,000, Membership 2,500,000. Largest churches – United Church 990,000 members, Anglican 627,000, Lutherans 145,000, Baptists 180,000, Presbyterians 190,000. Significant evangelical groups – Pentecostal Assemblies 80,000, some Baptist groups 40,000, **CMA** 16,000, Assoc. of Gospel Churches 7,000. Evangelicals 7% of population.

Points for Prayer

1) **Canada needs revival.** A localised revival in 1972 in the Prairie Provinces brought blessing to many churches. A deeper and more widespread work of God is needed.
2) **Unreached peoples are many.** The many immigrant peoples have tended to settle in communities that retain their customs and languages. Many of these groups must be evangelised – especially the Greeks and Italians in the east, and the Chinese and East Indians in the west. About 10,000 of the 300,000 Jews* in Canada have become Christians, but many more have yet to hear the Gospel.
3) **The French Canadians** are almost entirely Roman Catholic, and there have not been many who have come to a living faith. Persecution of preachers and converts was severe in the past. The last 10 years has seen many new attempts by evangelical groups to witness to them including CSSM, **CMA, OM,** yet there are now still more than 30,000 French Canadians for every evangelical worker (average for English, etc. – 1:900). Pray for the planting of many live churches.
4) **There is a drift away from the traditional Protestant Churches** where nominalism, non-Biblical theology and an over-emphasis on social concern is common. Pray that the Evangelicals within these denominations may be as salt and light in them.
5) **The evangelical witness is growing** – pray that it may become a mighty voice for God and righteousness in the land – this is much needed in this materialistic society. The Pentecostal Assemblies of Canada is the fastest growing denomination in the land. Other smaller denominations are also making a very valuable contribution – such as the **CMA,** Association of Gospel Churches, Evangelical Baptists, Nazarenes, etc. There is the ever present danger of divisiveness over various doctrines among Evangelicals. Pray for a greater concern for the evangelisation of the many minority groups of Canada.

6)   **The Bible School movement** is playing a major role in the growth of the evangelical
       witness. Pray for these schools – one such being the famous Prairie Bible Institute in
       Alberta.
7)   **The missionary vision has been great,** and there are probably about 2,000 Canadian
       missionaries serving all over the world. Canada is the H.Q. for the **SIM.** Pray that
       there may be no lessening of the contribution of Canada to the evangelisation of the
       world.
8)   **The Amerindians** have, to a great extent, been absorbed into the English speaking
       population in the south. Of the 61 tribal languages, only 25 are still in common use.
       Pray for the work of North Canada Evangelical Mission (100 workers), **CMA, WBT**
       in Bible translation and church planting ministries among these. Much of this work is
       in the harsh northern parts of the country. Many Amerindians are nominally Chris-
       tian, but drunkenness and degradation is common.
9)   **The Eskimos in the Arctic** are mostly Anglicans, but the impact of the worst of
       Western civilisation has greatly harmed their way of life, and a work of the Spirit of
       God among them is greatly needed.

THE UNITED STATES OF AMERICA

BACKGROUND

Area:	9,365,000 sq. km. – 4th largest land in the world in both area and population.
Population:	215,300,000. Growth 0.8% per year. People per sq. km. – 23.
Peoples:	**European origin** 87%. Mostly from the British Isles, but also from every other country in Europe.
	African origin 11%. Most of their forbears coming to America as slaves.
	Asian origin 2%. Japanese 1 million, Chinese 500,000, Filipino 350,000. Now also many Vietnamese and Cambodian refugees.
	Amerindians 0.4% – the original inhabitants of North America. About 5% of the U.S. population is foreign born.
Capital:	Washington 2,600,000. Other important cities – New York 16,400,000; Los Angeles 6,800,000; Chicago 6,700,000; Philadelphia 4,700,000; Detroit 4,000,000; Boston 3,300,000; San Francisco 3,000,000. Urbanisation 74%.
Economy:	The most wealthy state on earth with an immense agricultural and industrial production. Balance of payment deficits, inflation and the 1973–74 Oil Crisis have all helped to weaken the once stable U.S. dollar. Yet the world is immediately affected by any changes in the U.S. economy.
Politics:	After World War II the leadership of the free world fell upon the U.S.A. The military, diplomatic and propaganda victories of Communism have brought a dismaying spirit of defeatism, introspection and isolationism to the fore and weakened her in this leadership. This has been enhanced by internal divisions and the moral decline. Nevertheless the U.S.A. remains the most powerful nation in the world.
Religion:	There is complete freedom of religion.
	Roman Catholics 37%
	Orthodox 3%. **Jews** 4%
	Protestants 53%. There are probably 69,000,000 members of the over 200 different denominations (over one quarter of the world's Protestants). Major denominational groups: Baptists (25 groups) 34%, Methodists (17) 20%, Lutherans (11) 9%, Episcopal 5.5%, Presbyterians (8) 7%, Pentecostals (27) 4%. Conservative Evangelicals 27% (with a considerable degree of evangel- ical nominalism).

Prayer Points

1)   **The economic and political stability of the U.S.A. is of vital importance** to the whole
       world. Pray for the President, Congress and all in authority in these difficult times.
       Pray that there may be many men in high positions who have moral integrity and
       Christian principles.

2) **The U.S.A. is a divided and troubled nation.** The impact of television on American life is incalculable and has brought violence into every home – the bitter Vietnam War, racial hatred and programmes of pornography and bloodshed. Violence seems to have become an accepted part of life to many. The nation is divided over civil rights, the gap between the rich and the poor, the gap between the young and the old, and there is a revolt against all forms of authority. There are many evil people who desire to exploit these differences for their own ends and delight to help in the destruction of this great nation. Pray that the forces of evil at work may be bound in the name of the Lord Jesus.

3) **The very freedom that made the U.S.A. great** is being used by some to destroy that greatness. In the name of freedom every form of sinful perversion, drug abuse and filth is being more and more condoned. In the name of the freedom of the press the open betrayal of state secrets, and destruction of national security is made a virtue. In the name of freedom of religion the Christian heritage is destroyed. Such freedom only leads to bondage – drugs, immorality and alcohol, and possibly to the enslavement of the whole people under a terrible tyranny. Pray for the true liberty that comes only from the Spirit of God. Pray for revival. Pray that these things may drive the people of God to their knees before Him.

4) **Most of the modern missionary sects originated in this land.** The Watchtower, Mormons, Seventh Day Adventists, Christian Scientists, and now Scientology aggressively propagate their errors all over the world. The Mormons have 20,000 short term missionaries all over the world. There are probably about 7,000,000 adherents of these various groups in the U.S.A. Pray that believers may show the love of Christ to such, and bring them to the salvation offered by the Lord Jesus in His Word.

5) **The decline of many of the main traditional Protestant denominations is accelerating.** Some of these denominations are powerful in national and World Council of Churches politics, yet the spiritually deadening non-Biblical theology preached has led to declining membershp, lessening missionary outreach and opening the doors to the permissive standards of the world. Yet within these denominations the evangelical voice is becoming stronger. Pray that these believers may be given courage and wisdom as they seek to bring back these churches to a Biblical faith and emphasis on the winning of souls and building them up in the Lord.

6) **The evangelical witness in the States is growing,** and the voice of evangelical leaders is more and more listened to. Pray that the increasing respectability of believing the Bible may not lead to a cheaper and more superficial faith. Pray for another evangelical awakening that will restore the moral greatness of the country.

7) **The Evangelical denominations are growing** through vigorous and well organised programmes of evangelism. Pray that there may be no loss in spiritual depth because of a worship of success and numbers. It is estimated that there are about 40,000,000 evangelical believers, and that 68% of these attend church regularly. Pray that there may be a deeper love for the Lord and the brethren, and a hatred of worldliness. There is much superficiality in evangelical circles.

8) **There are tragic divisions among the Evangelicals which** greatly hinder the effectiveness of the witness. There are several major denominations in varying stages of bitter divisions. There are damaging disputes between the isolationists and ecumenists, about the authority of the Bible, about evangelical social involvement and the charismatic movement. Pray for spiritual unity and love.

9) **The young people** have immense problems in modern American society. The bitter fruits of humanistic philosophies are now being harvested in the immoral, drug-addicted and rebellious youth of today. Yet in the midst of all this degradation the Spirit of God worked a few years ago in what later became known as the Jesus Revolution. Many thousands were converted across the country. This movement is now largely a thing of the past. Many of these converts went into established churches through the influence of such as Campus Crusade and the Billy Graham Association, others formed their own charismatic house churches. Some sadly sank into grievous doctrinal error. Pray that the present tendency to emphasise experience and feelings may be replaced by a greater willingness to personal discipline and a study of the Word of God. One great result of the Jesus Revolution was the upsurge in missionary

interest among young people – many serving the Lord in groups such as Youth With A Mission.

10) **Student work** has been encouraging. Both the IVCF and Campus Crusade have been used of God in the conversion and discipling of many university students. Both groups have been strong in emphasising missions. Pray for this valuable work in the university campuses across the country. Pray for the leadership in the universities and also the outreach to the unconverted.

11) **Overseas students** number about 250,000 at any one time. These come from nearly every land – some closed to the Gospel. Pray especially for those from Muslim lands, and also for those from Japan*. Pray that these often lonely students may be befriended and won for Jesus.

12) **Bible Colleges and Theological Seminaries** play a very important role. Evangelical Colleges are usually full. Pray for high spiritual standards, and also that many students may make a valuable contribution to world evangelisation. There are about 60,000 Bible School students at any one time in the States.

13) **The missionary vision.** Much of the burden for world evangelisation rests on believers in the U.S.A. – about 54% of all missionaries, and 90% of all funds. Pray for a continuing concern in these days when many think only in terms of withdrawal and retrenchment. The world economic crisis is hurting mission work. Pray for the 36,000 U.S. missionaries serving all over the world, and for their adaptation to the land to which they are called, and also for their spiritual effectiveness. There are 465 agencies sending out missionaries to other lands.

14) **The Blacks** number 24,000,000; many living in the centres of the great cities. The 12 largest cities will be more than one half black by 1980. They are generally poorer than their white counterparts despite the achievements of the civil rights movement. There yet remains a legacy of bitterness and division. Pray for the healing of the wounds of the past, and a fair society for all sections of the community. Pray for the reviving of the many lifeless Protestant churches among them. Pray that the rising interest in foreign missions may be properly fostered and directed.

15) **The Amerindians** number 900,000 in about 150 different tribes (11 in Alaska), but many of these people (possibly 50%) now live in the cities. Only 42 of their languages are still commonly used. Pray for those living on the Reservations – often in great need, and hardened to the Gospel. Pray for outreach to them by many groups – SMA, GMU, WBT, etc. Especially needy are the Navajos (137,000), Lakota (20,000), Zuni* (6,000), Paiute* (5,000), Towa* (1,800) and Jemez Pueblo* (1,800).

16) **The Jews** (6,500,000) are influential in every part of U.S. life. One third of the Jews of the world live in the States. Witness among them is not easy. Pray for the various societies working among them. Pray for the Jews for Jesus – converted Jews who retain their Jewish links as Christians. They report 7,000 conversions a year.

B. Europe (Free)

AUSTRIA

BACKGROUND

Area:	83,000 sq. km. A landlocked central European state.
Population:	7,500,000 Annual growth 0.1% People per sq. km. – 90.
Peoples:	**German** speaking, but with minorities of Slovenes, Czechs and Hungarians. Migrant labourers – Turks (30,000), Yugoslavs.
Capital:	Vienna 1,700,000 (nearly one quarter of the population). Urbanisation 52%.
Economy:	Stable and growing.
Politics:	Once part of the great Austro-Hungarian Empire, but now a small neutral buffer state between the Communist Bloc and the West, but whose sympathies lie with the latter.
Religion:	**Roman Catholics** 88%.
	Protestants 7% Community 490,000 Denominations 10.
	Evangelische Kirche (Lutheran) 440,000, Reformed Church 26,000, also Assemblies of God, Baptists, Methodists with several thousand each. Conservative Evangelicals 0.5% of population.

Prayer Targets

1) **Austria is a mission field with only a small evangelical witness.** No more than 20% of the people are estimated to have ever had contact with the Gospel. Many have had dealings with the occult, and the illegitimacy and suicide rates are among the highest in Europe.

2) **Many areas are without a permanent witness,** though this lack is beginning to be met. It is reckoned that there are only about 160 of the 4,000 towns and villages with a group of believers that regularly meets together. There are still about 70 towns of over 5,000 people with no permanent witness. Most of the believers are found in the cities. Pray for the reaping of a great harvest of souls.

3) **The land is nominally Roman Catholic,** but there is a marked drift away from the church in the cities. Nevertheless, people still fear to have too much contact with Evangelicals, thinking them to be a sect. Pray that the barriers to the entry of the Gospel into their hearts may be broken down.

4) **There is much formality and lifelessness in the established Protestant Churches.** There are a number of Bible believing pastors, and their number is now being increased by graduates of the Free Evangelical Seminary in Basel, Switzerland. Pray for a move of the Spirit of God in these churches that will make them a force for the evangelisation of the land.

5) **The evangelical witness is small, but now growing.** There are now about 200 Bible Study or church groups meeting regularly – most being very young. There are now possibly 10,000 – 15,000 born again believers in the country. Pray for the growth of this church planting ministry.

6) **The believers need prayer** – for there is not much of a burden for the evangelisation of the lost, and they are too conscious of being a small and despised minority within the Roman Catholic majority. There are too few young Austrian believers coming forward for full time service for the Lord. The Association for the Evangelisation of Austria was formed in 1976 to co-ordinate evangelism and to pinpoint areas of special need for evangelism (13 Evangelical denominations and missionary societies cooperating). Pray for this new initiative.

7) **The cults are aggressive and growing.** There are now about 13,000 "Jehovah's Witnesses" and 2,000 Mormons. Their work does untold harm to the efforts of evangelicals to evangelise this needy land.

8) **There is a growing missionary force** of around 250 in around 20 agencies. Pray for a real adaptation to the Austrian situation among these missionaries. Most missionaries are involved in evangelism and church planting. There are a number of German based missions as well as **ECM, GEM, GMU, TEAM,** Bible Christian Union, etc. Pray also for the witness of **OM** in mobilising local and tourist believers in aggressive evangelism.

9) **The witness among students** is one of the most fruitful in the land today. There are strong groups in 5 of the 17 universities, and the groups are growing in depth and outreach. Pray that these young Christians may really have an impact on the land and its churches.

10) **Migrant labourers** – little has yet been done for the Muslim Turks. There is one small Yugoslav church in Vienna, but most of this large community has yet to be evangelised. This community is very strategic for the evangelising of Yugoslavia as that land becomes increasingly difficult for Christian work.

BELGIUM

BACKGROUND

Area: 30,500 sq. km. One of the Low Countries, forming part of the Benelux.
Population: 9,800,000 Annual growth 0.3% Densely populated – 320 people/sq. km.
Peoples: **Flemings** (Dutch speaking) 57% – largely in north and west.
                  Walloons (French speaking) 34% – largely in south and east.
                  Germans 0.65%. Immigrant workers 7%.

Capital: Brussels 1,100,000 – economic capital of Europe.
Economy: Highly industrialised and wealthy.
Politics: Political stability disrupted by disagreements between the Walloons and
             Flemings since the mid-1960's with fragmentation of most political parties
             along linguistic and regional lines.
Religion: **Roman Catholics 89%.**
             Protestants 0.9% Community 85,000 Denominations 12. Largest group
             Église Evangélique Protestante.
             About half of Protestants belong to the more evangelical confessions – Bel-
             gian Ev. Miss. **(BEM)**, Baptist, Brethren. Conservative Evangelicals 0.6% of
             population.

Prayer Targets

1) **Belgium is one of the less evangelised lands of the world.** Only 60 Km from the coast of
   England is a land that is as much a mission field as India, for the proportion of
   Evangelicals to the population is about the same. The former colony, the Belgian
   Congo (now Zaire), has nearly 200 times as many evangelical believers as Belgium
   itself. There are few Christians in the Ardennes region, and there are over 140 towns
   of over 10,000 people without a witness to the Lord Jesus. Pray for the evangelisation
   of Belgium.

2) **The majority of the people are Roman Catholic,** though few are ardent. The Roman
   Catholic Church is fast losing influence – dramatically illustrated when the **GEM**
   recently acquired one of the largest Jesuit colleges in Europe as a new and larger base
   for the Belgian Bible Institute. Vatican II and the theological turmoil within the R.C.
   Church has brought a new spirit of enquiry to the people.

3) **The Protestant witness is very small,** but growing slowly. Opportunities for evangelism have never been greater. Pray for the believers that there might be a more
   effective use of the opportunities and a greater boldness in outreach.

4) **Bible training** – pray for the greatly enlarged Belgian Bible Institute **(GEM)**
   increased from 30 students in 1970 to 140 in 1977 (though most are from Holland),
   and also for the Pentecostal Continental Bible School in Brussels. There are very few
   Belgian young people coming forward for the Lord's work. Pray that this lack may be
   remedied.

5) **Missions** – about 270 missionaries in 18 agencies, the most significant being the 103
   workers of the **BEM** who are making good use of summer campaigns, year teams, etc.
   to strengthen existing groups and also plant new churches where no evangelical
   witness exists. Pray for the extensive church-planting programme planned for the
   next few years.

6) **Literature** is being produced and used by many groups including **SU**, Scripture Press,
   Assemblies of God, and **OM**. **OM** handed out a piece of literature in every home in
   the country in 1972. The **BEM** has its own press at Genk and operates three Christian
   book shops. The Pocket Testament League distributed 40,000 Gospels of John in
   1976. Pray for fruit from all this literature evangelism.

7) **Operation Mobilisation** has its HQ for Europe in Zaventem, where over 40 workers
   administer the large operation necessary to train and send out young people for the
   summer and year programmes all over the needy areas of Europe, the Middle East
   and South Asia. Pray for these many young people as they go out distributing
   literature and evangelising. Pray that many may be called into full time service as a
   result of this temporary ministry. Many now in Europe's Bible Schools, and an
   increasing number of full time missionaries have been greatly influenced by this
   work. Pray for this ministry.

8) **Immigrant workers need to be evangelised**
   North Africans (55,000) and Turks (5,000) present a unique and urgent challenge for
   prayer and evangelism. Two **GMU** couples work among these people and there is
   now a small Arab fellowship of believers meeting regularly.
   Yugoslavs – there are several small churches among them.
   The many diplomats, businessmen, etc. from other European lands are neglected and
   are not able to be reached by normal evangelism.

CYPRUS

BACKGROUND

Area:	9,250 sq. km. – a small island republic in the East Mediterranian.
Population:	670,000.
Peoples:	**Greek** 80%. **Turks** 18%. **Armenians** 2%.
Capital:	Nicosia 115,000.
Politics:	Independent of Britain in 1960. This unhappy land has lived with violence and war for the last 22 years. The worst development was when the erstwhile military rulers of Greece overthrew President Makarios and replaced him with a guerrilla leader. This provoked a Turkish invasion of the island in 1974. Now 40% of the island is under Turkish military rule. This caused 200,000 Greeks to flee to the south, and 20,000 Turks to the north in this now partitioned island. The legacy of mistrust, bitterness and economic disruption is immense and the chances of settlement of the dispute are small.
Religion:	**Greek Orthodox** 80%. **Muslims** 18%. **Protestants** 0.04%. Community 250. Membership 120. Believers largely Pentecostals, Greek Evangelical and Brethren. There are also about 6,000 Anglican and 4,000 Free Church British troops based on Cyprus. Conservative Evangelicals 0.2% (including British).

Prayer Points

1) **Pray that this suffering land may have a fair chance to hear the Gospel.** Evangelical Christians are very few and there is only a handful of full time workers.

2) **The Turkish part of the island has no active Christian witness,** though several Turkish Christians have recently moved there from the mainland. Pray that it may be possible for some to enter the area to tell these Muslims of the Saviour. Pray for the entry of Christian literature from Turkey.

3) **Over one third of the Greeks are refugees.** Many still live in tents and much work of resettlement remains to be done. Christians helped much, and through their witnessing some outsiders have been saved. Pray that this disaster may open many hearts to the Gospel.

4) **The national believers** were much strengthened through the 1974 crisis. Pray for their growth in grace and for a continuing increase in their outreach to the lost. The believers are strongest in Limassol and Nicosia. Pray for the planting of new churches in other areas.

5) **Literature** is distributed through the Christian book store in Limassol, and also by British servicemen who love the Lord; the latter coming from the NATO military bases on the island. Pray also for the occasional Gospel advertisements placed in national newspapers.

6) **Cyprus is the new H.Q. for the MECO outreach** to Lebanon, Eritrea and possibly other lands in the Middle East. Pray that Cyprus may become a blessing to the Muslim world.

DENMARK

BACKGROUND

Area:	42,600 sq. km. – the most southerly of the Scandinavian countries.
Population:	5,100,000 **Danes.** Growth rate 0.4% p.a. People per sq. km. – 120.
Capital:	Copenhagen 1,380,000. Urbanisation 80%.
Economy:	Based on agriculture and light industry. Wealthy welfare state.
Politics:	Stable parliamentary democracy with a constitutional Monarchy. A member of the European Economic Community (EEC).

Religion: There is complete religious freedom.
Roman Catholics 0.5%.
Protestants 96%.
Lutheran (the State Church) 98%. The Church is supported out of state funds and is almost a government department. Other Protestants 1%. Community 53,000. Denominations 14. Largest groups are Baptists 20,000; Methodists 8,000; Pentecostals 6,000. Evangelical Free Church – the evangelical witness is very small indeed.
Conservative Evangelicals 4% of population.

Points for Prayer

1) **Denmark is reputed to be the pornographic capital of the world.** Liberal laws have legalised many social sins and there is no longer any censorship of literature, films, etc. The moral degradation of a permissive society has brought no peace or happiness to the people. Pray for an outpouring of the Spirit on this needy land.

2) **The Lutheran Church is largely formal.** There is a general belief in baptism as the only way to be saved. Pray for this Protestant nation that is so far from God.

3) **The evangelical witness is pitifully small.** There are a few isolated Lutheran pastors who seek to preach the true Gospel – some after contact with the charismatic movement. There are also Evangelical congregations in the other denominations. Pray for these few believers.

4) **Evangelical believers seem unconcerned about the unsaved around them.** Pray for revival to stir the believers into a vital witness.

5) **Higher unemployment** has forced many young people to go as "guest workers" to Sweden. Pray that some of these may have contact with Swedish believers.

6) **Although Protestant, Denmark is really a pioneer mission field today.** Few Danes have really heard the Gospel. Evangelistic and church planting ministries are needed. There are some denominational and non-denominational missionaries serving in the land, but reinforcements are needed. Child Evangelism Fellowship, Youth for Christ, Navigators, IVF and Campus Crusade have already made a valuable contribution. Pray for these ministries.

7) **There are no Evangelical Bible Schools or Seminaries in the country.** There is a great need for a good Bible teaching ministry and training in evangelism and church planting. This is the vision of the newly started work of GEM.

8) **The once significant missionary outreach of the Danish Church is now small.** There are now about 300 Danish missionaries serving in other lands – only a minority of these being evangelical.

9) **The Faroe Islands** between Britain and Iceland are a part of Denmark. There is a much higher proportion of true believers among the 40,000 people than in Denmark itself. The Brethren are strong – pray that these believers may have a greater burden for the evangelisation of the Mainland.

10) **The large island of Greenland** in the Arctic, N.E. of Canada, is also Danish. Greenland is 51 times larger than Denmark, yet only has a population of 50,000. The island is largely ice covered and inhospitable. The majority of the people are Eskimos. Some of these are true believers, but many little communities are without a witness. Most of the Christian work being done is by Pentecostals.

FINLAND

BACKGROUND

Area: 332,000 sq. km. This cold northern land is 70% forest and 10% lake.
Population: 4,700,000 Annual growth 0.4% people per sq. km. – 14.
Peoples: **Finns** 92%, **Swedes** 7% and some Lapps and Russians.
Capital: Helsinki 850,000. Urbanisation 58%.
Economy: Growing and increasingly wealthy despite unhelpful trade treaties with Soviet Russia.

Politics: West leaning, but Russian political pressures force neutrality.
Religion: **Attitude of Government** – The Lutheran State Church is freer from government interference than any other Scandinavian country.
                Orthodox 1.3%.
                Roman Catholic 0.06%.
                Protestants 93% – Lutheran State Church 97%; Free Churches 2.5%. Largest Free Churches – Pentecostals (2) 36,000 members; Finnish Free Church (Congreg.) 5,000; Baptists (2) 2,600; Conservative Evangelicals 30% of population.

Points for Prayer

1) **The threat of a Russian Communist takeover is always there** (Russia attacked Finland seeking territorial gain in 1939). Finland has a 1,300 Km frontier with Russia, and is bound rather tightly by treaty to Russia and there is a powerful Communist party.

2) **The people are more religious than most Scandinavians,** and very open to the Word of God. There is need for more open evangelism and soul winning. There is also a need for a deep national revival – the groundwork having already been laid by many smaller waves of revival affecting mainly the Lutherans over the past century.

3) **The Lutheran Church** has remained much more Evangelical than in most other lands because of this spirit of revival, and a high proportion of the ministers in this and the Free Churches are Evangelical. There are theologically liberal elements in the Theological Faculties in the universities, from where there is much pressure exerted on the many evangelical students to leave their position on the Word of God.

4) **The Free Churches** need to cooperate more in evangelism. The Pentecostals are the strongest by far, and have enriched the spiritual life of the country, and are open to the strong charismatic movement within sections of the Lutheran Church. There is a need for more evangelism among the Swedish speaking people – pray for the witness of the Swedish Free Covenant Church among them.

5) **The missionary vision** of the Finnish believers has grown considerably in recent years as a result of many young people coming to the Lord and seeking God's will concerning service overseas. There are now 522 missionaries serving in 51 countries. There are 253 Lutheran missionaries and 211 Pentecostals (i.e., one out of every 150 members is a missionary among these Pentecostal brethren!).

FRANCE

BACKGROUND

Area: 551,000 sq. km. The largest country in Western Europe.
Population: 53,100,000. Growth 0.8% (nearly one half through immigration). People to sq. km. – 99.
Peoples: **French** 92% including bilingual Bretons, Alsatians, Basques and Corsicans. **Immigrant Minorities** 7%. North Africans 1,200,000; Spaniards 600,000; Italians 650,000; West Indians 200,000; Africans 150,000; Vietnamese 200,000; Cambodians 50,000.
Capital: Paris approx. 10,000,000. The capital dominates the life of the country. Other major cities – Lyon 1,000,000; Marseille 1,000,000. Urbanisation 70%.
Economy   Economic stability and growth gave the country one of the highest standards of living in Europe. It is now affected by oil price rises.
Politics: Precarious hold by coalition of centre and right to keep out the powerful Communist-Socialist alliance. A member of the EEC.
Religion·   **Attitude of Government** – complete freedom of religion.
                Roman Catholics 85% but with about 21% practising their faith. The Church still has a very great influence despite the strong anti-clerical feeling.
                Muslims 3% – mostly Arabs and Berbers from N. Africa and the Black Africans.

Protestants 1¼%. Community approx. 800,000 but **attendance** approx. 180,000, which is split up among the less evangelical Reformed Church 50,000 and Lutherans 34,000; also the evangelical groups – Pentecostals 46,000, various independent and missionary Churches 9,000, Evangelical Independent Reformed 8,000, Open and Closed Brethren 7,000, Baptists 6,000, Gypsy Mission 14,000. Conservative Evangelicals 0.5% of population.

Points for Prayer

1) **France is one of the world's more important mission fields today.** It is reckoned that over 40 million French people have no real understanding of the true Gospel, and no connection with a church, though most are baptised Roman Catholics. The powerful influence of the Communist Party and also the dabbling of many in occult practices are symptomatic of the need. Pray that the present freedom to evangelise may be used to the full to bring many to a saving knowledge of the Lord Jesus Christ.

2) **There are many unreached peoples and areas in France.** Only about 1,500 of France's 38,000 communes (towns, villages, etc.) have a permanent evangelical witness. There is only a handful of believers to be found in many parts of North and Central France, and also Brittany and the Island of Corsica just to name a few areas. The many minority groups also must be evangelised – see point **n.**

3) **The influential Roman Catholic Church is in turmoil** with many tensions between the conservative traditionalists, liberals, modernists, radicals and now the growing charismatic movement. The latter has opened the hearts of many to the truths of God's Word and the acceptance of the need to be born again. Pray that there may be many won to the Lord through these pressures and influences.

4) **The Protestants have had a long and glorious history** of zeal and persecution. Later the Reformed Church had a great missionary vision with many missionaries going out all over the world with the old Paris Evangelical Missionary Society. Most of the pastors of the Reformed Church are liberal in theology and many radical in politics, so numbers have been declining for many years. Most of the Protestants are very nominal and never attend church, yet there are staunch believers in many congregations. The evangelical voice, muted for many years, is now becoming stronger. Pray for a move of the Holy Spirit in this and the Lutheran Church (the latter being strong in Alsace-Lorraine, but also rather nominal and formal).

5) **The Evangelical and Pentecostal Churches** are relatively few, but growing. Most of the growth has been in the very vigorous, nationally led Pentecostal movement, and less so among the Baptist and Brethren groups. There is generally not much real growth among the churches linked with the missionary groups. Pray for the mobilisation of believers for evangelism and church growth. Many believers find it very hard to witness to others due to the national reluctance to intrude into the private lives of others and also to the common indifference, materialism and even hostility to the things of God. Pray for revival among the believers.

6) **Pray for the 1978 National Evangelistic Campaign** organised by the leading French evangelical groups. The leaders hope to involve all the country's Evangelical Churches for this big enterprise. Pray that there will not only be a great ingathering of new converts, but that the believers may be inspired to greater faith and action in evangelism in the future.

7) **The teams of young people** from many countries conducting intensive evangelism with **OM** in specific areas in cooperation with local churches has been very beneficial to the unsaved and believers. Pray for these summer campaigns, using literature, open air and evangelistic meetings and door-to-door visitation.

8) **Foreign missions in France.** There are now about 43 different groups ministering with about 519 missionaries. There are 46 working among young people, 48 in technical ministries (largely **NAM**), and the rest in evangelism, church planting and Bible teaching. We mention a few: **ECM** and **WEC** (centre and north east), **TEAM** and **UFM** in many areas, **GEM** in Paris area, **GMU** in south. There is plenty of work for new missionaries prepared to work under French leadership and French ways. There

is a great need for missionaries to humbly adapt to the French culture. 38 of the 95 departments have no resident missionaries.

9) **There is a great need for Christian workers.** There are estimated to be 1,360 full time Evangelical Christian workers in the country, i.e., one worker for every 40,000 people. Pray for the raising up of spiritual men of God for the ministry.

10) **The Evangelical Bible Schools and Seminaries** are very important for the whole French speaking world. The significant ones: Lamorlaye Bible Institute (**GEM**) with 80 students from 20 countries, Nogent Bible Institute, Vaux Seminary for Free and Reformed Church students and Aix-en-Provence Seminary for Reformed students are all Evangelical and full. Pray for the staff and students – that the influence of these schools may be great in France and the French speaking lands all round the world. Many French believers also study at the Emmaus Bible School in Switzerland, and the Belgian Bible Institute in Brussels, Belgium.

11) **Young people are probably the most receptive group to the Gospel.** Many groups and missions have specialised in this ministry – Youth for Christ, Young Life, Eau Vive, **ECM, TEAM** in running camps, clubs, coffee bars and ministering in secondary schools; Teen Challenge among drug addicts; **SU** in schools and through Bible reading notes. Pray for many young people to be saved and integrated into good evangelical churches – the latter step usually being much harder than the former!

12) **There are 68 university type institutions,** but the evangelical witness is still very small. There are 29 only with a GBU (**IVF**) group, and most of these only have 5–10 students in them. Campus Crusade and the l'Abri Fellowship also have a significant impact. Much more remains to be done to establish evangelical groups in every faculty and to build up the believers for more effective witnessing among this rather receptive student population. There are several groups who are burdened for the overseas student population – **SIM, WEC, OM,** etc. There are about 100,000 foreign students in Paris alone. There are over 800,000 university students in France.

13) **Literature has been used of God.** Much evangelical literature has been written over the last few years, and used for intensive literature campaigns. Pray for the production of good, relevant, French written tracts, etc. Pray for the much used **WEC** Gospel broadsheet, Bientôt, that is distributed all over the world by post, etc. Pray for the 35 evangelical bookstores (5 of them of the **CLC**). There is a lack of good devotional, teaching and missiological books in French.

14) **Minority groups:**
 a) **North Africans** number 1,300,000 and are Arabs and Berbers from Algeria, Tunisia and Morocco. There are only about 100 Christians among them; the majority being Muslims. There is one little assembly of believers among them and others have joined French Evangelical Churches – one being pastored by a Berber. Pray for the ministry of the 54 **NAM** missionaries among these people in France – some in the radio and BCC ministry for North Africa, but others involved in personal ministries and a valuable youth centre in Marseille. It is hard to bridge the gap of culture and resentment against "Christians". Pray that God may raise up believers from among these people who will return with the Gospel to N. Africa.
 b) **Africans** 150,000 from former colonies in Central and West Africa. Several **SIM** missionaries witness to these people and have many opportunities among these receptive people, many being Muslims.
 c) **Portuguese** – these people are very open to the Gospel, but more must be done for them in Portuguese, for they do not adapt well to French ways of life.
 d) **Gypsies** – over one third of these people have come to the Lord over the last few years and there is now a community of believers of about 60,000. They have their own churches and methods, and aggressively reach out to their fellow Gypsies in other lands. **WBT** is translating the Bible into their language.
 e) Many **Vietnamese** and **Cambodians** have fled to France since the fall of their lands to the Communists. Many have been seeking the Lord. Pray especially for the ministry of **CMA** missionaries and pastors to their bodily and spiritual needs.
 f) **Jews** number 570,000 but there are very few Christians among them. Pray for the 10 missionaries of 4 missions who witness to them.

15) **The missionary vision of the French Church.** There are now about 350 French missionaries serving in other lands. Some work with the denominations, others with

international missions such as **SUM, SIM, TEAM, WBT,** etc. There have been six mission agencies founded in France since World War II. Pray for the growth and co-ordination of this vision.

GERMANY (West)

BACKGROUND

Area:	246,000 sq. km. – nearly half of Germany's pre-World War II territory was lost to the USSR, Poland and the Communist puppet state of East Germany.
Population:	62,100,000 (a further 17,000,000 in E. Germany). Annual growth 0.2%.
People:	**Germans** 95%. **Danes** 2%. **Immigrant workers** 3% (Turks 1,200,000; Yugoslavs 65,000; North Africans 30,000; etc.)
Capital:	Bonn 300,000. Berlin, the former capital, is divided; the western three quarters being an island of liberty 150 Km inside East Germany, but surrounded by the Communist built Wall of Shame. West Berlin 2,100,000. Other major urban areas – Ruhr area 5,200,000; Hamburg 1,800,000; Munich 1,400,000. Urbanisation 88%.
Economy:	Dramatic post-war recovery, and now one of the world's strongest economies.
Politics:	Federal parliamentary democracy made up of 11 "länder". Aligned with the Western World and a member of the EEC.
Religion:	**Roman Catholics** 44%. **Jews** 0.05% (was 4% before World War II). **Protestants** 47% – State Church (made up of 29 "land" churches, largely Lutheran but also Reformed) 30,000,000 community. Other denominations 30+; total community 1,100,000. Major groups – Baptists 255,000 community; Brethren 134,000; Methodists 169,000; Evangelical Community 80,000; Free Evang. 59,000. Conservative Evangelicals 9% of population.

Prayer Targets

1) **Germany's spiritual restoration.** Her spiritual decline has been one of the tragedies of history. The rise of humanism and destructive criticism of the Bible enfeebled the churches, and opened the door to militarism and Hitler's Nazi tyranny with its wars and massacres. Post-war materialism and the permissive society have further helped to erode the place of the Church in society.

2) **The need of Germany** is highlighted by the growing interest in the occult, the rise of the New Left, and the rapid growth of the sects such as the New Apostles, Mormons and Watchtower. There are many areas where the evangelical witness is very small or even unknown.

3) **The Roman Catholics** are predominant in parts of south and central Germany. Many are very confused by the tensions and divisions within the R.C. Church, and are more open towards the Gospel and the witness of evangelical believers than ever before. Pray for many R.C.s to come to a personal and Biblical faith.

4) **The State Church needs a movement of the Spirit of God.** The believing pastors are in a minority; for most are disciples of the successive non-Biblical theologians that have dominated in the seminaries over the last century. There is therefore much nominalism and deadness in German Protestantism.

5) **The Theological Seminaries** in the universities all teach the humanistic neo-orthodox theology that so cripples any evangelistic urge, or cultivation of a simple child-like faith in the Lord Jesus and His Word. Pray for those evangelical pastors who seek to help theological students to both come to and preserve a Biblical faith through prayer meetings and private seminars. There are only two conservative evangelical seminaries in the German speaking world – Seeheim (GEM) and Basel in Switzerland, but graduates from these are not so easily accepted by the State Church.

6) **The Free Churches** have, generally speaking, a stronger evangelical witness, but there is not much growth among them.

7) **There are some encouraging signs of an evangelical awakening.** The evangelical voice

is more listened to and respected as a result of the "No Other Gospel" and "Confessional" movements within the State Church. Pray that there may be an increasing unity and power among true believers as a result. All over Germany house groups are springing up for Bible study and prayer. The Evangelical Alliance and the well publicised Billy Graham campaigns are greatly strengthening the evangelical witness. The quantity of good evangelical literature and books has enormously increased over the last decade.

8) **There is a promising upsurge of interest in the Gospel among young people.** Many are turning away from the immorality, drug use and leftist radicalism that has so characterised German youth of late. The missionary emphasis of **OM** has passed on a vision for aggressive and successful evangelism to many young people through their mobilisation of young people in their teams. The Bible Schools are full, and a stream of keen young people are moving out into full time service at home and abroad – to mention several: Seeheim, Brake and Adelshofen. The SMD (**IVF**), with groups in nearly every university and expanding into graduate and high school work is now having a significant impact on the strongly Marxist-flavoured atmosphere of German universities.

9) **The vision for mission work has grown** as a result of the evangelical upsurge. More than half of the 1,300 German missionaries are now conservative Evangelicals. The Frankfurt Declaration by Free and State Church leaders in 1971 was a dramatic committal to Biblical mission work as opposed to the present theological emphasis on dialogue, universalism and social work as a substitute for evangelism and disciple making. Over 35 evangelical groups are now linked together in the A.E.M. (Assoc. of Ev. Miss.). There is a marked increase in the number of young people going out to the mission fields. Pray that many more churches and believers may see their responsibility for the winning of the world for the Lord.

10) **Christian Radio** – The German branch of **TWR** Evangeliums Rundfunk has made an immense impact on both Germanies and the German speaking world. Now programmes are being produced for the Italian, Spanish, Yugoslav and Turkish immigrant workers. Pray for the staff of 83 and their ministry.

11) **Immigrant labourers** number over 2,000,000. Pray for the strategic work by a number of German and international groups among the Turks – there are now more Turkish believers in Germany than in Turkey itself (**WEC, OM**). Others seek to witness to the 20,000 Albanian speaking Yugoslavs in Munich (the only sizeable Albanian speaking community in the world that is open to the Gospel). Pray for those engaged in this demanding ministry to these Muslim people.

GREAT BRITAIN

BACKGROUND

Area:	242,000 sq. km. A Union of four kingdoms (England, Scotland, Wales and Northern Ireland), The Isle of Man and the Channel Islands.
Population:	56,200,000. Growth rate 0.1%. People per sq. km. – 232.

England	46,800,000	359 people per sq. km.
Scotland	5,200,000	66 people per sq. km.
Wales	2,700,000	130 people per sq. km.
N. Ireland	1,500,000	106 people per sq. km.

Peoples:	**English** 83%. **Scots** 9%. **Welsh** 4%. **Irish** 3%.
	Immigrants 5% – West Indians 1,200,000; Indians and Pakistanis 900,000; Chinese 100,000.
Capital:	London 8,000,000. Other large cities – Birmingham 2,000,000; Glasgow 1,000,000. Urbanisation 76%.
Economy:	Very weak due to lack of raw materials, labour unrest, poor management and excessive government interference. The nation continues to live beyond its means, and has a falling standard of living.
Politics:	Parliamentary government is impotent in the face of militant leftist-Marxist trade unions that are seeking to impose their policies on the country through

their stranglehold on industry and transport. Britain is a member of the European Economic Community.

Religion: **Roman Catholics** 10%. **Jews** 1%. **Hindus** 1%. **Muslim** 1%. **Buddhists** 0.3%. **Protestants** 70%. The Church of England is the State Church; 80% of the Protestants are at least nominally Anglican, though only 3% attend church regularly. Other denominations (at least 45) – Methodists 6%; Church of Scotland (Presbyterian) 4%; United Reformed 1½%; Baptists 2%. Conservative Evangelicals 13% of population.

Points for Prayer

1) **Britain has a great spiritual need.** The nation has lost the sense of mission that made it one of the greatest moral and spiritual forces in modern history. The decline of true Christianity and the rise of the permissive society are characteristic of the age. There are now laws that permit homosexuality, witchcraft and abortion. The rise in the crime rate, immorality and the use of drugs is alarming. A beginning has been made through the interdenominational National Festival of Light to make the voice of protest of the Evangelicals to be heard, and to make the high standards of the Bible to be known. Pray for a national repentance and return to God. Pray that believers may be more concerned about the state of the country, and be more earnest in prayer.

2) **There is need for another revival.** The political and economic tensions have become so great that the disintegration of the whole country is not impossible. In similar national crises in the past, God has graciously sent revival, as in the time of Wesley. There has been a national revival every century for the past 800 years, but the revival for this century is overdue. Pray for it.

3) **Few nations have produced such a galaxy of great men of God** – such as Wycliffe, Tyndale, Latimer, the Puritans, Whitfield, Wesley, Carey, Hudson Taylor, George Muller, etc. Pray that Britain may continue to give such men to the world.

4) **The Church of England** is a strange body, for it is both Catholic and Reformed. The powerful Anglo-Catholic wing is very little different from the Roman Catholic Church. Many in the middle are liberal in theology. Then there is the growing evangelical wing that is reformed in theology. Three out of five of the top posts in the Church are held by Evangelicals, and more than one quarter of the ministers preach the true Gospel. Some of Britain's finest evangelical leaders, convention speakers, writers and theologians are found in this group. Pray that the Gospel may be more and more accepted and preached within this Church.

5) **The non-conformist Churches** are largely the fruit of former revivals, and now have about 6,000,000 adherents, but the number of true believers is now much smaller. There is much formalism and deadness. Few denominations are free from modern theology, yet in each one there is a minority of fine evangelical believers. Church unity and social issues are too often more important than the winning of souls; hence nearly every denomination has a declining membership. The great need is for a fresh move of the Spirit of God.

6) **The Evangelical movement** is now stronger and more respected than for many years. Many factors have worked together to make this so – Billy Graham's campaigns, the splendid work of **SU** in the schools, and the UCCF **(IVF)** in the colleges and universities, first class evangelical literature, and the many who have passed through Evangelical Theological Colleges and Bible Schools since World War II, etc. Pray that the believers may be a credit to the Gospel they seek to proclaim to their land. Pray for all efforts to win the lost – both from within local churches and through mass evangelism.

7) **Despite growth, there are serious weaknesses found among Evangelicals:**
   a) Lack of Bible teaching and personal study of the Scriptures have made the average believer hazy on doctrine, shallow in evangelism and undiscerning of error among those who claim to base their teachings on God's Word.
   b) A sad increase in worldliness and therefore, little real concern for world evangelism or the support of the missionary enterprise in prayer and giving.
   c) Divisions – denominational loyalty, ecumenism, neo-Pentecostalism, action on social

issues and the bitter Calvinist-Arminian dispute – these all damage the unity of believers and hinder their witness to the world outside.

8) **The Charismatic movement** has had a big influence on the churches and believers. There has been much disputing and even divisions in church fellowships on this issue. On the negative side there has been an overemphasis on gifts at the expense of holiness, and emotion at the expense of doctrine. On the other hand many churches and Christians have been brought to a Biblical faith. There has been a welcome emphasis on worship, fellowship and singing of Scripture. Largely through the charismatic movement, the house church movement has become a significant factor in the spiritual life of the country. Pray for balance, love, unity and evangelistic zeal among believers of all groups.

9) **Young people** have been turning to the Lord in fairly large numbers, but relatively few find a real home in Evangelical churches. Pray for the bridging of the very large generation gap – for many young people either never really become involved in the life of a church fellowship, or go off to form their own (often introspective) house groups.

10) **Students.** Pray for the excellent work of CSSM and **SU** among young people and also for the UCCF among the college and university students. The proportion of Christian students in the universities is far higher than the national average. There are now Christian Unions (UCCF) in 550 colleges, but there are yet 300 with no active group. Pray for the 35 travelling secretaries as they counsel student leaders and seek to establish new groups. Pray for the student leadership that they may have maturity. Pray for outreach to the unconverted students – often through evangelistic Bible studies. The believers are generally making a great impact on the spiritually fairly receptive student body.

11) **Overseas students** are a fertile field for missionary work by students. About 11.5% of the students in universities and colleges are from other lands (i.e., about 80,000 – of which 15,000 are Muslim, and from lands closed to the Gospel). Pray for all programmes to welcome and befriend overseas students, and pray that these may lead to the conversion of many – there have been some dramatic cases of conversions among these people.

12) **The West Indians** have immigrated from the poor islands of the Caribbean since World War II, and are now a very large minority in some cities. Too little has been done to make these nominally Christian people welcome in churches. There is increasing racial hatred which is made worse by Britain's economic plight. Pray for these frustrated people.

13) **The Muslims** now number about 500,000 and the number of mosques in Britain has grown from 1 to 300 in 30 years. Most of the Muslims are Pakistanis and Indians,but some English have been converted to Islam. A concerted attempt is now being made by Muslims to win Britain for Islam. Pray for these Muslim people. Pray that believers will seek out opportunities to befriend and win them for Jesus. Pray for churches to initiate an active programme aimed at teaching their members how to win Muslims and bring them into a Christian fellowship. A number of missionary societies have now appointed missionaries who have worked in Asia to witness to the Muslims and Hindus. Pray for the right strategy for the discipling of these people.

14) **The Chinese** number 100,000 and are mostly nurses and restaurant workers. Pray for several Chinese groups seeking to witness to these people, and win them for the Lord. Pray that such converts may become missionaries to Asia.

15) **The Missionary vision** has grown dim through pessimism and lack of enthusiasm, and few young people show much interest. There are still about 7,000 British missionaries serving in lands all over the world. There are also very many missionary societies operating from Britain (approx. 147). Pray for the return of a sacrificial concern to British Churches for the evangelisation of the world, for much yet remains to be done. Pray that more young people may be inspired to serve the Lord through such groups as **OM** in mobilising thousands of young people for evangelism in Europe, and beyond, every summer. Pray that British believers may have a greater concern for the other EEC countries such as Belgium, Luxembourg, Italy, France, etc.

GREECE

BACKGROUND

Area: 132,000 sq. km. Famed for its ancient civilisation and now for its attrac-tiveness to tourists.
Population: 9,000,000. **Greeks** 98.5%. **Turks** 1.3% (latter in Macedonia and Rhodes).
Capital: Athens 2,540,000 (including the port of Piraeus). Urbanisation 53%.
Politics: 7 years of military dictatorship ended in 1974. Now a multi-party par-liamentary democracy. Applying for membership of the European Economic Community.
Religion: **Attitude of Government** – Freedom of religious conscience but proselytism at the expense of the State Church is illegal.
           Greek Orthodox – the State Church 98%. Only 2% are churchgoers.
           Muslims 1.2%.
           Roman Catholics 0.5%. **Watchtower** 0.16% (15,000).
           Protestants 0.3%. Community 15,000. Membership 5,000. Larger groups – Greek Evangelical 2,000 members; Free Evangelical 2,000; 4 Pentecostal groups approx. 2,000. Evangelicals 0.2% of population.

Prayer Points

1) **The Orthodox Church dominates the religious life of the country.** Much superstition and tradition with little knowledge of the Scriptures is found everywhere. Pray that the people may be liberated by the preaching of the Gospel.

2) **Formerly there was much persecution of the Protestants,** but the influence of the Orthodox Church has been weakened since the restoration of democracy in 1974. The Protestants are now more likely to be harassed or suffer discrimination. Pray that the believers may be delivered from fear. They are all too often unwilling to use the many opportunities to witness because they are a despised minority.

3) **Much of the country is largely without an evangelical witness.** Pray for the evangel-isation of the country areas, the Aegean Islands and also the Muslim Turkish minority.

4) **The Protestant Church** is very small and is only growing at about the same rate as the population. Pray for the 60 or so Greek full time pastors and Christian workers. Pray for the mobilisation of the believers for the winning of those in their local com-munities and also to reach out to the many areas without a witness. Pray that all legal means may be fully used to win the lost.

5) **There is a great need for Christian workers to be trained locally.** Many young Christians, who seek Bible training elsewhere, do not return to their spiritually hard homeland. Pray for the **GEM** Bible Institute in Athens. There are now 15 part time students at the evening school. Pray that plans for this B.I. to become a fully residential day school may be realised.

6) **The small missionary force** of 25 or so has a majority of workers who are of Greek parentage or birth, but who were converted in North America or Australia and were led to return to witness in their native land. They need no residence visas, non-Greeks needing permits. Most of the missionaries are involved in pastoral, literature or Bible training ministries. Pray for more workers to be called to this land.

7) **University students** need to be reached with the Gospel. There is no permanent witness among them. Pray for such to be raised up.

8) **The printing of all forms of Christian literature is free,** but must, by law, be marked "evangelical", which is a derogatory term to most Greeks. Pray for the witness of the several Christian bookshops and the very active Greek Bible Society. The latter distributes Bibles in the Army, some schools and some other places. Advertisements of the Gospel placed in several national newspapers have proved fruitful – pray for this.

9) **Radio.** Both **TWR** and **IBRA** have many Greek broadcasts weekly, and there has been some response to this. Pray for this ministry.

10) **Expatriate Greek communities** are large in Germany (250,000), Australia (approx.

260,000) and the U.S.A. (around 2 million). These people have been much more systematically evangelised, and there are now assemblies of believers among them in all these and several other lands. Pray for these believers and their missionary vision – especially for their homeland. Pray for the considerable amount of literature that is handed out to Greeks in these lands.

ICELAND

BACKGROUND

Area: 104,000 sq. km. A large volcanic island in the North Atlantic; mountainous, largely barren, and many large glaciers.
Population: 221,000. Annual growth 1.3%. People per sq. km. – 1.
Peoples: **Icelanders** 98% – original settlers came from Norway 1,000 years ago.
Capital: Reykjavik 82,000. Urbanisation 82%.
Economy: Prosperous, but very dependent on the fishing industry.
Politics: Conservative coalition from 1974 that has stopped implementation of leftist policies of former government in which Communists participated.
Religion: **Roman Catholics** 0.6%.
                   Protestants 98% – almost entirely of the State Lutheran Church.
                   Free Churches 6% – the Free Church 10,000 community; Pentecostals 2,000. Also small groups of Brethren and Baptists, each with several hundred. Evangelicals 4% of population.

Prayer Targets

1)   **The Icelanders are nominally Christian,** but prosperity is causing a drift away from the churches and a growing interest in occultism, promiscuity and leftist ideology. Evangelistic work has been discouraging in this spiritual climate with much indifference shown to the things of God.

2)   **There is much nominalism in both the Lutheran and the Free Church today** and there are very few Bible based churches where the new birth is preached. Pray for the small churches now being planted by fairly recently arrived missions, such as Southern Baptists and Swedish Pentecostal missionaries. There are also two groups of evangelical believers indirectly linked to the State Church. Pray for the growth of the evangelical witness.

3)   **Immigrant labourers** – there are a number of Yugoslavs and others working on development projects. Pray that these people may be evangelised in their work camps.

IRELAND (Eire and Northern Ireland)

Note: Eire is an independent Republic, and N. Ireland under the British Crown and part of the United Kingdom. Both are politically, culturally and spiritually so different, yet their futures are inextricably intertwined, hence their combined coverage.

BACKGROUND

Area: Eire 68,000 sq. km., people per sq. km. – 45.
                   N. Ireland 14,000 sq. km., people per sq. km. – 107.
Population: Eire 3,100,000; N. Ireland 1,500,000
Capital: Dublin 575,000 in Eire; Belfast in N. Ireland 400,000
Economy: Eire rather poor and agricultural (member of EEC) and N. Ireland more industrial but plagued by high unemployment.
Politics: The centuries-old conflict of the Irish Catholics against English-Scots Protestants has not yet ended. The 1920 partition of Ireland between the 26 R.C. counties in the south, and 6 Protestant counties of Ulster in the north did not

provide a permanent solution. The Catholic minority started campaigning for civil rights in 1968, but this gradually degenerated into a war by the Communist-backed Irish Republican Army for the reunification of Ireland under a Marxist government. The Protestant backlash has brought virtual civil war to the unhappy land, between extremists of both sides, with the British army trying to keep them apart. The end to violence seems far off and the future dark and uncertain.

Religion: Eire – **Roman Catholics** 93%; **Protestants** 4.5%.
N. Ireland **Roman Catholics** 38%; **Protestants** 62%.
Protestant Community in all Ireland 954,000 (128,000 in Eire).
Major denominations: Church of Ireland (Anglican) 450,000 Community; Presbyterians (2) 410,000; Methodists 75,000;
Baptists 16,000;
Conservative Evangelicals – N. Ireland 30%; Eire 2%.

Prayer Targets

1) **Eire is the only R.C. country in the English speaking world.** Although not the State Church, Rome controls, or has a say in every aspect of the life of the country. There are 4,500 priests in Eire, and many thousands of R.C. missionaries have gone out all over the world. Since the Vatican II Council, the R.C. hierarchy has lost a good deal of its influence, persecution of Protestants has diminished, and there is a new spirit of openness and freedom to study the Scriptures and to consider the claims of the Gospel. More and more Roman Catholics are turning to the Lord and forming their own little groups for prayer and Bible study (few join the Protestant denominations). The charismatic movement has led to the conversion of some, but only confirmed others in their dogmas. Pray for a move of the Spirit in Eire.

2) **The separationist politics of the R.C.s in education and housing in N. Ireland** are a large contributory factor to the present communal (and NOT religious) violence. Pray for peace between the two communities and a fair integration. Pray that the deep bitternesses and resentments may be healed, and the plans of the Communists thwarted by a mighty turning of people to the Lord in revival.

3) **The Protestants in the north** are more Evangelical than their counterparts in England. The true believers are the only bridge of sanity between the nominal Protestants and the Catholics, yet some extremist sections of the Church have sadly provoked intransigence and also brought division to the Evangelicals on the difficult political issues. There are deepening divisions over the ecumenical movement and also the charismatic movement (the latter with its appeal to both Protestants and R.C.s to meet together for fellowship, but on the basis of an experience rather than the Cross of Christ). Pray for real Bible based unity among believers, and also for their witness in these troubled times, that many may be saved through their Christ-like lives. The missionary vision of the believers is far greater than that found in England today.

4) **The Protestants in Eire** are slowly decreasing through emigration. they have religious freedom and are the key to the evangelisation of the Catholic majority, but are isolated from them by social and cultural differences and prejudice. Pray that these believers may be revived and become effective witnesses to the now more receptive Catholics.

5) **The evangelistic outreach in Eire** by many denominations and evangelistic missions continues unabated despite the tragic shadow of the violence of the I.R.A. that hangs like a pall over all Ireland. There are a number of intrepid evangelists and colporteurs who witness through evangelistic meetings, open air meetings, personal witness and through Christian bookshops and literature displays in shows, fairs, etc. They face some opposition and converts are liable to suffer for their faith, yet the seed is sown and produces fruit in some lives.

ITALY

BACKGROUND

Area:	301,000 sq. km. – a long peninsula that dominates the Central Mediterranean.
Population:	56,300,000. Growth 0.8% p.a. People per sq. km. – 187.
Peoples:	**Italians** – descended from numerous different peoples.
Capital:	Rome 2,900,000. Other cities of note: Milan 1,800,000; Naples 1,800,000; Turin 1,200,000. Urbanisation 53%.
Economy:	Basically unstable due to a lack of raw materials, inefficient bureaucracy, industrial unrest and galloping inflation.
Politics:	Politically unstable since World War II. The well organised Communist Party only just failed to become the largest party in the National Assembly in the 1976 elections. Only short-lived coalition governments have been able to keep the Communists from power. Many fear the probability of a Communist dictatorship. Italy is a member of the EEC.
Religion:	There is religious freedom, but the still powerful R.C. Church can make things difficult for the Protestants. **Roman Catholicism** – the State religion – 94%. **Protestants** – 0.8%. Community 440,000. Denominations largely non-Evangelical: Waldensians 30,000. Community; Methodists 5,000. Evangelical groups: Assemblies of God 250,000; Brethren 10,000 (?); Baptists. Conservative Evangelicals 0.7%.

Points for Prayer

1) **Italy remains largely unreached by Evangelicals.** Possibly only 1,000 of Italy's 31,000 communities have an evangelical witness. There are many towns and cities without an effective group of believers. There are even whole provinces without a resident witness to the Lord. Most of Sardinia and Lecce in the S.E. have few Evangelicals.

2) **VATICAN CITY** is the last vestige of the Roman Catholic Pope's temporal empire in central Italy. It is an independent city-state with a population of 1,000. From here the Pope rules the world's 765,000,000 Roman Catholics. The Roman Church is in turmoil because of the conflict between the traditional and reforming factions, the impact of the ecumenical movement, the growing charismatic movement and the increasing use of the Bible by R.C.s. Pray that all these factors may be used of God to bring many R.C.s into the light of the Gospel.

3) **The Roman Catholic Church is increasingly despised and ignored by Italians** because of its interference in politics and efforts to preserve the privileges of the powerful. This is especially true of the youth. Sadly, few of these disillusioned people have had the chance to hear the Gospel clearly, and it is the false promises of Communism that are winning their minds.

4) **Pray for this land to remain open for the Gospel.** The gaining strength of Communism is most marked in the industrial north, and many have been hardened to the Gospel. A Communist takeover is likely, humanly speaking. Pray that the present opportunities for the Christians may not be lost.

5) **The Protestant witness is small and often not effective in outreach.** The centuries of R.C. persecution and discrimination, though now largely a thing of the past, has left its mark and made the Protestants feel inferior and reluctant to witness to the oppressively large R.C. majority. Several denominations are liberal in theology, and most denominations show little growth. Pray for revival to stir up these churches to the huge task of winning Italy for Jesus.

6) **There are encouraging signs for the Gospel.** There is a new and genuine interest in the Gospel in nearly all levels of society and parts of the country. Some believers and denominations are very active and are seeing people converted. The Assemblies of God is growing fast – especially in the poorer south, and now two thirds of all the

believers in the country are of this group. There is also a growing Fellowship of Free Evangelical Churches. The new Evangelical Alliance is just getting under way. Pray for continued growth.

7) **The need for foreign missionaries is very great.** There are now about 270 missionaries working in the land, but this number could be greatly increased. Believers from the U.S.A. and Australia of Italian descent and also Brazilians would probably be more easily able to adapt to the Italian way of life. There are many open doors for those willing to do a humble work of befriending people, overcoming their prejudices, and discipling them for the Lord and, above all, of working together with Italians to plant churches. Pray for the calling of such.

8) **There are over 50 missionary societies ministering in the land.** Pray for the evangelistic and church planting ministries of **ECM, GMU, UFM** in the north, **WEC** in Sardinia, **WIM** in Sicily and **GEM** in the Rome area.

9) **The need for dedicated Italian full-time workers has never been greater.** There are 4 Protestant Bible Schools and seminaries and only ONE interdenominational Bible School; the latter being run by the **GEM.** There are no more than 50 Italians studying for the Lord's work in Italy. Pray for the calling of students of the right calibre. Pray for the staff, their life and teaching ministry.

10) **Literature distribution has borne fruit.** Pray for the valuable work of Every Home Crusade and also the **OM** teams. **OM** has played an important role in stimulating Italian believers into aggressive evangelism.

11) **The follow-up of contacts** of mass evangelism presents real problems with the lack of spiritually qualified workers, and also the reluctance of new believers to associate with the despised Protestants. Pray for the increasing use of homes as neutral meeting places for Bible studies.

12) **Areas of special need:**
   a) **Sardinia,** an island with 1,600,000 people. There are only about 400 believers, some who are associated with the witness of **WEC.**
   b) **Sicily,** 5,000,000 people living in poverty. The Mafia gangster society affects much of the life of the island. There are small, but growing groups of believers.

13) **The 700,000 strong university student population** in 44 universities is more open to the Gospel than ever before, but has been largely ignored by Evangelicals. There are tiny groups of Christians totalling 80 believers only, in a handful of the universities. Several **IVF** workers in Rome and Padua and several other missionaries in Milan and Naples seek to witness to the students.

ANDORRA

A tiny independent principality of 465 sq. km. in the Pyrenee Mountains between Spain and France with a population of only 26,000. Only one third of the population is truly Andorran. The state depends on tourism and tax free concessions to banks and traders for its wealth. There are no known Evangelicals; the entire population is Roman Catholic. Some Gospel literature has been distributed in the land. Pray for the evangelisation of these people.

MONACO

A small independent principality on the south coast of France with an area of only 189 hectares (0.25 sq. km.) and a population of 24,000.

Points for Prayer

1) **This tiny land is almost entirely Roman Catholic.** No open evangelism is allowed. Pray that the Monagesque people may be evangelised.

2) **Trans World Radio has its home here.** This remarkable work of God has grown to a ministry that reaches out to the whole of Europe, the Communist lands and North Africa. Many of the lands in these areas are only able to be reached with the Gospel by means of radio.

Pray for the network of studios and programme producers in many lands – especially in Poland and West Germany (German **TWR**) where programmes are produced for Communist lands, and France (**NAM**) and Spain (**GMU**) where Arabic and Berber programmes are prepared for North Africa.

Pray for the many hours of programmes broadcast each week in 30 languages. Pray for the large staff and their walk with God.

Pray for the follow-up ministry through correspondence courses and linking seekers up with believers in their own countries.

SAN MARINO

A small 61 sq. km. republic with a population of 20,000 people. The state is an enclave in north central Italy. As far as is known all the people are Roman Catholic. There is no known Protestant witness in this little territory.

LUXEMBOURG

BACKGROUND

Area:	2,600 sq. km. – the smallest of the Low Countries (Belgium, Netherlands and Luxembourg).
Population:	360,000 **Luxembourgers** of mixed French and German origin.
Capital:	Luxembourg 80,000. Urbanisation 68%.
Economy:	Wealthy industrial state. A member of the European Economic Community.
Religion:	One of the most strongly Roman Catholic countries in Europe.
	Roman Catholics 98%.
	Protestants 1.7% who are mostly nominal Lutherans. The evangelical witness is confined to little groups of Mennonites, Free Evangelical Church, Assemblies of God. There are about 150 born again believers in the little land. Conservative Evangelicals 0.2%.

Points for Prayer

1) **The dominant position of the Roman Catholic Church** remains unchanged. The revolutionary changes within the R.C. Church elsewhere have not really made the Luxembourgers more open to the Gospel. Pray for the spiritual liberation of this dark land.

2) **The evangelical witness is very weak.** The believers are rather scattered and lack the fellowship they need. Pray for the planting of a vigorous Church in the land. Pray for the believers and their growth in grace. Pray that they may have a vision for the winning of the lost.

3) **There are only about 7 full time workers for the Lord** in the land, i.e., one for every 50,000 people. Pray for others to be called. Teen Challenge run a coffee bar – pray for outreach to the youth. **OM** teams made a special effort in 1975, through which good contacts were made, but few were added to the Protestant denominations.

4) **Pray for the Mennonites** – their small group needs wisdom and strength to continue their evangelising of Luxembourg. There has not been much encouragement for them in the past. Pray for the break-through for God.

MALTA

BACKGROUND

Area:	316 sq. km. – three small, but strategic islands in the central Mediterranean Sea. The site of the Apostle Paul's shipwreck.
Population:	322,000 Maltese. Growth 0.4% p.a. People per sq. km. – 1,018.

Politics: The Labour Government is seeking to end the dependence of the economy on British and NATO use of Malta as a military base, and make the land politically neutral.
Religion: Very limited religious freedom for non-Roman Catholics.
Roman Catholics 99.9%.
Protestants – about 20 believers.

Prayer Points

1) **Malta is Europe's least evangelised land.** The very dominant Roman Catholic Church opposed any Protestant missionary activity before independence in 1964. Pray for the Maltese people to come to a living faith in Jesus through the preaching of the Gospel.

2) **Pray for complete religious freedom.** There was no religious freedom before 1964, and all converts to the Lord had to leave the country. There are still many legal and social difficulties for the few Maltese believers, although the situation is improving.

3) **Much friendship has been shown by some in authority for the cause of the Gospel.** Pray that this may lead to the opening up of the land for the Lord Jesus.

4) **The Roman Catholics have shown more interest** in the study of the Bible and in the need of a personal faith. The visit of the Gospel ship M.V. Logos (**OM**) in 1976 greatly increased this. Pray for their salvation.

5) **The few national believers** are associated with the little Brethren assembly and the Elim Pentecostal Christian Centre. Pray for the few Maltese church leaders that they may be strong and bold for the Lord in the face of opposition.

6) **Pray for new converts** who find it very difficult to identify with and integrate into the despised little groups of believers. Pray for the combined outreach of believers as they hold informal meetings in private homes seeking to win people in this tactful manner.

7) **Several missionaries visit the country on tourist visas.** Pray that some may be able to obtain residence visas.

8) **Literature.** Pray for the 500 copies of the Maltese N.T. now in circulation, and also that the problems hindering the completion of the O.T. may be removed. Several thousand Maltese have written in for Bible correspondence courses. The believers aim to start a second coverage of every home in the land with Christian literature. Pray for the **SGM** portions so used.

NETHERLANDS

BACKGROUND

Area: 34,000 sq. km. – over one quarter of the land is below sea level and there is a continuing dramatic programme for reclaiming land from the sea.
Population: 13,800,000. Growth Rate 0.9%. People per sq. km. – 405.
Peoples: **Dutch** 97%. Immigrants from Indonesia and Suriname 1.3%. Guest workers 1.2%.
Capital: Amsterdam 1,002,000. Other cities: The Hague – seat of government 685,000 and Rotterdam 1,040,000 – the world's busiest port. Urbanisation 77%.
Politics: Dramatic recovery and readjustment after World War II and the loss of East Indies (Indonesia) in 1949. A member of the E.E.C.
Religion: There is complete freedom of religion.
Roman Catholics 38% – largely in the southern provinces.
No Church Connection 26%. **Muslims** 1%.
Protestants 36%. Community 4,695,000. Denominations 25+. Largest groups – Dutch Reformed Church (state supported) 900,000; other Calvinistic groups (13) approx. 500,000 members. The more Evangelical denominations – Baptist, Free Evangelical, Brethren, Pentecostals (most fairly small). Conservative Evangelicals 9%.

Points for Prayer

1) This land has a great history of revival and suffering for the sake of the Word of God. The Protestant Church has seen great decline with much deadness and formalism evident. The younger generation is generally leftist, free-thinking and churchless, and increasing in political power. Holland has gained a reputation for open immorality in Europe. **Revival is the land's greatest need.**

2) **The Roman Catholic Church** has been growing at the expense of the Protestants for decades, but now is also declining in numbers. The R.C. Church is possibly more vital and rebellious of the Pope's authority than in most countries in Europe. In the growing declension, few are being won to a living faith in the Lord Jesus.

3) **The Protestant Churches are generally dead,** formal, legalistic and losing people. Nearly every denomination has a great variety of theological beliefs – liberal, neo-orthodox, orthodox and a few evangelicals. Sadly, many pastors are more Marxist than Christian in their thinking. The churches need prayer that they return to a warm evangelical faith, separation from the world, good Bible teaching and a burden to evangelise the many Dutch and immigrant peoples in their own land.

4) **There is a growing shortage of full-time workers in the churches.** Most seminaries have few students. Only the few Evangelical Bible Schools continue to maintain their numbers.

5) **The Evangelische Omroep** is an interdenominational Christian Broadcasting Corporation that produces many hours of television and radio programmes for the state broadcasting service every week. These broadcasts and the E.O. magazine are greatly strengthening the evangelical voice in the land. Pray for the leadership of this excellent organisation and its outreach.

6) **The evangelical witness is growing in effectiveness** and there are some encouraging signs of the Lord's working. There are many prayer and Bible study groups springing up all over the country – largely through E.O. and the Pentecostals. These house meetings are where most of the real Bible teaching and conversions occur. Pray that this movement may continue to grow, and be kept free from error and byways of doctrine.

7) **Foreign missions are few,** and workers from other lands number no more than 30, yet their influence is out of all proportion to their numbers. Pray for the witness of Youth for Christ. **IVF, ECM.**

8) **Missionary interest** is not very great and could be much increased. There are now about 120 missionaries in the denominational societies, and a further 250 in the interdenominational missions serving round the world.

9) **Young people need much prayer.** Christian youth groups are generally weak, worldly, lacking in discipline and possibly more dangerous than useful. Yet God has been working among young people in the last few years, but quite apart from the churches. Pray that such converts may make a useful contribution to the churches, and not be led into error.

10) **The immigrant population needs to be evangelised.** A little work is done among the Chinese, Portuguese (7,400) and Yugoslavs (12,000), but the Turks (54,000). Moroccans (30,000) and Spanish (32,000) have little opportunity to hear of the Gospel. Pray also for the Ambonese* (30,000) and Surinamese (150,000) communities which do not really fit into the national life, and need specialised attention to win them.

NORWAY

BACKGROUND

Area: 324,000 sq. km. – one of the 4 Scandinavian countries, a long, fjord-indented, mountainous land stretching into the Arctic.

Population: 4,000,000. Minority of 20,000 **Lapps** in the far north. Population growth 0.7% p.a. People per sq. km. – 12.

Capital: Oslo 469,000. Urbanisation 45%.

Politics: A constitutional monarchy with a stable democratic government.

Religion: Protestants 99%.
The state Lutheran Church 94%. Other Protestants 4%. 10 Free Churches. Community 160,000. Membership 115,000. Largest: Pentecostals 40,000; Lutheran Free Church 17,000; Methodists 14,000; Baptists 12,000; Mission Covenant 8,000. Conservative Evangelicals 25%.

Points for Prayer

1) **Almost the entire population is Protestant,** but there are very many who do not understand about the new birth. The believers long for revival.
2) **The Lutheran Church** being the State Church, has many nominal members. Yet the evangelical witness is very strong in contrast to the situation in Sweden and Denmark. Nearly half the leaders and pastors are evangelical. Many voluntary organisations have sprung up within the State Church with a burden for home and overseas evangelism. Many fine missionaries have gone out from these groups. Pray for this large Church, its leadership and the growth of true spirituality in its congregations.
3) **The dissenting, or free, churches** are stagnant and need to come out of their isolation to evangelise. Only the Pentecostals and the Mission Covenant Churches are growing. Pray that the leadership may continue to be evangelical in theology and Biblically grounded.
4) **The charismatic movement** seems to have brought much new life to many congregations of both the State and Free Churches. Many young people have found the Lord as a result. Pray that this movement may remain Scriptural and not be divisive.
5) **Norway has made a great contribution to world evangelisation.** This little land has probably more missionaries than any other nation on earth for the size of its population. There are 23 Norwegian missionary societies, and about 1,500 Norwegians in these and international missions have gone to serve the Lord in other lands.

PORTUGAL

BACKGROUND

Area: 91,631 sq. km. – Europe's most southwesterly country.
Population: 9,500,000. Growth rate – 0.4%, due to much emigration and job-seeking as "guest" workers in other European countries. There are 2,000,000 **Portuguese** in France, Germany and Britain, 103 people per sq. km. There are 900,000 Portuguese refugees from former colonies in Africa.
Capital: Lisbon 1,100,000. Urbanisation 26%.
Economy: The 1974 Revolution disrupted the stable, but poor economy. Communist disruption of the economic life and the spirit of freedom, together with the world economic recession, has brought the country to starvation and ruin.
Politics: The fifty year dictatorship ended in April 1974. In the following year the Communists virtually gained control of the country, though they were ultimately thwarted through the election of a democratic government in 1976. Yet the Communists succeeded in quickly handing over power in the overseas territories of Mozambique, Angola, Guinea Bissau, Sao Tomé and the Cape Verde Islands to minority Marxist regimes. Portuguese Timor was later taken over by Indonesia. Macao (China) is Portugal's last colony.
Religion: Complete freedom of religion since the revolution.
Roman Catholics 90% – the State Church until 1974. Now somewhat discredited because of support for the former regime.
Protestants 1.3% are increasing very rapidly in the new freedom. Estimated community 140,000. Membership 60,000. Denominations 15.
Largest groups: Assemblies of God (3 groups) 15,000 members; Baptists (2 groups) 4,000; Presbyterians 2,000; Brethren 10,000(?) members; Gypsy Evangelical 9,000 community. Evangelicals 1%.

Points for Prayer

1) **Pray for peace and stability** as well as freedom for the Portuguese people. The Communists still have much power despite their recent setbacks. The new political freedom has generated much division and bitterness. Pray for the conversion of many who now claim to be atheists.

2) **The terrible sufferings of many Portuguese** over the last few years have made them more open to the Gospel. Pray for a mighty harvest of souls in these days.

3) **The refugees from the former colonies** came to Portugal in 1975 possessing nothing, and with little prospect for many of making a living in Portugal. They are bitter, frustrated and angry. Pray for the evangelisation of these people, for few have ever heard the Gospel.

4) **Unreached peoples in Portugal** – in both the far north and south there are many areas with no real evangelical witness. The many new city dwellers and the middle and upper classes have largely been passed by and need to be evangelised. Pray that the believers may get a vision for winning these people.

5) **The extraordinary freedom since 1974** has given the Evangelicals an amazing opportunity to evangelise openly by all means – open air meetings, house visitation, literature and extensive use of Christian and commercial broadcasting. Pray that the believers and missionaries may be bold to use these means now.

6) **The churches are growing rapidly.** Most of the larger denominations are evangelical, and work together in the Portuguese Evangelical Alliance. In 1975 there were 600 churches and 45,000 believers associated with the E.A. Pray for the effective discipling of the many young believers in the churches. The great need is for mature leaders and Bible teachers. There is much growth in the Assemblies of God, Baptist, Nazarene and Brethren.

7) **Bible training assumes new importance in today's Portugal.** There are a number of good denominational Seminaries and Bible Schools, but little on an inter-denominational basis. Pray for the vision of **GEM** to launch a residential, inter-denominational Bible School – there are now about 100 students studying in the TEE courses.

8) **Missionaries are now much needed** after the years of restriction on their activities. Pray for **TEAM** in evangelistic and church planting ministries and the expanding ministries of **GEM**. There is a growing number of Brazilian missionaries entering the land. Pray for reinforcements to seize the present opportunities.

9) **Student work is yet in its infancy.** Pray for the GBU (**IVF**) in the three universities where Communism and anti-religious feeling is strong. Pray also for the excellent work of **SU** and **CEF** among school children.

10) **Literature** has been much used in the conversion of Portuguese. Pray for the CEDO Gospel broadsheet (see p. 30) and the tract ministry of "NUCLEO". Much more needs to be done to produce good Portuguese Christian literature.

11) **Pray for the evangelisation of the very receptive Portuguese** in other European countries (over 1,000,000 in France, 500,000 in Germany). Many live in barracks and hostels, and only a few with their families. Many have been converted (5% estimated to now be Protestant), but the need is for more workers to bring the Gospel to them and plant churches among them.

SPAIN

BACKGROUND

Area: 505,000 sq. km. – occupying the major part of the Iberian Peninsula.
Population: 36,000,000. Growth 1.1%. People per sq. km. – 71.
Peoples: **Spanish speaking** – several dialects: Castilian 30%, Catalan 21%, Andalusian 17%, Galician 13%.
                     Basques 17%. They live in the 4 provinces on the north coast adjoining France. Strong separatist movement for the creation of an independent Basque State used as a pretext for terrorism by the Marxist ETA group.

Gypsies 1%. A strange nomadic people found in nearly every country in Europe.

Capital: Madrid 3,146,000. Other major cities: Barcelona 1,745,000. Urbanisation 61%.

Economy: Relatively poor, but rapid improvement through industrialisation and tourism. Labour unrest and the world recession now hindering growth.

Politics: Increasing democratisation and liberalisation since the death of Dictator Franco in 1976. King Juan Carlos spearheads the gradual reforms. The Communists are seeking to use the greater freedom to disrupt the life of the country through their many front organisations, trade unions and the strong separatist movements among the Basques and Catalonians.

Religion: **Attitude of the Government.** The Franco regime persecuted the Protestants and gave them no legal recognition for 30 years. In 1968 discriminatory laws were eased. The Roman Catholic Church is still the State Church though the rapid liberalisations since 1975 have eroded its privileged position. A complete separation of Church and State in a few years is not an impossibility. There is now more religious freedom than ever before.

Roman Catholics 99% but only about 8% could be considered faithful. There is a strong anti-Rome sentiment right through the country.

Protestants 0.3%. Community about 55,000 membership 35,000 – most of whom are evangelical in theology. There are about 19 denominations. Largest – Assemblies of God 10,000 members; Brethren 8,000; Baptist 5,000; Independent Evangelical 5,000.

Evangelicals 0.2%.

Points for Prayer

1) **The ending of the dominance of the Roman Catholic Church** and the new spirit of freedom in Spain is bringing an openness to disillusioned Roman Catholics to new ideas. Sadly, many are attracted by Communism, for few have had the opportunity to hear the true Gospel. Pray that there may now be a great harvest for the Kingdom of God.

2) **Spain is now one of the countries most open to the Gospel** after centuries of ruthless persecution of non-Catholics. This is an answer to prayer. Pray that there may now be a period of freedom for the Gospel. There is a real threat of a Communist revolution or takeover.

3) **The Protestant Church is very small,** but growing fairly rapidly and spreading into new areas. Only Greece, Cyprus and Malta in Free Europe have a proportionately smaller number of believers. The growth is most marked in the Assemblies of God, and to a lesser extent in the Baptist and Independent Evangelical Churches.

4) **There are serious weaknesses among believers** which hinder the churches from taking full advantage of the many opportunities:
   a) The feelings of inferiority after years of being a despised, oppressed minority that was officially rejected by society.
   b) The lack of both education and Bible teaching among believers which makes it very hard for most to give a reasonable account for the faith that is in them.
      Pray for their spiritual liberation and empowering so that they may beome a mighty force for the evangelisation of Spain.

5) **The leadership in the churches.** Pray that they may be able to both teach and inspire their fellowships to action as they plan the strategy to win their country for the Lord Jesus. Pray for the continuing ministry of **OM** which has already had a very marked effect in mobilising and enthusing young Spanish believers into aggressive evangelism through open air meetings, literature and door-to-door evangelism.

6) **There is an acute need for more and better trained national pastors.** Many of the 350 pastors have had little formal Bible training. There are now about 8 Bible Schools and Seminaries (some part time). Pray for th **GEM** Spanish Bible Institute and others that a growing stream of mature men of God may go out to serve the Lord. Pray that Spanish believers may give more liberally for their support, for too many are supported entirely by funds from other lands.

7) **Areas of greatest need.** The evangelical churches are more concentrated in certain areas – Catalonia in N.E., Andalusia in the S.W., Valencia on the east coast and Madrid. The rest of the country is under-evangelised. Especially needy are the central provinces south of Madrid, Galicia in the N.W. and the Basque provinces in the north. Pray that the whole country may soon be covered with live and powerful churches.

8) **There are now about 300 missionaries** in 54 different organisations, but what are so few when faced with the great need? Pray that the Lord may raise up many more willing to pour out their lives for the salvation of Spain. This could be a very fruitful field for believers in Spanish speaking America. Pray for the right relationships between the national believers and missionaries, and that the latter may have the right strategy for the planting of strong churches. There are now a number of different ministries open to missionaries – evangelism, church planting, Bible teaching, literature, etc. There are good evangelical missions now expanding their witness in the above ministries – **OMS, CAM, GEM, GMU, TEAM, WEF, WEC, WIM.** Pray for these brethren!

9) **Literature has proved to be the most potent weapon** for the conversion of Spanish people. There is now freedom to print and sell literature in the country. Pray for the publishing and colportage ministries. There are, as yet, few Christian bookshops in the country. Pray for the evangelistic literature distributed by **OM** every summer.

10) **Radio ministry.** The short wave **TWR** transmissions from Monaco can only be received by a minority of Spanish radio sets. Pray that there may be complete freedom to use the state and commercial medium wave stations in Spain for broadcasting the Gospel.

11) **Student ministry.** Both the GBU (**IVF**) and Campus Crusade have three university groups with a few students associated with them. There are 10 universities with no evangelical group. The 180,000 university students are now open for the Gospel as never before.

12) **The Gypsy people movement** is as noticeable here as in France, Germany and Rumania. Many thousands of these people are turning to the Lord and little Gypsy churches are springing up all over Spain. Pray for the continuation of this work of God. Pray also that these enthusiastic believers may be able to play a part in evangelising Spain.

OTHER AREAS

Ceuta and **Melilla** (170,000 population) are small Spanish ruled enclaves on the north coast of Morocco. 10% of the population is Muslim. It is not known if there is any evangelical witness in this potentially strategic bridgehead for the Gospel in North Africa.

Canary Islands 1,200,000 – a barren group of islands off the N.W. coast of Africa that form two provinces of Spain. There are only about 500 scattered Protestants and several small church fellowships. Pray for the handful of **WEC** missionaries witnessing there. Pray for the many lonely believers on islands without an established evangelical group, and for efforts to teach them through visitation and cassettes. Pray for a greater concern among the believers to reach out in evangelism. Pray for missionary reinforcements.

Gibraltar is a tiny British ruled 4 sq. km. peninsula on the south coast of Spain. Britain captured this strategic Rock in 1704 and have used it as a military base ever since. The tiny population of 27,000 has resisted all attempts hitherto by the Spanish government for the return of the territory to Spain. Since the passing of Franco there is more likelihood that Britain will hand over Gibraltar to Spain. The people are a mixture of Spanish, Moroccan, Maltese and English, and 77% Roman Catholic. Pray for:

1) **The Protestant witness.** There are three churches for the English speaking people – Methodist, Presbyterian and Church of England, and two for the Spanish speaking – Pentecostal and Evangelical. The last two maintain a lively witness to the Gibraltans.

2) **The witness to the Muslim Moroccans.** There are about 7,000 migrant labourers from Morocco. Pray that some of these may be won for the Lord. There is now a small group of Arab believers who meet regularly.

3) **CLC has a small bookshop** with several workers who seek to witness to both Arabs and Gibraltans.
4) **Pray about the political future of Gibraltar** – that the best for the Gospel may be done.

SWEDEN

BACKGROUND

Area: 450,000 sq. km. – the largest of the Scandinavian countries.
Population: 8,200,000. Growth Rate 0.4%. Density 18 people per sq. km.
Peoples: **Swedes** 95%, **Finns** 2.5%, also **Germans** 50,000, **Danes** 40,000, **Lapps** 10,000, a largely nomadic people in the far north. Migrant labourers: Yugoslavs 30,000; Greeks 12,000.
Capital: Stockholm 1,500,000. Urbanisation 81%.
Economy: Paternalistic welfare state with highest standard of living in the Western World.
Politics: Strict neutrality has kept Sweden out of all wars for 150 years. 44 years of Socialist governments ended in 1976, halting the increasingly leftist drift.
Religion: **Attitude of Government** – very secular in the past. Religious freedom. **Roman Catholics** only 0.7%. **Orthodox** 1.3%. **Protestants** 90%. Lutheran Church (92%) is the State Church. Other Protestant denominations 7% with 260,000 membership. Largest groups: Pentecostals 94,000; Covenant Church 85,000; Baptists 25,000; Independent Baptists (Orebro) 20,000; Swedish Alliance Mission 15,000. Conservative Evangelicals 10% of population.

Points for Prayer

1) **National revival is Sweden's greatest need.** Great revivals have swept over the land in past years. Yet now the country is well known for its welfare state, wealth, materialism, very permissive society, suicides, immorality and drunkenness (42% increase in the latter in 10 years). Yet there are signs of a new interest in spiritual things among young people during the last 7 years.
2) **The new government needs prayer,** for the damage of years of permissive legislation and erosion of respect for the things of God by those in high authority must be rectified.
3) **The State Lutheran Church is very formal** and has become little more than a department of the government Civil Service. Nominalism and neo-orthodox theology have become almost universal, and church attendance averages less than 3% of the membership. Yet some of the leaders and laity in the Church are Evangelical and the number is growing, largely through the charismatic and Jesus movements.
4) **The Free Churches** are larger than in any other Scandinavian country. Many of these congregations were born in past times of revival but are losing people apart from the Pentecostals, Independent Baptists and Swedish Alliance Mission. Much of the Covenant Church is weak and formal, yet some of the country's finest evangelical leaders are to be found in it. Pray for a move of the Spirit and a greater evangelistic concern.
5) **Needy areas** – past revivals were often very localised, and some areas have many believers, yet others virtually none. Many of the newer urban areas have no churches, and their people have never been effectively evangelised.
6) **Young people have been very adversely affected** by the permissive society, and a recent survey indicates that 41% do not believe that there is a God. Pray that there may be an effective outreach to them.
7) **Bible Schools** are not common in Scandinavia and much more must be done to provide good evangelical teaching for believers. Pray for the strategic Scandinavian Bible Institute of the **GEM** now with 60 students.
8) **Missionary outreach** has been exceptional. Outstanding has been the role of the Pentecostals in South America and elsewhere and also the work of the Swedish

Alliance Mission and Orebro Mission. There are now about 1,700 Swedish missionaries serving all over the world. Pray for a quickening of this vision, for Sweden's unusual stand in world politics makes her strategic for bringing help to the believers in Communist lands and also evangelising many other areas of the world closed to most western missionaries.

9) **Pray for the evangelisation of migrant labourers** – especially for the Greeks and Yugoslavs – a little is now being done to reach them.

SWITZERLAND

BACKGROUND

Area: 41,000 sq. km. – the mountains of Switzerland are one of the greatest tourist attractions in the world.
Population: 6,333,000. Growth rate 0.7%. 153 people per sq. km.
Peoples: **Swiss** 83.5% – German speaking 70%, French 19%, Italian 9% and Romansch 1%. There are four national languages.
               Migrant labour 16.5% – mostly Italian, German, Austrian, Spanish, Yugoslav, Greek and Turkish workers.
Capital: Berne 282,000. Other cities: Zurich 715,000. Urbanisation 55%.
Economy: Strong, but inflation due to overproduction and high value of Swiss franc.
Politics: Federal democracy with much power vested in the 22 Cantons. Neutral since 1815.
Religion: **Roman Catholics** 49% – are dominant in 12 Cantons.
               Protestants 47% – are dominant in 10 Cantons. The Cantonal Reformed Churches make up 98% of all Protestants.
               Other Free Churches 2% – various Free Evangelical Churches 21,000 members; Methodists 11,000; Brethren.
               Conservative Evangelicals 8% of population.

Points for Prayer

1) **There is a marked drift away from the churches.** There is little active evangelism so this means that the majority of Swiss people have little knowledge as to what the true Gospel is. **Pray for the revival** for which Switzerland awaits.

2) **There are very few evangelical believers in the Roman Catholic Cantons** – pray for these areas to be effectively evangelised, and for the prejudices among the R.C.s against the Gospel which are rooted in the turbulent history of the country. Pray for those in the R.C. Church who are searching the Scriptures for the Truth and who are moving away from papal infallibility – there are some true evangelicals among them.

3) **The Reformed Churches have relatively few evangelical believers,** but the number is growing. The neo-orthodox theology of the Swiss theologians, Barth and Brunner, rob pastors of assurance of salvation and evangelistic concern. There are now more and more evangelical theological students going into the ministry; pray for these men that they may not compromise the Truth. Pray that these churches may return to the doctrines of their great founders, Calvin and Zwingli, etc.

4) **The small evangelical witness is becoming stronger,** mostly in the Free Churches. The Swiss Evangelical Alliance is becoming a rallying point for Evangelicals within the state and the Free Churches. Pray for a greater unity and desire for the evangelising of the Roman Catholic areas and the many foreign workers as well as the many unconverted and nominal Protestants. There is a growing hunger for spiritual reality among the believers.

5) **Switzerland is the home of the L'Abri Fellowship.** This Fellowship has become a mighty force for the Gospel among intellectuals throughout the world. Pray for the personal and literature ministries that these may continue to stimulate evangelical revival in universities all over the world.

6) **The Fellowship of Evangelical Missions** (founded in 1972) has greatly strengthened the missionary interest of the Swiss churches. This fellowship is formed of 25 national

and international mission groups representing 500 Swiss missionaries. Pray for a continuing growth of this vision. There are a further 260 missionaries of the Cantonal Churches.

7) **There are a number of good Bible Schools:** Beatenburg, Le Roc, Emmaus, Aarau and St. Chrischona who have sent out many graduates all over Europe and the world. Pray for the very vital ministry of the Free Evangelical Theological Seminary in Basle and its influence on the whole German speaking world.

8) **The immigrant labour force** is mostly Roman Catholic, Orthodox or Muslim. Pray for them – especially the 21,000 Greeks and the 17,000 Muslim Turks. Pray for the 8 missionaries of the interdenominational M.E.O.S. mission working among these foreigners together with many part time helpers. The Swiss Tent Mission also gives considerable time to evangelism in the various languages.

9) **Liechtenstein** is an independent Principality of 18,000 people between Austria and Switzerland. It is now virtually a 23rd Canton of Switzerland. The people are almost entirely R.C., and the legal position of the very few Protestants is difficult. There is one small group of evangelical believers in this mini-state. Pray for these wealthy but unreached people.

III. COMMUNIST BLOC

For the purpose of this survey, we define the Communist Bloc as those lands that form a single unit of 16 nations across the Eurasian land mass. We do not include the Communist lands of Africa, America or the Middle East. For Asian lands see map on page 96.

BACKGROUND

Area: 35,676,000 sq. km. – 24% of the land surface of the world.
Population: 1,300,400,000 – 32.4% of the world's population.
            Eastern Europe and Russia (including Siberia) 9.7% of world's pop.
            Communist Asia (largely China) 22.7% of world's pop.
Peoples: **Europeans** and **Asiatics.** Largest peoples: **Russians** 133,640,000; **Chinese** 778,000,000; **Ukrainians** 43,600,000; **Vietnamese** 39,000,000. Many hundreds of minority peoples in Russia (48% of population), Vietnam (16%), Rumania (15%), China (7%). Urbanisation 33%.
            Cities of over 1 million people – 34 out of world total of 163.
Religion: All governments hostile to all religions, but varying degrees of persecution. Hence religious statistics are only estimates.

	E. Europe and USSR	Communist Asia
Buddhists 9%	1%	12%
Muslims 6%	9%	4%
Jews 0.3%	1.1%	
Christians 16%	51%	0.8%
Orthodox 9%	29%	
Roman Catholics 5.4%	16%	0.7%
Protestants 1.7%	5.5%	0.1%
Evangelicals 1.1%	3.3%	0.2%**

**Higher than Protestants because of China's peculiar situation. *q.v.*

Other lands with fully fledged Communist governments – also year of Communist takeover.

Cuba (1959), Zanzibar (1964), South Yemen (1968), Congo (1970), Mozambique (1975), Angola (1976), Ethiopia (1977). With a total population of 54 million people.

There are now 1,354,000,000 people under a Communist tyranny in 23 lands. Just over one third of the world's population is now ruled by 50,000,000 Communist Party members. In 1975–76, seven countries were seized by the Communists. The advances continue with Thailand, South West Africa and Rhodesia under direct military attack. There are other lands with Marxist-inclined governments, but that are not wholly committed to Russian or Chinese Communism such as Benin, Guinea, Guinea-Bissau, Madagascar, Sao Tomé and Principe, Cape Verde Is., Somalia, Algeria and Iraq, etc.

The Expansion of Communism

Ruthless promotion of wars, revolutions, guerrilla movements, subversion and propaganda has brought many nations round the world under the shadow of a Communist takeover – in fact the world itself is threatened by this tyranny. This expansion has taken place in only 60 years with untold misery and death to millions. Some reckon that nearly 150,000,000 have been killed or died as a result of this advance. Despite these depressing statistics, severe internal weaknesses are evident: –

1) The serious economic failures of Communist policies in industry and agriculture.
2) The growing power and sophistication of the intellectual revolt in the U.S.S.R.
3) The restiveness of the East European Satellite states and U.S.S.R. national minorities in the face of the arrogance of Russian colonial rule.
4) Dissension between Communist states – the Russian-Chinese confrontation, etc.
5) The total inability of materialist Communism to satisfy the deepest longings and desires of the human heart.

The spiritual and moral decline of the West greatly assists the expansion of Communism. Only a prayer-born revival in the West can stem this tide – as has been proved in Brazil (1964), Indonesia (1965) and in Chile (1973).

The Confrontation between Christianity and Communism

Communism and Christianity are incompatible. Christianity is the only ideology with mass appeal that has been able to stand up to Communism and expand under its persecution. Hence the Communist's bitter hatred of the Gospel. Communism's vain hope that Christianity would die with its advent has proved to be foolish. With the possible exception of Albania, the number of believers with a living faith has increased in every country since the coming of Communism. The Communists have officially proclaimed religious freedom, but in practise have sought to destroy all forms of religion that they could not control. The advances of the Gospel have been many – the movement of the Holy Spirit among Communist-indoctrinated young people, the touches of revival in different places, and the rapid growth of the churches in Romania and USSR where the persecution has been most severe.

The Persecution of the Church in Communist lands

Conditions vary widely between the different countries and even within a country. There are, basically, four different situations: 1. **Lands where organised Christianity has been blotted out and the Church is completely "underground".** This is so in China, N. Korea, Laos, Cambodia, Mongolia and Albania. 2. **Lands with strict control of registered churches.** This leads to much compromise on the part of some Christian leaders and to the multiplication of unregistered or "underground" churches. This is so in the USSR, Romania, Bulgaria, Czechoslovakia, Vietnam, Zanzibar, South Yemen, Angola and Mozambique. 3. **Lands with limited freedom to worship,** but where believers are persecuted through job discrimination, lack of education opportunities and economic hardship – Cuba, East Germany, Hungary and Yugoslavia. 4. **Lands with considerable freedom** and little open persecution at present – Poland, Congo.

The hard-line countries such as the U.S.S.R. practise every kind of cruelty on Christians. Many are in prison, deprived of parental right, exiled, thrown out of work, heavily fined or committed to mental institutions for such "crimes" as teaching children about the Lord, evangelising, distributing literature, attending prayer meetings, etc. Persecution has markedly increased in nearly all countries after the Communist victories in Asia and Africa since 1975 and also since the successful tricking of the lands of the West into signing the 1975 Helsinki Agreement which, among other things, guaranteed religious freedom.

The Help Ministries from the Free World to Communist Lands

1) **Prayer** – the first appeal from believers behind the Iron and Bamboo Curtains.
2) **Publicity** – making known the sufferings of the believers has influenced these governments from some excesses and protected the Christians.

3) **Importation of literature and practical help.** The desire to gain foreign currency from the 5 million tourists that annually visit these lands makes this a valuable means of getting help to the believers. Pray for the safety of all involved in this hazardous ministry.

4) **The Printing of Literature and Bibles** is forbidden or severely restricted in all countries. The huge demand makes illegal importation from other lands essential.

5) **Christian Radio** has proved a most potent means of evangelism, church planting, and of teaching Christians. The Communist Bloc is ringed by many powerful Christian broadcasting stations. These broadcasts are hated and feared by the Communists. The number of listeners is very high. This ministry is worthy of prayer.

For further information – **CMI, OD, UE** and **CFC.**

A. Eastern Europe

ALBANIA

BACKGROUND

Area: 28,700 sq. km. – a mountainous Balkan State on the Adriatic Sea.

Population: 2,500,000. Growth 2.4%. People per sq. km. – 87.

Peoples: **Albanians** speaking widely differing dialects – Gheg in the north, Tosk in the south.
Greeks 2.5%.

Capital: Tirana 175,000. Urbanisation 34%.

Economy: Europe's most poor and backward country. Much dependent on Chinese economic aid.

Politics: Became a Communist Republic in 1945. The most harsh and ruthless Communist regime in Europe. Sided with China against U.S.S.R. from 1961 onwards. Now virtually a satellite state of China seeking to gradually end its political isolation by making contacts with the West.

Religion: **Attitude of Government** – it proudly claims to be the world's first atheist state. The land's extreme isolation from the outside world enabled the rulers to eradicate all organised religion in a "cultural revolution" in 1966 (modelled on that of China). All 2,169 mosques, churches and religious buildings were destroyed or converted to secular use. All those known to have religious beliefs are now killed, imprisoned or in hiding.
We quote the pre-world War II strengths of the religious groups:
Muslim 70%. Europe's only Muslim country.
Orthodox 19%.
Roman Catholics 10%.
Protestants Several thousand Lutherans; Evangelicals approx. 1,000.

Points for Prayer

1) **Albania is Europe's most closed and least evangelised land.** Pray for the miraculous opening of this needy land for the Word of God.

2) **Pray that the spiritual vacuum in the hearts of the people may be filled** – Communism can never do this. Most of the people knew no religion but Islam.

3) **There are still believers meeting together in secret** – despite the claim that all religious superstitions have been eradicated. The Albanian press complained in 1975 that there was a remarkable increase in the public and secret practice of religion! Pray for these isolated and persecuted believers and their continued secret witnessing.

4) **There is a growing concern in Western countries** for the evangelisation of the Albanian people. There are about 1,000,000 Albanians who live in southern Yugoslavia where there has been a limited freedom to preach the Gospel, and there are now several groups of Albanian believers there. Many of these Albanians go to Western European lands temporarily for work. Pray that some may be converted there. There are Christian workers seeking to reach the large community of Albanians working in Munich, West Germany where several have come to the Lord.

5) **Christian literature in Albanian** has been almost totally lacking since World War II. The N.T. was reprinted in 1972, and a number of books and booklets have been produced since then. Pray for fruit among the relatively few Albanians in the Free World, and for the Albanians in Yugoslavia. Pray that some of this literature may find its way over virtually sealed borders into Albania itself from Greece and Yugoslavia. It is almost impossible for the few well-guarded tourists to distribute any literature inside the country as in other Communist lands. Pray that the slight thaw in relations with the West may result in more openings.

6) **Christian Radio broadcasts** are the only way, at present, to get the Gospel into the land. Pray for the raising up of more believers in the West who are fluent in Albanian

who can help the brother who prepares programmes for **TWR** for transmission from Monaco. There are now 5 programmes beamed on Albania every week. Pray that the news of these broadcasts may reach those who need the message of the Gospel.

BULGARIA

BACKGROUND

Area: 110,900 sq. km. – one of the Balkan States.
Population: 8,800,000. Growth 0.7%. People per sq. km. – 79.
Peoples: **Bulgarians** 86% – a Slavic people related to the Russians.
                    Turks 8% – these people ruled the land for 5 centuries. Bulgaria became independent of Turkey in 1908.
                    Macedonians 4%.
                    Gypsies 2%.
Capital: Sofia 950,000. Urbanisation 59%.
Economy: Poor and totally dominated by the inefficient Communist state.
Politics: The presence of Russian troops in the country aided the takeover of the country by the Communists in 1946. A hard line Communist regime that is faithful to the U.S.S.R. Bulgaria is sometimes called "Little Russia".
Religion: **Attitude of Government** – severe limitation and control of all organised religious groups. Many church leaders are government appointees.
                    Bulgarian Orthodox Church 75% – this church was the chief preserver of the national culture during the centuries of Turkish rule. It still plays an important role in the country, but is heavily infiltrated by Marxists.
                    Muslims 9% – largely Turks, but also a minority of Bulgar Muslims (15%).
                    Roman Catholics 0.5% 50,000. **Armenian Church** 22,000.
                    Protestants 0.6% 15,000 members. 30,000 community. There are also other "underground" believers not included in these figures. Most denominations are Evangelical – Pentecostals 6,000 members; Baptists 800; also Reformed, Congregational, Brethren groups. Evangelicals 0.6%.

Points for Prayer

1)   **Many Bulgarians have never had a chance to hear the true** Gospel; their land is one of the more needy of Eastern Europe. Pray that they may hear of the Saviour.

2)   **Propaganda against believers is extreme.** Pray that this continual assault on believers and the Bible may cause the many disillusioned Communists to seek for the Truth.

3)   **The persecution of believers** has been very severe. Many Christian leaders suffered long terms of imprisonment and death in the early years of Communist rule. Since 1972 the level of persecution has again been stepped up, and many believers are suffering in prison for their faith. Pray for Christian prisoners and their witness in prison. Pray for their families who are subjected to intimidation and discrimination.

4)   **Pray for the leaders of the churches** who face constant harassment from the authorities and betrayal at the hands of informers who have been infiltrated into both official and underground groups. There are now about 40 Pentecostal and 23 Baptist pastors in the official churches, and others who live a hunted life ministering to the secret groups. Pray for their ministry. It is impossible to obtain an adequate Bible training for those who would enter the ministry.

5)   **The churches** are not restricted by law from holding meetings, but the long working hours and lack of Sunday rest greatly limit their activities. The limitation on registration of new churches forces many groups to meet illegally. Pray for these believers that their faith may be strong, and that their witness may win many to the Lord.

6)   **Young people** are now more receptive to the Gospel despite the years of indoctrination in Marxism, but there is a strict restriction on their attendance of church services (except in the tourist season!). There is also a problem of a generation gap between the enthusiastic young believers and the older people in the churches.

7)   **Literature.** No literature for believers is allowed to be printed or distributed in the

country. The famine of literature is so great that there is much hand copying of the Scriptures and good Christian books. Pray for those who seek to bring literature from the West to these believers.

8) **Christian Radio** – pray for the broadcasts to the country from **TWR** Monaco and others, and also for those who prepare the programmes.

CZECHOSLOVAKIA

BACKGROUND

Area: 128,000 sq. km. – a federal republic of two nations – Czechs (Bohemia, Moravia and parts of Silesia) and Slovaks in the east.

Population: 14,900,000. Growth rate 0.8%. People per sq. km. – 116.

Peoples: **Czechs** 63% in centre and west, **Slovaks** in east 32%, **Magyars** 4%.
Other Minorities – Gypsies 2%, some Germans, Poles, Russians, Ukrainians.

Capital: Prague 1,091,000. Urbanisation 62%.

Economy: Highly industrialised and efficient before the Communist takeover. Now economy tied to that of Russia by disadvantageous trade agreements.

Politics: Although a minority party, the Communists seized power in 1948. The hard line Communist regime that followed brought great hardship. The liberalising policies of the Dubcek Government (1966–68) were ended by the Russian invasion of 1968. The hated Russians still occupy the country and manipulate the government and economy to their own ends.

Religion: **Attitude of Government** – the remarkable freedom of the "Prague Spring" of 1968 has been replaced by increasing repression and persecution of the churches to almost Stalinist proportions.
Roman Catholics 65% – are more strong in Slovakia.
Protestants 10%. Community 1,540,000.
The larger denominations are more formal and in subjection to the state. Czech Hussite Church (broke away from Rome 1918) 650,000 members; Evangelical Church of Czech Brethren (Presbyterian) 270,000 members; Lutherans 480,000; Slovak Reformed 100,000.
The small, but growing evangelical groups: Baptists 11,000; Church of Brethren 8,000; Moravians 8,000; Methodists 8,000.
Conservative Evangelicals 0.8%.

Points for Prayer

1) **The Czech Protestants** have been persecuted for nearly 6 centuries (since the martyrdom of the great early Reformer Huss in 1415). The Communist regime has followed a carefully stepped up programme for the erosion of the influence and ultimate liquidation of the Church since 1973. Pray for our suffering brethren that they may stand firm and continue to win people for the Lord.

2) **The religious freedom of 1966–68 was a gift of God.** The rather discouraged Christian witness was revived by a move of the Spirit right across the country. The churches were filled, many were converted and new churches built. The move was especially marked among the young people. There has been a great deepening of spiritual life since the Russian invasion and the subsequent sufferings.

3) **Communism has been completely discredited** in the country by the Russian occupation of the land. Pray that this will lead to a great turning to the Lord in spite of the high cost of following the Saviour.

4) **The pressures are especially great upon the pastors.** They are only allowed to preach if approved by the state and have taken an oath of loyalty. The number of legal meetings has been greatly cut, and some pastors are now in prison for exceeding that number. Pastors are not allowed to send out pastoral letters, own duplicating equipment or do visitation. Many are now in prison, forbidden to preach or subjected to harassment and intimidation. Pray for these leaders and their ministry in such trials.

5) **Pray for the larger and more formal churches** that have been dominated by non-

Biblical theology and formalism. There are born again believers among them – pray that their number may increase as the persecution increases.

6) **There are relatively fewer believers in Slovakia.** Pray for the evangelisation of every part of the land.

7) **Very much literature was taken into the country** before the Russian invasion, but this could not meet the great and growing need. No literature is now permitted from the West – some Christians from the West have been imprisoned for seeking to bring Bibles to the believers. Pray for all involved in this dangerous ministry. Over 120,000 Bibles were printed between 1969–73 in the country, but now no more. There is now a severe lack of Bibles despite permission for a few small consignments of Bibles to enter the country recently.

8) **Radio ministry.** Pray for those producing and broadcasting Czech and Slovak programmes in the West.

EAST GERMANY (German Democratic Republic)

BACKGROUND

Area: 107,000 sq. km.
Population: 16,800,000. Population growth 0.3% – steadily decreasing since the end of World War II. People per sq. km. – 157.
Peoples: **Germans.**
Capital: Berlin (East) 1,200,000. Urbanisation 75%.
Economy: The most efficient and industrialised of the Communist satellite states.
Politics: Germany lost much of her eastern territories to the U.S.S.R. and Poland at the end of World War II. The remaining third of the country was occupied by the Russians (who still maintain a very large military presence). Although theoretically independent, the world now recognises it as a separate state. The German people showed their hatred of the Communist regime in an uprising in 1953, and by nearly 4 million fleeing to West Germany over the last 30 years. The infamous Berlin Wall was built in 1961 to stop this flow. This wall surrounds the free enclave of West Berlin, and is a permanent reminder of the spiritual and moral failure of Communism.
Religion: **Attitude of Government.** Thirty years of subtle pressures on the powerful Protestant State Church have, since 1975, become far more acute. The time of relative freedom for the churches seems to be passing.
                Roman Catholics 7%.
                Protestants 50% (80% in 1947) – almost entirely the state supported Evangelische Kirche (Lutheran and Reformed). Much nominalism, but a growing Evangelical minority. Federation of Evangelical Free Churches (mainly Baptist and Methodist) are about 2% of all Protestants. These churches are growing.
                Conservative Evangelicals 15%.

Points for Prayer

1) **Nominal Christianity is waning rapidly** under the pressures of vigorously propagated atheism, increasing materialism and discrimination against believers. Few of the Protestants go to church and the number of baptisms in the State Church is declining dramatically. Pray for a move of the Spirit among the many discouraged and nominal Christians.

2) **There are still many more freedoms** for German Christians to worship and witness than is usual for a Communist state. Pray that the true believers may be courageous and strong to use the opportunities that they have to evangelise whilst it is still possible.

3) **Persecution is increasing.** More and more discrimination against believers and their children in job and education opportunities is being applied. It is now virtually impossible for a believer to obtain a university education. There is the ever present danger of compromise for the sake of their families.

4) **There seems to be a plan to force the Church** into the same situation as in Russia. This may mean loss of legal status for the Church, expropriation of all church owned land and institutions, and ultimately the destruction of the Church as a witnessing body. Pray that the devil's plans may be thwarted.

5) **The pastors are coming under severe pressures.** There are now some Christians in prison. There is increased surveillance and interrogation of pastors – especially effective ones. Many younger pastors are now seeking to go to free West Germany – the Communists help them to leave. Pray for stability and faithfulness to the Lord and their flocks among the pastors.

6) **Youth.** It is extremely costly for a young person to follow the Lord Jesus – mocking in school, deprivation of education opportunities and poverty, yet there is a growing and enthusiastic response to the Gospel among young people. The charismatic movement is said to be very strong.

7) **Literature** is more freely available than in any other Communist land. Bibles and some Christian literature (censored) are sold in the shops, though there is a great lack of good, new evangelical literature. Pray that this freedom may continue – for there is real danger that this may be stopped.

8) **The Churches are still able to give theological training** to potential pastors. The University Theological Faculties are increasingly dominated by Marxist staff, but the Seminaries are still free of state interference. There is now an independent theological faculty for Evangelicals connected with Seeheim (q.v.) in West Germany. Pray for this freedom to continue.

9) **Christian Radio.** The large and effective German branch of **TWR** produce a number of daily programmes for broadcasting to both Germanies. Pray for this ministry.

HUNGARY

BACKGROUND

Area: 93,000 sq. km. – a landlocked, Central European State on the River Danube.
Population: 10,600,000. Growth rate 0.6%. People per sq. km. – 114.
Peoples: **Magyars** (Hungarians) 93%.
Minorities – Germans 2%, Gypsies 1½%, Slovaks 1% & Croats 1%.
Capital: Budapest 2,000,000. Urbanisation 49%.
Economy: The 1974 recession has hit the development of the land's growing economy.
Politics: A Russian engineered coup brought the Communists to power in 1947. The Hungarian uprising of 1956 brought terrible revenge from the Russians. 80,000 were killed and 400,000 fled to the West. The hard line puppet regime that followed has gradually softened through the years until 1975. Russian pressure behind the scenes seems to have now reversed this.
Religion: **Attitude of Government.** Limited freedom for many church activities, but there is a very tight control of the leadership of the official churches. Since 1975 there has been more government interference and limitation of earlier freedoms.
Roman Catholics 60%.
Jews 1% (80,000).
Protestants 25%. Community 2,700,000.
The two largest churches are more liberal in theology and have greatly compromised with Marxism.
Largest denominations – Reformed 2,000,000; Lutheran 430,000. Other more evangelical denominations – Baptists 35,000 members; Pentecostals more than 8,000; Methodists 2,500; Brethren 2,000.
Conservative Evangelicals 10%.

Points for Prayer

1) **The Reformed and Lutheran Churches** are very much under state control with leaders who toe the Party line. These leaders seek to enforce government policies on

the pastors and churches that are often detrimental to the Gospel. All pastors must take an oath of loyalty to the state in order to minister. Yet there are many pastors and leaders who resent this leadership, and speak out. A number have been forbidden to minister as a result. Pray that Christian leaders may put loyalty to God and His Word first.

2) **There are a number of fine Evangelical Reformed and Lutheran pastors** and believers who seek to witness within the many restrictions imposed on them. God is working in some congregations. Pray for a move of the Spirit in these largely formal and theologically liberal denominations.

3) **The smaller Free Churches are almost all Evangelical** and were born largely out of the revivals in Hungary in 1939 and 1946. There is evidence of a new wave of revival now despite increasing persecution. The number of believers and congregations is growing, but many of the newer groups are not recognised by the government, and are forced to meet illegally. Pray for the further increase of the Church. Pray for the believers, whose lot is increasingly hard, especially for the unregistered pastors and groups.

4) **Persecution used to be more by threats,** harassments and discrimination. This is now changing with more pastors being interrogated, watched and dismissed. Some unofficial Christian workers are now in prison. Uncertainty and fear pervades the country. Pray for the believers in these difficult circumstances.

5) **Bible training for the Evangelicals is very hard to obtain.** The Council of Free Churches (Baptist, Methodist and Pentecostal) has now been permitted to run a correspondence course for prospective Christian workers. Pray for this ministry, and also for the raising up of more labourers willing to pay the high price of serving the Lord full time.

6) **Young People are turning to the Lord all over the country.** They are compelled to meet illegally in most cases. There are some large and enthusiastic groups. Pray that these young believers may remain faithful under the many pressures to which they are subjected. To be a Christian endangers their future livelihood.

7) **There is an awakening among the Gypsies** in the east of the country. Pray that this movement may grow and spread to other areas.

8) **Christian literature** is sometimes available in limited quantities, but there is a great inadequacy of supplies. Some Bibles have been printed in the land, others have been legally imported; yet it is now virtually impossible to buy a Bible and now illegal to transport or receive literature from the West, so pray for those who seek to bring such greatly needed literature from the West to this land.

9) **Christian Radio** broadcasts from the **TWR** station in Monaco are very valuable for evangelism and teaching.

POLAND

BACKGROUND

Area:	313,000 sq. km. – sandwiched between Germany and Russia.
Population:	34,400,000. Growth rate 1%. People per sq. km. – 110.
Peoples:	**Poles** 96% – over 10,000,000 live abroad, 6,500,000 in U.S.A.
Capital:	Warsaw 1,388,000. Other major cities – Lodz 800,000, Cracow 660,000. Urbanisation 55%.
Politics:	Tragic history of wars and partition among powerful neighbours over last 200 years. One quarter of the population died in World War II. Russian Army forced a Communist puppet regime on the country in 1944. The present Communist leaders seek to walk the difficult path of appeasing the watching Russians and the enduring hatred of the Polish people for the Russians and their Communism.
Religion:	**Attitude of Government.** The Roman Catholic Church is too strong for the Communists to dominate or destroy, so there is more religious freedom than in any other Communist state. The Protestants have more freedom than for centuries because they are considered a counterbalance to the Roman Catholics.

Roman Catholics 95% – numbers and power undiminished after 30 years of Communism. There are over 20,000 priests (one for every 1,700 people). **Orthodox** 1½% – largely of the Ukrainian and Byelorussian minority. **Protestants.** Community 206,000. Denominations 7. The largest Church – Lutheran, but mostly German speaking and declining through emigration to West Germany. Largest denominations – United Evangelical 6,000; Pentecostal 5,000; Baptists 3,000; Methodists 4,200 members. Evangelicals 0.35%.

Points for Prayer

1) **This land is one of the least evangelised countries** in Communist Europe, yet it is the most open for Christian work. Many areas of the country are without an evangelical witness. Pray for the evangelisation of this land.

2) **The Roman Catholic Church is very powerful,** and has successfully blocked all attempts by the atheist government to deprive it of its independence and freedom to work through its churches and institutions. Many Communist Party members remain R.C. The Church is really the centre of Polish nationalism and culture in the face of Russian imperialism. The Church is very conservative, not in favour of the use of the Bible. The effects of liberal theology, and the charismatic movement are still small, but growing. Pray for the salvation of many Polish people.

3) **The many freedoms for both Roman Catholics and Protestants** could be taken away. Increasing government efforts to weaken the influence of religion are evident. There is little persecution of believers, but restrictions and difficulties are often placed in the way of their witness. Pray that there may be continued freedom for the propagation of the Gospel to this needy land.

4) **Literature** – there is a well used Bible Society depot in Warsaw which sells many Bibles and some Christian literature. Pray that this ministry may be continued and expanded. Literature is also able to be sent to some other Communist lands from this depot. A new Polish translation of the Bible is now being printed in Poland – pray that many may be converted by this new version. The government allows one evangelical Christian book to be printed every year – pray for the wisdom from above for those who write and those who choose those books that must be printed.

5) **The Evangelical Churches** are very small, but slowly growing. Pray for a greater evangelistic fervour among the believers and a more open mind among the Roman Catholics. Pray for the planting of many more churches in hitherto unreached areas. Pray for government building permits to be issued more readily to churches seeking to put up new meeting places.

6) **Radio programmes are prepared** by the United Evangelical Church in Warsaw for broadcasting from **TWR** Monaco. The government has reluctantly given permission for this, but this privilege could easily be withdrwn. There is such a good response to these broadcasts that the evangelical churches have difficulty in finding enough mature Christians to follow up the contacts.

ROMANIA

BACKGROUND

Area:	237,000 sq. km. – area much reduced by Russian seizure of Bessarabia in 1940.
Population:	21,500,000. Growth rate 1%. People per sq. km. – 91.
Peoples:	**Rumanians 85%, Hungarians 7%, Germans 2%, Gypsies 4%, Jews ½%.**
Capital:	Bucharest 1,643,000. Urbanisation 42%.
Economy:	Much use made of Western economic and technical aid to develop economy.
Politics:	Communist coup in 1947 with Russian support. The very harsh and repressive Communist regime has followed a nationalistic anti-Soviet line since 1963.
Religion:	**Attitude of the government** – the registered Churches are very strictly controlled. The leaders are Communist inclined by choice or compulsion. Many

evangelical believers are forced to worship in illegal groups because the government refuses to allow the registration of new churches.
Romanian Orthodox 80%. **Muslims** 1½%. **Roman Catholics** 7%. **Jews** ½%. **Protestants** 10%. Community 1,650,000. Denominations 6. Largest denominations: Hungarian Reformed 700,000; Lutheran 200,000. Other groups: Baptists 200,000 members; Pentecostals 200,000; Brethren 20,000. Conservative Evangelicals 7% and growing 13% per year.

Points for Prayer

1) **The Romanian people are very hungry for God.** Intense atheistic propaganda and severe persecution have only stimulated this interest and refined the Church. Every year there are reports of many thousands of baptisms in the evangelical churches (these figures are greatly minimised so as to avoid more opposition from the Communists). Pray that many more, even Marxists, may be converted.

2) **The Romanian Orthodox Church** is very formal and the leadership servile to the state. The Church is a form of national protest against Communism, and churches are always full. Suffering has brought many Orthodox to a living faith. Pray for an evangelical awakening in this Church.

3) **The Roman Catholics, Reformed and Lutherans** are largely found among the Hungarian and German minorities in Transylvania in the west. These churches are also formal and controlled by the government. Yet there has been revival over the last few years in the area. Pray that all congregations may be affected.

4) **The Baptists and Pentecostals** are singled out for especially hard treatment by the authorities because of their extraordinary success in winning Romanians. Very severe limitations were imposed on their activities – forcible reduction in number of churches, baptismal lists to be submitted to government beforehand, banning of all evangelism, etc. This has led to the formation of many underground groups who are savagely persecuted, for they do not adhere to the government limitations. Pray for the relatively few pastors and their difficult ministry. Pray for the believers.

5) **Persecution in the 1950s was very severe.** Many believers were martyred and imprisoned. Latterly persecution has been more in the line of frequent house searches, interrogations, very heavy fines, dismissal from work and imprisonment. The intensity of persecution has markedly increased since 1974. Pray for Christian prisoners and their suffering families.

6) **New laws have made the life of believers much harder.** All people in responsible positions must now take an oath of loyalty to the furtherance of Communism, which is, in effect, for Christians, a denial of their faith. Refusal to take the oath leads to dismissal from work. Pray for the believers when faced with this agonising decision. It is easy to compromise.

7) **There has been a remarkable people movement among the Gypsies.** Many thousands of these little understood people have been converted since 1972. Pray for these new believers, and their fine leaders, some who have already suffered much for their faith. The Bible is now being translated into their language, Romany.

8) **The small Baptist Theological College** is now allowed 40 students. Pray for this valuable ministry. Pray for raising up of more full time workers for all churches. The Pentecostal Church was given permission in 1976 to build a Bible School and new churches.

9) **There is a critical lack of literature.** The much publicised 100,000 Bibles printed in Rumania in 1971 never reached the Protestants. The only source of Bibles and Christian literature is from the West, and much has been smuggled into the land. Now the government has passed a law forbidding the receiving, transporting, storing or distributing of literature from abroad. Heavy sentences have been meted out to those doing so. Yet the believers continue to plead for more literature from the West despite the risk. Pray for those who risk their lives and those of their families in getting the Word of God out to the believers. Pray for the preservation of Bibles already in the land. The police continue to arrest believers with Bibles and destroy all Bibles and literature that they find.

10) **Christian radio broadcasts** from Monaco (**TWR**) are a source of immense comfort and blessing to the believers and a means of evangelising the lost.
11) **The severe earthquake of March 1977** gave the believers closer contact with those from the free world, less persecution and unparallelled opportunities to witness.

YUGOSLAVIA

BACKGROUND

Area: 256,000 sq. km. – a federal state made up of 6 republics: – Bosnia & Herzegovina, Montenegro, Croatia, Macedonia, Serbia and Slovenia.

Population: 21,500,000. Growth rate 0.9%. People per sq. km. – 84.

Peoples: Major nationalities – **Serbs** 42% and **Croats** 22%. Much of Yugoslavia's present political instability is due to the mutual hatred of these two peoples that differ in culture and religion, but little in language.
Other minorities – Slovenes 8%, Macedonians 6%, Albanians 6%, Bosnians 6%, Montenegrins 3%, Hungarians 2%, Turks 1%, Bulgarians 1%, Czechoslovak 1%.

Capital: Belgrade 1,204,000 – also Zagreb 602,000. Urbanisation 39%.

Economy: Poor but expanding. Much hurt by inflation and world recession. Nearly one million Yugoslavs have sought work in Western Europe.

Politics: Tito, the wartime guerrilla leader against the Germans, formed a Communist government in 1944. The measure of unity achieved was seriously harmed by the appearance of a strong Croatian independence movement in 1971. Tito has been able to maintain his nation's neutrality in the Cold War in the face of Russian anger at his independence. The death of the sickly and octogenarian Tito and the appeals by Croatian nationalists for Russian help could lead to a Russian invasion.

Religion: **Attitude of Government** – confrontation with the Roman Catholics, control of the Orthodox, and the smaller Protestant groups allowed considerable freedom until recently.
Orthodox 40% – largely among the Serbs and Macedonians.
Roman Catholics 32% – largely among Croats, Bosnians and Slovenes.
Muslims 12% – Turks, Albanians and some Montenegrins.
Protestants 1% Community approx. 310,000 – though half of these are found in small national minorities. Largely non-Evangelical: 4 Lutheran groups (largely Slovak and Slovene) 150,000; Reformed (Hungarian) 60,000; Seventh Day Adventists 20,000.
Evangelical groups (10% of Protestants): Baptists 6,000 members; Pentecostals 6,000; Methodists 3,000; Brethren 1,500. Conservative Evangelicals 0.2%.

Points for Prayer

1) **The political future is dark** – the shadow of repressive Russian Communism falls over the land. The present relative freedom to preach the Gospel is ending. Pray for more freedom for the Gospel. Pray that believers may use the opportunities that there are.
2) **Unreached peoples** – many areas of the country are without an evangelical witness. Pray especially for the reaching of the two and one half million Muslims, the million Albanians (many of whom are Muslim), the Montenegrins and Macedonians. The Dalmatian coast, so well known to tourists, is largely unevangelised. Pray for the believers witnessing to these groups – there have been a number of conversions of Albanians recently and there are now several little groups of believers among them.
3) **The Government is reversing the previous liberalising trend** in the face of the dangerous political situation. There has been increasing pressure on all church groups since 1971. There has been more discrimination against believers in schools and work, more police harassments and some imprisonments. It is now much harder to register a church group, and there have been cases of church buildings being

destroyed. Illegal meetings have been broken up. Much harsher laws against religious groups were introduced in 1976. Pray for the believers in this time of fear and increasing uncertainty.

4) **The evangelical believers are relatively few.** Their witness is spoiled by disunity for there are several damaging splits among the Baptists and Pentecostals. The churches are not growing as fast as in some other Communist lands although they have had a greater freedom to witness. Pray that these believers may be effective for God.

5) **The training of pastors is legal.** The Baptists have a Bible School with an average of 10 students. As a result of the 1974 Lausanne Congress the Lutherans and other Evangelical groups have started a theological faculty in Zagreb. Pray for these institutions, and for the calling of many into the Lord's service.

6) **Literature** has been fairly freely sold in the country. Bibles are printed in Yugoslavia in the 4 main languages. Yet a recent law makes it difficult for literature to enter the country from other lands. Pray for the lifting of this restriction. There is a Bible Society depot in Belgrade.

7) **There are nearly a million Yugoslavs working in Western Europe,** for longer and shorter periods. Many live in special barracks or hostels in Germany, Holland, Switzerland, etc. Pray for those seeking to win these people for the Lord there.

B. Asia (Communist)

UNION OF SOVIET SOCIALIST REPUBLICS (U.S.S.R.) – Russia

BACKGROUND

Area:	22,400,000 sq. km. – the world's largest country, stretching 9,000 Km across Eastern Europe and Asia. The Asian portion is much larger (Siberia).
Population:	257,000,000 of which 63,000,000 live in Siberia, the latter being very sparsely populated away from the southern borders. Population increase 0.9%.
Peoples:	**Slavic Peoples** 73%; the dominant **Russians** 52%; **Ukrainians** 17%, etc. **Minority peoples** 27% – many **Turkic** peoples and **Yakut tribes** as well as **Letts, Lithuanians** and **Estonians,** etc. There are 54 major national groups and over 127 languages used in this vast land. The Russians are just over half of the population, but rule a vast colonial empire over many peoples who do not appreciate this domination. Since 1940 the Russians have seized the lands of Estonia, Latvia, Lithuania and parts of Finland, Poland, Czechoslovakia and Rumania.
Capital:	Moscow 7,528,000. Other large cities: Leningrad 4,243,000; Kiev 1,887,000; Baku 1,359,000; Kharkov 1,350,000. Urbanisation 60%.
Economy:	Overemphasis on heavy industry and armaments has deprived all but the Communist Party elite of most comforts and poverty is widespread. Bureaucratic inefficiency and the collectivisation of farmland lead to constant economic crises and food shortages.
Politics:	The 1917 Revolution brought Communism to power. In the '30s Stalin's brutal purges and enforced collectivisation of farmlands caused the death of about 66 million people in labour camps and through starvation. Communism is but a tool for the expansion of the growing Russian Empire. The leaders of Russia are openly and totally committed to world domination and the destruction of all who oppose them. The U.S.S.R. is the strongest military power on earth and is opposed by an increasingly demoralised West. Yet internally there is a growing instability. The hatred of the people of East Europe and the oppressed national minorities for their Russian overlords and the very sophisticated intellectual revolt are a real threat to the power base of the Communist government.
Religion:	**Attitude of Government** – very harsh repression of unofficial Christian bodies and rigid control of registered denominations. 60 years of Communist rule has not led to the withering away of religious "superstition" as they had expected. The constitutionally guaranteed right of freedom of conscience is but a propaganda smokescreen behind which every form of persecution, infiltration of agents and control of the leadership of the churches is used to destroy the influence of Christianity and other religions. These efforts have proved a signal failure despite the enormous efforts and expenditure. **Muslims** 30,000,000 are still many despite persecution. They are mostly found along the southern borders and in Central Asia among the many Turkic peoples and others. **Jews** 4,000,000. Many are actually atheists. Much persecuted by the Communists in the last 10 years. Many seek to emigrate to Israel to where over 120,000 have gone in this period. **Russian Orthodox Church** 50,000,000 (approx. 25%). The leadership is under Communist control. Despite the traditionalism, formalism and non-Biblical doctrines of this Church, persecution has brought many Orthodox believers to a warm personal faith in the Lord Jesus. This Church retains a very important place in the life of the Russian people. **Protestants** 3,000,000 – 8,000,000, number unknown but could be higher. There are two major types of Churches: –

The Registered Churches
Lutherans 800,000 – largely in Latvia and Estonia and among Volga Germans.
Reformed 100,000 – mostly Hungarians near the Hungarian border.
Evangelical Christians – Baptists (ECB) 3,000,000 (membership officially 500,000 but actually much more). A union of Baptists, Brethren, Pentecostals and Mennonites enforced by the government to facilitate rigid control of its activities.
Smaller registered groups of Seventh Day Adventists, Pentecostals, etc.
The Unregistered Churches (estimated 4,000,000 adherents). Deliberate limitation of the number of registered congregations in the recognised denominations force many to meet in illegal groups. Other groups refuse to seek registration because of the desire to be free of government limitations on evangelism, etc. These groups are found all over the country and some reckon that there are 10 times as many unregistered as registered congregations (though the illegal groups are naturally smaller).
Evangelicals 3% and growing markedly.

Points for Prayer

1) **Praise God for the spread of the Gospel to** every corner of the land despite 60 years of possibly the most severe persecution of Christians that the world has ever seen. Sometimes the very persecution endured has spread the Gospel to unevangelised areas and among unreached peoples. One hundred years ago there were hardly any Evangelicals.

2) **Pray for the suffering peoples of Russia** that many may see the barrenness and failure of Communism and turn to Christ. Pray that more of the leaders of the country may be saved. There have been some very remarkable conversions to Christ in recent years – Stalin's daughter, Kosygin's wife, Solzhenitsyn and some of the most brilliant writers and scientists Russia has produced.

3) **Pray for the triumph of the Gospel over Communism.** The Bible provides the only viable alternative to the philosophy of Communism, and hence is bitterly opposed by the rulers of the land. The intellectual revolt daily gains in power, influence and sophistication; it derives much of its inspiration from Christianity.

4) **The persecution of believers continues** to this day with increased ferocity. No one will ever know how many died for their faith under Communism through torture and ill treatment in prisons and labour camps – probably millions. Some estimate that there are now about 1,000,000 people in prison or exile in Siberia for their faith. Pray for these believers that they may remain strong in the Lord in the awful conditions under which they must live. Pray for the families of believers who are left behind – often in great hardship and poverty.

5) **The Russian Orthodox Church** is showing great vitality despite the closure of two thirds of all the churches in 1960–64, and the duplicity of some of their leaders. There is a trend towards a simple Biblical faith among these people in both the registered and illegal groups.

6) **The Evangelical Christians-Baptist leadership** submitted to extreme government pressure and accepted severe restrictions on their activities – no evangelistic work, or any children's and young people's work, severe limitation on the number of baptisms and the forbidding of people under 18 from attending worship services. Despite this the churches carry on and are usually packed at every meeting. Pray for both the pastors and believers and their witness.

7) **The Reform Baptists and many Pentecostals** refused to accept these limitations and broke away to form their own unrecognised group, or independent churches. These churches are growing rapidly and spreading all over the country. On them falls the full weight of Communist persecution. Many of their leaders and most spiritual men are now in prison. Pray for these brethren who carry on such an effective witness. It is from this group that most news comes to the West.

8) **The legal position of Christians** is now more difficult than ever before. The law is so ambiguously worded that Christians are easily sentenced as criminals. In 1975 new

laws made it illegal to hold house meetings without permission. The authorities turn a blind eye to unlawful breakings-up and molestation of believers attending meetings. A vast organisation is being built up to co-ordinate the destruction of the "underground" Church. Pray that God may give both wisdom and strength to our brethren in these conditions. The registered churches are also coming under more and more harassment in spite of their legality.

9) **The individual Christian** faces many terrible forms of persecution – pray for them. Constant propaganda and crude attempts at conversion to Communism at work and in the home. Discrimination in job opportunities and in education, so believers are thus condemned to a life of poverty and deprivation even greater than average. Heavy fines are levied for attending "illegal" meetings. Imprisonment and deportation to Siberia. Many refined methods of torture and "treatment" in mental institutions for those who obstinately persist in believing.

10) **The children of believers** are singled out for persecution if they follow their parents in believing and refuse to join the Communist Youth groups. It is illegal for parents to teach the children about their faith, and the state often removes children from their families and deprives the mothers and fathers of their parental rights for this. Pray for the Christian families and their preservation. Pray for those parents weeping for their children, and children suffering in harsh atheist orphanages. There has been a recent increase in the number of children removed from their parents.

11) **There appears to be revival** spreading across the country. Young people are turning to the Lord in large numbers. Many villages with 2–3 believers three years ago now have large groups of 50–100. There are reports of a move of the Spirit in the Baltic States and Armenia. Pray for the deepening and widening of the work of this revival. The authorities are said to be very alarmed by this. Many Russian believers pray and fast every Friday for the reviving of the Church.

12) **The training of pastors** is virtually impossible by normal means. Pray for the raising up of mature leaders well acquainted with the Scriptures to replace those now being imprisoned in increasing numbers. Pray for the ECB Bible correspondence course permitted for the training of some ministers.

13) **There is a famine of Bibles** in the country. Despite official claims to the contrary, no Bibles have been printed in the U.S.S.R. recently for distribution to the public. Pray for the many worthy organisations and individuals from non-Communist lands who use many strange ways to get Bibles into the hands of the believers – this is a dangerous ministry: pray for it! Pray also for the underground presses now producing hymn books and Bibles with growing efficiency despite the seizure of the underground press in Latvia in 1974 (which produced 220,000 Bibles and portions in 8 languages in 1973). There is reckoned to be, on average, only 1 Bible for every 25 believers. Many will go to extreme lengths in order to obtain a copy.

14) **Bible translation.** It is reckoned that 60,000,000 people do not have anything of the Word of God in their language. Pray for the work of **WBT** and others working in surrounding lands on new translations in 8 languages. Some other languages are being revised. The Bible has been translated into 11 languages, the N.T. into 17 and portions in a further 18, though many of these are out of date and out of print.

15) **Unreached peoples** – it is almost impossible to obtain facts about peoples that have not intelligently heard the Gospel. Pray for the following: – **The Jews** have been severely persecuted over the last few years, yet there are many finding the Lord Jesus in Moscow and other places. Pray that their hardships may bring them to Christ. Pray for the evangelising of those who have emigrated to Israel. **The Muslims.** Some estimate them to even number up to 50,000,000, speaking a great variety of languages, never having been adequately evangelised.

16) **Help from the West.** Much can be done by believers in the Free World to alleviate the suffering of the believers. **Practical aid** for families of prisoners and pastors (through publicising of the needs by the Council of Prisoners' Relatives in U.S.S.R.) – pray for the organisations and couriers who arrange this. **The publicising of the persecution of believers** in the U.S.S.R. has made the Communists afraid to go too far.

17) **The Radio ministry** has grown phenomenally. There are 10 missionary stations that ring Russia (to name a few – **TWR** (Europe), **WRMF** (S. America), **FEBC** (E. Asia)). There are now about 243 hours of broadcasting time a week from these stations to

the U.S.S.R. One out of every two people in the U.S.S.R. has a radio, and millions listen in. Some believe that there have been over one million people converted through these broadcasts, and many new churches planted as a result in hitherto unevangelised places. Pray for the production of the right programmes that are relevant to the needs of believers and atheist-indoctrinated unbelievers.

18)   **The 1980 Olympic Games in Moscow** will be a big Communist showpiece to the millions of visitors expected. Pray that there may be no limitations on the entry of Christians to witness there. Pray that the new and unusual opportunities may be used to the full for the helping of the believers and also to witness to the people of the U.S.S.R. Pray that the Communists may raise no illegal (according to the rules of the Olympic movement) barriers to the freedoms accorded to visitors.

CAMBODIA (Khmer Republic or Kampuchea)

BACKGROUND

Area: 181,000 sq. km.
Population: 7,735,000 – reduced by the nearly 1,000,000 killed in the year following the Communist conquest of the country.
Peoples: **Khmer** (Cambodians) 85%, **Chinese** 6%, **Cham** 3%, **Vietnamese** 2%, **Mountain Tribes** 3% – about 11 small tribes, some overlapping into the neighbouring lands of Vietnam, Laos and Thailand.
Capital: Pnomh Penh 200,000. Just before Communist victory, the city contained 2,500,000 (swollen with many refugees). The Communists immediately and brutally drove out the entire population, young and old, sick and dying into the jungles – very many to their deaths.
Economy: The most drastic and radical of revolutionary changes immediately put into effect in April 1975. There is now no money, private land or possessions. Virtually the entire country is a vast forced labour camp.
Politics: The new Communist leaders are pro-Russia and Vietnam and anti-Chinese. These leaders have ruthlessly destroyed all links with the past. All birth and death records and graveyards have been destroyed, family names cancelled and family life deliberately broken up. The entire army of the defeated government, all teachers, former government employees, those with secondary education and above, and all wealthy persons have been brutally murdered. The surviving population has been cowed into submissive slavery. The Chinese minority has been singled out for especially harsh treatment – many killed.
Religion: **Attitude of Government** – all religions that contributed to the "ruin" of the country are banned (i.e., Christianity). Leaders of all religious groups murdered.
               Buddhists 97%. **Muslims** (Chams) 3%. **Roman Catholics** 1,000 (?)
               Protestants 0.1%. Community in 1975 – 12,000. Now very much less

Points for Prayer

1)   **Pray for the tragic people of Cambodia.** The vast majority have never had a chance to hear the Gospel. Nearly all the little mountain tribes are unevangelised but for those reached in refugee camps in Pnomh Penh or in neighbouring lands.

2)   **Pray for the conversion of the Communist rulers** – men who have been more savagely cruel and vengeful than possibly any in modern history.

3)   **Praise God for the growth of the Khmer Church** from 700 believers in 3 churches in 1970 to 6,000+ in 42 churches in 1975. The CMA worked for 42 hard years with little fruit until expelled in 1965 by the hostile government. A pro-Western government coup opened the door for evangelism again in 1970 and a mighty harvest among the Khmer and Chinese resulted. Over one half of the believers were saved in the last year of freedom. Nearly all the believers were associated with the Evangelical Church born out of the work of **CMA**, and three quarters lived in Pnomh Penh.

4) **The persecuted believers** have now been scattered all over the country, and probably all the leaders and older Christians have been martyred but for the few who managed to escape to Thailand. Nearly all the Christian literature in the country has been destroyed. The believers are few, very young in the faith and most without the comfort of the Word or fellowship. Pray that they may be given grace to follow the Lord and also to win others in spite of all.

5) **The Muslim Cham* people** were beginning to show interest in the Gospel in 1975. **WBT** was seeking to translate the Scriptures for them, and a few had sought the Lord.

6) **The Khmer people** in Vietnam number 2,000,000 and through the missionary work of **CMA** and the Khmer Church in Cambodia, 700 believed in the last few months before Vietnam fell to the Communists. Pray for these new believers.

7) **By the end of 1976 about 60,000 Cambodians had managed to flee** from their land. The great majority of escapees died or were killed before reaching Thailand. Most of these refugees are going to live in France, U.S.A., etc. There are 10,000 refugees in poverty stricken conditions and in a state of traumatic shock in 5 refugee camps at any one time in Thailand. Pray for **CMA, OMF,** and **WEC** as well as other missionaries seeking to minister to the bodily and spiritual needs of these poor people. Pray for the ministry of literature, cassette messages and personal work. Over 2,000 Khmer have sought the Lord in these camps.

8) **The majority of the Khmer are going to France and U.S.A.** There are some Khmer pastors and also former missionaries to Cambodia seeking to help the believers to form fellowship groups and witness to the uprooted unconverted in both these lands. Others are constantly being converted. There is a critical lack of Khmer speaking Christian workers to do this work. Pray for the efforts made to train young Khmer believers for leadership.

9) **There are now daily broadcasts** prepared by Khmer pastors and transmitted from **FEBC** Manila. Pray that believers may be strengthened and the lost and the Communists converted thereby.

10) **Cambodia For Christ (CFC)** is a support agency for publicising the spiritual needs of the Khmer people, and to help in aiding refugees, supporting the training of leaders and preparing literature and broadcasts – above all, calling God's people to PRAY for Cambodia and Indo-China. Pray for **CFC**.

CHINA

BACKGROUND

Area:	9,562,000 sq. km. – the third largest country in the world.
Population:	857,000,000 – by far the largest nation in the world; this one country contains one fifth of the world's population. Most people live in the better watered coastal provinces in the east. Population growth 1.7%. Average no. people per sq. km. – 88.
Peoples:	**Chinese** 93% speaking 8 major dialects but with one written language common to all. The ancient script has now been simplified and the number of characters greatly reduced. Mandarin (spoken by 70% of the population) is the national language and is the only one taught in the schools. **Minorities** 7% – Major national groups: **Chuang** 9,500,000; **Hui** 5,200,000; **Uighur** or Turki 5,200,000; **Yi** 4,700,000; **Tibetans** 4,000,000; **Meo** 3,600,000; **Manchu** 3,500,000; **Mongolians** 2,100,000. Minor tribes total about 150 and are mostly found in the south.
Capital:	Peking 10,000,000. Largest city – Shanghai 11,300,000. There are 13 other cities with over one million inhabitants. Urbanisation 23%.
Economy:	The whole population has been mobilised for the raising of agricultural and industrial production. Strenuous efforts are being made to bring China economically and militarily to superpower status. The land has vast untapped mineral resources. The devastating 1976 earthquakes were a great setback to the economy.
Politics:	This mighty and ancient nation is regaining an important place in the world

after 800 years of decline and humiliations at the hands of foreign invaders; latterly the Western Powers. The hatred for foreigners aided the rise to power of the Communists between 1921 and 1949. The former Nationalist government was driven from the Mainland in 1949, and found refuge on the island of Taiwan. The Communist government under Mao Tse Tung ruthlessly sought to eradicate all traces of the pre-Communist economy, religions and culture and to re-mould the nation in the concepts of Marxism. The 1966 Cultural Revolution instigated by Mao and promoted by the teenage "Red Guards" led to 3 years of unparalleled chaos and suffering. China's political isolation began to end with her admission into the United Nations in 1971. The political eclipse of Mao since then and his death in 1976 has intensified the power struggle among his successors between the radical left and the pragmatic moderates. The latter seem to have gained the upper hand at the time of writing, and to be largely supported by the people, tired of a generation of continuous revolution. The rapid rise of China with its nuclear weapons, confrontation with the U.S.S.R., and growing influence in the world, is one of the most significant political events of our time.

Religion: **Attitude of Government:** By the end of the Cultural Revolution all organised religion had ceased but for several propaganda "show" churches. All church buildings have been destroyed or put to other uses, and all religious groups disbanded. This was achieved with consummate skill by a gradual infiltration and takeover of control of the churches, and then making it increasingly difficult for them to function and preach the truth. All Christian and other religious groups can only function "underground" now. Yet there is evidence that there is more freedom for little groups to meet together informally now. It is impossible to obtain figures for the adherents of the different religions in China. We can only give a rough estimate.

Confucianism 150,000,000 – now under severe attack by the Communist propaganda machine.

Buddhism and Taoism – altogether about 130,000,000.

Muslims 36,000,000 – mostly found in the west and north-west.

Christians 4,000,000 – at the Communist takeover there were 3,000,000 Roman Catholics and 1,000,000 Protestants (about half not Evangelical). The destruction of all denominational groups and systems has forced all Christians to simply meet as Christians where they have opportunity. Suffering has brought Christians to a common Bible based faith in the Lord Jesus. Evangelicals – possibly 0.2% and growing.

Points for Prayer

1) **Praise God for the purified and growing Church in China,** despite severe persecution and isolation from believers in other lands and also the death and imprisonment of nearly every outstanding Christian leader. The number of Bible believing Christians may have increased more than six fold since the Communist seizure of power. There is now hardly a town or village without a Christian group.

2) **Pray for the leaders of the new post-Mao China** that they may grant more freedom for Christians to meet together. Pray that this land may be freed from tyranny and fear. Pray that the Gospel may be freely preached.

3) **Christians in other lands ought to be more concerned** for the spiritual need of China. Pray that there may be much fruit from the "Love China" Conference in Manila in 1975 and the 1976 Hong Kong Conference in rousing Overseas Chinese believers and believers of other lands to prayer for the evangelisation of China.

4) **Nearly 600 million Chinese** have never known anything but Communistic atheism. For nearly all, life is a drab and purposeless struggle, constant revolution with much fear and insecurity and no hope for the future. More and more young people are looking for a deeper meaning to life than Communism offers. Pray that many may turn to the Lord Jesus. Pray that the believers may be alert to seek out such.

5) **The Church in China** is completely "underground". Believers meet whenever they can in homes or outside in little groups – sometimes only in twos and threes, and in

some areas in larger groups. The believers have been purified by great suffering. Their high spiritual standards shame the believers in the free world. Pray that they may be protected from betrayal by informers and from giving way to compromise when under pressure. Pray that God may give them courage and the openings to testify to others and win them for the Lord. Pray for the children of believers that they may not be hindered from believing in a society where family ties are deliberately weakened or even broken due to the regimentation of the life of the people.

6) **Revivals** have occurred all over China since 1930. These prepared the believers for the suffering that was to come. There are continuing reports of local revivals bursting out in answer to the earnest prayers of some believers. Pray for a greater work of the Holy Spirit that will demonstrate the power of our Lord over atheistic Communism.

7) **Persecution of believers is severe.** No one will ever know how many Christians were martyred for their faith. It is estimated that 50,000,000 people were liquidated by the Communists after they took power – many of the Christians would be in this number. Many other believers were deported to inhospitable regions as slave labour, thus spreading the Gospel to hitherto unevangelised regions. Pray for Christians in prison today, and also for their families who remain behind. Pray for the believers that their faith may remain strong under seemingly impossibly heavy pressures.

8) **There are very few Bibles** left in China. Many Bibles were destroyed by the Red Guards in the cultural revolution. Pray that these precious Bibles may be preserved. The believers are now beginning to print Bibles and Christian literature on primitive presses in secret – pray for this dangerous ministry. It is very difficult to get Bibles into the land from Hong Kong and other lands. Pray for the several Chinese and Western groups seeking to prepare, print and introduce the new script New Testaments into China (the Old Testament will be ready in 1980), and also pray that the Lord may show these brethren ways of getting the Bibles to those who need them so much. Pray for the radio programmes in which Bible passages are read at dictation speed for believers to write down by hand.

9) **Praise God for the missionary work** done before the door closed to missionaries in 1951. The 100 years of missionary work in a time of great unrest and hatred for all foreign influences was a miracle. The Gospel was preached in nearly every part of the land, and many churches were planted. At one time there were about 8,500 Protestant missionaries serving in China (1,000 being of the well known China Inland Mission – now **OMF**). There were failings in this work – too many non-evangelical missionaries, too much emphasis on institutional work, and not enough evangelism, church planting, careful training of Chinese Christian leaders and teaching of believers. As a result the Church was ill prepared for the Communist holocaust. Pray that the warnings of China may be heeded by missionaries in other lands.

10) **The opening of China for missionary work again** is not impossible but pray that the Lord may give the right strategy for the evangelisation of the land; the old methods cannot be used again. Believers in other lands must be ready to stand behind the Chinese believers on whom the great burden will fall.

11) **The training of new leaders** for the Church is almost impossible. There are hardly any pastors or leaders left who have had any formal Bible training. Pray that the present leaders may be taught the deep things of God by the Spirit, and be able to minister to the real needs of the believers. Pray for those who live the dangerous life of an underground pastor. Pray for the opening of the way for more believers to be able to obtain training in Hong Kong and return to China; there was one such in 1977.

12) **The unreached peoples of China.** Many of the minority groups in China have been only very slightly influenced by the Gospel due to their inaccessibility or resistance to the Gospel. It is unknown what the present situation is, but all these groups now must use Mandarin Chinese, and are thus more open to the witness of Chinese believers. Pray that every one of the 150 or so minority groups may be reached with the Gospel. We mention several areas and peoples for prayer:

a) **The many peoples of Sinkiang** – the vast desert and semi-desert northwest where many different peoples live as nomads or in cities and oases. The main groups being the Muslim Uighurs, Buddhist Mongols, etc. Most of the smaller groups like the Uzbeks, Kazakhs, etc. are Muslim. The land was only partially open for the Gospel in the 1930's and some outstanding evangelistic work was done by the CIM (**OMF**), etc., and a few churches planted.

b) **Tibet** was an independent Buddhist nation until invaded by China in 1950. A systematic attempt to destroy the Tibetan people has reduced the population to 1,300,000, but 500,000 of these are now Chinese. A few missionaries were just beginning to penetrate this closed and unevangelised land when Communism came. Pray for this needy and tragic people. Pray for the 85,000 Tibetans who fled to India and other lands. Among these latter there are now groups of believers in Ladakh (Kashmir) and North India. **TEAM** have a fine work among them. Pray for the emerging of a strong Church, and also for the reaching of Tibetans in China through literature smuggled over the Himalaya passes and by Radio from **FEBC** Manila.

c) **Inner Mongolia and the Mongolians.** These strongly Buddhist people live all along China's northern border with the U.S.S.R. and the U.S.S.R. puppet state of Mongolia (with a further 1,500,000 Mongolians). Only a few little churches were known to have been planted in Chinese Inner Mongolia. Most have never really heard the Gospel.

d) **The many southern tribes** of Yunnan, Kweichow and Kwangsi were opening up to the Gospel in a wonderful way between 1930–1950 and fine church groups were growing among the Meo, Lisu and other tribes. Many more were never evangelised, and have nothing of God's Word. Many of these tribes are also found in the neighbouring lands of Burma, Thailand, Laos and Vietnam where work was continued when China closed to the Gospel (**OMF**).

13) **The Overseas Chinese** number nearly 40,000,000. Many have fled from Communism to other S.E. Asian lands. The large Chinese communities in Indonesia and Philippines as well as the Chinese lands of Taiwan, Hong Kong and Singapore are open to the Gospel, and a mighty harvest of souls is now being reaped, and strong churches developing. Pray for the growth of the missionary vision among these people both for Mainland China and the many needy Chinese communities all over the world where materialism and the old religions of China with their demonic powers are still keeping many from the Lord.

14) **The Ministries of Help for China from the Free World.**

a) **Prayer** – the most important, but this is not an easy ministry with the lack of information coming out of China.

b) **Literature** – pray that more and more Bibles and Christian literature may be printed and taken into China. Pray for the writing and printing of the right type of literature for the new Communist-indoctrinated China. There are a number of good Christian organisations working on this ministry in the strategically placed Hong Kong (**OD, UE,** Asian Outreach, etc.).

c) **Radio** – many hours of programmes are beamed into China each day from Cheju (**FEBC,** Korea), Manila (**FEBC,** Philippines), Guam, etc. Direct contact with people by post is now impossible, so follow-up work, obtaining feed-back on the effectiveness of programmes and publicising the times of programmes is very hard. Pray that God may overrule in this to make these programmes as effective as possible, despite these hindrances. Occasional reports do come from tourists and refugees as to the value of these broadcasts.

d) **Christian Tourists** – it is very hard for non-Chinese tourists to enter and meet people, yet Overseas Chinese are now given a very warm welcome (one million in 1975), and are permitted to visit relatives. There have been wonderful accounts of such visitors being converted in China on finding their relatives now following the Lord. Other Christians have been used of God to bring encouragement and blessing to their people. Through these Christians a trickle of literature is now going all over China (very little can be taken in by each individual). There have even been teams of believers who have entered to contact the groups of believers and minister to them.

KOREA (North)

BACKGROUND

Area: 122,000 sq. km. – larger than South Korea, but has harsher climate.
Population: 16,300,000. Growth rate – 2.7%. People per sq. km. – 134.
Peoples: **Koreans** 100%.
Capital: Pyongyang 1,500,000. Urbanisation 41%.
Economy: Fairly highly industrialised, highly regimented and inefficient.
Politics: Liberation from the Japanese in 1945 did not result in a free united Korea due to Russian objections. A Communist puppet government was installed in the North and a democratic government in the South. The North invaded the South in 1949. The resulting war dragged on until 1953. The very large and well-equipped Korean Communist forces continue to threaten a second invasion of the South. The government of Kim Il Sung, the Communist Dictator, is one of the most oppressive in the world.
Religion: **Attitude of Government** – harsh repression of all religions. Nowhere has the Christian Church been more violently oppressed than here. During and after the Korean War many thousands of pastors and believers were murdered. The Christian Church had been stronger in the North during the Japanese occupation, but now nearly all the believers have fled to the South.
Roman Catholics 40,000 (?) **Protestants** a few thousand (?)

Points for Prayer

1) **The remaining believers** are forced to worship in great secrecy. There are occasional reports of the discovery of a group of believers and their subsequent martyrdom or imprisonment. Pray for these few remaining believers and their witness.
2) **Pray for a change in the attitude of the government** towards believers.
3) **A little literature still enters the land** – these methods are often ingenious: floating little packets in the sea, balloons, the post, etc. Pray that more of the written word may enter this closed land by some means.
4) **Radio** is the only direct way to reach the people. Pray for the broadcasts in Korean from the **TEAM** and **FEBA** stations in South Korea. Pray that people may hear of these programmes and start listening in.

MONGOLIA

BACKGROUND

Area: 1,565,000 sq. km. – largely grasslands and the great Gobi Desert.
Peoples: **Mongolians** 95% – largely Khalkhas.
           Kazakhs 5%
Population: 1,500,000. Growth rate 3.0%. Population Density – one per sq. km.
Capital: Ulan Bator 350,000. Urbanisation 46%
Economy: Largely based on agriculture, especially livestock; some mining and light industry. The people were largely nomadic until formed into collective and state farms.
Politics: Virtually a satellite state of the U.S.S.R. since the proclamation of a People's Revolution in 1921.
Religion: **Attitude of Government** – all religions have been suppressed.
Buddhism was the national religion, but only one monastery remains active.
Christians – no evidence of national believers.

Points for Prayer

1) **There has never been permanent missionary work in the land.** The Brethren, Pentecostals, **CIM, CMA** and **TEAM** all had mission stations in Inner Mongolia and the influence of their witness extended into the present state of Mongolia. Pray that this land may somehow be opened for the Gospel.

2)   **There are no copies of the old translation of Mongolian Bible** still circulating. It is
      almost impossible to get new Bibles into the land from the free world. **TEAM** in
      Hong Kong revised the N.T. in 1952 but this is unusable in the Mongolian People's
      Republic.
3)   **There are two small groups of Mongolian believers** in the free world – in Hong Kong
      and Taiwan – and they are the only source for new programmes broadcast by
      TEAM from Korea and **FEBC**, Manila. Pray for this valuable radio ministry – one
      of the few means at present of reaching this unevangelised nation.

LAOS

BACKGROUND

Area: 236,800 sq. km. – a landlocked, jungle-covered land in Indo-China.
Population: 3,400,000. Growth rate 2.4%. People per sq. km. – 13, but with the majority
               living in lowlands along Mekong River.
Peoples: **Lao-Lum** 40% and **Lao-Tai** 15% – are related to the Thai people.
               Mountain tribes 30% – about 50 small and very small groups scattered
               throughout the country and more especially in the mountainous areas.
               Meo-Yao 13% – mainly in the north of the country.
               Vietnamese 6%. **Chinese** 1%.
Capital: Vientiane 150,000. Urbanisation 15%.
Economy: Very poor country with most people living in a subsistence agricultural
               situation. Very undeveloped and also greatly hindered by the long Indo-China
               War.
Politics: The Rightist government collapsed in 1975 before the Communist Pathet Lao
               forces and massive military aid and direction from North Vietnam. The land is
               virtually a satellite state of Vietnam that is being mobilised for the subjugation
               of free Thailand. There is still much internal resistance from non-Communist
               forces in the country, especially among the Meo.
Religion: **Attitude of Government** – unclear at time of writing. Great pressures being
               placed on all Christians.
               Buddhists 75% – but a thin veneer over the older animistic religions.
               Animists 24% – more among the tribal and Meo peoples.
               Roman Catholics 1% – majority among the Vietnamese.
               Protestants 0.3% (?) – possible community of 12,000 and membership 4,000
               (about half the Christians have fled to Thailand since June 1975).
               Largest Evangelical groups – Evangelical Church (CMA) once 7,000
               members; Brethren (Swiss, British and **OMF**) approx. 1,000 members.
               Evangelicals 0.3%.

Points for Prayer

1)   **The Laotian people** are under the iron heel of Communism. The whole nation is being
      forcibly indoctrinated in Communism, with even Christians being compelled to lead
      indoctrination classes. Few of the people have believed in the Lord Jesus. Pray that
      somehow these people ·may be able to hear the Gospel.
2)   **The Protestant Church** among the Lao has been weak, lacking in effective leadership
      and largely illiterate. The rate of backsliding has been high. Converts were generally
      from the socially rejected elements of society. Humanly speaking, this Church has
      little chance of surviving the onslaught of Communism. Pray that the fires of perse-
      cution may refine the small company of believers into an effective soul-winning force.
      Many of the strongest leaders have had to flee for their lives.
3)   **Most of the Christians in the country** are among the Meo where there has been a great
      turning to the Lord through the witness of the **CMA**. The N.T. in two dialects was
      ready just in time for distribution before the Communists came. Pray for this

suffering people who have proved a hated thorn in the flesh to the Communists for many years, and are therefore in great danger now. Many Meo have fled to Thailand, where 10% of them are Christians.

4) **About half the believers and Christian leaders** have fled to Thailand, and there are many large refugee camps in N. E. Thailand with a high proportion of believers. Pray for the pastors ministering to these uprooted people, and that this tragedy may lead to strong churches developing among the 50,000 Laotian refugees. Pray for the relief and spiritual work of missionaries of CMA, OMF and WV among these people, and the resettlement of believers in areas useful for witness.

5) **The persecution of the believers in Laos** is building up in intensity. All land buildings, crops and livestock have been nationalised, and there is starvation. A very close watch is kept on Christians, though services are still continuing in two churches, all others having been closed. Many young people have been drafted into the army and some pastors are in prison. Pray for these harassed believers. All evangelism is now strictly forbidden. The two Bible Schools (CMA and Brethren) are closed.

6) **The many tribes** of the country are largely unevangelised. CMA, OMF and Brethren missionaries were able to do a little evangelism between 1957 and 1961 before Communist incursions made it too dangerous. Some of these people were won for the Lord in refugee camps subsequently. Only among the Khamu (100,000), Ngeq (50,000) and Nyaheun (15,000) are there churches. Pray for the unreached Alak*, Brao*, Galler*, Jeng*, Kasseng*, Loven*, Makong*, Oi*, So*, Phu Tai*, Ta Oi*, etc. Only a few have anything of God's Word. These tribes alone total 700,000 people. Some may have escaped to Thailand.

7) **There were only about 10 believers** among the Vietnamese, and 150 among the Chinese in 1975. Pray that these people may be evangelised.

8) **There are now daily broadcasts** from FEBA Manila prepared by CMA. There are few radios in the land and these are closely watched by the Communists. There is little electric power and batteries are almost unobtainable. Pray that despite this, many may hear the Word by this means.

VIETNAM

BACKGROUND

Area: 336,000 sq. km. – lying along the entire 2,000 Km Indo-China eastern coastline.

Population: 46,400,000. Growth rate 2.2% – very high population density in Red and Mekong River deltas, and very low in the inland mountains.

Peoples: **Vietnamese 84%. Cambodians** (Mekong Delta) 3.5%. **Chinese** (cities) 6%. **Mountain tribes** (about 57) – 5% related to similar tribes in China, and others to the peoples of Polynesia.

Capital: Hanoi 1,400,000 – also Ho Chi Minh City (Saigon) 4,000,000. Urbanisation 12% in the North, 37% in the South.

Economy: Productive agricultural economy gravely damaged by the War. Communists mobilising the entire country for reconstruction and development.

Politics: The tragic 30-year Vietnam war ended in April 1975 with the complete victory of the Communist North over the Western aligned South. This Communist-ruled nation is strenuously working to gain political control over all of Indo-China, Thailand and beyond.

Religion: **Attitude of Government** – very strict control of Catholics and Protestants in the North. There is still relative freedom in the South but future government action is likely to be harsh.
Buddhism 70% – but shot through with animism.
Hoa Hao 3% – a Buddhist sect. **Cao Dai 6%** – a Buddhist-Catholic sect.
Roman Catholics 8% – very influential in the South before Communism came.
Protestants 0.4%. Membership approx. 73,000. Community 200,000.
Evangelical Church of V.N. 54,000; United World Mission 4,000 members; Baptists 1,200; and a further approx. 10,000 believers in the North.
Evangelicals 0.4%.

Points for Prayer

1) **The subjugation of the South** by the Communists was followed by a systematic looting in Saigon of all the vast military and consumer goods left by the U.S.A. Poverty and famine as well as the sending of over one million politically "unreliable" people to "re-education camps" has driven many to despair and suicide. There is the possibility of a massive massacre of a rumoured two million people when all direct links with the outside world are severed. Pray that the ministry of many servants of God through the years may bear fruit in this hour of darkness.

2) **Missionary work in the land has ended.** The CMA gave 64 years of service to the land (50 years as the only Protestant Mission) and a wonderful foundation was laid for the establishment of a strong national church. Other missions came in the '50s and later, notably **WEC,** UWM and the Southern Baptists. There were 280 missionaries serving in 1974. Pray for these servants of God as they settle in other ministries and other lands.

3) **The Protestant Church** has grown steadily and strongly. In recent years the growth has been dramatic among the mountain tribes, who now make up one third of the membership. This growth has been in a time of terror, intimidation, murder of pastors by Viet Cong terrorists and massive movements of population fleeing the war. There were about 800 Evangelical churches in the South when the Communists took over.

4) **The present situation** for the believers in the South is not yet one of severe persecution. Yet, about 50 pastors have been killed, many believers are in prison, and all suffer the economic hardships of the whole people. Yet churches are now free to meet, Christian workers to minister and Bibles are still openly sold. There are tensions within the churches, between the leftists and rightists. Pray that the believers may remain true to Jesus and not be beguiled into compromise. Pray that they may maintain their daily communion with the Lord and shine for Him, and be spared the ghastly slaughter seen in Cambodia.

5) **The believers in the North** are free to meet together, but pastors are strictly controlled in what they preach and are forced to report to the Communists on their activities and also on their members. The few Christians are under great pressure through the 7-day week and the use of Sundays for indoctrination classes. There is discrimination against believers in education and employment.

6) **The pastors and church leaders** need great wisdom in this dangerous situation. Pray that they may remain true to their calling whatever this may cost.

7) **Several Bible Schools** are still open – pray for the staff and students in this tense time. Pray for the raising up of more spiritual men of God to lead the Church.

8) **The Church in many of the mountain tribes** has grown fast through some remarkable people movements, often in refugee camps. To mention a few: the **CMA** among the Chrau*, Jarai, Katu, Raday, etc., UWM among several others, **WEC** among the Hray. The majority in some of these tribes would now call themselves Christian. Pray for these isolated believers; so many so ill-taught and without much of the Word of God, who must face the ruthless atheism of Communism.

9) **The young people** face acute trials in the new Vietnam – not the least being the permission granted to the Viet Cong soldiers to take any unmarried girl in marriage. Pray for the Christian girls that they may find a believing partner.

10) **Bible translation** was in progress in 24 of the smaller language groups, mainly by **WBT.** By the time of the Communist take-over, 7 tribes had the N.T. and a further 17 had portions of the N.T. Pray for the distribution and preservation of this precious treasure in the years to come.

11) **Unreached peoples in Vietnam.** It is hard to see how these people can now be reached with the Gospel. Pray that the Lord may open up a way. We mention a few:
    a) Cham* 50,000 – a mixed Hindu and Muslim tribe in the Mekong delta – very few believers.
    b) The Mountain tribes of the North – Muong 400,000, Tai 400,000, Tho 150,000 and Yao. Some refugees were evangelised in the South. Pray that these may be free to go back to their unreached fellows in the North.

c) The Chinese – only about 2,000 believers in 10 congregations are known among these 3,000,000 people in Vietnam.

12) **About one half million Vietnamese fled** to other lands in 1975; many are seeking the Lord in refugee camps in Asia, and also in the lands to which they have gone – especially in France and the U.S.A. Pray for the brethren ministering to them.

13) **Radio broadcasts** from **FEBC** Manila in cooperation with **CMA** are the only direct contact with the believers now. Pray for the two-hour daily broadcast in Vietnamese, one-hour daily in Cambodian and Laotian.

14) **Thousands of Vietnamese continue to flee from oppression by boat.** Only about 30% – 50% ever reach a non-Communist land. The surrounding countries cannot absorb this flow of refugees, and refuse them sanctuary. Pray for these tragic people.

IV.   ASIA (Free)

For this survey we define Asia as those countries of Asia east of Iran and not under Communist rule (for the latter see "Communist Bloc").

ASIA 1978

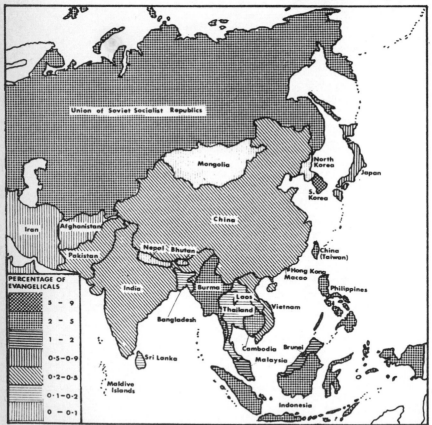

PERCENTAGE OF EVANGELICALS

	5 – 9
	2 – 5
	1 – 2
	0·5 – 0·9
	0·2 – 0·5
	0·1 – 0·2
	0 – 0·1

BACKGROUND

Area: 9,106,000 sq. km. – this is 6.3% of land area of the world. The whole of Asia proper, including Siberia, China and the Middle East is 29%.

Population: 1,254,000,000 – 31% of the world's population in the 21 nations and territories of our area.

Annual Growth 2.2%. People per sq. km. – 141.

Urbanisation 25.6% and increasing rapidly – these lands have 36 of the world's 163 cities of over one million inhabitants.

Economy: Industrialisation and improvement of living standards gravely hindered by the population explosion, political instability, etc. Most of these lands are desperately poor but for Japan, Hong Kong, Taiwan and Singapore. The richer states are becoming more rich and the poorer more poor. The long-promised "green revolution," with increased food production, has not succeeded as hoped due to the exorbitant rise in cost of fertilisers, inefficient methods and bureaucracy.

Politics: Asia is in a ferment. Great changes have come over the last 30 years. Factors contributing to this turmoil:

1) **The ending of the political dominance** of the Western nations. In 1945 only 4 of these nations were not under colonial rule – now only 3 territories are not independent – Macao, Hong Kong and Brunei. Independence has led to the renewal of ancient hostilities, between Muslims and Hindus in the Indian sub-continent and between China and India, etc.

2) **Nationalism** – often with an anti-western stance in international politics due to a rejection of everything resembling western dominance, yet, at the same time, retaining the doubtful benefit of western materialism. Nationalism has also stimulated the resurgence of the national religions, discrimination against Christian minorities and closing of some lands for missions.

3) **The presence of racial minorities** in all Asian lands. These minorities are a constant source of friction and instability, with many opportunities for the Communists to fish in these troubled waters. These minorities are of three types:

Aboriginal tribes, often many and small, they are usually the original inhabitants of the country who have been driven into the more inaccessible interior by invaders. These people are usually animistic and there has generally been a greater response to the Gospel among them. They generally have little political influence.

National minorities, existing within national borders that were arbitrarily drawn, that strive for independence. This has led to the shedding of blood in Pakistan (Bengalis, and also Sindhis), India (Nagas), Burma (Karens and Kachins), Philippines (Moros in Mindanao), Malays in Thailand, etc.

Immigrant populations: the most significant – **the Overseas Chinese** in these lands number 38,000,000 (including the Chinese Province of Taiwan and also Hong Kong). They control 4 territories and wield enormous economic power in 8 others. They are often disliked and feared by their host countries. Their national pride makes them a potentially subversive element to aid Red China's expansionist policies. The large Chinese minority in Malaysia is restive under Malay rule. Yet it is among these Overseas Chinese that the Lord has worked in power in this generation. **The Indians** are a significant minority in Malaysia, Singapore and Sri Lanka.

4) **The expansion of Communism in Asia** was greatly advanced by the fall of Laos, Vietnam and Cambodia to Communist forces in 1975, and now 975 million people in Asia live under this tyranny. Many other lands are now the victims of Communist aggression in the form of terrorist infiltration. Communist subversion feeds on the immense economic and social problems and inequalities. National governments can do little about it. The idealistic youth looks more to Communism for solutions than to the religion of their parents. The rise of China to super-power status is one of the most significant political developments in Asia today. God can halt Communism as He did in Indonesia in 1965, or use Communism for the purification and expansion of the Church as in Indo-China and China.

This is a critical time for Asia, and a strategic one for the Gospel, for we are beginning to see unprecedented expansion in the churches in the midst of the unrest and uncertainty, yet the time is also possibly very short.

Religion: **Hinduism 41%** – dominant in India, Nepal and Bali (Indonesia).

Islam 27% – dominant in Afghanistan, Bangladesh, Brunei, Indonesia, Malaysia, Maldive Islands and Pakistan.
Buddhists 1.7% – dominant in Burma, Bhutan, Hong Kong, Japan, Nepal, Sri Lanka, Taiwan and Thailand.
Animists 4%. **Sikhs** 1.1% (mostly in N.W. India).
All Christians 7%:
Roman Catholics 4.3% – majority in Philippines, strong in Hong Kong, Sri Lanka and Macao.
Syrian Churches 0.15% – mainly S.W. India.
Other Churches 0.3% – mainly in Philippines.
Protestants 2.3% – strong in Hong Kong, Korea, Singapore and in parts of Indonesia and Philippines.
Evangelicals 1.1% – Protestant Missionary force 13,787 (both Western and Asian), i.e. one missionary for every 90,955 people. Missionaries from Asia 2,260.

The Advance of the Gospel in Asia

After nearly 200 years of Protestant missionary endeavour, the Gospel has been preached in nearly every part of Asia. There is now a living Church in every country in our area but for Afghanistan and the Maldive Islands. In some areas the response has been minimal and the field hard, and in others there are large and vital churches that are beginning to contribute much to the spread of the Gospel in their own and other lands. We stand at the threshold of greater and more effective advances in the last part of the 20th Century than seen hitherto, whether Communism comes or not.

The Challenge of the Unfinished Task

Much remains to be done and the pressing needs of this continent deserve a greater effort by the Christians of the world to finish the task given by the Lord Jesus Christ. We mention a few points to illustrate the urgency and challenge: –

1) **The time is short** – some fields are closing to missionary work, such as Malaysia; there are mounting pressures on foreign missionaries in Indonesia and India. Other lands hitherto open for normal missionary work are now closed – Burma (1966), Cambodia, Laos and Vietnam (1975). There is urgency to do all possible to evangelise, plant churches and strengthen believers whilst there is time and opportunity. The Church must be prepared for likely persecution.

2) **The Church needs reviving** – as it has been in New Guinea, Timor (Indonesia), Korea, Nagaland (India) in recent years. In many areas, third and fourth generation Christians are nominal and need to be saved. This is a major problem in Pakistan, parts of India and Indonesia, Japan, and is a growing problem in Burma, Hong Kong and Taiwan. Much can be done by foreign missionaries in standing alongside these churches and helping them to come to a vital outgoing faith.

3) **There are specific peoples that remain unreached** that are a challenge to us to pray that the door may be opened for a witness. The following nations are closed to normal mission work: Afghanistan, Maldive Islands, Bhutan, Nepal, though in each but the Maldives there is a Christian presence. The penetration of the Gospel has been greatest among the animistic peoples, but the major religious blocs such as the Hindus, Muslims and Buddhists remain intact, and have lost relatively few to Christianity. To illustrate: –

    Muslims – there are probably no more than 300,000 converts out of Islam in Asia, 95% being in Indonesia and a small trickle of converts in Pakistan, Bangladesh and South Thailand. There are very few missionaries involved full time in working among Muslims.

    Hindus – about one quarter of the Christians in India come from the tribal peoples that only constitute about 7% of the population and the majority of the rest are descendants of the lowest castes of Hinduism. Only about 1% of all Protestants are converts out of Hinduism. The main body of Hinduism remains virtually untouched and out of reach of present Christian activity.

Buddhists – except for the conversion of many weakly Buddhist Chinese and the increasing turning to the Lord of Buddhists in Cambodia and Vietnam in the early '70s, fruit for the Lord in the predominantly Buddhist lands has been disappointing. Only 2% of Burmese Protestants are Burmese speaking and of these only a small fraction are converts out of the Buddhist majority. In Sri Lanka there are more reversions of Christians to Buddhism than converts out of it.

Asia needs our prayers and concern!

The Missionary Vision of the Asian Church

The missionary vision and outreach has grown and matured in the last decade, but only a small proportion of the believers have become actively concerned in cross-cultural missionary work, or have even seen their responsibility for world evanglisation. Much praying and teaching is required before the full potential of the Asian Church for missions can be realised.

There are about 2,260 (and possibly many more) Asian believers engaged in cross cultural missionary work. There are 4 major types of missionary: –

1) Those sent out by churches in Sarawak, Indonesia, New Guinea, India, Philippines and Burma to evangelise and plant churches in adjoining tribal areas. For example, the Danis of New Guinea, the Mizo and Naga of India, etc.

2) Those commissioned by churches to evangelise and plant or strengthen churches among those of their own race and language in other lands. Much of the Chinese and Japanese missionary effort is of this type.

3) Those joining international missions of Western origin, such as **OMF, BMMF,** etc.

4) The increasing number sent out by denominational and interdenominational missions of Asian origin for mission work within their own country or in other lands. International missionary work by Asian bodies is hindered by political and financial limitations. Interdenominational missions of this type: – Indian Evangelical Mission, Japan Overseas Missionary Assoc. and the Indonesian Missionary Fellowship.

More thought is now being given to preparing missionaries with special Bible Schools and missionary orientation courses in some lands, especially in Korea, Japan and Hong Kong.

AFGHANISTAN

BACKGROUND

Area	657,000 sq. km. – dry and mountainous, but with fertile valleys.
Population	19,500,000. Growth rate 2.2%. Population density – 30 people per sq. km.
Peoples	**Pushtoons** (related to Pakistani Pathans) 55%
	Tajiks (speaking Dari, a Persian dialect) 27%
	Uzbeks and **Turkomans** 9%, and also 36 other smaller tribes 5%
Economy	Very poor and undeveloped and dependent on foreign aid.
Politics	Autocratic monarchy overthrown in a coup in 1973, and replaced by a Republic. The land is a key buffer state between Iran, U.S.S.R., China and Pakistan.
	Note – pro-Communist coup in April 1978.
Capital	Kabul 600,000. Urbanisation 15%. Over 15% of the population is nomadic.
Religion	**Attitude of Government** – an Islamic state that does not tolerate the evangelisation of Afghans.
	Muslims 99%. A few **Hindus** and **Sikhs** have immigrated from India.
	Christians – several hundred foreigners and a handful of Afghan believers.

Points for Prayer

1) **Afghanistan is to all intents and purposes unevangelised.** Pray that this land may be opened for the preaching of the Gospel. Though there has been religious freedom since 1964, proselytisation is forbidden, but all kinds of witness goes on quietly.

2) **Unreached peoples** – this includes all the 40 peoples of this country. Special mention must be made of the Uzbeks, the many tribes north and east of Kabul living in the rugged mountain valleys of Nooristan, and also the nomadic peoples of the west. There are translations of the Scriptures in versions of the two official languages, but nothing is available in the minor languages.

3) **Missions** – there are a number of societies interested in the land who co-ordinate their activities as the International Aid Mission. Pray for all linked with this fellowship. Pray for the right strategy to fulfil the Great Commission. There are about 50 workers associated with the I.A.M.

4) **There are Christians serving the Lord** from other lands as doctors, teachers, etc. Pray that their lives may recommend the Saviour to those with whom they come into contact, and that they may obtain opportunities to witness and see fruit for their labours. Most of these workers are, at present, working in Kabul; pray that some may be able to work in other parts of the land. There is one Community Church that serves these ex-patriates, but no Afghan is allowed to attend any meetings.

5) **Afghan believers** – pray for some who are secret believers, and have little opportunity to share with other believers. Pray that their faith may grow strong and be without compromise in a very hostile environment.

6) **Witness to Afghans in other lands.** Pray for the witness in mission hospitals in Pakistan to which many Afghans go. There they have the opportunity to hear the Gospel and take back literature and Gospel records to their homes. Afghan university students in the West have proved quite responsive to the Gospel, and a number have sought the Lord in North America and Europe. Pray for these Afghans who have believed but who find it very difficult to remain in their own land on the completion of their studies.

7) **Many hippies and drug addicts come to Afghanistan** (150,000 per year and 3,000 at any one time) where they can obtain cheap drugs. These derelicts come from all over the world. Some Christians (**YWAM**) have been given permission to set up a Christian rehabilitation centre for them. Pray for this ministry – that it may lead to some being delivered from both drugs and sin by trusting in the Lord Jesus.

BANGLADESH

BACKGROUND

Area: 143,000 sq. km. – occupying the delta and floodplains of the Ganges and Brahmaputra Rivers, with high rainfall and prone to floods.

Population: 76,100,000. Annual Growth 2.7%. People per sq. km. – 532. Literacy 23%.

Peoples: **Bengalis 97%. Biharis 1%. Tribal peoples 2%** – 28 tribes in north and east.

Capital: Dacca 1,400,000. Urbanisation 9%.

Economy: One of the world's poorest nations, suffering from gross overpopulation and periodic natural disasters such as devastating floods and cyclones. The nation is still recovering from the widespread destruction caused by the war of independence. There seems little hope that the poverty of this unhappy land will ever be substantially alleviated.

Politics: Formerly East Pakistan – independent in 1971 after bitter civil war and defeat of Pakistan by Indian and Bangladesh forces. Instability and corruption have marked the subsequent years culminating in the coup that brought in the military government of 1976.

Religion: **Attitude of Government** – secular state declared in 1971 despite large Muslim
majority – due to revulsion against the cruelty of the Muslim Pakistani
repression in the civil war. Present freedom could be limited.
Islam 85%. Hindus 14%. Buddhists 0.5%. **Roman Catholics** 0.2%.
Protestants 0.2%. Community 130,000.
Largest: All Baptists (5) 45,000 community; All one in Christ (indigenous)
15,000; Anglicans 13,000. Evangelicals 0.15%.

Prayer Targets

1) **Bangladesh has been a hard and neglected field** but is now open for the Gospel.
Receptivity is due to national disasters, disillusionment and the good testimony of
Christian aid organisations. Pray that this golden opportunity may be seized by
believers. This land is reckoned to be still 80% unevangelised.

2) **Missions have neglected this land in the past** – the people were unresponsive, the
climate difficult and most mission work was channelled into institutions and not
evangelism. Many international workers are urgently needed but visas are not always
easy to obtain. There are now about 250 missionaries in 17 agencies, over half being
Baptists and 30 of **ICF**. This means one missionary for every 400,000 people. There
is much cooperation between missions to conserve limited manpower. The **ICF** is
specialising in the very successful BCC ministry and also Muslim and Hindu evangelism.

3) **Christian aid** has proved a dramatic stimulus to church growth in some areas due to
the impartial love and sympathy of the Christians. There is a great degree of
cooperation between the 10 mission agencies working in this field. Funds, etc., have
been provided by **WV, TEAR** Fund and others, and administered through missions
such as **BMMF** and national churches. This has led to a surge of people into the tribal
churches and a large number of Hindu enquirers as well as a trickle of Muslim
converts (there are now about 2,000 Muslims and Hindus converted every year).

4) **The Church** is very small and half of the community is among the tribal peoples that
make up only 2% of the population. Pray for the Bengali speaking believers as they
emerge from their spiritual shallowness, introspective inferiority and dependence on
missionary aid and initiative. The present opportunities have brought in a new spirit
of evangelism, cooperation and expectancy of a future harvest among Hindus and
Muslims. Pray for the conversion of whole families – most necessary in the close-knit
Muslim and Hindu societies.

5) **Leadership in the churches** is the biggest bottleneck to growth. There is still no major
Bengali Bible School (though one is being planned), yet scores of believers are
seeking to prepare for full time service. Ten groups are cooperating to launch a TEE
programme but this has limited value and effect at present.

6) **The tribal churches** have been growing through people movements and perhaps up to
15% of these peoples are now Christian, though there is much nominalism and lack of
understanding about the Gospel. Only 4 of the languages have been reduced to
writing and most of these tribes have nothing of the Scriptures. The work has grown
among the Garos 60,000 (Baptists), Santalis and Khasi (Lutherans), Tipperah
37,000 (Baptists and Methodists) and Bawm 10,000 (N.E. India Gen. Miss. formerly
working). Many tribes are still unreached – Koch* 40,000, Banai* 2,000, Hajong*
17,000, Murung* 22,000 (all above being animist) also the Buddhist Mogh 90,000.

7) **Bible correspondence courses** have proved the best way to reach Muslims and
Hindus. The most significant work is that of **ICF** with a full time staff of 30 nationals
and missionaries working from 6 centres and processing over 12,000 papers a month.
Enrolment has doubled since 1971. More is being done to personally follow up
students and hold follow-up rallies. Pray for many to be saved and brought into the
churches.

8) **Literature** – unprecedented demand; Bible Society reports tenfold increase in distribution of Scripture portions, and also there is a large increase in sales of all
Christian literature. This is largely due to the successful BCC programmes and the
very effective mass distribution of evangelistic literature by **OM** (the work now being
carried on by national brethren). Pray that this literature, and also the two new

versions of the Bengali Bible (one for Hindus and one for Muslims), may lead to conversions and church growth.

9)   **Other needy groups:**
   a) **Students** – several missions and also two **IVF** workers are starting a witness among them. Pray for the establishment of strong, witnessing groups in the universities.
   b) **The Biharis** – despised and rejected, and many living in vast and squalid refugee camps, these Muslim people are now more open to the Gospel because of their sufferings. Pray that conversions among them may lead to the evangelisation of the large Muslim Bihari population in India.

BHUTAN

BACKGROUND

Area: 47,000 sq. km. – a small kingdom in the eastern Himalaya Mountains.
Population: 1,200,000. Annual Growth 2.3%. People per sq. km. – 25 (mostly living in the rich central valleys).
Peoples: **Bhotia** 67% – related to Tibetans and speaking two major languages.
               Nepalis 25% – minorities of Santalis, Lepchas and Tibetan refugees (4,000).
Capital: Thimpu. Urbanisation 3%. Literacy 3%.
Economy: Undeveloped subsistence economy but with potential for future wealth.
Politics: Isolated from outside world until the trade and cultural links were severed with Tibet after the Chinese Communist invasion. India plays a dominant role in foreign affairs of Bhutan and also in its development.
Religion: **Attitude of Government** – hostile to all foreign cultural influences, but desirous of help from other nations, which may change things.
               Lamaistic Buddhism 65% – the state religion – a veneer over spirit worship.
               Hindus 27% – largely Nepalis and Santals; **Muslims** 5%.
               Christians 0.02%. Community possibly about 300.

Points for Prayer

1)   **Totally closed and without Christian witness until 1965,** but now a small Christian witness is growing. Pray for the full opening of this land for the Gospel.
2)   **The number of believers** among the Nepalis has grown dramatically since 1970 through the work of several Nepali pastors, with regular meetings in two places. Pray for spiritual and numerical growth, and also a reaching out to the Bhotia.
3)   **Missions** have been allowed to operate several small leprosy hospitals – pray for the silent witness of the workers of the Leprosy Mission and the Danish Mission to Lepers. These missions were forced to promise that they would not proselytise. The German Christoffel Mission hopes to open a blind school soon. Pray for a relaxation of limitations on witnessing.
4)   **Christians in government service** – mostly Indians and some westerners have good opportunities to witness all over the country. Pray that they may lead some to Christ.
5)   **Indian believers** are active in the border region in evangelism and literature distribution among visitors from Bhutan. Pray for conversions. There is also one Bhotia Pentecostal pastor in India who is translating the N.T. into the major Bhotia language, Dzongkha. Pray for the unreached Bhotia in their isolation and need.
6)   **Pray for the launching of proposed BCCs in both Bhotia and Nepali.**

BRUNEI

BACKGROUND

Area: 5,800 sq. km. – two small enclaves in East Malaysia on island of Borneo.
Population: 160,000. Growing at 3.5% per year. People per sq. km. – 27.
Peoples: **Malays** 54%. **Chinese** 26%. **Tribal people** 17%. **Expatriates** 3%.

Capital: Bandar Seri Begawan. Literacy 50%.
Economy: Wealth and rapid development through large revenues from oil.
Politics: Refused to join the Malaysian Federation; theoretically still a British Pro-
             tectorate. A Malay Sultanate.
Religion: **Attitude of Government** – Islam is the state religion. Missions are not allowed,
             but existing churches allowed to continue to operate.
             Muslims 60% – all the Malays and some Tribal people.
             Animism 10% among Tribal people. **Buddhism,** etc., among Chinese 20%.
             Roman Catholics 3%.
             Protestants 1.3%. Community 2,000 – Anglicans 1,000; others (5 groups)
             1,000.
             Evangelicals 0.6%.

Points for Prayer

1) **Unreached peoples** – there are no known Christians among the Malays and open
   evangelism of them is not allowed. There are few believers among the tribal Bisaya,
   Kedayan and Iban peoples – these are a potential mission field for the Chinese
   believers in Brunei (there is some outreach from one group), and Iban missionaries
   from Sarawak, East Malaysia. Local Christians must do the evangelism with the ban
   on missions.
2) **The churches are entirely led by immigrants,** mostly Chinese, and most of the
   believers are expatriate Westerners, Koreans or Chinese. The Anglican Church is
   not an evangelistic body, and very ritualistic. There are two very lively Evangelical
   Fellowships with three congregations that cater for Chinese, Indian and English
   believers. Pray for their witness and outreach. Pray that all opportunities for witness
   may be fully used – such as literature, camps and visiting Asian evangelists (all being
   legal).

BURMA

BACKGROUND

Area: 678,000 sq. km. – isolated from India, China and Thailand by a ring of
             mountains.
Population: 31,200,000. Annual Growth 2.4%. People per sq. km. – 46. Literacy 60%.
Peoples: Over 125 languages and dialects.
             Burmans 68%. **Minority Tribes** 24% – largest groups of tribes: Karens 10%,
             Shans 5%, Chin/Lushai 2%, Kachin/Lisu 2%. Other smaller tribes 10%.
             Immigrant minorities – Chinese 3%, Indian-Bangladeshi 1%.
Capital: Rangoon 3,400,000. Other major city – Mandalay 1,000,000. Urbanisation
             20%.
Economy: Very poor due to years of unrest, inefficient socialism and extreme isolationist
             policies of the government. Severe inflation.
Politics: Independent of Britain in 1948. Turmoil in country since Japanese occu-
             pation in 1942; there are now 4 tribal uprisings and 2 Communist revolutions
             in progress affecting 40% of the country. Military coup of 1965 following
             Burmese (Marxist tinted) Socialism.
Religion: **Attitude of Government** – Atheistic, yet afraid of religious leanings of the
             people. Buddhism no longer state religion. Officially religious freedom.
             Buddhists 75% (shot through with animism) – mainly Burmans, Mon and
             Shan.
             Animists 14%. **Muslims** 4%. **Hindus** 1%. **Chinese Religions** 2%. **Roman Cathol-
             ics** 0.9%.
             Protestants 2.5% – 2% Burman, 98% ethnic minorities (Kachin and Lisu 50%
             Christian, Chin and Lushai 38%, Karens 25% and Shans 0.5%). Community
             780,000. Denominations 15 – largest: Baptists 650,000 adherents; Anglicans
             (BCMS) 30,000; Assemblies of God 35,000; Methodists 22,000.
             Evangelicals 2.5%.

Points for Prayer

1) **Pray for peace,** religious freedom and a mighty turning to God in this divided and suffering land.

2) **Missions have done a wonderful work,** especially the American Baptist work pioneered by the great Adoniram Judson from 1813 onwards. So, when the government expelled all Protestant and most R.C. missionaries in 1966 (400 left the land), the Church was able to speedily make the many painful adjustments and carry on the ministry. Since that time the believers have been almost completely isolated from contacts with Christians outside the country. Pray for the removal of restrictions.

3) **The churches have continued to grow steadily** at about 3% a year. Almost the entire Church in all denominations is Evangelical and evangelistic. Church leaders have gained immensely in maturity and also in standing in the eyes of the authorities and people since the expulsion of the missionaries, for Christianity did not collapse, but proved to be truly rooted in the hearts of the people. Many Christians are well educated and to be found in positions of responsibility all over the country. Many young people are being converted and form a large proportion of many of the congregations. The charismatic movement has made a significant impact in many areas. Pray for the continued witness, spirituality and growth of this Church.

4) **Opposition to the Christians** has been more for political reasons – links with other lands, so loyalty to state and socialist policies doubted; also nearly all Christians are among restive minority groups with a recent history of uprisings against the central government. Pray for the believers in their very difficult situation facing hostility from both the government and also the Chinese Communists who exploit the national chaos to make military incursions into Burma. In some border areas the Christians have suffered much – isolation, poverty, disease and death. Generally there is still freedom for evangelism in areas away from sensitive border areas, but this could change to become open and general persecution.

5) **The missionary vision** of the believers is outstanding. There is much outreach to the unevangelised all over the country. Nearly all pastors and evangelists do much evangelistic work in animist and Buddhist villages. Most churches have vigorous lay-training schemes to get believers winning souls. Young peoples' evangelistic teams are greatly used. There are more trained full time workers than churches, despite the poverty of the congregations, so many go out as missionary evangelists to plant churches in new areas. There is a growing outreach to the Burmans and all Buddhists, as well as to tribes in Thailand. Pray for these believers as they evangelise the unreached peoples of their land.

6) **Leadership training** is an important part of the ministry of the Church – the Baptists having 26 Seminaries and Bible Schools with nearly 1,000 students, and the Anglicans, Methodists and Assemblies of God a further 5 Bible Schools.

7) **Unreached peoples**
   a) **The Burman people** are resistant. There are only 20,000 Protestants among them. It is not easy for the tribal believers to witness to them because of the years of mistrust between them. There is a new outreach run by the Baptists in Rangoon. Pray for the conversion of Buddhists.
   b) **Resistant tribal peoples** include the Shan, Mon and Palaung* (Buddhists), Moken* (see Gypsies), also the Kayah and Arakanese peoples.
   c) **The Chinese and Indian communities** – some work has been done by the Methodists but the response has been small. Many of the Christians among them have emigrated because of the harsh and discriminatory policies of the government.

8) **Bible translation** – 7 languages have the whole Bible, 9 the N.T. and 12 have portions. There is an urgent need for the completion of the Pa-O N.T. and Lahu O.T., as well as three important revisions. It is virtually impossible to import Christian literature and the government makes it very hard for the believers to obtain paper to print Bibles and Christian literature locally. Government censorship further complicates the production of literature. Pray for the critical lack of Bibles and literature to be supplied. A small amount of **SGM** literature is entering the country. Pray also for the entry of the valuable Gospel records – records in 59 languages.

9) **Christian Radio** – there are daily broadcast in Burmese or Karen through **FEBC** and also S.E. Asia Radio. The response is good, but all letters appeal for literature.

HONG KONG

BACKGROUND

Area:
1,045 sq. km. – two larger islands and a mainland peninsula on the S. China Coast (9/10 of the area, known as the New Territories, leased from China until 1997).

Population: 4,600,000. Annual Increase 2.1% (0.7% immigration). People per sq. km. – 4,300.

Peoples: **Chinese** 98% (88% of these being Cantonese speaking).

Economy: Rapid growth – one of Asia's major trading ports and industrial areas.

Politics: A Dependent Territory of Britain, dominated yet tolerated by the awakening giant of Communist China for its usefulness as a door to the world and source of foreign exchange – future very uncertain.

Religion: **Attitude of Government** – freedom of religion.
Chinese Religions (Taoism, Buddhism, Confucianism) 86%.
Roman Catholics 7%.
Protestants 6.5%. Community 260,000. Growth rate in '70s – 4%. Denominations 52, with about 600 congregations (about one quarter being non-denominational church groups) – Largest: Church of Christ in China 23,000 members; Baptists (5–6 groups) 30,000; Anglicans 20,000; Lutherans 21,000; non-denominationals approx. 20,000; Alliance Church (**CMA**) 5,000.
Evangelicals 5%.

Points for Prayer

1) **Hong Kong** is one of the most important centres strategically for the Gospel in Asia, with its close links with Communist China, the Overseas Chinese (42,000,000 outside Communist China) and all Asia. Yet the threat of Communist takeover is ever there.

2) **The churches** have grown in number and maturity with outstanding Christian leaders in denominations, theological training, literature and mass media. The expense of land, and overcrowded state of the country has compelled many groups to meet in homes, roof-top churches, or build high-rise multi-purpose, church-school-hostels. Materialism is slowing church growth. Pray for the leadership and outreach of the churches to the many unreached Chinese. Pray that the believers may be well taught and well prepared for the possibility of a Communist takeover.

3) **Outreach by the churches** – some older denominations are less enthusiastic in evangelism, though most are Evangelical in theology, but some younger, indigenous and mission oriented churches are vigorously evangelising. The 1975 Billy Graham Crusade drew a dramatic response.

4) **Leadership training** – there are over 20 Seminaries or Bible Schools – we make special mention of the Seminaries of the Southern Baptists, Alliance Church and Evangelical Free Church. A new interdenominational Graduate School of Theology was opened in 1975, and promises to be a great boon to the Church of S. E. Asia as well as to the churches and pastors of Hong Kong.

5) **Missions** – many agencies with over 452 Protestant missionaries – many serving in Asia-wide ministries, and the minority actually serving the Hong Kong Church in evangelism, Bible teaching and church planting. Pray for a happy relationship in humility between the expatriates and Chinese believers, and also for the most effective use of the former for the building up of the Church. Many missions work in a support capacity in literature (Asian Outreach, **CLC**), evangelism and church support (**OMF**) and ministries involving Red China.

6) **Refugees from Communist China** continue to arrive illegally (and often with great

danger) at the rate of about 30,000 a year. Some are repatriated by the government to China and an unknown future. Two out of every three in Hong Kong are refugees. These needy and despairing refugees often become embittered and disillusioned in the overcrowded and difficult conditions of Hong Kong. Some local Chinese groups and several missions have made a real effort to win these people, such as **CMA**, Evangelise China Fellowship, etc. There are also many Christian welfare agencies (e.g. **WV**).

7) **Christian communications** are very developed. There are many publishing groups (Christian Communications Ltd., Asia Outreach, etc.) producing new translations of the Bible in "Mao" script (4 new translations), and literature – both for Asia and also for Mainland China. Pray for the entry of this literature into the closed lands of Asia. **CLC** has now a new literature base. Much work is done in preparing Christian films and radio programmes (transmitted via **FEBC**, etc.). This extensive ministry needs to be covered in prayer.

8) **Youth – SU** has a very active programme in the many secondary schools, and the IFES **(IVF)** a good evangelistic outreach in the increasingly leftist universities.

9) **Missionary vision** – increasing through greater maturity of the Church, and boosted by the 1976 China Conference on World Evangelism in 1976. There are now more than 10 Chinese sending bodies or churches with over 50 missionaries serving in other lands. Pray for the increase of this vision and its better co-ordination and support.

10) **MACAO** is Portugal's last remaining colony – a 15 sq. km. peninsula 30 Km from Hong Kong, with 400,000 people. The Communists virtually control the colony, yet a little Christian work continues. 15% are Roman Catholic, and 1% Protestant – mainly Baptist. Pray that these believers may be well prepared for a Communist future. There are few Christian workers. More could be done by Hong Kong believers to evangelise these people – many being refugees*.

INDIA

BACKGROUND

Area:	3,268,000 sq. km. – 21 Union States and 10 Union Territories.
Population:	620,700,000. Annual Growth 2% (13,000,000 annual increase). People per sq. km. – 190. Indians in other lands 5,000,000. Nearly one sixth of the world's population is Indian.
Peoples:	Great racial and linguistic diversity with over 800 languages spoken. **Official languages** – Hindi and English.
	National languages (14): – Hindi 31%, Telugu 8%, Bengali 8%, Marathi 8%, Tamil 7%, Urdu 5%, Gujarati 4.6%, Kannada 4%, Malayalam 4%, Oriya 4%, Punjabi 2.5%, Assamese 1.6%, Kashmiri 0.5%.
	Tribal peoples 7% – mainly in N.E. and inland hills and mountains.
Capital:	New Delhi 4,100,000. Cities of over one million: – Calcutta 7,000,000; Bombay 6,000,000; Madras 2,500,000. Urbanisation 25%.
Economy:	Crippled by high birth rate, ignorance, prejudice, resistance to change, bureaucratic inefficiency and corruption as well as the oil price rises since 1974. India faces a future of possible famines and social upheaval.
Politics:	Independent of Britain in 1947 – the world's largest democracy. The new Government (Mar. 1977) faces immense task in domestic and foreign policies and needs courage and unity to overcome the many problems, but with the ever present danger of a collapse of the present coalition.
Religion:	**Attitude of Government** – central government seeks to guarantee religious liberty in the face of powerful pressure from Hindu radicals that have obtained the passage of anti-conversion laws in several states.
	Hindus 80% – a religion that is a social system, plus a philosophy as well as a religion that readily absorbs aspects of any religion with which it comes into contact. Much of popular Hinduism is just idolatry and spirit worship. Philosophical and mystical Hinduism is becoming popular in the Western

World. India suffers under its fatalism, caste system, 200 million holy cows, etc., to its economic and spiritual detriment.

Muslims 11% – an influential minority, but in majority in Jammu and Kashmir. There are as many Muslims in India as in Muslim Pakistan.

Sikhs 2%, **Jains** 0.5%, **Buddhists** 0.7%, **Animists** 3%.

All Christians 3.4%: **Roman Catholics** 1.5%, **Syrian Orthodox** 0.3% (the latter mainly in Kerala and founded by the Apostle Thomas in 1st Century.

Protestants 1.5% – mainly in south and north east. Community 6,000,000. Denominations 100+.

Largest: Baptists (11) 734,000 adherents; Church of North India (CNI) 700,000; Church of South India (CSI) 1,200,000; Lutherans (12) 363,000; Salvation Army 200,000; Methodists (3+) 600,000; Presbyterians (3) 144,000; Pentecostals (15+) 100,000; Fed. of Ev. Churches (**CMA, TEAM, ICF,** etc.) 80,000; Mar Thoma 250,000.

Evangelicals 0.4%. Annual Growth rate of Christians 3.26%. This map below clearly shows the uneven distribution of India's Christians in the different states and territories: –

INDIA 1974

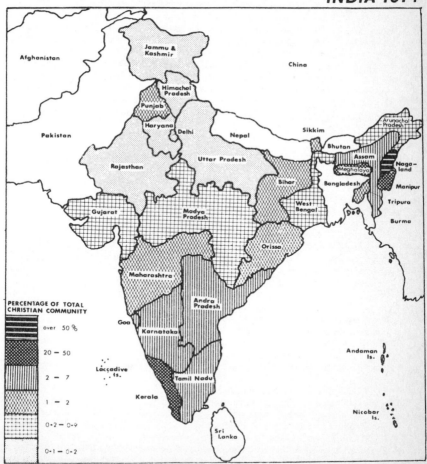

Note: – These figures, and the shading are **not** for Evangelicals only, but the whole Christian community – using the Government Census figures of 1971.

Prayer Targets

1) **Pray that India may remain open for the Gospel** in the face of **Communism** which exploits India's social and economic woes, and **militant Hinduism** that bitterly opposes the advances of Christianity. Anti-conversion laws are in operation in two states and are being contemplated for three more. Much of the country is still a pioneer mission field. Pray for the Christians that they may use present opportunities to evangelise.

2) **The missionary force** in India has declined by 40% in the last 15 years. Entry and re-entry visas for missionaries are hard to obtain. Few new missionaries are entering the country. The entry and use of mission funds from abroad are strictly scrutinised. There are about 2,000–2,500 missionaries in India. Pray for the issuing of visas to expatriates needed for the Lord's work, and also for the most effective use of the present missionary force. Pray that these limitations may stimulate outreach by Indian Christians.

3) **Missions** have done an immense amount of work since 1706, and many large and independent Churches are the fruit of this labour. Some missionaries are still in pioneer work and evangelism, but most work within the national churches in church planting, lay and pastor training, Christian education, rural uplift and technical ministries. Pray for missions such as **BMMF, CMA, ICF, RBMU, WEC, OMS,** etc. Pray for individual missionaries – those in sensitive areas where every action and every soul won for Jesus can be a pretext to end their ministry in the land. Pray for those who may be discouraged by lack of visible results, carnality among the Christians and the frustrating restrictions under which they work.

4) **Many of the larger and older denominations** are the fruit of mass movements to Christianity in the last century that were inadequately discipled. There is now much nominalism. Yet there is a growing evangelical voice with some outstanding Christian leaders in them. The churches are generally in decline in Uttar Pradesh and Gujarat, growing by natural increase in most states, and growing through conversions in the north east. Revival is needed to rid the churches of introspection, petty squabbles, social climbing and sin, and to get the believers out to evangelise. The people are now more receptive to the Gospel, but there are too few Christians in a position to witness to them. There are too many Christians who are still bound by Hindu caste loyalties, prejudice and superstitions; court cases are common among Christians. Pray that the Church in India may soon shine brightly for the Lord.

5) **Outreach by the Christians has been very poor,** but much is being done to rectify this and impart a vision to the churches: – **The 1977 All India Congress on Evangelism** – pray for its outworkings that this may lead to a better co-ordinated and more determined evangelisation of India.

   Every Home Crusade is now visiting every home in India for the second time in order to leave a portion of Christian literature. Pray for conversions. **OM** has had a very important impact on many churches in the large denominations by mobilising local believers for evangelism and literature distribution. Pray for the large numbers of Christian young people involved, and their aggressive evangelistic coverage of many of India's most poorly evangelised areas.

6) **The Evangelical witness needs prayer: –**
   a) **In giving the Bible its rightful place** both in the theologically liberal denominations and in the Evangelical churches. In the former, dialogue and universalism have replaced evangelism and conversion. In the latter there is little solid teaching or expository preaching or application of Bible answers to the real and pressing needs of India today.
   b) **The Evangelical Fellowship of India,** with more than 100 cooperating Evangelical bodies, is having a significant impact on maturing, stabilising and mobilising the believers through weeks of prayer, conventions, pastors' retreats and co-ordinating missionary outreach, literature production, Sunday School courses, TEE (under title TAFTEE) as well as backing the Yeotmal Seminary.
   c) **The newly formed Fellowship of Evangelical Churches of India(FECI)** is the fruit of the work of over 15 of the smaller Evangelical societies (both denominational and interdenominational). Pray that this new body may overcome internal problems to become a mighty force for the evangelisation of the land.

d) **The more indigenous Indian denominations** such as the Assemblies associated with the name of Bakht Singh and the Pentecostals are growing. Pray for them.

7) **Leadership training** is critically important. The lack of dedicated Christian workers prepared to leave all for the sake of Christ is the biggest single factor limiting the growth of the Church. There is now an average of one pastor for 8 churches and 400 villages over the country, though some pastors have oversight over 200 churches. Pray for all lay-training schemes, TAFTEE (run by many churches and missions) with many thousands of students. Pray also for the 40 degree-level seminaries and the students being prepared for the ministry; only a few are truly Evangelical – one such being the Yeotmal Seminary (soon to move tọ Poona). The latter is backed by 26 evangelical bodies and is sending out a stream of well-trained evangelical leaders into India and Asia. Pray also for the very many Bible Schools in India.

8) **The missionary vision of the Indian Church** is small, but growing. The denominations have some mission work both in India and in other lands – CSI (to Orissa and hill tribes), Methodists (Sarawak, Malaysia), Mar Thoma (N. India and Arabian Gulf), Mizo Baptists (to Assam Hills), Naga Baptists (Burma border, N. E. Frontier). There are several interdenominational societies of note – the National Miss. Soc., with 40+ workers in 6 fields in India and Nepal, and the EFI-supported Indian Evangelical Miss. with 65 workers in 10 Indian and 3 foreign fields. There are now about 600 Indian missionaries in cross-cultural mission work. Pray for the cultivation of missionary concern in the churches. Pray for effective missionary training programmes, such as that launched by **BMMF-IEM** in 1976.

9) **Specialised ministries: –**
a) **Young people** are, unfortunately, largely neglected by many churches due to lack of manpower and interest. Pray for such agencies as Youth for Christ, **SU** and **CEF** who are seeking to do something about winning and discipling India's youth.

b) **University students** – over 2,500,000 in 32 universities (Calcutta has 120,000!). The only effective evangelical witness on a national level is the Union of Evangelical Students of India (UESI-**IVF**) with 20 full time workers and 4 missionaries. Most universities have a group meeting regularly – pray for their witness to the many unconverted, and also pray for their purity of life, spiritual growth, and their involvement in local churches. There are no UESI groups in Kashmir, Punjab, Bihar or Rajasthan.

c) **Literature.** Pray for the mass distribution work of EHC and **OM** (the latter distributing 12–14 million pieces a year), and also for the Scripture distribution of the Pocket Testament League. Pray for conversions and church growth thereby. Christian bookstores and literature agencies (most of the Evangelical groups associated with the EFI related Ev. Lit. Fell. of India) face major problems with importation of literature, lack of local writing talent, high costs in a poor land.

d) **Bible correspondence courses** have proved most successful. 60–70 centres send out courses – one of the largest being **TEAM** who send out courses in 22 languages and have seen over 2 million people completing at least one course.

e) **Bible translation.** Of India's 800 languages, only 26 have the Bible, 48 the N.T. and a further 48 portions of the N.T. Work is now in progress in 35 languages, but many more await translators. More Indian believers need to be raised up for this exacting ministry.

f) **Gospel Recordings** – now with records in 187 of India's languages. This is a valuable tool together with Cassettes for evangelising and teaching the smaller or less accessible peoples of India.

g) **Christian medical work** has had to be greatly streamlined with the run-down of missionary staff. **The Christian Medical Assoc.** has oversight over 430 institutions with both Indian and expatriate medical workers. **The Emmanuel Hospitals Assoc.** now has responsibility for all the hospitals, etc. that were run by Evangelical missions. Pray for the witness that goes out from these hospitals to the many patients, and that this may lead to many seeking the Saviour. Pray for the Evangelical Nurses Fellowship with groups in many hospitals. Pray also for the specialised ministry of the Leprosy Mission to India's millions of sufferers from this disease.

h) **Christian Radio.** There is no Christian broadcasting in India, but over 20 studios produce programmes for transmission by **FEBC** Manila, **FEBA** Seychelles and Back to the Bible Broadcasts and **TWR** in Sri Lanka. There is an increasing audience, but

pray for a greater impact and response among Hindus and Muslims.

10)   **Unreached peoples and areas** – please prayerfully study the map of India on p. 107. We mention a few areas and communities: –

a) **The North Indian Plains** with their teeming millions have far fewer believers than better evangelised South India. **Uttar Pradesh's** (95,000,000) population has increased 300% in 50 years, but the number of Christians of all kinds has decreased from 200,000 to 133,000 and most of these are only nominal and rarely attend a church service. There are 6 small Bible Schools in the state and few Christian workers. **Bihar** (60,000,000) is prone to droughts and famines and is very needy spiritually – the 8 million Muslims and 65,000 schools have no Christian witness.

b) **The 68,000,000 Muslims** are found all over India, and are more willing than ever before to listen to the Gospel, but there are only about 20 Christian workers seeking to witness to them. Pray for a greater concern for these people among the believers.

c) **The rural population** is generally poor, backward and unevangelised. Very few of the 700,000 villages of the land have any evangelical witness. In North India there is an average of ONE church for every 2,000 villages.

d) **The upper and middle class Hindus** tend to despise the Christians for their low caste or tribal origin, and there are very few believers among them.

e) **States seeking to limit Christian evangelism** – Orissa (21,000,000) and Madhya Pradesh (41,000,000) have both passed laws making it very hard for anyone to change his religion. Pray that this may stimulate prayer and action by the believers, and also raise the quality of discipleship in the churches.

f) **Gujarat** (30,000,000) – most of the Christians are of the lowest castes (road-sweepers, weavers and the tribal Bhil*); 32 higher Hindu castes remain unreached, and the number of Christians (many nominal) is declining.

g) **The North East** (The old Assam), now made into 6 States: **Assam** (15,000,000) – there is a considerable turning to the Lord among the 3,200,000 Santal and the 1,100,000 Oraon peoples. Most of the peoples remain unreached. Small Nepali fellowships are springing up in some centres. **Manipur** (1,250,000) – most of the tribal people have become Christian, but the valley Meitei* (700,000) despise them, but are tired of Hinduism. **Arunachal Pradesh** (500,000) on the north eastern frontier is made up of 40 different tribal peoples. The area is closed to all open Christian work. Most people are animists or Buddhists, but God is moving through children converted in mission schools in Assam and Christians from Nagaland. In spite of official persecution, there are growing churches with over 4,000 believers. **Nagaland** (516,000) – 16 Naga tribes now 66% Christian (mostly Baptist). For years a war of independence by the Nagas has hindered the great potential for a great missionary movement from these people to the 43 million tribal peoples of all India. Revival broke out in some areas of Nagaland in 1976.

h) **Kashmir** (5,300,000) is largely Muslim. Several missions work in the Kashmir Valley, but very few Christian groups. There are probably no more than 6 people converted out of Islam. A number of Indian missionaries from S. India have seen a turning to the Lord in neighbouring Jammu. Ladakh, once evangelised by the Moravians, has a weak Christian community that is inter-marrying with Muslims. Pray for the conversion of nominal Christians and Muslims.

i) **Sikkim** (200,000) in the sensitive mountainous border region between Bhutan and Nepal was taken over by India in 1975. Largely unevangelised and closed to mission work. The Nepali and Bhotia majority is virtually without an evangelical witness, but there are about 1,500 believers among the minority ruling Lepcha people.

j) **The Laccadive Islands** (31,000) west of India are Muslim and unevangelised.

INDONESIA

BACKGROUND

Area: 1,491,000 sq. km. – 5 large and 3,000 small inhabited islands.
Population: 134,700,000 – the world's 5th most populous nation. Annual Growth 2.1%. People per sq. km. varies from Java – **644** to Irian Jaya's **2.**

Peoples:	25 major language groups, and a further 750 languages in use (over 500 are in Irian Jaya). Increasing use of Indonesian is unifying the people. **Largest groups: Javanese** 40%, **Sundanese** 15%, **Madurese** 8% all on Java. **Chinese** 4% number 6 million and are scattered throughout Indonesia.
Capital:	Jakarta 6,000,000 – Main cities: Surabaya 2,900,000. Urbanisation 18%.
Economy:	Potentially rich with vast mineral resources and good agricultural land, but catastrophic economic policies of former President Sukarno brought great poverty and inflation. Dramatic recovery under President Suharto since the abortive Communist coup of 1965, but overpopulation in Java a brake on hopes for raising living standards.
Politics:	Independent of Netherlands in 1950 after 350 years of Dutch rule. Revulsion against Communists after their unsuccessful coup in 1965 led to the massacre of 400,000 Communists and their sympathisers at the hands of enraged Muslims. There has been political stability since then.
Religion:	**Attitude of Government** – a religious state with equal rights for Islam, Hinduism, Buddhism and Christianity, though with growing pressures from Muslim leaders to limit the notable advances of the Christian Church. **Muslims** 84% officially. Strong in parts of Sumatra and Sulawasi and especially so in Java. Islam is often a veneer over animism and Hinduism. Some would therefore reckon that true Muslims are only 45%. **Hindus** 3.3% largely on Bali, and some in E. Java. **Buddhists** 2% – mostly Chinese. **Animists** 1% – mostly Irian Jaya. **Christianity** 10% – **Roman Catholics** 2.3%, majority on Flores; **Protestants** 7%, majority on Timor, West Irian, Moluccas and in parts of Sumatra, Kalimantan and Sulawesi. Community 8,500,000. Denominations – 63. Linked with the National Christian Council – 42 (80% of all Protestants and mostly of Reformed and Lutheran traditions). ther groups: "KINGMI" (**CMA**) 250,000 community, Baptists, etc. Evangelicals 4% annual rate of growth of Protestants 5.5% since 1948.

Map of the islands mentioned and an indication of the progress of the Gospel.
Please note that the system of shading here has no relation to that used elsewhere in this book.

INDONESIA & MALAYSIA 1978

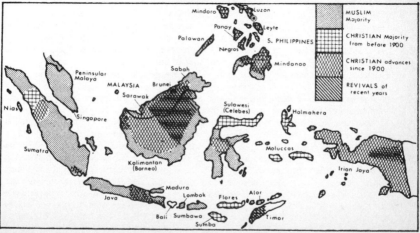

Points for Prayer

1) **One of the most significant movements** to Christianity in history is occurring in this great and diverse land with a great ingathering of souls. This is the only country in the world where significant numbers of Muslims have turned to Christ. Pray for a continued open door in the face of the Communist threat and rising Muslim opposition.

2) **The great people movements** seen in Sumatra, Java and Kalimantan over the last 15 years were accelerated by the events surrounding the 1965 coup. The cruelty of the Communists and bloodthirsty Muslim reprisals caused revulsion among many, and the virtual outlawing of animism further helped to bring thousands of Muslims, ex-Communists and animists into the churches or open to the vigorous evangelistic work of many churches and missions. The number of Christians increased 40% in 1963–66. Pray for a continuing of this movement of the Spirit of God.

3) **There are acute dangers** in this rapid growth. Although God also gave revival to the churches in some areas, much of the Indonesian Church is nominal, and most do not yet understand about the new birth because earlier people movements were not well discipled due to the lack of Bible teachers. The same danger is there in the present movement. Pray for the raising up of many leaders and teachers who are able to bring these hungry souls into a living relationship with the Lord. Unless this is done, many may be open to sects or bring heathen thought patterns and practices into the churches.

4) **The Muslim backlash,** stimulated by over-enthusiastic reporting in the Christian press about the great turning of Muslims to the Lord in Java, has led to some persecution, rioting and destruction of some churches. The government has bowed to this pressure a bit, and is beginning to limit the numbers and spheres of ministries of missionaries. There is also increased police surveillance of Christian activities in Java. Pray that Christian leaders may have the tact and wisdom to avoid unnecessary provocation, and yet not draw back from the quiet winning of Muslims. Pray that they might know the Lord's plan for evangelising Muslims.

5) **The churches** are strong and revived in some areas, nominal in others and virtually non-existent in yet others. Please look at the brief coverage of the various areas below. There are some general prayer points: –

   a) **Nominalism** is rife in the islands which have been Christian for centuries, such as Halmahera, the Moluccas, N. Sulawesi and Timor. Pray for revival to sweep these islands – so far only Timor has experienced this. Even areas evangelised in the last century such as N. Sumatra, Nias, E. Java, etc., have many 3rd and 4th generation "Christians" that need to be evangelised. There are also many pastors in these churches who are unconverted. The evangelisation and mobilisation of these people is essential if a harvest of souls is to be won and retained. Pray for the timely ministry of **OMF** missionaries within the older churches.

   b) **Liberal Theology** is having an increasing influence through the W.C.C. to which many of the larger Churches belong. The younger pastors and the theological institutions are more affected than the older and senior leaders. Pray that the Bible may have its rightful place in the affections and teaching of the leaders.

   c) **The training of leaders** – there is a desperate shortage of Christian workers, due to the explosive growth of the Church recently. Many pastors are ill-taught but the number and quality of the Bible Seminaries and Schools has grown. There are now over 35 Seminaries in the country – some definitely not evangelical. The great need is for the conversion of many who come for theological training, and then for the development of their walk with God and vision of the need of the lost. **Evangelical missions** have some first-class Bible Schools – notably the 16 Schools of KINGMI **(CMA)** in the eastern half of the country, and the outstanding Batu Bible College (Indonesian Missionary Fellowship and **WEC**). From these latter a stream of evangelistic teams have gone out all over the country and to other lands and these teams have been the cause of people movements in Irian Jaya, Kalimantan, S. Sumatra and Java, and the dramatic revival in Timor. **TEE is now being profitably used in many areas,** but lack of suitable staff and teaching materials and the sheer size of the field has limited its impact. The dominance of the pastor in Indonesian congregations greatly inhibits the development of good lay leadership – a real hindrance to growth. **The OMF seeks to establish a Graduates Training School** for those in the professions with one and two-year courses – pray for the launching of this promising project and the provision of staff, etc.

d) **The evangelical witness** has been strengthened by the formation of the Indonesian Evangelical Fellowship – largely supported by at least 65 lay-evangelistic organisations. Pray that this may lead to better co-ordination of the evangelisation of the country and all the many support ministries.

e) **Outreach** – the dramatic growth rate is now falling (probably for the many reasons outlined above). Pray that the churches may all have a vision for outreach locally and to other unreached areas and islands. Much of Sumatra, parts of Java, Bali, Sumba, Sumbawa, Flores and E. Timor (former Portuguese) remain unreached.

f) **Missionary vision** has resulted in the formation of the Gospel teams (see point 5-c) that have spread the Gospel to other language groups. Teams from Batu have had great results in Pakistan, S. Thailand, West Africa, etc. Pray for the development of this vision – Indonesia could mean much for world evangelisation, especially the great unreached Muslim world. Pray for the small but growing number of missionaries going out with the **IMF,** Evangelise China Fellowship, and now through the Indonesian Home Council of **OMF.**

6) **The Chinese believers** are a large minority of the scattered Chinese population. The great work of John Sung and the resulting revivals led to the planting of many Chinese churches 40 years ago. There are many fine leaders and strong missionary-minded congregations in Java. There are also Chinese churches in W. Kalimantan, etc. Many Chinese believers are now being absorbed into the Indonesian churches. Pray for the work of the **ECF** and its S. E. Asia Bible School with its outreach to other lands. Over 12% of the Chinese are now Christian.

7) **Missions** – early efforts by Dutch and German missions were highly successful in the areas where they were permitted by the Dutch authorities. There are now about 1,300 missionaries serving in 72 agencies. Pray for them in the hot, humid climate, with time-consuming and difficult travelling conditions and in their need for tact and patience in frustrating situations. Many more are needed to do pioneer work, church planting, church support work and Bible teaching, etc. Pray for work permits. **Some Missions such as OMF** with their 70 workers seek to humbly help the long-established Churches by loaning workers to them. Pray for this delicate ministry of winning the confidence of pastors and people so as to bring in helpful programmes of teaching and outreach to often lethargic congregations. **Other interdenominational missions seek to evangelise new areas and plant churches,** such as **WEC** with 70 missionaries in Sumatra, Java and Kalimantan; **CMA** in East Indonesia (50 missionaries in 9 fields), **TEAM, RBMU** and **UFM** in Irian Jaya, etc.

8) **Student witness** – a largely neglected, but ripe harvest field. There are wonderful openings to teach the Bible in primary and secondary schools, and also to witness to the 250,000 university students in 24 universities, but the labourers are too few.

9) **Christian literature** – there is a colossal appetite for any evangelistic literature – pray for the many printing presses working on this, and for the distribution thereof. Pray for the ministry of the SGM booklets in this needy land. Books are not easy to sell. Indonesians are both poor and poor readers. There is a great dearth of good evangelical literature for theological students – pray for the **OMF** project of translating the New Bible Commentary into Indonesian. Pray also for the publishing work of **CLC** and bookstores, now expanding to many of the major islands.

10) **Bible translation** is still a pressing need for the many small languages of Irian Jaya. The rapid spread of the use of Indonesian lessens the need for many more translations of the Bible, but much primary translation and also revision is still needed. Of the 838 languages, 9 have the Bible, 19 the N.T., and 28 have portions. There is work in progress in 33 (mostly in Irian Jaya).

11) **Prayer needs of the major islands:**
a) **Sumatra** 23,000,000 –
The 2.4 million ardently **Muslim Atjeh** in extreme north are unevangelised.
The 5 million **Menangkabau** in Centre are also strongly Muslim, and only a handful

of Christians among them (one congregation in W. Java). There are some Christians in the area, but all are from other language groups.

The **Toba Bataks** and people of Nias have been Christian for decades, now there is much nominalism. Pray for revival. The Toba Batak Church has one million members.

The **Karo Bataks** are turning to the Lord in large numbers – pray for this growing church and the work of **OMF** missionaries assisting it.

The **16 tribes of the South** – only one now reached with the Gospel – live in rugged country and most are Muslim. One tribe is turning from Islam to the Lord (**WEC**). The **UFM** is working in three tribes in the area.

b) **Java** 90,000,000 –

Unreached peoples – the Banten and Sunda (15 million) in the West (with a few churches) and the resistant Madurese in the East (6 Madurese Christians on Madura Is.) are all Muslim. Pray for the difficult ministry of **WEC** among the latter. Pray also for the evangelisation of the largely unreached Hindu Tennger* in the mountains of E. Java.

The **Church** (2% of population) has seen hundreds of thousands of Muslims coming into the fellowships in spite of being generally weak and immature. The Christians are not fully able to take advantage of the great openness of the 50 million Muslim Javanese to the Gospel. Pray for the **OMF** missionaries working among the Christian Reformed Churches, and also for the evangelistic and church planting ministries of many other groups. The need of the growing cities is great.

c) **Bali,** a 3,000,000 tourist-infested Hindu island in great spiritual darkness, demonic oppression and witchcraft. The progress of the Gospel has been slow, with only about 10,000 Christians until recently. The great volcanic eruptions over the last decade have brought a great change because of Christian love shown to the victims, and whole communities are turning to the Lord. Pray for the ministry of **CMA** in Bali.

d) **The lesser Sunda Islands** (Lombok, Flores and Sumbawa) are virtually without an evangelical witness. Lack of workers hinders their evangelisation. **CMA** is burdened to reach out to them through the few Christian congregations there. There are no Protestant missionaries there.

e) The **Moluccas** have been Christian for 3 centuries, but there is little true spiritual life on these many small islands.

f) **Timor** 2,500,000 – recently reunited when Indonesian troops crushed a Communist takeover after the collapse of Portuguese rule in 1976. The 700,000 people of the former Portuguese E. Timor are unevangelised but for one group on tiny Atauro Island. Pray for Timorese evangelists who pray for an entrance from W. Timor as soon as the continuing war ends. W. Timor has been nominally Christian for 300 years, but the large church was riddled with nominalism, witchcraft and sin until revival came in 1965. Remarkable happenings with many miracles led to deep repentances and 200,000 baptisms in 1964–67. Batu teams (**IMF-WEC**) helped to consolidate the work on a Biblical basis, and hundreds of witness teams went out all over the island and beyond. The cooling ardour was greatly revived again in 1976. Pray for greater maturity, spiritual depth and growing missionary vision (over 28 missionaries from Timor in 1973 serving in Indonesia, South America, etc.).

g) **Kalimantan** (Indonesian Borneo) 6,000,000. A vast underpopulated land of rivers and forests and very few roads. There are many nominal Christians in the south, but a great people movement is in progress among the majority Dayak tribes in the east (**KINGMI* CMA**), centre (**WEC**) and west (**RBMU**) with thousands seeking the Lord every year. Strong, nationally-led churches are springing up and also helping to reach out to the many other unreached tribes. **TEE** is being profitably used with the aid of **MAF** planes to train leaders in their villages. The Dayak revolt of 1967 led to great suffering for the many **Chinese** in the west where there has also been a significant turning to the Lord in recent years, though these Chinese churches planted by the **OMF** need more systematic Bible teaching and unity, in face of divisive trends.

h) **Sulawesi** (Celebes) 10,000,000.

Unreached peoples – the Muslim Bugi* (300,000) – a few believers now among them, also many smaller tribes in the interior (**NTM** opening up a witness). **Minahassa** in the north has over one million Protestants, mostly nominal. **OMF** is praying for openings to loan workers to help these churches.

The **Toradja** people in central Sulawesi have emerged from much Muslim persecution for their turning to the Lord some years ago as a strong Church reaching out to the unsaved. **OMF** supports the large Christian Reformed Church, and the **CMA-KINGMI** have a growing church planting ministry among these people.

i) **Irian Jaya** (West New Guinea) 1,000,000. See **Papua-New Guinea** for more detail. A wild, undeveloped land with many small tribes emerging from the stone age. Yet God has moved in a remarkable way through the sacrificial work of many missions, and now 70% of the population is Christian. There were great people movements on the coast in the last century, and in the interior in this. Pray for the continuing work of **TEAM, UFM, RBMU, WBT** in evangelism, church planting, Bible teaching and Bible translation (over 500 languages!). Their ministry would be impossible without the services of the 10 **MAF** planes working from 5 bases in one of the most difficult areas for flying on the mission field – pray for safety. The **Church** needs more trained leaders, but many of the tribespeople are illiterate. Pray for the many basic Bible Schools in tribal languages and also for the increasing numbers of students able now to study in Indonesian language schools in Irian Jaya and Indonesia itself. The large people movements characteristic of this field need to be well discipled to avoid error, heathen practises and nationalistic splits within the churches. Pray for the growing number of missionaries going out to unevangelised tribes from these tribal churches, especially for the many Dani evangelists; the large Dani tribe in the interior turned to the Lord in a dramatic people movement a few years ago.

JAPAN

BACKGROUND

Area:	372,500 sq. km. – a 3,000 km. arc of 4 large and 3,000 small islands, including the Ryukyu Islands (returned by the U.S. government to Japan in 1972).
Population:	112,300,000. Annual Growth 1.2%. People per sq. km. – 302. Literacy 99%.
Peoples:	**Japanese** 98% and 20,000 **Ainu,** the original inhabitants. **Foreigners** 2% – including Koreans 700,000.
Capital:	Tokyo 11,000,000. Other major cities: Osaka 2,600,000; Yokohama 2,400,000; Nagoya 2,000,000. Urbanisation 72%.
Economy:	Rapid and dramatic post-war growth now somewhat blunted by over-dependence on increasingly expensive imported oil. One of the world's most powerful economies, despite lack of raw materials and limited agricultural land.
Politics:	A constitutional monarchy with a democratic government which is under much pressure from leftist elements and weakened by accusations of corruption.
Religion:	**Attitude of Government** – Freedom of religion and entry of missionaries. **Shintoism** and **Buddhism** 83% – both religions intertwined in Japanese society, together with shamanistic animism and Confucian ancestor worship. **Sokka Gakkai** 15% – a militantly nationalistic offshoot of Buddhism that is very anti-Christian and seeks political power. **Sects** such as Dr. Moon's Unification Church, Mormons and Watchtower are small, but very active. **Roman Catholics** 0.5% numbering about 390,000. **Protestants** 1.2%. Community 800,000. Membership 500,000. Denominations 114. Largest: United Church of Japan (Kyodan) 145,000 members; Spirit of Jesus Church 62,000; Anglicans 60,000; Non-Church movement 50,000; Baptists 21,000; Lutherans 15,000. Some larger churches in decline, evangelical churches growing 10% per year. Evangelicals 0.6%.

Points for Prayer

1) **This talented people** are materialistic, unresponsive and hidden in a centuries-old cocoon of culture and bondage to demonic powers and multiplied varieties of Buddhism. Few are willing to make the decisive break with the past despite many being sympathetic to the claims of the Gospel. Pray for a mighty work of the Holy Spirit to break down these barriers and liberate these people through the Gospel.

2) **The Church in Japan** needs our prayers. We mention some points: –
   a) **The United Church of Christ,** the largest Church, is basically a government imposed union of Presbyterian, Reformed, etc., churches of nearly 40 years ago. The Church is crippled by liberalism and violent controversy stirred up by leftist young pastors over social action. The Church, and other larger liberal denominations, are in serious decline, and only kept going by a few faithful believers who carry on in spite of the leaders. Pray for a moving of the Spirit and a return to Biblical theology.
   b) **The smaller and younger Evangelical Churches** are growing both in numbers, evangelistic zeal and missionary vision. The Japan Evangelistic Fellowship links most of these denominations for cooperative programmes. There is a new surge of evangelism in progress which is being ably led by some of Japan's finest Christian leaders and evangelists, using saturation evangelism methods (laity mobilisation) and mass evangelistic campaigns under the title **Total Mobilisation Evangelism Movement.** Pray for a great harvest of souls to be both won and retained in the churches.
   c) **The needs and problems in the churches** – it is reckoned that around 90% of all those who seek the Lord later backslide through the pressures of family, society, unequal marriages and the pervasive influence of the spiritual darkness of Japan. Revival is the great need – to bring Christians to a point of total abandonment to the Lord Jesus, and rid them of the cloying power of their background. Only revival can get the ordinary believers out evangelising and from under the overlordship of the pastors.
   d) **The training of leaders** is being ably done through many denominational and inter-denominational Seminaries – worthy of especial mention: those of **TEAM** (Tokyo, Chr. Coll) and **OMS.** There are also some fine Bible Schools that emphasise the spiritual life of the students, such as that of the **JEB.** Pray for the calling of dedicated young people into the ministry and also for missionary service.
   e) **Missionary vision** is growing. There are now about 140 Japanese missionaries serving the Lord in 24 countries. About 40 of these serve with the 14 small societies linked together in the Japanese Overseas Missionary Association. **JOMA** seeks to co-ordinate the preparation of missionary candidates, and the enthusing of the local churches with the responsibility for the evangelisation of the world. Pray also for the new, and yet small, Missionary Orientation Course which is backed by a number of Japanese churches and missions, and for the sending of more students with a call to the mission field.

3) **Missions** – there are about 140 agencies serving with 2,560 missionaries. There is complete freedom for the entry of missionaries, but adaptation to the culture and learning what is reputed to be the world's hardest language is a barrier to effective service that takes years to cross. **Pray for first term missionaries** as they seek to prepare themselves for future usefulness, and pray that they may not be discouraged, but filled with faith and power for their difficult task. It is impossible to do justice to all good missions working – we mention a few: **OMS, TEAM, OMF, JEB, WEC** who are both evangelising and planting churches in different parts of the country. These, and others such as the JMHE are more involved in church-support ministries – hospital evangelism, radio and literature work. **There are many opportunities for both career and short-term missionaries,** the latter in teaching English and using this as a door for evangelism; many missions use this method to great profit. There remains the most pressing need for adaptable evangelist-church planter missionaries.

4) **Student witness** is a strategic ministry – Japan has 933 colleges with two million students. The largest work is that of the KGK **(IVF)** with groups in 200 colleges. The 14 national staff workers are insufficient to take advantage of the many opportunities for growth and expansion. The Campus Crusade and Navigators also have a good witness to students. The greatest hindrances are apathy and Marxism (90% of

students claim to be atheists, though most express themselves more favourable to Christianity than to any other religion). Young people, generally speaking, are unwilling to fully commit themselves to the Lord. There is a need for a witness like SU to be started in the secondary schools.

5) **Unreached peoples:**
   a) **Okinawa and all the Ryukyu Islands** need pioneer evangelism and there are very few Christians among the Ryukyu* people.
   b) The majority of the people in the **cities,** have never really had a chance to understand the Gospel. 65% of the **towns** and 85% of the **villages** have no witness for the Lord.
   c) **The 700,000 Koreans** form an unpopular and dispersed minority. About 60% are Communist and there are only 6 Korean churches in Japan (all in Tokyo). They are not welcome in Japanese churches.
6) **Literature** is widely used and increasing in quality and range of coverage in subject matter. 70% of converted students attribute their conversion to Christian literature. There are 70 Christian bookstores (9 of **CLC**), 90 publishers and 25 printing presses.
7) **Ministry in hospitals** has proved an especially fruitful field – there are many long-term patients in the large number of T.B. hospitals among whom many have come to the Lord. Pray for the outstanding hospital, literature and radio work of the JMHE.
8) **Christian Radio** has had a great impact. The Pacific Broadcasting Assoc. prepares 4 weekly and 3 daily programmes transmitted over 92 Japanese stations, and also programmes for **FEBC** Manila. There is an amazing response to Japanese broadcasts from **HCJB** in Ecuador where three Japanese speakers are fully employed replying to those who write. The average Japanese spends 6 hours a day watching television; brief 3 minute T.V. advertisements on commercial stations have proved very profitable for reaching needy people. Pray for all follow up work through BCCs, personal visitation and linking contacts with a local church.

<u>KOREA</u> (South)

BACKGROUND

Area: 98,500 sq. km. – a mountainous peninsula of which only 20% is arable.
Population: 34,800,000. Annual Growth 2%. People per sq. km. – 353. Literacy 90%.
Peoples: **Koreans** – an ancient and cultured people.
Capital: Seoul 7,000,000. Other major city – Pusan 1,900,000. Urbanisation 41%.
Economy: Rapid recovery and industrial growth since 1949–51 Korean War.
Politics: Strong military-civilian government in face of ever present threat of invasion from Communist North Korea. Gen. Park's autocratic rule is resented by many.
Religion: **Attitude of Government** – freedom of religion, but a hard line taken against church leaders who protest about government policies.
               Buddhists and **Confucianists** approx. 16% – despite small following these religions have made a deep impact on Korean culture. Most people are influenced by the ancient religion of superstitions, witchcraft and appeasing the spirits, though in a rather undercover way.
               Roman Catholics 2.3%. **Marginal sects** 3% – Olive Tree 700,000 adherents; World Unification Church (Dr. Moon) 310,000 with a vigorous worldwide missionary movement that is irritatingly aggressive.
               Protestants 10% – the strongest organised religion in Korea Community 3,500,000. Denominations – 54 divided into three major groups: **Ecumenicals** (6 groups) 2 Presbyterian Churches with 532,000 and 194,000 adherents respectively; Methodists 300,000; Salvation Army 50,000; Episcopal 20,000; though many members are strongly evangelical. **Anti-Ecumenicals** – Haptong Presbyterian 727,000; Koryo Presbyterian 102,000; the schismatic Methodists and Holiness churches (21,000 and 71,000 respectively).
               Independent Evangelicals – Christian Holiness (**OMS**) 177,000; Baptists 52,000; Assemblies of God 30,000+, etc.
               Evangelicals 9%.
               Annual growth of Protestants 10% (5 times population growth).

Point for Prayer

1) **The receptivity of the Korean people** for the Gospel has been unmatched in this century, with rapid growth, dramatic revivals and strong indigenous churches that have shown great faithfulness in years of persecution under the Japanese and later the Communist invaders (over 600 pastors were martyred between 1945 and 1951). Communism remains a serious threat. Pray that this uncertainty may be used of God to keep the believers praying and the people hungry for spiritual things.

2) **Christianity has made a vital impact on Korea.** There are 2,000 churches in Seoul alone. One third of all parliamentarians are Christian. Revival in the 600,000 strong army has raised the number of believers from 16% in 1965 to 51% in 1977. The largest Christian gatherings in history took place in Seoul with one million attending both Billy Graham's 1973 Campaign and Campus Crusade's 1974 Explo.

3) **The Protestant Church,** founded on sound indigenous principles, blessed with many periods of revival, and refined by years of suffering has emerged as a mighty praying, evangelising army of believers. Early morning prayer meetings attended by hundreds are still the pattern in many denominations. Pray that materialism and present ease of being a Christian may not blunt their earnestness and outreach.

4) **Division** has sadly caused major splits in every large denomination – over earlier compromise under Japanese rule, liberal theology and ecumenism. The Presbyterians are now split into 4 major and 8 splinter groups. These bitter divisions have led to authoritarianism among ministers and an emphasis on right doctrine at the expense of fellowship with the Lord and His Word. Pray for a spirit of love and reconciliation among all true believers.

5) **Theological education** has made remarkable progress with over 100 Seminaries and Bible Schools (12 degree level and 3 post-graduate) with over 9,000 students. Pray that these men may go out into the ministry and the mission fields full of the Power of the Holy Spirit.

6) **There is a growing missionary vision** which Christian leaders are seeking to foster and co-ordinate. There is a need for more to be done to train workers for the mission field. Pray that all the churches may become enthusiastic for missions. There are now about 280 Korean missionaries in many lands of the world in both denominational and interdenominational societies, and there are plans to send out many more.

7) **Missions** have placed a healthy emphasis on Korean leadership and initiative. Most missions today are involved in leadership training programmes or in specialist ministries. There are about 53 agencies operating in Korea with 700 missionaries. **TEAM** has 30 missionaries in radio and an extensive BCC work. **OMF** loans workers to the Presbyterian Churches and also seeks to launch the infant and vitally needed SU programme. **OMS** has been used of God to plant one of the largest faith mission originating churches in the world. Missionaries who go as servants of the Korean Church are both needed and welcome.

8) **Student work** in the 97 colleges and universities and among the 190,000 students has made great progress through the University Bible Fellowship. The UBF emphasises Bible study and personal evangelism, and now has workers who have gone out to the USA, Germany, Switzerland and other lands to witness among students. There are many Christian schools all over the country in which the Gospel is preached.

9) **Christian broadcasting** has a strong base with two missionary stations in the country broadcasting to both the Koreas and the closed lands of China and Russia from the **TEAM** station HLKX and also the **FEBC** transmitters on Cheju Island. Pray for these key installations, their staff and the impact of these programmes in the target areas.

MALAYSIA

BACKGROUND

Area: 326,000 sq. km. – two distinct parts: West Malaysia or Peninsular Malaya 40%, and East Malaysia – Sabah and Sarawak in Northern Borneo 60%.

Population: 12,400,000 (84% in W. Malaysia). Annual Growth 2.9%. People per sq. km. – 94 in P.M., 10 in E.M.
Peoples: **Malays 48%** – a rural people, but dominant in government and civil service.
Chinese 36% – largely urban and dominate commercial and business world.
Indians 9% – largely Tamil, many working on rubber estates.
Tribal peoples – over 170 tribes 7%; predominantly in Sarawak and Sabah.
Capital: Kuala Lumpur 800,000. Urbanisation 17%. Literacy 50% in P.M., 30% in E.M.
Economy: Steadily expanding and prosperous – world's largest exporter of rubber and tin.
Politics: Independent of Britain in 1957 after defeat of Chinese Communist insurgents. Tensions between Chinese and Malays in W. M. and reappearance of Communist terrorism, and tensions between Malays, Chinese and indigenous peoples in E.M. dominate the political scene and could lead to trouble.
Religion: **Attitude of Government** – Islam is the state religion in P.M. and there are pressures to enforce the same in E.M. All Christian witness to Muslims is illegal and missionary work among other races being severely limited.
Islam 45% – Malays and a few Indians and tribal peoples.
Chinese religions 20%, Hindus 9%, Free thinkers 17%, Animists 8%, Roman Catholics 3%, Protestants 2.1% (11% in E.M.). Community 242,000 (51,000 in P.M. only). See separate areas below for figures for denominations. Evangelicals 1.1% (in P.M. only 0.2%, in E.M. 9%).

Prayer Points for Malaysia

1) **Pray for interracial peace and harmony** and freedom for the Gospel in the face of increasing unrest and creeping limitations on Christian activities by Malay rulers.
2) **The Malay Muslims** cannot be evangelised by normal means. The few who have trusted the Lord have suffered severely and generally leave the country. Pray for the Christians who have contacts with Malays that they may have opportunities to tactfully tell them of Jesus and pass on literature in spite of the hindrances. It is only possible to openly evangelise Malays in S. Thailand (where OMF is seeing a Malay Church coming into being) and also in Singapore. This witness is helped by the increasing use of Malay as a language in all churches and by all races.
3) **The state-aided Muslim missionary outreach** to the tribal peoples has had some success – through bribery and subtle coercion – among the interior tribes of Malaya and also in Sabah and Sarawak. Pray that Christians may not give way to intimidation but rather be strong and alert to forestall this effort by winning the uncommitted to Christ.
4) **There are increasing limitations** on mission work, and the number of missionaries is dropping rapidly. There are still 60 missionaries in P.M., but it is now impossible for any missionary to remain in the country for more than 10 years. There is therefore a great dearth of the vitally needed mature missionary advisers. 20 **BEM-OMF** missionaries in Sarawak have had to end their work in 1976, and nearly all missionaries have had to leave Sabah. Pray that needed missionaries may be allowed to enter and that the national believers may be able to take over and maintain the evangelistic, teaching and missionary impetus. It is a little easier for Asian missionaries to enter the country.

Prayer Points for Peninsular Malaya

1) **The churches** are almost entirely Chinese and Indian in composition. There are 51,000 Protestant adherents (largest of the 12 denominations – Anglican 7,500; Baptists 2,000; Brethren 3,200; Presbyterians 6,000; Lutherans (2) 4,300; Methodists 15,000; Assemblies of God 3,000). Growth is slow, and rate of backsliding high, due to the hostile environment for all races with many social and family pressures on young Christians. Most growth is seen among the Presbyterians among the Chinese with CCC help and in the Assemblies of God. Revival is needed and a greater willingness to suffer shame for Jesus and to witness to the unsaved.

There is a lack of well trained church leaders and good Bible teaching, so many congregations are weak and spiritually shallow.

2) **Unreached peoples** – not only have many of the Chinese and Indians never heard the Gospel, but great sections of the population are untouched – especially the poorer and older people. The **Malays** are totally unreached. The **13 small tribes** are considered to be Muslim, but are actually animists and open to the Gospel. The Sarawak SIB desire to do mission work among these people (known as the Orang Asli) who number about 120,000.

3) **Young people** are the most receptive among the Chinese and Indians. IFES (IVF), CCC and Navigators are doing a good, steady work of winning souls among students, but there is little conservation of fruit of these efforts, and few really contribute much to local churches as they grow up. There is also a widespread work of the Inter Schools Christian Fellowship in the secondary schools.

Prayer Points for Sabah, E. Malaysia

Formerly North Borneo, this 81,000 sq. km. territory has a population of 773,000 (Malay 14%, Chinese 21%, Indigenous peoples (13) 64% – largest Kadazans 218,000) and became part of Malaysia in 1963.

1) **Unreached peoples** – Malays, many of the indigenous peoples; some of the latter becoming Muslim.

2) **National Church** – Protestants 11% (Anglican 20,000; Lutheran 40,000; Baptist, Brethren, etc., 22,000). Over half the Chinese Christians are nominal. There is a growing work by independent missionaries (linked with SIB-BEM) and Lutherans among the indigenous peoples. Pray for greater unity and power among believers in the face of Muslim opposition. Very few missionaries are left in Sabah, though 2 BEM (OMF) workers were granted a 10 year permit in 1976.

Prayer Points for Sarawak, East Malaysia

This 121,000 sq. km. territory has 1,270,000 people (Malay 19%, Chinese 30%, Dayak (Iban and Bidayuh) 40%, Kayan, Kelabit, Kenyah, etc. (140) 10%) also became part of Malaysia in 1963.

1) **Sarawak** has been the scene of one of the most wonderful people movements this century. The movement began in the 1930s among the Murut people and has spread over much of Sarawak through the splendid work of the **BEM (OMF)** missionaries and enthusiastic national evangelists. As a result of this work of God, the SIB Church has over 50,000 members among more than 10 peoples, a national-led Bible School, outreach to the coastal towns and a vigorous missionary outreach programme. Pray for the continued maturing of these believers as they come more and more into contact with the outside world – many of these believers are from primitive and illiterate backgrounds. Pray that the evangelistic vigour of the believers may not be blunted by the rising second generation of Christians, with all the temptations of materialism and need of a personal faith. Revival has recently brought blessing to some areas.

2) **Missionary work seems to be drawing to a close** but, praise God, the churches are rapidly reaching the position of being able to manage. Pray for the **BEM (OMF)** missionaries (60 in 1975, but reduced to 40 in 1977) and others, that they may use their time strategically – some involved in lay training, Bible translation and evangelistic outreach in 10 unreached peoples. The difficult terrain makes it essential to depend on the **MAF** plane. Pray for this ministry. Bible translation work is in progress in 7 languages.

3) **Unreached peoples** – many of the smaller and more inaccessible groups must still be contacted and evangelised. Pray that SIB missionaries may be successful in this. Pray for a growing missionary vision among believers for these people. Also the larger Iban and Bidayuh tribes have proved unresponsive, though the Methodist Church has a number of churches among them. Pray for their evangelisation.

4) **The coastal churches** are predominantly Chinese, with some indigenous believers as well, and are largely Anglican (30,000 adherents) and Methodist (40,000) with some

Baptists also. Revival is needed among these Christians, for outreach is not their strong point. There are growing churches of the SIB also in the towns on the coast.

NEPAL

BACKGROUND

Area: 140,000 sq. km. – a mountain ringed Himalayan state between China and India.
Population: 12,900,000. Annual Growth 2.3%. People per sq. km. – 92. Literacy 14%.
Peoples: The Nepali language increasingly used. Over 70 tribes and peoples. The major groups: Gurung 200,000 and Magar 300,000 in west; Tamang 240,000 and Newar 400,000 in centre; Limbu 150,000 and Sherpa in east; Tharu and Maibili 1,100,000 in south.
Capital: Kathmandu 250,000. Urbanisation 4%.
Economy: Underdeveloped but progress being made in education and building roads in this isolated, mountainous land.
Politics: Constitutional monarchy since 1951 with the King holding executive power. The land has opened to the outside world since 1951.
Religion: **Attitude of Government** – Hinduism the state religion. Christian Missions permitted so long as they do not seek to convert people or plant churches. **Hindus and Buddhists** 97% – a strange fusion of the two in this land. **Muslims** 2% along southern border region.
            Christians – a few hundred Nepalis and a further 150 Santali believers.

Points for Prayer

1) **This long-closed land** opened up a little for the Gospel in 1951, but the conversion of people is illegal and those seeking the conversion of others are liable to punishment. Some workers were expelled from the land in 1976, probably from complaints about infringing this law. Pray for complete freedom of religion.

2) **Missions** in Nepal need great tact and wisdom in their very delicate relationship with the Government, which carefully watches their activities. Expatriate workers with the United Mission to Nepal (a fellowship of over 28 Asian and Western missions) now number 180 and seek to live for Christ through their ministry in 5 hospitals, dispensaries, communal health programmes and leprosy control. There are a further 50 workers associated with several other mission groups in similar ministries. Pray that these brethren may be a vital witness in their limiting circumstances, and also a real strength to the national brethren as they fellowship in the little congregations around the country.

3) **The Church is small,** but steadily growing with 30 or so little unorganised groups linked together as the Nepal Christian Fellowship. These groups were planted by Nepalis returning from surrounding lands where there are many Nepali churches and about 10,000 believers. Nepali Christian workers itinerate much, and every Christian home is used as a point of contact with the people around. Pray for these believers who have suffered many difficulties and inconveniences for their faith, and some have even been imprisoned for infringing the conversion law. Pray for the growth in grace of the few believers and their witness under difficult circumstances.

4) **Unreached peoples** – very few of the peoples of this land have any believers among them. The large investment of **WBT** with 100 workers in 21 languages was suddenly terminated, and it is hard to see how this Bible translation programme can be continued. Pray for these many peoples without a witness or the Scriptures.

5) **Pray for the radio broadcasts** in Nepali. Pray that this may lead to conversions and the building up of the Church.

6) **Literature** has been much used of God – through books sold in the several little bookstores, Bible correspondence courses to Nepalis inside Nepal and in surrounding lands. Pray also for wide distribution of the Scriptures. The O.T. is being revised and should be ready in 1977. The new N.T. has been translated, but a dispute about dialect differences is holding up printing.

7)   **Nepalis outside Nepal** number about 8,000,000. A number of Indian and Western Christians have prayed and worked for a harvest among these people, and now there are many Nepali Christian Fellowships all over N. India, and some in Sikkim and Bhutan. There is a Bible School in Darjeeling in India where Nepali believers are trained for pastoral work. Pray for this ministry and for the men who go out from it to evangelise the Nepali people.

PAKISTAN

BACKGROUND

Area:	801,000 sq. km. – arid mountains in north and west and vast irrigation schemes in the fertile Indus Valley.
Population:	72,500,000. Annual Growth 2.9%. People per sq. km. – 90. Literacy 25%.
Peoples:	Over 41 languages – **Urdu,** the national language spoken by most of the population. Major groups: **Punjabi** in centre, **Sindhi** in south, **Baluchi** in west, **Pathan** in north west, **Kashmiri** in north.
Capital:	Islamabad 235,000. Other cities: Karachi 4,600,000; Lahore 2,300,000. Urbanisation 26%.
Economy:	One of the world's poorer countries, but now some economic progress.
Politics:	Independent from Britain at partition of India in 1947. Much greater stability and progress since the 1971 war with India and loss of East Pakistan to become Bangladesh.
Religion:	**Attitude of Government** – despite being an Islamic state, freedom of religion is maintained, both to practise and to propagate. **Islam** 97%. **Hindus** 1.5% – largely weakly Hindu tribes in the Sindh. **Roman Catholics** 0.5%. **Protestants** 1.4% – mostly in the E. Punjab. Community 533,000. Membership 120,000. Denominations 17. Largest denominations: Church of Pakistan (Anglicans, Methodists, Lutherans, Presbyterians) 58,000 members; United Presbyterian 53,000; Salvation Army 31,000; Other Presbyterian (2) 17,000; Brethren 2,000; Pentecostals 2,300; Various Evangelical Churches (fruit of missions such as **ICF, TEAM, ABC** and 3 Baptist groups) approx. 2,000. Evangelicals 0.25%.

Points for Prayer

1)   **This needy Muslim land is wide open for evangelism** and the entry of missionaries. Pray for a continued open door despite pressures from the Islamic World Conference in 1976 recommending the ending of all Christian missions. Pray that Asian and Western churches may use these opportunities to send in more workers.

2)   **Response among Muslims** is slow, but growing markedly. Few are prepared to take the costly step of open discipleship and associate with the Christians, who are usually socially poorer and basically of low-caste Hindu origin. Possibly only one tenth of the missionary force give much time to this 97% of the population. Pray for more missionaries well equipped for Muslim work, and for the winning of Muslims.

3)   **The greatest response** in the land now is among the scheduled caste Hindu tribes of the Sindh where there has been a considerable turning to the Lord of late. There are about 30 tribes, each with its own dialect, and most are semi-nomadic. Pray especially for the Mawaris, Kohlis*, etc. More national and missionary workers are urgently needed. Pray for the development of a strong, well-led Church.

4)   **Unevangelised areas** and peoples abound. Pray for Baluchistan with its very small Church, and the many warlike Muslim tribes of the North West Frontier with Afghanistan (including the 2 million Pathans). Pray also for the many peoples living in the isolated valleys of the north that have begun now to open up for the Gospel – Chitral 15,000 people; Hunza 100,000; Kohistan 500,000; Gilgit 150,000; Nagiri 50,000; Baltistan 50,000; who are all Muslims, and also for the 6,000 animistic people of Kafiristan. Several national evangelists and the **ABC** have made occasional

visits to these northern regions, but there is no permanent work and the people remain in darkness. Medical work may provide the key to these areas.

5) **The Protestant Church** has some outstanding leaders and fine congregations but, generally, there is a dead orthodoxy in most of the older churches. Pray for:

a) **A greater openness and concern** for the evangelisation of Muslims and their reception in the churches. The cultural and social barriers are high and make it hard for the believers to be bold with their low social standing.

b) **Illiteracy** is higher among the Christians than the national average. Hence the churches are often weak and spiritually immature.

c) **Nominalism** is the greatest hindrance to growth, due to the large people movements of the last century and succeeding generations remaining unconverted. Much of Christian work is aimed at evangelising "Christians" and building them up through the various means of literature, teaching and discipleship training. **BMMF** and **ICF** play an important role in this field through their service ministries.

The greatest need is for revival that liberates, emboldens and mobilises the Church.

6) **Leadership training** – both at pastoral and lay-worker level is vital. Pray especially for the developing **TEE** programme into which a number of missions have entered. This is a valuable tool for leadership training in the context of Pakistan's many small, scattered groups of Christians. The development is hindered by lack of personnel and time to prepare the teaching materials in local scripts.

7) **The potential of the Pakistani Church** for world evangelisation is great. Some churches have a vision, such as St. Andrew's, Lahore, who already have 5 missionaries serving with **IVF, SU** and **OM**. Large numbers of Pakistanis (including many Christians) now work in lands right across the Middle East, some totally closed to the Gospel, such as Qatar, Saudi Arabia, Libya, etc. Pray that they may truly be tent-maker missionaries.

8) **Missions have been working in the land since 1833.** Many new evangelical missions entered the land after World War II such as **TEAM,** Pak. Christian Fellowship, International Missions, **BMMF, ABC** and various denominational groups. Most of these have emphasised evangelism and church planting ministries and work in fellowship together in the Pakistan Evangelical Fellowship. Other missionaries come from Korea, Japan and Indonesia either temporarily in evangelistic teams or as full time workers. These, together with the older denominational missionaries, now number about 480. There are many opportunities in evangelism, church planting, Bible teaching and in various service ministries such as literature, BCCs and health services. Pray much for more labourers – especially from Britain and Canada, for these nations need no visas. Pray also for a more concerted, prayer covered assault on the need of the Muslim majority, and the unevangelised Muslim peoples.

9) **Christian literature** – much excellent material of all kinds is produced by the Brethren MIK and interdenominational Christian Printing House in Lahore – problems are: a dearth of good national writers, distribution and the high level of illiteracy among the Christians. Pray for the evangelistic broadsheet "SOON" in Urdu, and all Muslim-oriented literature that there may be conversions as a result. Pray also for th ministry of occasional Gospel advertisements in the secular press – which has led to an unusually big response.

10) **Bible correspondence courses** run by **TEAM** and **ICF** are very useful for the evangelisation of Muslims and nominal Christians and building up converts. Pray especially for the follow-up of students.

11) **Youth work** – a little is done by CSSM, **CEF, CCC,** but the most significant work is that of the Pak. Fellowship of Evangelical Students (**IVF**) with an expanding work in universities throughout the country with real outreach to non-Christian students. Pray for the 8 national staff workers and the little groups. **SU** has not really developed much yet, but the need is there for this type of ministry.

12) **Bible translation** – most of the major languages have the Bible or N.T., but many languages have yet to be reduced to writing and translation work begun. Work has been initiated in 4 languages – pray for those involved.

13) **Christian Radio** has not had a great impact due to the lack of short wave receivers in the country. Pray for the recording studios in Rawalpindi, and also the stations transmitting to Pakistan – **FEBA** Seychelles, **TWR** Sri Lanka, etc.

PHILIPPINES

BACKGROUND

Area:	300,000 sq. km. – 11 larger and 700 smaller inhabited islands.
Population:	45,000,000. Annual Growth 3%. People per sq. km. – 150. Literacy 83%.
Peoples:	Tagalog and English both official languages, but 9 major and over 70 minor languages are in use.
	Filipinos (related to the Malays and Indonesians) 96% – major groups: Tagalog 12 million; Cebuano 12 million; Ilocano 4 million; etc.
	The Tribes 2% – usually found as many small units in the more inaccessible areas of Luzon, Mindanao, Mindoro and Palawan – about 100 tribes.
	Chinese 1% – a very important people in the commercial world.
Capital:	Quezon City – Manila 5,000,000. Urbanisation 32%.
Economy:	In good shape since the declaration of martial law in 1973, with real progress.
Politics:	A Spanish colony for 377 years (hence the R.C. majority and many Spanish customs), then ruled by the U.S.A. until independence in 1946. Martial law imposed in 1973 to combat Communist insurgents in Luzon, and Muslim separatists in Mindanao. The latter war continues.
Religion:	**Attitude of Government** – full religious liberty.
	Roman Catholics 83% – Martial Law and the spirit of Vatican II has weakened the hold of the priests on the masses.
	Aglipayan Church 5% – breakaway from Rome now more influenced by the Gospel than ever before.
	Muslims 6% – mostly in Mindanao, Sulu Islands and Palawan in the south.
	Syncretic Sects 3% – over 200. Largest: the aggressive Iglesia ni Cristo with over 500,000 adherents. SDAs also strong and growing (114,000 adherents).
	Protestants 5% Community 1,500,000. Denominations 70. United Church (Presbyterian, Congregational, United Brethren, etc.) 150,000 membership; Methodists 100,000; All Baptists 80,000; All Pentecostals 150,000; Alliance Church (**CMA**) 30,000; Assoc. of Bible Churches (**OMF**, FECC) 10,000. Evangelicals 3%.
	Growth of Protestants – very small overall until 1970s.

Points for Prayer

1) **The Philippines** is now one of the most open and also receptive countries in Asia. Pray that this opportunity may be fully used by nationals and missionaries.

2) **Roman Catholics** are more tolerant, desirous of reading and studying the Bible and open to the Gospel than ever before. Pray that believers may be open to help these seeking people to know the Lord Jesus.

3) **Unreached peoples** – the Philippines has been patchily covered with the Gospel, pray for the needy Muslims, many unreached little tribes and large lowland areas that have little evangelical witness – pray especially for the planned **OMF** advance to S. E. Luzon and Samar Island which fall in the latter category.

4) **The Protestant Church** is emerging as a significant force in the life of the country: –

    a) **Growth through evangelism** has been stimulated by various conferences on evangelism (Philippines in 1970, Lausanne 1974, etc.), and is most marked in several Baptist groups, the Pentecostals and the Alliance Churches. There is increasing evangelical cooperation in outreach in local, nation wide and mass evangelism. Some methods have been more successful than others. The younger evangelical groups started since World War II are increasingly important. It is planned to plant as many churches from 1976 to 1980 as in all the previous 75 years.

    b) **Some of the older and larger denominations** have stagnated through an overemphasis on institutions and dialogue with Roman Catholics, rather than on evangelism, though many of the congregations are unhappy about these developments. Revival is needed.

    c) **Problems to be prayed over** – Evangelical churches and leaders are often too dependent on funds and initiative from the U.S.A. Although there are some outstanding pastors and leaders in the ministry, there are too few to meet the need, especially in the rural areas. The rapidly growing cities are inadequately covered with the Gospel. A greater spiritual depth is needed in the congregations for more effective outreach.

5) **Leadership training** – over 71 Seminaries and Bible Schools, most being Evangelical. Number of graduates for all levels of pastoral ministry is very inadequate. Greater emphasis now on TEE – pray that this may be effective and not just a new fad that does not really meet the need.

6) **Missionary vision of the Filipino Church** is growing – now with 13 sending agencies and 170 missionaries serving in other lands or areas.

7) **Missions** – many new groups and missionaries have entered the land of late, and now there are around 1,500 (84% in evangelical missions). There are far more opportunities than there are labourers to use them – in evangelism, church planting, pioneer work, as well as in teaching and helping in the churches, etc. The **CMA** urgently need 55 more workers and both **OMF** (103 workers in field) and **WBT** (170) need reinforcements for their many vital ministries. There are many needs in Bible translation work, student outreach and in technical ministries such as radio.

8) **Literature** is extensively used and is largely run by Filipino Christians – Pray for the publishing and distribution ministries of **OMF** (16 stores), **CLC** and **CMA**, etc., and for the expansions planned by them. There are severe difficulties with the distribution of Bibles, and there is a great lack of Scriptures. Pray for the speedy removal of these difficulties. Government censorship also delays publication of needed literature.

9) **Bible translation** is being undertaken in 54 languages; **WBT** is working in 43. Another 34 need translators. Most of these languages are fairly small.

10) **Student ministry** among the 1,500,000 students in the many universities has developed well despite the strong leftist element. Many worthy groups are involved – **CMA, CCC,** Navigators and also the **IVCF** (**OMF** assisted) with 30 keen young staff workers. Pray for the development of strong witnessing groups in the universities.

11) **Minority groups**
 a) **The Chinese** number 500,000 but only 3% are Christian. There are over 40 Chinese churches in the Manila area that are strong and with a missionary vision, but many are still in darkness.
 b) **The Muslims** – major groups: Yakan* 50,000; Tausug 300,000; Samal* 600,000; Sama-Badjaw* 400,000; Moranao 1,000,000; Magindanao 450,000. The **CMA** have long worked among them but with little response, though praise God that there are 5 or so congregations made up almost entirely of converted Muslims. Much of the **CMA** thrust has been among the pagan and R.C. people in the area. Work among Muslims has been greatly hindered by the continuing guerrilla war (armed and financed by Libya) in which the Muslims seek to secede. Pray for peace and open hearts among these Muslim people. Pray also for the new outreach of 6 **OMF** missionaries to Muslims in Mindanao. **WBT** have several translation teams among them.
 c) **The animist tribes** – pray for the work of **NTM** in Palawan and Luzon, **OMF** in the Mangyan* tribes (50,000) of Mindoro and **CMA** and Baptists in various tribes in Mindanao. **CMA** pray about reaching out to the unevangelised Manobo and Subanen in Mindanao, and also the 50,000 Kalinga in N. Luzon. Pray for these tribal churches and their spiritual growth and raising up of mature leaders able to teach their people and prepare them for their ever increasing involvement in national life – many are primitive, timid and exploited by the lowland Filipinos.

12) **Christian Radio** – extensive use has been made of both the radio and T.V. media by denominations and interdenominational groups. The largest is the work of **FEBC** with Headquarters in Manila, with a staff of over 200 in radio, printing, programming and follow-up ministries. Pray for these brethren that they may know the blessing of the Lord on their lives as they serve – often behind the scenes. **FEBC** has 23 broadcasting stations in the Philippines (10 for internal use, the rest for transmissions to S. E. Asia, etc.) and also others in other parts of the continent. Pray for the smooth running of equipment, the supply of funds and programmes, for the spiritual impact in the Philippines and also in the closed lands of Asia. **FEBC** broadcasts in 63 languages and for 1,890 hours per week.

SINGAPORE

BACKGROUND

Area: 581 sq. km. – 1 larger and 40 small islands off the southern tip of Malaya.
Population: 2,400,000. Growing at 1.6% a year. People per sq. km. – 4,200.
Peoples: **Chinese 76%, Malay 15%, Indian 7%, Others 3%.**
Economy: This city state is one of the cleanest, richest and most progressive states in
              Asia, with a standard of living second only to Japan. Its important and
              strategically placed port and growing industries providing its wealth.
Politics: Singapore left the Malaysian federation in 1965. Increasing wealth and a
              stable, popular government has diminished the influence of Communism.
Religion: **Attitude of Government** – complete freedom of religion. **Chinese Religions**
              38%. **Free Thinkers 30%. Muslims 15%. Hindus 7%. Roman Catholics 4%.**
              Protestants 6%. Community 110,000. Denominations – 15 – the largest:
              Methodists 13,000; Anglicans 7,200; Brethren 2,500; Baptists 1,500; vari-
              ous independent groups 7–14,000.
              Evangelicals 3.5%.

Points for Prayer

1) **Singapore** has, proportionately, one of the largest Christian communities in Asia
    today, with many young people seeking the Lord. Most of the Protestant Churches
    are Evangelical and evangelistic and now number around 250. House churches are
    multiplying rapidly to cater for the nearly 60% of the population living in high rise
    flats. Pray for a continuing harvest among people of many races who are being so
    uprooted from their cultural past and thrust into the modern materialistic age.

2) **The Church in Singapore** is largely divided along ethnic lines, but an increasing
    number of people are using English. There is a need for more full time workers who
    are able to minister to the many house churches (church buildings are too expensive
    due to the lack of land) and really give Bible teaching. The charismatic movement has
    had a beneficial effect on the leadership of the liberally inclined Anglicans and
    Methodists. Some feel that the foreign influence in the churches is still too great and
    initiative is stifled. The churches are filled with young people and there is a real
    movement of the Spirit of God among them. The growth rate is not as high as one
    would expect with the favourable conditions prevailing.

3) **Bible training** is given in 7 Seminaries and Bible Schools. Worthy of especial mention
    is the **Singapore Bible College** from where many young people have gone out to serve
    the Lord in Singapore Churches and also to the mission field. Also, the strategic
    Discipleship Training Centre (OMF) where Christian graduates from many Asian
    lands come for a highly concentrated course in preparation for service in their own
    lands and also some as missionaries.

4) **Young people** are open to the Gospel. It is reckoned that 30% of all university
    students claim to be Christian. **SU** has 92 school groups, and 90 church groups and
    exerts a very wholesome influence on the evangelical witness. The **IVF** groups in the
    universities have a successful programme of evangelism and Bible teaching. Pray that
    converted young people may make a powerful impression on church and national life
    when their education is over – many fall away.

5) **Singapore** has become one of the most strategic centres for the evangelisation of
    Asia. It is the headquarters of **OMF, SU** in Asia, Co-ordinating Office for Asian
    Evangelism (COFAE), the Asian office for EiD and the Bible Society. Singapore has
    also great potential as a missionary sending base. A number of missionaries have
    gone out to other lands – 5 with **OMF.** The Singapore churches have the means to
    support them too. There are now about 50 Singaporean missionaries serving in other
    lands.

6) **Missions** – There are now about 188 missionaries in 13 agencies. Notable is the
    contribution of **OMF** which, apart from its HQ staff, has 30 missionaries serving with
    local churches in evangelism, Bible teaching, etc. It is not easy to obtain visas for new
    missionaries if the intended work is able to be done by a Singaporean.

7) **Unreached peoples.**
  a) **The Muslim Malays** are not responsive and too little is done in prayer and evangelism to win them, but there is one Brethren missionary working full time among them, and there have been some saved.
  b) **The older Chinese** who speak over 6 different non-Mandarin dialects are largely by-passed by most evangelistic efforts.
  c) **The 1977 Outreach programme by Christians** is intended to present every Singapore inhabitant with the Gospel. Pray for this programme, the effective mobilisation of believers and also for a harvest of souls to be gathered into the churches.

SRI LANKA (Ceylon)

BACKGROUND

Area: 64,600 sq. km. – a large island 80 Km south east of the southern tip of India.
Population: 14,000,000. Annual Growth 2%. People per sq. km. – 216.
Peoples: **Singhalese** 71% – who are almost entirely Buddhist.
                Tamils 21% – largely Hindu; 10% are immigrants from S. India.
                Moors 7% – The Muslims of Sri Lanka, descended from Arabs, Indians and Persians.
                Burghers 0.5% – descendants of mixed marriages between Dutch and Singhalese in the 18th Century. They are mostly Presbyterian.
Capital: Colombo 600,000. Urbanisation 22%. Literacy 72%.
Economy: Falling commodity prices for tea and rubber as well as socialist and nationalist policies have impoverished the country.
Politics: After 450 years of Portuguese, Dutch and British colonial rule, land independent in 1948. Recent years marred by communal violence between Singhalese and the economically deprived Tamil.
Religion: **Attitude of Government** – officially freedom of religion, but Buddhism actively promoted by the government.
                Buddhists 67% – very active in seeking the reconversion of Christians and stimulating Buddhist mission activity round the world.
                Hindus 18%. **Muslims** 7%. **Roman Catholics** 7%.
                Protestants 0.8%. Community 103,000. Denominations 7. Major groups – Anglicans 54,000 adherents; Methodists 26,000; Baptists 5,000; Presbyterians 2,000; Church of S. India (Tamil) 6,000. All these denominations seeking to agree on Church union as Church of Sri Lanka. Pentecostals 7,000; Salvation Army 3,000.
                Evangelicals 0.2%.
                Rate of Growth – both Roman Catholics and Protestants in serious decline.

Points for Prayer

1) **The land is very poorly evangelised** and much prejudice and misunderstanding about the Gospel must be broken down. The colonial powers suppressed national culture and language and imposed national forms of Christianity in the past. Independence has brought in a backlash against Christianity and a "revival" of Buddhism. Pray for the evangelising of this needy land.

2) **A greater openness to the Gospel** has been evident in the last three years. The lessening of resentments against the West and the growing economic privations of the land have made people more ready to listen to the Good News. Literature is in great demand and people are being won thereby. Every Home Crusade has had a very successful house to house distribution of literature.

3) **The Protestant Church** is one of the weakest and most nominal in Asia. Few know about the new birth. Non-evangelical theological colleges and literature have not produced committed Christians or soul-winning evangelists. Church union is seen as a better solution than a vital personal union of individuals with the Lord. Many "Christians" have reverted to Buddhism because of the loss of privileges and

difficulties in education and employment because of bearing the name of Christ. Revival is very much needed.

4)   **Evangelistic outreach** is, however, more noticeable now than for many years. Evangelicals within the larger denominations are concerned at the lethargy prevalent in the churches. Evangelical groups inside and outside the churches are now more aggressively reaching out. Youth for Christ is having an impact on youth. Efforts are being made to win the university students. Since the nationalisation of all schools, Christian teachers have been making an impact in government schools. Yet all these are but small beginnings. Pray for the Evangelical Fellowship of Sri Lanka as it seeks to strengthen and co-ordinate the evangelical witness. The Pentecostals have been fairly successful in winning souls.

5)   **Christian Radio** – the **TEAM** "Back to the Bible" broadcasts via **FEBC** and Radio Sri Lanka have been very successful – 700,000 follow-up BCCs have been sent all over the island. **TWR** now has a powerful transmitter reaching out to all of South Asia.

6)   **Missions** – entry is very difficult. Only 50 missionaries remain. Pray that they may have a fruitful and strategic influence in this needy land.

7)   **Students – CCC** has had a big impact on the students – pray for the young believers.

REPUBLIC OF THE MALDIVES

This tiny land with 130,000 people on 220 small coral islands 600 Km east of Sri Lanka is one of the smallest United Nations members. It is a Muslim Police State, undeveloped and desperately poor. The people are related to the Singhalese and Arabs. **There are no Maldivian Christians** – the only totally unevangelised nation in Asia. No Christian propaganda is permitted, for Christianity is abhorred by the people. Pray for these people in their sin and need – it would appear that their major hobby is immorality.

TAIWAN (Republic of China)

BACKGROUND

Area:	36,000 sq. km. – an island 150 Km off the coast of Mainland China.
Population:	16,500,000. Annual Growth 1.9%. People per sq. km. – 460.
Peoples:	**Malayo-Polynesian mountain tribes (2)** 1.7% totalling 300,000 people.
	Chinese – Hakka speaking 13%, Hoklo speaking 74%, Mandarin speaking 11%. Though with Mandarin as the national language, others being superseded.
Capital:	Taipei 2,200,000. Major city – Kaohsiung 1,000,000. Urbanisation 63%.
Economy:	Very rapid development and emergence as an industrial nation.
Politics:	The last refuge of the Nationalist Chinese Government since the fall of Mainland China to the Communists in 1949. Increasing political isolation since exclusion from the United Nations in 1972, though the people wait for the day when they will be able to liberate the mainland.
Religion:	**Attitude of Government** – Freedom of religion. Traditional religions of Confucianism, Taoism and Buddhism predominant, but in decline before secularism and Christianity.
	Roman Catholics 2%.
	Protestants 3%. Community 410,000. Communicants 200,000. Denominations 42 – the largest: Presbyterians 70,000 members; Baptists (4) 12,000 members; and the indigenous "Little Flock" 33,000 (Brethren) and True Jesus Church (Pentecostal) 22,000.
	Evangelicals 2.5%.

Points for Prayer

1)   **The outstandingly Christian testimony** in the will of the late Pres. Chiang Kai-Shek in 1975 gave fresh impetus to believers to evangelise among a more responsive people.

Pray that this land may be fully evangelised while there is time. The growing power of Communist China may be used to occupy Taiwan.

2) **Between 1945 and 1960** there was great growth in the Church – both due to the influx of Christians and many experienced Christian workers at the fall of the Mainland, and also a remarkable people movement among the mountain tribes. Growth has slowed due to increasing materialism, the over-dependence of many of the smaller churches on overseas funds and failure to teach and mobilise the church members for outreach and personal evangelism. The need of the Church today is for systematic Bible teaching and revival to bring unity and zeal for outreach.

3) **The Protestant Church** today is stronger among the Mandarin speakers (largely the post-war refugees), but weaker among the Hoklo (though this is the main language group of the Presbyterians), and very weak among the Hakka* (only 0.3% of this group are Christians). There are fine national leaders of maturity and many Bible Schools and Seminaries training workers for the churches. **OMF** have a valuable ministry assisting some of the older denominations in teaching and outreach. Greatest growth is seen among the two larger indigenous Chinese Churches because of a high degree of loyalty to the Lord and their fellowship and the involvement of the whole membership in outreach.

4) **The Tribal Church** now claims 80% of the people and nearly half the Christians in the Presbyterian Church. In recent years there has been spiritual decline due to poverty (unable to support pastors adequately), inadequate Bible teaching and ensuring of a personal relationship with the Lord for each Christian. The breakdown of tribal life has been speeded by the drift of many to the cities and increasing education among the young people. Immorality among the youth, and inability of parents to control and raise up their children in a changing society have led to the loss of many young people. Pray for the pastors in this critical time that they may give the lead the people need. God graciously gave revival to the Tayal people in 1973 – pray that this movement may affect other tribal areas.

5) **Missions** – pioneered by the Presbyterians, but since 1950 over 100 other church planting, evangelistic and service missions have entered. There are now about 770 missionaries in the land. There are many openings for new missionaries in evangelism, church planting, and inspiring of believers to action, but national believers are increasingly shouldering the leadership, administration and burden of the work.

6) **The witness to students** – the 300,000 university students are probably the most open section of the community now. Many churches have student centres that are well used. The Campus Evangelical Fellowship (**IVF** related) has a good outreach and 20 dedicated full time workers. **CCC** continues with bold plans for mobilisation of students and young people for evangelism, and are, at present, training 4,000 teams of two for in-depth personal evangelism in Taipei and other centres under the title "Here's Life movement."

7) **Literature work is now extensive. CEF (IVF)** and others have plans to penetrate the secular book market with Christian books as well as publishing new books translated from other languages and encouraging local writers.

8) **Needy areas and peoples.**
   a) **The 2 million Hakka speaking people** need to be evangelised in their own language despite increasing use of Mandarin. They have no Bible and there are only about 6 or so missionaries able to minister in this language.
   b) There are still about **500 small towns and larger villages** without a resident evangelical witness.
   c) **Factory workers** of the lower income group are relatively unreached – most believers coming from a middle class background. Pray for the factory evangelism of **OMF** workers and others.
   d) **The fishing villages** are poor, and the people work long hours and few have ever witnessed to these needy and superstitious people.

9) **The missionary vision** of the national Church is only seen in a few groups and congregations. There are stirrings of greater things – such as through recent conferences on evangelism, but this burden is not seen to be part of the life of the Church. Some tribal pastors have gone as missionaries to Sarawak, Malaysia, other denominational workers have gone to pastor Chinese congregations in other lands (but this is

hardly mission work!). Up to 200 "tent-making" missionaries have gone out to other lands to plant churches from the two large indigenous churches. Pray that the little Chinese Missions Overseas may really get launched.

THAILAND

BACKGROUND

Area:	514,000 sq. km. – a fertile agricultural land and a large exporter of rice.
Population:	43,300,000. Annual Growth 2.5%. People per sq. km. – 84. Literacy 70%.
Peoples:	**Thai** 86% – subdivided into the related Thai 53%, Thai-Lao 30%, Khmer 3%; also the Shan 50,000 and Karen 160,000 tribes in the west.
	Chinese 10% – the great majority living in Bangkok. **Malays** 2% in the south.
	Tribal peoples 1% – about 30 tribes; most in the northern areas.
Capital:	Bangkok 4,000,000. Urbanisation 18%.
Economy:	Steady growth, but poverty in the north east, and inadequate roads.
Politics:	Constitutional monarchy. Serious increase of Communist terrorism from Communist subdued Laos and Cambodia since 1975 and both Communist and Muslim separatist guerrillas in the far south. Corruption and political spinelessness of the democratic government in the face of Communism provoked the military coup of 1976 with the resulting restoration of morale and the end of defeatist talk of an imminent fall to the Communists.
Religion:	**Attitude of Government** – Buddhism is the state religion, though there is freedom of religion. Christianity regarded as a buffer against Communism. **Buddhism** 94% with a strong hold on people with Buddhism and Thai nationality closely linked. Considerable animistic practices also found. **Muslims** 3.9% (mostly the Jawi Malays). **Animists** 2% – tribal peoples.
	Roman Catholics 0.6%.
	Protestants 0.4%. Community 130,000. Membership 45,000+. Denominations 17 – the largest: Church of Christ in Thailand 25,000 members; Baptists (4 groups) 8,000; Pentecostals 6,000; Various Evangelical Churches associatd with **OMF** 2,000+; **CMA** 1,700; **WEC** 700.
	Evangelicals 0.2%.

Prayer Targets

1) **A very marked increase in interest in the Gospel** since 1968 after 150 years of very discouraging and hard mission work. This interest has been caused by a number of factors working together – the grave Communist threat, the excellent witness of Christian medical mission work, and also a breath of revival and spiritual deepening among the few Thai believers.

2) **Pray for the breaking of the demonic powers behind the entrenched Buddhism** and widespread fear of the spirits among both Thai and tribal peoples.

3) **Needy areas** – the whole of the country is still a pioneer mission field, but more needy is rural central Thailand and also the poor north east where the density of Christians is one tenth of the low national average.

4) **The churches** have not grown as fast as the population for decades, until the last several years. The rather nominal and older C.C.T. (largely Presbyterian) was in decline, but there is a new surge of life with some spiritual evangelistic church leaders emerging that has been stimulated by revival in northern Thai congregations. The younger churches (the fruit of the newer Evangelical missions) are showing steady growth – especially among the tribal people. Pray that the believers may become strong and effective witnesses for the Lord. 1978 has been made a year of Evangelism.

5) **The problems faced by the churches** – lack of mature pastors, most believers only semi-literate or illiterate and many are converts from among "outcast" leprosy patients at mission hospitals and clinics. Thus many are open to aggressive propaganda by sects and not able to really form an effective evangelistic force. Pray for all

literacy work and lay training programmes. Pray also for a greater earnestness among believers to follow the Lord, come what may.

6) **Leadership training** – there are a number of good denominational and inter-denominational Bible Schools – just to mention the Phayao B. S. (**OMF**) and the growing Bangkok B. S. (**OMF-CMA**) as representative of these. There are a number of talented young men coming into the Lord's work. Pray also for TEE (Presbyterians, **OMF** and **CMA**) and also for the much used cassette ministry for the training of local leaders. The latter is vital with the poor communications and widely scattered Christian community.

7) **Missions** – a rapid post-war increase from 2 groups to 35. There are now over 800 missionaries, mostly with the newer evangelical groups (**OMF** has 200 workers, **WEC** 39) and the majority in evangelism and church planting ministries among both the Thai and minority groups. There is a pressing need for more to use the present receptivity of the people and build them up into strong churches. Communist and Malay insurgency has limited missionary activity in some areas – 2 **OMF** missionaries being martyred in 1975. Pray for safety and strategic usefulness in the possibly limited time for working.

8) **Medical work** has proved a valuable key and many owe their conversion to the loving witness in these institutions. There are about 30 Protestant hospitals – 3 of **OMF**. Pray for the witness to the many non-Christian nurses (some are seeking the Lord), and for the raising up of Christian Thai medical workers. Leprosy control and treatment among the 400,000 sufferers of this disease has resulted in the planting of many small churches among the Thai, and one even among the Malays.

9) **Student witness** is yet small, but growing. The Christian Students Fellowship has 200 members in 6 of the 12 universities and 50,000 students.

10) **Literature** – a number of publishers are producing more and more Thai books and much is distributed through the 10 Christian bookstores. Several groups plan massive Bible and literature distribution programmes in the light of Thailand's exposure to Communist aggression.

11) **Minority groups:**
   a) **The Chinese** number around 3 million, but fewer have put their trust in the Lord than in other overseas communities of Chinese such as Singapore, etc. There are about 17 churches with 3,500 believers only, i.e., 0.1% of the people.
   b) **The Malays** (1,000,000) live in the 5 provinces adjoining Malaysia. There is much political tension and unrest. This is the only Malay community open to evangelism in Asia, thus is strategic – especially for the Malays in Malaysia who are legally not allowed to be evangelised. After years of work by **OMF** missionaries a little Malay Church of 20 believers and 30 almost committed believers has been born. Many others have heard the Gospel and believe, but hold back because of fear. Pray for the growth in numbers, power and ability to witness of these few believers. Pray also for the completion of the Jawi Malay N.T. by 1980.
   c) **The tribal peoples** are generally very poor (unless they illegally grow opium), illiterate and under terrible domination of the spirit world. Many missions have laboured and wept for a harvest which is now beginning to appear. Among the Meo (100,000 – supplemented by many refugees from Laos – most Christian), Lisu (20,000) and Lahu strong, well led churches are emerging, but the Yao*, Pwo Karen*, Akha* and Shan (**OMF** teams) and the Kui* (160,000) and Khmu (**CMA**) and also the Lawa*, etc., (NTM – 5 tribes) the work is slow and hard, with believers lacking in incentive to learn to read or to better themselves. Bible translation, literacy work and the encouraging of potential leaders are the great needs. Conditions are hard for the missionaries and now worsened by Communist infiltration.
   d) **Refugees from Laos and Cambodia** have proved a very receptive field of labour for **OMF, WEC, CMA** and denominational missionaries with thousands seeking the Lord from both lands. Many of these new believers have moved on to other lands such as the U.S.A., France, etc. Pray for continuing evangelistic and relief ministries. **W.V.** and **TEAR** fund have done much to alleviate the sufferings of these people.

V. MIDDLE EAST

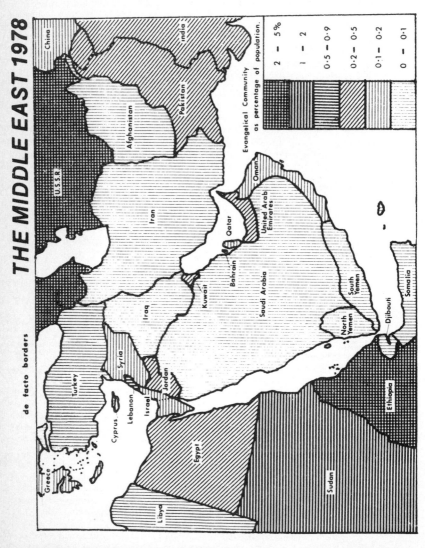

THE MIDDLE EAST 1978

Evangelical Community as percentage of population.

- 2 – 5%
- 1 – 2
- 0·5 – 0·9
- 0·2 – 0·5
- 0·1 – 0·2
- 0 – 0·1

de facto borders

China, India, Pakistan, Afghanistan, U.S.S.R., Iran, Oman, Qatar, United Arab Emirates, Bahrain, Kuwait, Saudi Arabia, South Yemen, Somalia, North Yemen, Djibouti, Iraq, Syria, Turkey, Lebanon, Cyprus, Israel, Jordan, Greece, Ethiopia, Egypt, Sudan, Libya

NOTE for Arab N. Africa, see p. 157.

132

BACKGROUND

Area: 15,836,000 sq. km. – 11.1% of land surface of the world. Only 5% of this area has sufficient water for cultivation. In this survey we define the Middle East as the Arabic speaking lands of North Africa and South West Asia together with Turkey and Iran. There are 22 lands in this area.

Population: 221,000,000 growing at 2.8% per year. Population density – 14 per sq. km.

Peoples: **Arabs 60%** – the Arabs conquered the entire region but for Asia Minor (Turkey) in the 7th and 8th Centuries, Arabising the Egyptians and Aramaeans (Syria). The North African Berbers (15,000,000) still resist this process.
Non-Arab nations 34% – Turks, Kurds, Iranians.
Africans 2% – almost entirely in S. Sudan.
Jews 1% – almost entirely in Israel, some in Iraq, Iran, Syria, etc.
Immigrant Minorities 2% – Armenians and Circassians in Jordan, Iraq, Egypt, etc. – Asians and Westerners wherever oil is produced. Urbanisation 36% – 9 of the world's 163 cities of over one million in Middle East.

Economy: The Oil Crisis of 1974–5, in which the world was held to ransom, and the price of crude oil raised fourfold has caused a major redistribution of the world's wealth to these lands that produce 70% of the world's oil. Some states have become fabulously wealthy, while others remain in grinding poverty. Oil wealth is bringing enormous development and industrialisation in many areas.

Politics: The Middle East is the most strategic area on earth due to its geographical position, control of trade routes and vast reserves of oil. The Russians have exploited the tensions of the area in order to gain control of it. The festering political sore of Israel divides the whole Middle East into two, and yet is the only factor that unites the Arabs. The Arab-Israeli war has continued from 1948 until today – 4 times erupting into violent shooting wars. This conflict shows little sign of abating.

Religion: **Muslims 92%** – 203,000,000 of the world's 701,000,000 Muslims.
Jews 1% – 2,200,000 – 15% of the world's Jews live in the Middle East.
African Traditionals 1.7% – in South Sudan.
Hindus 0.13% – mainly immigrant workers in the Arabian states.
Christians 4.5%.
Eastern Churches 3%; Roman Catholics 1.2% – almost entirely descendants of the Christians of the pre-Muslim era. Generally formal, decadent and lacking in spiritual life. Most of the Roman Catholics belong to the "Uniate" churches – adhering to the rites of various Eastern Churches, but acknowledging the authority of the Pope.
Protestants 0.3% – totalling 683,000, but of these, 400,000 are Black African Christians in the Sudan. A further 152,000 live in Egypt, and only 131,000 Protestants in all the other 20 lands of the area.
Evangelicals 0.23%.
Missionaries to Middle East 1,300, i.e., 1 missionary for every 170,000 people. Middle Eastern Missionaries 230.

The Challenge of Islam

The home of the First Century Church is now the most needy mission field in the world. The Muslim conquests virtually wiped out the decadent Christianity prevailing in these lands, leaving a despised and harassed remnant of a great variety of ancient churches that did not succumb to Islam. No trace of the North African Church remains. The life style of many of these "Christians" is rarely a recommendation of the Gospel to Muslims, but these are virtually the only Christians a Muslim would meet. Islam reigns supreme where once the Gospel was preached. May believers be stirred to pray that the Lord Jesus Christ may be glorified and honoured in these lands! Islam has proved to be Christianity's most successful and bitter opponent. Few MUSLIMS HAVE EVER BEEN FREED FROM THE SHACKLES OF Islam by the liberation that there is in Jesus. Islam's missionary fervour has greatly increased since the 1974 Oil Crisis. With vast funds at its disposal, a big effort is being made to evangelise Europe, Asia, Africa and the Americas for Islam, and at the same time to end Christian missionary work in Muslim lands. Islam is now beginning to make some notable advances.

Paradoxically, Muslims are more open to the Gospel than ever before. This is due to the dramatic political and social changes that are revolutionising their lives. The teachings of Islam cannot meet the deepest needs of the human heart in these crisis times. Islam is now very divided because of doctrinal differences, attitudes to Communism, Western materialism, and the failure of Muslims to settle national and international problems among themselves, and above all, the extraordinary survival and expansion of the little state of Israel. In all this confusion, more Muslims are seeking for truth. Yet perversions of Christianity entrenched in their holy book, the Koran, and social pressures all help to keep the would-be seeker from coming to Christ – even if he were able to find a witnessing Christian to help him.

Missions

Early Protestant Missions in the last century frequently turned from the difficult Muslim majority to evangelising the more receptive nominal Christians. Few of the present Protestants are from a Muslim background. Yet the sacrificial labours and tears of many missionaries among Muslims will surely yield the longed-for harvest. Missionaries need much prayer, for this is Satan's territory; discouragements, lack of visible fruit and hostility of many can cause some to give up the struggle. Pray for adaptability to new cultures, acceptability among the people, perseverance, and provision of the love of God for the people they seek to win.

There are encouraging signs of a growing concern in Western lands for the evangelisation of the Muslim world:
1)   The number of missionaries in the Middle East has risen to over 1,300.
2)   The increasing numbers of Christians in secular employment in the Middle East (CSOs), who give up good prospects in their homelands to witness in this way. These need much prayer.
3)   The growing army of permanent and short term workers witnessing among immigrant Muslims in Europe. There are 3,000,000 Muslims from the Middle East now working in Western Europe. There are now more Turkish and North African Christians in Europe than in their own countries.
4)   The increasing use of Western, Asian and Middle Eastern young people as short term evangelists – especially pray for the work of **OM** and **YWAM.** Many of these short term workers later return for a full time ministry.

The National Believers

They are few and scattered, and much in need of prayer as they live in very difficult circumstances. It is easier for them to emigrate to lands with greater religious freedom – as many have done. Probably the majority of converts out of Islam have left their homelands for this reason, for they face extreme pressures. There is a great need for the planting and growth of vigorous churches all over the region. Trained leaders are few and there is only one Bible School giving instruction in Arabic in the world (in Lebanon). TEE is being developed as a useful tool to train the lay leaders. Pray for: –
1)   **Converts out of Islam** – for a close walk with the Lord, deliverance from all the erroneous Muslim thought patterns, a desire and opportunities for helpful fellowship with believers, acceptability by other Christians who are often suspicious of such converts, and boldness in the face of threats, ostracism, physical danger, etc.
2)   **The witness of the believers** – deliverance from fear of witnessing, life style that recommends the Gospel, tactful winning of Muslims where the law forbids such a witness.
3)   **The need for Christian homes** – these are very few. Unequal marriages between Christians and Muslims are the major cause of backsliding. The Muslim world needs to see the beauty of a Christian home.
4)   **The cultivation of a missionary vision.** Arab missionaries would be more acceptable than Westerners in many lands. There are now about 230 Middle Eastern missionaries – largely from Egypt, Jordan and Syria, who are serving the Lord in other

Middle Eastern countries. Many other Christians also work in lands closed to normal mission work – in Libya, Arabia, etc. This vision needs to be encouraged. Pray for the excellent work done in this respect by **OM** and **YWAM** in mobilising young people in Jordan, Sudan and Egypt.

The Most Effective Means of Reaching Muslims

1) **Medical work** – this opens up countries and hearts to the Gospel. This is the only way in which missionary work can be done in Yemen, some Gulf States and Afghanistan. Pray for this ministry – that it may create opportunities for a witness to Muslims. There is a continual cry for more medical workers.

2) **Personal witness** by nationals, missionaries and CSOs is the most effective way – but this needs a high degree of self-giving, much love and patience and a great faith.

3) **Literature** – more and more good evangelistic literature for Muslims, and Arabic teaching literature for Christians is now being produced by such groups as the Carmel Mission, **MECO,** etc. Pray for ex-Muslims engaged in writing these materials, for publishers and bookstores, etc., who seek to get this literature into the hands of those who need it. **OM** has distributed much literature all over the Middle East in recent years. Pray for fruit.

4) **Radio** – the most effective (and sometimes the only) means of witnessing to Muslims in many areas. There are studios for the production of programmes in Spain (**GMU**), France (**NAM**), Lebanon (**FEBA**) for broadcasting by **TWR** in Monaco and Cyprus, ELWA (**SIM**) in Liberia, and **FEBA** in Seychelles. The response has been good, and very effective when able to be followed up by BCCs and personal contacts with Christians.

5) **Bible correspondence courses** (BCCs) have been used of the Lord to win more Muslims to Christ than any other means. This is especially true of North Africa, Turkey and Iran. Pray for Missions involved in this ministry – **GMU, NAM, ICF,** etc. This witness is subject to much opposition by Muslim authorities – postal censorship plus harassment of students. Pray for these students, that they may be won for Christ and brought into living fellowships of believers.

6) **Gospel Recordings, and Cassette Tapes** are proving a splendid tool of evangelism and Christian teaching in regions that can never be visited by missionaries.

7) **Muslims in other lands** are more accessible – pray for all involved in ministry to students and workers in Europe and North America. Pray that converts from this ministry may become effective evangelists when they return home.

The Great Unmet Need

Unreached peoples – many! Countless villages and towns have never welcomed a preacher of the Gospel; Muslim women in many lands are virtually inaccessible in their prison-like seclusion; the nomadic tribes of the deserts of North Africa, Arabia and Iran; the expanding student population (only in Egypt is there an established witness in the universities); the expatriate Asian and Western communities, etc.

Closed lands – Mauretania, Libya, Saudi Arabia, Qatar, South Yemen, which are only able to be penetrated by CSOs at present.

Lands with no fellowships of national believers – Mauretania, Saudi Arabia, Qatar, Libya, Yemen (though in each are communities of expatriate believers). 15 of the 22 lands have less than 500 national believers. There are probably less than 5,000 Christians in the Middle East converted out of Islam.

There is a great lack of Christian workers to use present opportunities to the full. The Middle East has the lowest missionary/people ratio of any major region of the world, yet it is the area most needing pioneer work. These lands continue to defy our Lord Jesus and we cannot remain complacent about this state of affairs.

Further Information

We have had to refrain from giving much specific information that could bring harm to the Lord's work in the Middle East. If the Lord leads you, we suggest that you avail yourself of the prayer information given out by: **FFM** – outstanding prayer information covering the whole Muslim world; **NAM** – North Africa; **MECO** – Lebanon, Syria, Arabia; **OM** – Middle East; **WEC** + **RSMT** + **TEAM** – Arabian Peninsula.

ALGERIA

BACKGROUND

Area:	2,293,000 sq. km. – the greater part of the country is in the Sahara Desert.
Population:	17,300,000. Growth rate 3.2%. Population Density 8 people per sq. km.
Peoples:	**Arabs and Arabised Berbers** 70% – mainly along the more fertile coast. **Berbers** 29% – mostly in the Atlas mountains and speaking three major languages – Kabyle*, Riff and Tamazight. Also in the deserts to the south – Mzab dialects and the famous nomadic Tuareg. **Europeans** 100,000 – all that remain of the 1,000,000 French settlers of pre-independence times.
Capital:	Algiers 1,200,000. Urbanisation 50%.
Economy:	Poor, but more wealth with development of Sahara oilfields.
Politics:	Independence from France in 1964 after devastating 8 year war. Revolutionary leftist Muslim government now in power.
Religion:	**Attitude of government** – Islam is the state religion, but recent relaxations now permit 8 Protestant missions to operate legally within defined limits. **Muslims** 99%. **Roman Catholics** 72,000 (mostly French). **Protestants** 5,000 – mainly French and English speaking; only about 150 Arab Protestants meeting regularly in 6 little groups.

Points for Prayer

1) **The Government stopped renewing residence permits for missionaries in 1977.** Most of the 15 **NAM** and also other missionaries have had to find secular employment in order to remain in the country. Both missionaries and unbelievers need wisdom in this tense situation. Much of the ministry of missionaries is in encouraging believers in personal contacts, little Bible Study groups and camps. Pray that they may have wisdom in their ministry so as not to offend unnecessarily, yet to use all possible openings to the full. Servants of God have wept for the yet unseen harvest of souls in this land. Pray for it!

2) **The believers are generally younger** and the little groups less strong than in Morocco. Many of the believers are young people, largely girls. There are therefore many pressures on these young people – early arranged marriages for the girls to Muslims, and hostility in schools and at work for the young men. There are many backsliders. Pray for the establishment of many strong, witnessing fellowships of believers all over the country. Many of those who seek the Lord are unable to have fellowship with other believers due to the hostility of relatives or husbands – pray for such. Pray that there may be a more courageous witness from among these believers despite the problems.

3) **There is a critical lack of leaders** among the Algerian believers. Pray for the few doing TEE, and also for the calling of North African or other Arab Christians willing to minister there (possibly from among those in France).

4) **There is a reading room and student centre in Algiers** run by the NAM. This provides useful contacts with non-Christians and a haven for believers. There is a small **IVF** group in the university. Pray for the growth of this student witness among one of the most enquiring and open sections of the nation.

5) **Literature work** has been greatly hindered by the government closure of the one remaining Christian bookshop because it was offering Kabyle New Testaments for sale. Pray for its re-opening. Pray that the increasing demand for literature may be met, and that the right literature may be allowed to enter the country.

6) **Unreached peoples** – some specific groups ought to be mentioned: –
   a) **The Kabyle*** – these people number nearly 2 million. In the past a number believed, but most later emigrated to France. There are a number of independent missionaries

working among these resistant people. There are increasing difficulties in the use of their language due to government pressures to Arabise them – pray that even this may cause some to turn to Christianity, which their forbears followed.

   b) **The Oasis dwellers** in the Sahara – many different Berber tribes still unreached.

   c) **The Tuareg** – these nomadic people are very difficult to reach, but attempts are being made by the Sahara Desert Mission and **SIM** (in Niger).

7)   **The Algerians in Europe** – at any one time there are nearly 2,000,000 working in France, Belgium, Holland, etc. Pray that those of **NAM + WEC** in France, and **GMU** in Belgium may see many turning to the Lord who will, in turn, become missionaries to their own people.

8)   **Radio and Bible correspondence courses** with careful follow-up of those so contacted by visits from believers is still the most effective means of outreach. Pray that literature may not be intercepted in the post and that those receiving BCCs may be free from harassment.

EGYPT

BACKGROUND

Area:	1,001,000 sq. km. – all but the fertile Nile banks and some oases is desert.
Population:	38,100,000. Growth Rate 2.3%. People per sq. km. – in fertile areas **1,000.**
Peoples:	**Egyptians 94%** – the Biblical people, with admixture of Arab blood.
	Nubians 4% – mostly living in the southern part of the country.
	Minorities 2% – Desert Bedouin 80,000, and some Berbers in the W. Desert. Immigrant minorities of Armenians, Palestinians and Lebanese.
Capital:	Cairo 6,588,000. Other major cities – Alexandria 2,200,000. 14 other cities with over 100,000 people. Rapid urbanisation – now at 43%.
Economy:	Poor and crippled by high birth rate, lack of agricultural land, the expensive confrontation with Israel.
Politics:	President Sadat's diplomacy has ended the dominance of the USSR and won control of the valuable Suez Canal and Sinai oilfields from Israel as a result of the 1973 Yom Kippur War.
Religion:	**Attitude of Government** – Islam is the state religion. Christians free to worship, but not to evangelise Muslims – heavy penalties for the latter.
	Islam 86% – one of Islam's most important centres.
	Coptic Church 13% – one of the ancient churches that has survived 1,300 years of Muslim Arab persecution and discrimination.
	Roman Catholics 0.4% – 120,000 in 7 different groups and traditions.
	Protestants 0.4%. Community 150,000. Denominations 10. Largest groups: Coptic Evangelical (Presbyterian) 100,000; Assemblies of God 16,000; Free Methodists 16,000; Brethren 10,000 adherents.
	Evangelicals 0.3% of population.

Prayer Targets

1)   **Pray that the promise of Isaiah 19:19-22 for Egypt may be fulfilled.** There are encouraging signs of a turning to God from among Muslims, despite legal barriers. Several hundred Muslims are turning to Christ every year. Pray that Egypt's troubles, and Islam's emptiness may turn many to the Lord Jesus.

2)   **Unreached peoples.** Few Muslims have ever heard a Christian testify. Pray that the Christians may win opportunities to speak through their Christlikeness. The Desert Bedouin and Berber peoples remain unreached.

3)   **The Nubian people** are now more receptive to the Gospel than ever before. Most are Muslim, but many are Coptic Christians. The great need is for more Christian workers to learn their language and to live and witness among them.

4)   **Pray for the evangelisation of the cities** – many rural people are being compelled by poverty to go to the cities. Pray that these uprooted people may be evangelised somehow.

5) **The Coptic Church** is largely nominal, but an extraordinary revival within it since 1930 has gained momentum and the present leadership is highly educated, articulate and Bible based. The present Patriarch gives weekly Bible studies to 7,000 people. The charismatic movement is also making a deep impression. These 5,000,000 Coptic Christians, if revived, could have a decisive impact on the Middle East.

6) **The Protestant Churches** have not grown much for many years. There is some nominalism in the older churches and a considerable drift back to the Coptic Church from where the original converts came. Pray for a deepening of the spiritual life and a more consistent life-testimony before the Muslims. There are many young people now coming into the churches. There are several interdenominational groups who seek to stimulate Bible Study and outreach among the young people. Pray that, despite the difficulties, Muslims may be reached and welcomed into the churches. One church actually gained 100 converts out of Islam in 1975.

7) **The Christian witness among university students** is encouraging. There is now a group in every faculty of Egypt's 4 big university complexes; even in the Al Azhar Muslim University where Muslim missionaries are trained. Pray that these believers may find open hearts among the 250,000 students and win them in the relative freedom found there. Pray for the building up of these believers in the Lord for future usefulness in service.

8) **Missions** – there are only about 20 agencies with 80 missionaries serving in the land. There are now more opportunities for the entry of expatriate Christians for service than for many years. Pray for workers. Pray also for the growth of the missionary vision of the Christians in Egypt. Missionaries from Egypt would be more acceptable than Western missionaries in many Muslim lands. The greatest limitation is not the willingness of believers, but the difficulty of supporting them financially when they go.

9) **Christian literature** is freely printed and sold. Many Christian groups have moved their literature ministries from war-torn Lebanon to Egypt. There are many Christian Bookstores (10 in Cairo). Pray for the effective use of this literature, and also for the raising up of more local believers who are able to write suitable evangelistic and teaching materials.

ARABIAN (PERSIAN) GULF STATES

BACKGROUND

Area: 396,000 sq. km. – five small desert states along the east and south east coasts of the Arabian Peninsula.

Population: 2,520,000 – over 1,000,000 of these being immigrants from other lands:

State	Area sq. km.	Population	% Foreigners	
Bahrain	652	220,000	17%	Groups of Islands off Arabian coast
Kuwait	24,000	1,100,000	53%	Between Iraq and Saudi Arabia
Oman	269,000	800,000	20%	S.E. corner of Arabian Penin.
Qatar	11,000	180,000	68%	Penin. Arabian Gulf
United Arab Emirates	92,000	325,000	48%	Between Qatar and Oman

Emirates – Dubai 100,000, Abu Dhabi 95,000, Sharjah 55,000; Ajman 8,000; Ras al Khaimah 45,000; Fujaira 15,000; Umm al Quwain 8,000.

Peoples: **Local Arabs 57%. Immigrants 43%** – mainly Iranians, Pakistanis, Indians, Jordanians, Palestinians and Europeans.

Economy: The richest states in the world due to the immense oilfields now being exploited. A large number of skilled and unskilled expatriate workers needed for oil exploitation and many huge development projects.

Politics: All these states originally under British protection, but now all are independent and gradually emerging out of feudalism and autocratic rule. There is growing leftist unrest in some areas and a Communist war in East Oman that is masterminded from Communist South Yemen.

Religion: **Attitude of Governments** – remarkable freedom for all forms of Christian activity in all but Qatar and, to a certain extent, Kuwait.

Muslims 85% – many different sects – extremist Wahhabi, Sunni, Shia, Ibadhi.

Christians 5% – mainly Roman Catholic and Eastern Church Christians that have immigrated from other Middle Eastern countries.

Protestants approx. 15,000 but with only about 500 converted from out of the local Muslim Arab population. Evangelicals 0.2% (mainly Asian and European expatriates).

Points for Prayer

1) **This area is a strategic bridgehead for the Gospel** – pray for a continued open door for Christian work. A strong Arab Church here could affect the whole Middle East, for few countries in the area do not have some of their nationals working here.

2) **There are several lands that do not permit Christian work** at all or among the local people. Pray that expatriate workers in these lands may shine for Jesus.

3) **Unreached peoples** – specific mention must be made of the following: **Local Arabs*** – very few have been clearly presented with the claims of the Gospel. **Baluchis** from Pakistan are many, but there are no Christian workers availble to witness to these Muslim people in their own language. **Iranians** – very few of these Muslim people are Christian and little is done to win them for the Lord.

4) **The churches are growing** and a considerable number of Indians and Pakistanis are being won to the Lord. There are strong churches in Kuwait, Bahrain, Oman and U.A.E. (Presbyterian and Evangelical). Most of the churches are composed of some local Arab believers and many of the immigrant minorities – Indian, European, Jordanian, etc. Most are pastored by Arabs and Indians from other lands. Pray that the unity of the Spirit may be maintained in all this diversity. Pray that these believers may have a very clear testimony to the non-Christians around them.

5) **Pray for new programmes of outreach** being started for more effective evangelism. Pray for the effective use of house visitation, literature and personal work to win Muslims. There is now considerable interest in Christianity among educated Arab young people.

6) **Pray for the Christians** who have gone to witness for Christ in a secular job. There are unlimited opportunities in this line for Western Christians where Western skills are so needed to develop these countries.

7) **Christian missions** – long years of pioneering work by the U.S. Presbyterians through medical and educational work has opened the lands for other missions. There are now about 80 Protestant missionaries serving the Lord. Most are using medical evangelism to reach the hearts of the people. There are now about 9 medical centres run by missions, and in all there is complete freedom to evangelise the patients. There are 5 hospitals run by three U.S. Presbyterian groups (Bahrain, Muscat, Oman, Sharjah and Ras al Khaimah). There is the excellent **TEAM** hospital at the Buraimi Oasis between Oman and UAE and the **WEC** medical work in Fujaira. There is a critical need for dedicated Christian workers (especially men) to use the many opportunities. This is a wonderful opening for Arab missionaries. Pray for the health of missionaries working in this very hot and often humid climate. Pray for eternal fruit in a field that is unusually hard and discouraging.

8) **Christian Radio** – reception from **FEBA** Seychelles is now quite good. Pray that the daily Arabic broadcasts may bear fruit in the hearts of many.

9) **Christian literature** – there are little Christian bookstores in Kuwait, Oman, Bahrain and Abu Dhabi that are performing valuable service.

ISRAEL

BACKGROUND

Area:	Increased in 1967 Six Day War from 22,700 sq. km. to the present approx. 86,000 sq. km.
Population	4,500,000 including the 1,000,000 Arabs in territory conquered in 1967.
Peoples:	**Jews** 66% and growing at 1.7% per year. Immigration (especially from USSR) just about balancing emigration now. Immigrants from over 70 nations. **Arabs** 33%, growing at 3.9% per year. Arabs were 11% of population in 1967.
Capital:	Jerusalem 320,000. Tel Aviv 380,000. Urbanisation 86%.
Economy:	Modern industrial state; self sufficient in food production. The very high cost of maintaining strong armed forces is hurting the economy.
Politics:	The founding of Israel in 1948 ended 1,900 years of exile for the Jews. Four wars against the displaced Palestinians and surrounding Arab states in 1948, 1956, 1967 and 1973 have left Israel today occupying the Syrian Golan Heights, the Jordanian West Bank and Jerusalem, and most of the Egyptian Sinai. Military and diplomatic successes of the Palestinian terrorists and Arabs since 1973, and the growing unrest of the Israeli-ruled Arab population make a settlement imperative for Israel.
Religion:	**Attitude of Government** – freedom for all religious groups to work unhindered among their own communities, but proselytisation of Jews actively discouraged. **Jews** 57% – 25% Orthodox, others are Liberal and non-religious Jews. There are many tensions between the different groups. **Muslims** 39%. **Christians** 3% – about 100,000 non-Protestant Arab Christians in Eastern, Orthodox and Roman Catholic Churches. **Protestants** – only about 5,000 (almost entirely Arab). There are only about 300 Hebrew Christians, but possibly 10,000 – 20,000 secret believers. Evangelicals 0.1% (almost entirely Arab).

Prayer Points

1) **The Jews in Israel** are more resistant to the Gospel than those of the Dispersion. Pray for this hardness to be removed (Rom 11:25), and for the promised harvest (Rom 11:31). Pray for the removal of social and legal barriers to their conversion.

2) **Pray for the peace of Israel** and for all Arab and Israeli leaders in this critical time that there may be an equitable peace with justice for all peoples.

3) **The legal position** is not helpful to believers or missions among the Jews. It is not allowed to seek the conversion of a young person without the written permission of the parents. The legal position of a Jew who becomes a Christian is very difficult. It is hard for the Protestant Churches to gain government recognition.

4) **The Hebrew Christians** are considered almost traitors to their nation, and suffer ostracism and some discrimination from other Jews. There are about 4 Hebrew assemblies that meet on an interdenominational basis, and some other believers that fellowship with some of the many small mission groups. Some of the latter are all too ready to "sponsor" promising believers – often not for the best motives. Pray for the planting of strong independent churches all over the country.

5) **The Arab believers** are mostly Anglican, Baptist and Brethren, and also smaller numbers in the Alliance and Nazarene Churches. There are some fine, lively fellowships in Jerusalem and Galilee with a considerable outreach. Pray for their witness in the present difficult political situation. Pray for a greater outreach to the less evangelised West Bank, and especially the 350,000 Palestinians in the Gaza Strip. Pray for closer links between the Hebrew and Arab believers.

6) **The hostile environment** for both Arab and Hebrew believers with limited opportunities for the future tempts many to leave the country. Many young people emigrate and the witness they could bear is lost.

7) **A large proportion of the Israelis have immigrated** from countries all over the world.

Each group comes to Israel with its own language and culture and each must be reached with the Gospel in a meaningful way. Especially needy are the over 120,000 (often atheistic) Jews now coming from Russia, where they are suffering considerable persecution. Pray for the reaching of these **Immigrant Jews***.

8) **Israel needs more men and women who humbly and simply live for Jesus** and witness personally to the very many who have not responded to the Gospel. Pray for all groups seeking to help and encourage the national believers in this ministry of personal evangelism and distribution of literature. There are surprisingly few Christians doing this and the opportunities for this ministry are many.

9) **The missionary force** is variously estimated to be 120–250. There are over 37 societies – often very small and ineffective. Many are inspired by their own particular interpretations of the prophecies relating to the Jews and the Lord's return. Pray for the Lord's servants who labour among the Jews where there is so little encouragement that they may not succumb to discouragement, and that they might know the Lord's will as to how best to minister.

10) **Missionary work among Jews** could be legally stopped. Unwise methods and tactlessness by certain more extremist groups has stimulated Jewish demands for the ending of all Protestant mission work. Pray for humility and tact for all serving the Lord from other lands.

11) **The Jews of the Dispersion.** There are about 16,000,000 Jews living in other lands (only 3,100,000 in Israel). These people are more receptive to the Gospel than those in Israel. There are 7,000,000 in North America, 4,000,000 in Russia and about 500,000 in Argentina, Britain and France, etc. Many societies work specifically among the Jewish people in the U.S.A. and Britain, but little work is done in Argentina and France. Pray for this ministry – usually more in personal witness and patient caring for individuals – that it may bear fruit in the conversion of Jews to their Messiah. There are reports of many Jews now seeking the Lord in the U.S.A. and in the U.S.S.R., especially young people.

IRAN (Persia)

BACKGROUND

Area:	1,648,000 sq. km. – a central desert ringed by mountains.
Population:	34,100,000. Annual Growth 3%. People per sq. km. – 21. Literacy 50%.
Peoples:	**Persians** (speaking several major dialects) in the great majority.
	Minorities – Kurds 1,500,000; **Armenians** 300,000; Arabs, Turks and many smaller and often nomadic peoples – Bakhtiari, Qashqai, Baluchi, Brahui, etc., numbering about 27, each with its own language.
Capital:	Tehran 4,000,000. Urbanisation 43%.
Economy:	Huge oil-financed programme of land reform, education, industrialisation and build-up of armed forces which is rapidly changing the whole country.
Politics:	Constitutional monarchy, with the Shah having much power. The government is seeking to make Iran a second "Japan" economically and politically.
Religion:	**Attitude of Government** – Islam the state religion, but freedom of religion for the 4 long-standing faiths of the land.
	Zoroastrians 19,000 – the religion of the ancient Persian Empire.
	Christianity 0.5% – replaced above soon after Pentecost. The missionary minded Nestorian Church and other ancient Churches virtually wiped out in the 8th Century Muslim conquest of Persia. There remain: – **Armenians** 108,000; **Nestorians** 25,000; **Roman Catholics** 21,000; **Muslims** 98% – materialism and westernisation is weakening the hold of Islam on young people.
	Jews 81,000 – descendants of those who lived in Persia in Daniel's day.
	Protestant Christians – community of only 8,500, membership 5,000 but about 80% nominal. Major groups – Presbyterian 3,000 members; Assemblies of God 700; Anglicans 400.
	Evangelicals 0.006%.

Prayer Targets

1) **This needy Muslim land** is wide open for the Gospel and Muslims have never been so receptive to the Gospel message. There can still be considerable and violent opposition to any attempts at converting Muslims at a local level and converts can suffer much for their faith. Pray for a great turning to the Lord among Muslims – especially among the young people.

2) **Unreached areas and peoples:**
   a) Of the land's 55,000 villages, only half a dozen have a Gospel witness. There are 178 towns and cities, but there are only 78 Christian groups and about 30 little organised churches in the whole country.
   c) Many sections of the population are unreached – the nomadic people, the middle class, university students, women and children, etc.
   d) The linguistic minorities – the 200,000 Muslim Baluchi and Brahui are more open now, but no one is working full time among them. Many other minority peoples have never been evangelised and have nothing of the Word of God.

3) **The "Christians" of the ancient churches** are all too often living lives that cause Muslims to despise Christianity. Yet it is from these groups that most of the conversions have come. Very few of the believers have been converted out of a Muslim background, so are not really equipped to evangelise the Muslims, nor are they always welcoming to converts out of Islam. Very rarely does a Muslim meet a true believer who is willing to witness to him.

4) **The Protestant Church** is very small and weak. The 5 Pentecostal churches have real life and an outreach to all groups. Many of the little churches suffer from personality clashes, divisions and problems. Many are second and third generation Protestants and nominal. There are only about 500 believers in the whole country that meet together with any regularity. Pray for the believers and churches to be revived, become Bible based, and to be mobilised for the winning of the lost. What a tragedy that the Church is such a hindrance to the Gospel in a time like this.

5) **Leadership training** is virtually non-existent. There is a small TEE programme that has now been launched. Pray for the raising up of strong, spiritual men of God to lead the churches into a new era of growth. There is one small Bible School.

6) **Missions** – There are now about 130 missionaries and a further 150 Christians from other lands who seek to evangelise through their secular employment. Pray for a great increase in the number of the Lord's servants in this land, and also for the issuing of visas – these are not too easy to obtain. Much of the work of missions is in literature production and distribution and also in medical work (there are three Christian mission hospitals in the country – run by the CMS (Anglican)). There are many opportunities for service for those with qualifications that satisfy the government.

7) **The Kurdish people** in the north west need to be evangelised. Their number has greatly increased with a large influx of Iraqai Kurds fleeing their land since the Iraqi government crushed their uprising with great ferocity in 1975. There are just a few seeking to reach these unfortunate people – pray for the planting of churches.

8) **The university students** are neglected – pray for the raising up of a witness to them. Pray also for the conversion of Iranian students studying in other lands.

9) **Literature** has been widely distributed by **OM** teams all over the country, and there has been an encouraging response from areas that have no Christian witness. Pray for this hard ministry and also for the work of these pieces of literature in the hearts of the readers. The **Iran Literature Association** (supported by 7 church and Gospel agencies) runs three Christian bookstores and is planning bold new moves to distribute good Christian literature – pray for this.

10) **Bible correspondence courses** have a very fruitful ministry among Muslims. The largest, run by International Missions, has handled 45,000 applications to date and applicants come from every religious background. This ministry has been greatly stimulated by the literature drives of **OM**, etc.

11) **Christian radio broadcasts** from the Seychelles (**FEBA**) have had an encouraging response. Pray for the preparation and broadcasting of these programmes.

IRAQ

BACKGROUND

Area:	438,000 sq. km. – much of country is desert but for the banks of the Biblical Tigris and Euphrates rivers.
Population:	11,400,000. Growth rate – 3.3%. Average people per sq. km. – 26.
Peoples:	**Arabs** 78%, **Kurds** 18% in the north. A 15 year civil war between these groups ended in 1975 with the ruthless crushing of Kurdish aspirations for recognition as a national entity and ending of Arab exploitation.
Capital:	Baghdad 1,300,000. Urbanisation 61%.
Economy:	Very dependent on exploitation of large oilfields.
Politics:	Revolutionary military dictatorship that leans to Marxism. The Russian influence has been very strong.
Religion:	**Attitude of Government** – surveillance and harassment of non-Muslim religions that sometimes degenerates into open persecution. Some Jews and Christians have been executed in recent years.
	Muslims 97%.
	Eastern Churches 170,000 – various ancient churches such as the Chaldean, Assyrian, Jacobite and Orthodox Churches.
	Roman Catholics 125,000 who still run some educational institutions.
	Protestants 0.2%. Community 2,300. Membership 1,300. 5 denominations – largest being Presbyterians and Evangelical Church.
	Evangelicals 0.015%.

Points for Prayer

1) **This land is now closed** for mission work and no open preaching of the Gospel is allowed, yet only a very small proportion of this Muslim country has ever had a chance to hear the Gospel. Pray for the barriers against the Word of God to be broken down.

2) **Muslims are very hard to evangelise** – just a handful are known to have believed and this more often through hearing the Gospel while studying in other lands. For a Muslim to believe, it could mean certain death.

3) **The tragic Kurdish people,** now in the despair of defeat and oppression, have had little chance to hear of the Prince of Peace. There are virtually no believers among this 9,000,000 people scattered over Turkey, Iraq, Iran and the U.S.S.R., and there is only one group of believers known – in N. W. Iran. Pray for the evangelisation of the many thousands of refugees from Iraq now in Iran, where a few Christian teams are seeking to give material aid and the Gospel to them. There have been some who have sought the Lord. Pray for the Kurds in Iraq where it is rumoured that many thousands are being brutally murdered in reprisals.

4) **The national believers are very few.** They are mostly from a nominal Christian background. There are a few church fellowships in Baghdad and Basra but there is little witness elsewhere. Quite a few believers are not linked with any fellowship. New converts are being added to the Church despite the harsh and repressive conditions in the country. Pray that the believers may have courage to stand for the Lord and continue to witness. Many believers emigrate to other lands.

5) **The believers are constantly under pressure** from the authorities and it is dangerous for them to have contacts with foreigners. Pray that their testimony before the Muslim authorities may recommend the Gospel of Christ.

6) **Pray that the way may be opened for Jordanian and Lebanese believers** to enter for witness into this land, for they would be less under suspicion.

7) **The entry of literature** has been difficult, but since the Lebanese Civil War much more literature has been entering the country legally from Jordan. Pray for the wise and careful distribution of this literature. There are still several Christian bookrooms operating in the counry.

8) **Christian radio broadcasts and follow-up correspondence courses** remain virtually the only avenue for getting the Gospel to these needy people. Pray for the Arabic broadcasts from **TWR** (Monaco and Malta) and **FEBA** (Seychelles).

JORDAN

BACKGROUND

Area: 95,000 sq. km. – but the 5,650 sq. km. West Jordan (part of Palestine) has been under Israeli military occupation since the 1967 "Six Day" War.

Population: 2,800,000 (600,000 in the territory controlled by Israeli). Growth rate 3.3%.

Peoples: **Trans-Jordanian** and **Palestinian Arabs** in about equal numbers, but 42% of the latter still in West Jordan.
              Minorities – recently arrived Lebanese refugees and some Circassians.

Capital: Amman 600,000. Urbanisation 43%.

Economy: Severely crippled by the loss of the West Bank with its rich agricultural produce and lucrative tourist industry, and also the huge influx of Palestinian refugees in 1967 and the lack of oil.

Politics: Constitutional monarchy with King Hussein retaining his throne despite numerous leftist, Palestinian and international plots to overthrow him.

Religion: **Attitude of Government** – great tolerance for the Christian minority for all forms of Christian activity.
              Muslims 90%. **Roman Catholic** and **Eastern Churches** 9%.
              Protestants 0.5%. Community 14,000.
              11 denominations – largest: Arab Episcopal 6,000; Lutherans 1,800 adherents; also Assemblies of God, Nazarenes, Baptists (2), etc.
              Evangelicals 0.25%.

Points for Prayer

1) **The long-lasting Middle East Crisis** has brought 30 years of suffering to Jordan. This has made many nominal Christians and Muslims more open to the Gospel. Pray for a great harvest to be reaped for God in this land.

2) **Many areas are inadequately evangelised** – to mention several: the south of the country, the nomadic Bedouin and the refugee camps.

3) **There has been much Christian work** on the West Bank among the Arabs. Some of this work continues under the Israeli occupation. Pray that there may be fruit for the Lord there despite the tense political situation and the rising influence of the Communists among the Arabs. (See Israel).

4) **The Palestinian Refugees** are embittered by their years of fruitless struggle to regain their lands in Israel. Some have been absorbed into the economic life of Jordan, but others live in refugee camps financed by the United Nations. Jordanian Christians are free to distribute literature and witness in these camps, and some do, but this can be dangerous. Despite the immense difficulties, there are some who have believed in these camps; pray that they may stand for God.

5) **The Protestant Church.** There is much nominalism among the second and third generation Christians in the Episcopal and Lutheran Churches. Yet among the more Evangelical groups there is revival in some congregations and many people are being converted – especially Muslims. The most common source of new converts is from the many home fellowships where the unsaved feel more at ease. Pray that the believers may be sensitive, open and loving to those converted out of a Muslim background, for many of these converts find it hard to settle in a church fellowship.

6) **Outreach by believers** has increased of late. More and more young people have been enthused and involved in door-to-door visitation and tract distribution. The work of **OM** in inspiring Jordanian believers for this has been decisive. Pray for the right Christian leaders to be raised up who can continue to teach young believers how to reach out to others with the Gospel.

7) **Christian leadership** – mature Christian leaders are urgently needed for the many opportunities for ministry that there now are. Unfortunately too many of the best men tend to go to well-evangelised North America.

8) **Missionary work** is still needed and is a great encouragement to the national believers. Great tact and a low profile is needed in these times when a foreigner is under suspicion and often far less free to minister than the nationals. Several missionaries

have recently been expelled. There are now about 14 mission agencies and 60 missionaries in the country. This number is increasing since many literature, radio and other ministries could no longer carry on in strife-torn Lebanon.

9) **Many Lebanese took refuge in Jordan** in 1975–6. Pray that many may be brought to the Lord through their insecurity and sorrow. Many of these people are nominally Christian. Pray that the true believers among them may have courage to testify.

10) **Literature** – Jordan could become the new literature base for the whole Arab World. Jordanian believers have lately been taking Christian literature into such closed lands as Iraq and Saudi Arabia.

11) **The Missionary vision of the believers is growing,** but more could be done. There are already Jordanian believers serving the Lord in secular work all over the Middle East – some in closed in lands such as Saudi Arabia, Yemen, Libya, etc. Others have become well known all over the Arab World as evangelists and radio preachers.

LEBANON

BACKGROUND

Area: 10,400 sq. km. – small land north of Israel; site of Biblical Phoenicia.
Population: 3,100,000. People per sq. km. – 300. About one million people fled to other lands in the 1975–76 Civil War and some are now returning.
Peoples: **Lebanese Arabs** 80%, **Palestinian Arabs** 12%, Armenians and Kurds 5%.
Capital: Beirut 939,000 (before its partial destruction in war). Urbanisation 61%.
Economy: Civil War has played havoc with Lebanon's position as the commercial centre of the Middle East. Enormous destruction will take years to repair.
Politics: Delicate communal balance between Muslims and Christians upset by leftists (mostly Muslim) and refugee Palestinians seeking a power base against Israel which led to the Civil War. Over 60,000 have died. Syrian forces have now destroyed much of the Palestinians' military power and have occupied the country.
Religion: **Attitude of Government** – formerly there was religious liberty – the Syrians may not allow such liberty again.
Muslims 42% (generally the poorer section of community);
Druzes 7% (a Muslim sect).
Maronites (R.C.) 36% (generally wealthier).
Eastern Orthodox (5) 13%.
Protestants 1.4%. Community 40,000. Denominations 15. Largest: Presbyterians 18,000; Baptists (2) 6,000; Nat. Ev. Ch. 6,000.
Evangelical Community 0.5%.

Prayer Targets

1) **The tragic events since 1975** have brought suffering and economic disaster. Pray for a lasting peace and the restoration of religious freedom.

2) **Lebanon was once the most important base for Christian work in the Middle East.** These ministries have been greatly disrupted and many literature, radio and evangelistic organisations have had to move elsewhere. Pray for wisdom for such, as they seek bases in other lands, and also pray for those who hope to return and repair the extensive damage to their properties so as to resume their former activities. (MECO – LEM has moved to Cyprus, literature agencies to Egypt, etc.). Pray also for the strategic radio studios of **FEBA** and **TWR** in Beirut where Arabic programmes are prepared for the whole Middle East.

3) **Missions** – once 45 agencies with 300 missionaries, but now relatively few remain. Pray for the 21 workers of **MECO**. Pray for the right strategy for missions in the new and changed Lebanon. Pray for the opening again of the strategic Lebanon Bible Institute, the only Arabic speaking Bible School in the world.

4) **The national believers** have been shaken out of their complacency and coldness by their sufferings. Many have fled to other lands together with their pastors. Pray for

those who remained that they may have the love of Christ for men and be used to win many to Him – both nominal Christians and Muslims. Pray for the few overworked pastors and their ministry. Pray for the immense work of reconstruction before the believers – many churches were destroyed or damaged. Pray that through this suffering, the Lebanese Church may gain a vision for the evangelising of the Middle East. Pray for the Christian refugees and their witness in such lands.

5) **The Muslims** are embittered and resentful. Pray that their hearts may be made more open for the Gospel, despite the emotional and social barriers. Pray also for the Palestinians and their evangelisation. About 10% of the Protestant Christians are converted out of a Muslim background. Pray that they may win some and be able to help them feel at home in a Christian fellowship.

6) **The Arab peace keeping force** of 30,000 comes largely from unevangelised and closed lands such as Saudi Arabia, Libya, etc. Pray that they may hear the Gospel in Lebanon.

7) **Literature** – pray for the ministries of CALL (Christian Arabic Literature League) and **MECO** in producing much literature for the Arab world – **SU** notes, magazines, books. Pray that this literature may continue to be produced in the quantities needed. Pray also for the Carmel Mission and its work to produce good evangelistic and teaching materials for Muslim readers.

LIBYA

BACKGROUND

Area:	1,760,000 sq. km. – largely desert but for the thin agricultural coastal strip.
Population:	2,500,000. Growth rate 3.7% (0.7% immigration). People per sq. km. – 1.5.
Peoples:	**Libyan Arabs** approx. 76%.
	Berber tribes (4) approx. 4% – including some nomadic Tuareg.
	Expatriate workers 19% from many nations: – Europeans, Pakistanis, Egyptians, Jordanians, Eritreans, etc.
Capital:	Tripoli 500,000. Urbanisation 40%.
Economy	Oil has made the Libyans the wealthiest people in Africa. Oil wealth subsidises all other industries and agriculture, as well as many leftist or Muslim insurrections around the world.
Politics:	The revolutionary government of Col. Ghaddaffi with its zeal for traditional Islamic culture, Arab unification through subversion and destruction of all that originates from the West, is increasingly resented by Libyans and all surrounding nations.
Religion:	**Attitude of Government** – violent opposition to all that could oppose Islam. No form of Christian witness to Libyans is permitted.
	Christians – there are about 10 house churches for expatriates in several centres. Egyptian Copts (3,000?), Pakistanis (1,000+).

Points for Prayer

1) **The land is closed to all normal means of evangelism.** The last remaining outpost of missionary activity was closed in 1960. There is no church or group in which Libyan Christians meet. It is not known if there are now any Christians among the Libyans. Pray for this land to be opened up for the Gospel.

2) **Christian literature** can only enter the country by devious means, due to the strict controls and censorship of mail. This is the only country in N. Africa in which it is virtually impossible to use BCCs.

3) **There are Christians** among the European oilmen and experts, Eritrean and Egyptian technicians and the Pakistani labourers. Pray for the establishment of strong witnessing groups among these people that will reach out to the many unconverted expatriates, many of whom are Muslim. Pray that the believers may gain opportunities to witness to Libyans – not at all easy to find.

4) **Pray for the conversion of Libyans working in other lands.** Some studying in Western universities are being reached by local Christians.

5)   **Christian Radio** is the only direct means of witness to Libyans. Yet even this ministry is of more limited value since it is impossible to help and follow up seekers. Pray for a deep work of the Holy Spirit in the hearts of those hungry for the truth so that they may come to the Lord Jesus.

MAURITANIA

BACKGROUND

Area:	1,030,000 sq. km. + approx. 100,000 sq. km. ceded by Spain in 1976 to Mauritania in the Western Sahara. The land is almost entirely desert but for the north bank of the Senegal River on the southern border.
Population:	1,300,000. Growth rate 1.4%. People per sq. km. – 1.
Peoples:	**Settled Moors** 20%; **Nomadic Moors** 65% speaking a dialect of Arabic, and also some speaking several Berber dialects.
	Africans 14% – three tribes settled along the Senegal River: – Fulas 50,000; Toucouleur 90,000; Soninke 44,000.
Capital:	Nouakchott 70,000. Urbanisation 10%.
Economy:	Very poor underdeveloped country of nomadic pastoralists and subsistence farmers, but some wealth from the large iron ore deposits now being mined.
Politics:	Independent from France in 1960. Acquisition of southern Spanish Sahara has embroiled the country in an expensive war against Saharan insurgents based in Algeria.
Religion:	**Attitude of Government** – an Islamic state and no open mission work allowed. **Muslims** 99%.
	Roman Catholics 5,000 (all expatriates – mostly French).
	Protestants – approx. 20 (all European and African expatriates).

Points for Prayer

1)   **There are no known Mauritanian believers** and no mission work can be carried out among them. Pray for the opening of this land for the Gospel. There are several missions that have been praying for this entrance for years.

2)   **There is one small group of believers** among the expatriates, about half European and half African that meets for fellowship. Pray for the witness of these believers in this unreached land. Pray that a Mauritanian Church may become a reality.

3)   **There are possibilities for witnessing** to Mauritanians in Senegal and Mali, but there are no workers set aside for this ministry. Many Mauritanians visit these lands and others are permanently resident in Senegal.

4)   **Evangelism is further hindered** by the illiteracy of the people and the total lack of any Scriptures in either the local Maure dialect or of the African tribes in the south.

MOROCCO

BACKGROUND

Area:	458,000 sq. km. + further approx. 160,000 sq. km. added in 1976 through Spain's handing over of north and central West Sahara to Morocco.
Population:	18,000,000 (50,000 in Spanish Sahara). Growth rate 2.9%. People per sq. km. – 34.
Peoples:	**Arabs and Arabised Berbers** 59% who largely live in the agricultural north and west.
	Berbers 40% – the original inhabitants of the land who were conquered by the Muslim Arabs 1,300 years ago. There are 3 distinct languages. They live largely in the Atlas Mountains in centre and south.
	Europeans 1%.
Capital:	Rabat 703,000 – Other large cities: Casablanca 1,900,000; Marrakesh 1,650,000; Kenitra 1,415,000; Fez 1,140,000. Urbanisation 37%.

Economy: Overwhelmingly agricultural, but much mining of phosphates in the more barren Sahara and South Morocco where the world's richest phosphate ore deposits are found.

Politics: Constitutional monarchy with the King the supreme religious and civil authority.

Religion: **Attitude of Government** – Islam is the state religion. It refuses to recognise the legality or existence of a Church made up of North Africans.
Islam 98% – it is legally impossible for a Muslim to change his religion.
Roman Catholics 0.7% – almost entirely French and Spanish.
Protestants 0.02% – mostly French (3,000) and possibly only 200 Moroccans; many more secret believers. The number of believers is increasing more now than ever before. Estimated ratio of believers to population **1:500,000.**

Points for Prayer

1)   **The Government has been very hostile to missions.** Legislation passed in 1963 made almost any successful missionary work illegal and nearly all missionaries had to leave. Some missionaries, as individuals, have remained, using teaching, nursing, etc., as a means to remain in order to continue quietly ministering to the believers and contacts of the radio ministry. Pray for both tact and effectiveness for their ministry despite the very many restrictions and the close watch kept by the authorities on all their activities. Pray for the valuable ministry of these brethren in seeking to make disciples. There is opportunity for others to enter for this very personal ministry.

2)   **Pray that this land may be opened up again for the Gospel.** Most of the country has yet to be evangelised. Young people are disenchanted with Islam, but they have few opportunities to hear the Gospel. Pray for a change of attitude in the government.

3)   **The Berber tribes were once Christian,** but were forced to accept Islam. They resent increased efforts to Arabise them and there is something of a revival of the ancient Berber culture and script. Pray that the New Testament revision of one of the languages by **GMU** and others in the old script may cause many to seek for the Truth therein. Pray for the Berber radio programmes prepared by **GMU** in Malaga, Spain for transmission by **TWR** Monaco in two languages of these people. The Berbers have had even less chance than the Arabs to hear the Gospel.

4)   **The national believers** are few and scattered. There are groups to be found in most of the cities, though no organised churches yet. Many of the believers regularly gather from all over the country for conferences; these are a great source of strength to them in their isolation in very hostile situations at home and at work from the large Muslim majority.

5)   **The believers suffer much for their faith.** They face continual ostracism, discrimination and hatred from those around them. It is most difficult to find employment as a Christian. There have even been cases of punishment and imprisonment of some who did not keep the Muslim fast of Ramadan. Pray that they may be protected in all troubles and not compromise through fear of man.

6)   **There are very few Christian families** among the believers because of the common Muslim practice of parents choosing the bride and because of the lack of converted girls. Pray for the establishment of more Christian homes.

7)   **Few leaders in the church groups have had any formal Bible training.** Pray for the few now doing TEE and leadership training courses by post, and for those seeking to help them. There are at least three Moroccan believers who have completed Bible training in other lands and who are now seeking to return to minister. Pray for them and for the right strategy for their ministry.

8)   **The combined Radio and Bible correspondence courses ministry** is the most successful means available for the evangelising of Muslims. Pray for the extensive ministries of **GMU** in Spain and **NAM** in France, in preparing and sending out programmes and literature. Both **TWR** and **ELWA** (SIM) transmit daily Arabic programmes.

9)   **Many Moroccans work in Western Europe,** others are reachable in Gibraltar and the Spanish North African towns of Ceuta and Melilla. Pray for all efforts made to evangelise them in these areas.

SAUDI ARABIA

BACKGROUND

Area: 2,400,000 sq. km. – largely desert and much of the land thinly populated.

Population: 6,400,000. Growing at 2.9% per year. People per sq. km. – 3. Most of the people are nomadic, but rapidly being settled on government agricultural and industrial schemes.

Peoples: **Arabs** approx. 86%.
Negroes 7% – the descendants of African slaves; many still living in slavery today. Slavery is still legal and practised.
Immigrant workers approx. 7% – largely Pakistanis, Iranians, Turks, etc.

Capital: Riyadh 350,000 (Royal capital), Jeddah 300,000 (administrative capital), Mecca 250,000 (religious capital, and centre of the Muslim world).

Economy: Enormous and ambitious development and industrialisation using the vast wealth from exporting oil. The Middle East's largest producer.

Politics: Absolute monarchy under King Khalid with government wisely leading this feudal state into a balanced development for the future.

Religion: **Attitude of Government** – utterly dedicated to the preservation of traditional Islam. All other religions are denied the right to hold meetings or to propagate their faith.
Muslims 98% – the extremist Wahhabi sect has great power.
Christians 1% (?) – only among the expatriates from Pakistan and West. There are no known national Christians.

Points for Prayer

1) **Islam swept away the decadent Christian Church of Arabia** in the 7th Century and now reigns unchallenged. Let us pray that this land may once more hear the Gospel – even in the city of Mecca where no Christian is allowed to enter.

2) **The vast oil wealth is now being used to propagate Islam** all over the world. Mosques are being built with Saudi Arabian money in all continents. It was largely Saudi initiative and money that launched the large Festival of Islam in London in 1976. Pray that the government may accord similar privileges to Christian missionaries that they have themselves claimed in other lands.

3) **The expatriate believers are not officially allowed to hold any meetings.** Pray for those who regularly visit the country to minister to the believers of the various national groups. Pray for their tactful witness to Muslims and that their lives will make the Muslims hungry for the Lord.

4) **There are many opportunities for Christians to enter the land** in secular employment and to use this as a base for witnessing. Pray for those from the West who do so, and also for the entry of others to strengthen this witness.

5) **Pray for all means used to witness to Saudi Arabians** who travel outside their country – some to hospitals in surrounding lands run by Christian missions (Yemen Buraimi Oasis, etc.), others to study overseas. Pray for the planting of a church. Any convert to Christ would probably be killed immediately.

6) **Pray for Christian broadcasts** from FEBA (Seychelles).

SUDAN

BACKGROUND

Area: 2,580,000 sq. km. – desert in north merging into tropical bush in south.

Population: 18,200,000. Annual growth 2.5%. People per sq. km. – 7. Literacy 20%.

Peoples: **Sudan Arabs** and **Nubians** 70% – in the centre and north.
Africans 29% (130 tribes, 47 major languages) – largest: Dinka 2,000,000; Nuer 900,000; Koelib 350,000; living in the south.

Capital: Khartoum 675,000 – other large cities: Omdurman 305,000. Urbanisation 13%.

Economy: Considerable recovery since end of Civil War in 1972 and swing away from
            socialist-Marxist policies. Great agricultural potential.
Politics: Independent of Britain and Egypt in 1956. The present Military government
            came to power in 1969 and negotiated an uneasy peace with the African
            secessionists in the south after 17 years of bitter fighting. The South is now an
            Autonomous Region of the Sudan. President Nimeiry is popular in the south
            but has many enemies in the north (hence many attempted coups).
Religion: **Attitude of Government** – it was attempts at Muslimising the south that
            provoked the Civil War. Now officially religious freedom with no restriction
            on Christian activities in the south.
            Muslims 72% (Arabs and Nubians and a few Africans).
            African Traditionals 20% (Southerners) – many now turning to Christianity.
            Roman Catholics 4% (though possibly double this, in fact).
            Protestants 2.2%. Community 400,000. Denominations 11.
            Largest: Anglicans (Evangelical) 250,000; C.E.C.S. (SIM) ca. 18,000; Pres-
            byterians 8,000; C.C.N.M. (SUM) 4,000; A.I.C. (AIM) 3,000.
            Evangelicals 2% (6% in southern three provinces).

Prayer Targets

1) **Pray for a lasting peace in the land** – much mistrust and extremism still evident.
    Nearly one million died, and one half million became refugees in the Civil War.
    Political changes in Khartoum could lead to renewed fighting.
2) **All missionaries in the south were expelled** in 1964 after years of hard pioneer work,
    with relatively little fruit to be seen. SUM, AIM, MAF, etc., had to withdraw from the
    country, but SIM, CMS and Swiss Nile Ev. Mission retained some work in the
    Khartoum area with some 20 missionaries, from where a valuable work has con-
    tinued and where churches with converts from among Arabs, Nubians and Africans
    grew slowly. Pray for an open door for African and Western missionaries to enter
    again. This looks possible.
3) **ACROSS** (Africa Committee for the Rehabilitation of South Sudan) formed by the
    above missions has been invited by the Government to help in the economic recovery
    of the devastated south. There are now over 65 missionaries serving in specific
    government approved projects such as teaching, agriculture, practical ministries and
    even Bible training and teaching. Pray for the calling of others to take up the many
    opportunities for witnessing and church work within these practical ministries. Pray
    that the goodwill generated by these ministries may open the doors for more
    church-related ministries. Pray for these workers labouring in very difficult and
    unhealthy conditions.
4) **The sufferings of the believers** in the War were great, with many leaders losing their
    lives, churches were destroyed and congregations scattered. The spiritual deepening
    was great in many areas, with revival in some. There has been a marked increase
    among the Anglicans and in the SIM areas, but decline in the Presbyterian areas.
    Large numbers of little churches have sprung up in East Equatoria. The believers
    need much help in their poverty, lack of the Scriptures and lack of education to build
    a sound basis for evangelism and missionary advance.
5) The national believers in the south need prayer for: –
    a) **Leadership** – that the few leaders may prove both mature and faithful in the radically
        changed situation and where clear spiritual leadership is essential.
    b) **Leadership training** has been non-existent for years. SIM opened a Theological
        School in Omdurman in 1975 and now have 43 students. AIM is building a Bible
        School in the S.W. and the Anglicans are now training 10 men for the ministry in
        Juba. The Nubian Mountain region churches (SUM) are hoping to obtain Nigerian
        missionaries to commence a Bible School. These and other projected programmes
        need prayer.
    c) A vision for the **evangelisation of unreached tribes** and the Muslim north.
6) **Bible translation** is much needed in many languages (at least 20). Two languages have
    the Bible, 18 the N.T. and 10 have portions. WBT is entering this field in 1977. Pray
    also for the ministry of the records of GR and Bible portions of SGM.

7)   **Young people** – great opportunities in secondary schools in the south for missionary Scripture teachers and for **SU** work. Pray for the salvation of youth.
8)   Unreached areas and peoples: –
a) **Over 30 tribes** in the south remain unevangelised and many unoccupied. To mention some – Lotuka* 258,000; Topotha 60,000 (**AIM** area); Meban 130,000 (**SIM** area); Koalib 320,000 (**SUM** area); Nuer and Murle 121,000 in Presby. area; also the Dinka.
b) **The Red Sea Coast and Eritrea border** – these Muslim tribes need to be reached. **RSMT** and **MEGM** are negotiating entry. Pray! there are many who oppose this advance.
c) **The large Western Darfur Province** (pop. 1,700,000) bordering on Chad with many Muslim tribes.

SYRIA

BACKGROUND

Area: 186,000 sq. km. – the Golan Heights, adjoining the Sea of Galilee occupied by Israel in the 1967 Six Day War.
Population: 7,600,000. Growth rate – 3.0%. People per sq. km. – 41 (mostly in W. & N.W.).
Peoples: **Arabs 93%, Kurds** (in north east) 4.5%. **Armenians 2%.**
Capital: Damascus 840,000. Urbanisation 44%.
Economy: Poor, with little revenue from oil. Further impoverished by ruinous confrontation with Israel and over-entanglement with Russia.
Politics: Much instability since independence from France in 1949. Very strong Russian presence and influence in Syria was rather weakened by Syria's invasion of Lebanon and attempts to curb the Palestinian terrorist organisations.
Religion: **Attitude of Government** – the large Christian minority has forced the rather hostile Muslim government to give some freedoms to the churches, but more and more pressures being now applied to the Christians.
             Muslims 90% – 5 different sects, but mainly Sunni Muslims.
             Christians 10% – 10 different **Orthodox, Catholic, Nestorian, Jacobite** and **Armenian** Churches that pre-date the Muslim era.
             Protestants 0.2%. Community 22,000.
             9 denominations – Arab Episcopal 6,000; Presbyterian 10,000; Nazarene 1,200; Alliance (**CMA**) 1,500.
             Evangelicals 0.1%.

Points for Prayer

1)   **Syria is one of the most needy countries in the Middle East.** The evangelical Christian witness is very small and localised. Most of the country has never really been evangelised.
2)   **The Muslims are forbidden by law to change their religion.** Pray for the tactful witness of believers to their Muslim neighbours and for eternal fruit through it. Those converted out of Islam usually leave the country for their own safety. Pray that legal and social barriers to conversion to Christ may be broken down.
3)   **Pray for the witness of Lebanese believers** to the many Syrian troops in their land. Pray that the influx of refugees into Syria from Lebanon may give good opportunities for Lebanese believers to witness.
4)   **The Kurdish people** in the north east are unreached; there being only a handful of believers among these Muslim people.
5)   **The Protestant Church** has a measure of freedom and is slowly growing and expanding into new areas. Pray that the believers may make good opportunity of every legal means of witness open to them. There are some fine Syrian leaders in the churches, especially in the Alliance and Nazarene Churches. There are no longer any foreign missionaries permitted to work in the country, so pray especially for these key men, and that others may be raised up by the Lord to serve Him.

6) **There is a spirit of uncertainty and even fear** among the believers due to increasing pressures being put on them by the government. Pray that they may be strengthened by the Lord to stand up to persecution and continue to witness.

7) **There are some very lively Evangelical congregations** among the Armenian people. Pray for the very strong congregation in Aleppo, which is also being pressurised by the authorities.

8) **It has been very hard to import literature into the country,** especially if it was successful! Pray that the new channels being opened up from Jordan for the entry of Christian literature may prove useful.

9) **Christian Radio Programmes** from the Cyprus station of **TWR** Monaco are easily heard in Syria. Pray for the seed sown in many hearts through these programmes.

TUNISIA

BACKGROUND

Area: 164,000 sq. km.
Population: 5,900,000. Growth rate 2.4%. People per sq. km. – 36.
Peoples: **Arabs** 93%, **Berbers** 5%, **Europeans** (French, Italian, British) 1%.
Capital: Tunis 1,000,000. Urbanisation 40%.
Politics: Independent of France in 1956. The pro-Western line of Bourguiba, the ageing President, is not popular with Arab and Third World countries.
Religion: **Attitude of Government** – Islam is the state religion. No open mission work is permitted and there is a strict surveillance of all Christian activities.
                 Muslims 98%. **Roman Catholics** (French and Italians) 0.6%.
                 Protestants – 400 expatriates (Anglicans, French Reformed and Pentecostal). Tunisian believers – around 75 isolated believers, some meeting in little house groups.

Points for Prayer

1) **The land is closed to all open mission work,** though a number of Christians related to several mission groups work in a secular capacity as teachers, nurses, etc. Pray for all their ministries in teaching and helping believers, and following up contacts of radio and literature work. Pray for their spiritual walk in the midst of many frustrations and discouragements, and that their longing for the establishment of a strong, independent, national church may be realised. Pray for the entry of more Christian experts and students from the West and Arab world that would strengthen the Christian witness among the more influential Tunisians.

2) **The believers are very isolated** and all too often weak in their faith. There are only two known Christian families. Most of the believers claim to be Christian, but are afraid to live openly for Christ, and there are others who never really break with the errors of Islam through fear of man. Many backslide when foreign help is no longer available, or when forced into unequal marriages with Muslims. Pray for the establishment of these believers in the faith – especially those who are illiterate. Pray that they may become a strong evangelistic force for the Lord.

3) **There are a few little groups of believers** that meet in Tunisian homes – an essential step if an indigenous church is to come into being. Most of the believers are very isolated.

4) **TEE has been a useful means for instructing** some of the more earnest believers. Pray that other believers may join the programme, and that from this an effective leadership for the church groups may emerge. Pray for those working hard to prepare the teaching materials and help the students.

5) **BCCs were so successful in this land** that the missionaries running it were expelled from the country. Pray for correspondence courses now sent from France and Belgium. There are thousands who have applied for these courses over the last few years. Pray that this may result in new believers being added to the Church.

6) **Literature** has been distributed in considerable quantities in special efforts during

1976. Pray for the continued entry of Christian literature and for fruit from this ministry.

TURKEY

BACKGROUND

Area: 781,000 sq. km. – 3% in Europe, 97% in Asia – a strategically placed land.
Population: 40,200,000. Growth rate 2.6%. Average no. people per sq. km. – 51.
Peoples: **Turks 80%, Kurds** 13%, **Arabs** 5%; **Minorities** of Armenians, Assyrians, Greeks, Georgians, etc. 2%.
Capital: Ankara 1,500,000. Largest city – Istanbul 3,000,000. Urbanisation 20%.
Economy: Agricultural with some industry. Seeking to prepare for E.E.C. membership.
Politics: A republic with parliamentary democracy that rules this remnant of the once mighty Ottoman Empire. The Communist Party is outlawed but the universities are saturated with all shades of Marxist thought among staff and students. Tomorrow's generation is likely to be politically leftist.
Religion: **Attitude of Government** – although secular in law, is very much Islamic in practice and profession.
Moslems 98% officially, but the **Aleirs** (14%) refuse to be recognised as Muslim and their identity with Islam is purely coincidental.
Orthodox and **Roman Catholics** – hardly 100,000 (from Armenian, Assyrian, Greek, Arab and Latin elements). Their numbers are steadily diminishing.
Protestants – barely 1,000, with about half converted, but only about 50 believers out of Islam from the Turk and Kurd majority.

Points for Prayer

1) **Turkey is the largest unreached country in the world.** Some missionary work began in 1821, but was directed to the less resistant minorities. By the 1950's there were only about 10 Turkish believers. Things are changing with more being done to evangelise Turks. Pray for an even greater effort to spread the Gospel.

2) **The 5,500,000 Kurdish people** are even less evangelised than the Turks. There are probably only 2–3 known believers among these people that live in the east.

3) **The non-Muslim minorities** need a spiritual awakening. From among these groups most of the Christians have come. There are a few evangelical congregations among them – mostly in Istanbul (Greek, Armenian) and near the Syrian border (Arabs). Some outstanding Christian leaders have come from these groups. A number are bold witnesses for the Lord. Pray for those who seek to preach the Gospel to them.

4) **There is officially religious freedom** in this secular state, but the law is often not properly applied, due to deep-seated official and public resistance to Christian Truth. Pray for the authorities and for a general change in attitudes.

5) **Teams of young people visit the country every summer** to distribute literature. Great tact is needed because the term "Christian propaganda" is very odious in the press and in the thinking of the people. Readers are invited to send for a correspondence course to a foreign address; some have written. Conversions have come through this effort. Pray for the summer teams, for recipients of literature, for interest to write and the effectiveness of correspondence courses.

6) **Christian literature** – the Bible Society has one store in Istanbul from which an increasing number of Bibles are sold (now about 1,000 per year in Turkish). The present Bible is archaic but no translators can be found. One individual is translating a modern N.T. A Living New Testament is also planned. Pray for the translation, production and effective distribution of the Scriptures. Scriptures are now advertised in a major tabloid on Sunday, and many respond.

7) **The few Turkish believers need much prayer** for they are under constant pressure, in that –

   a) **There are no Turkish speaking churches** –only 3–4 very small and unstable fellowships in several cities. They lack a warm protective fellowship where they can feel at home. Pray for the planting of Turkish churches in all cities.

   b) **Extreme pressures are applied** by families, employers, etc., to those who are known to have become Christians. Thus many of the converts do not abide in Christ because of fear to live openly for the Lord. To most, to be a Turk is to be a Muslim; it is legally impossible for a Muslim to re-register as a Christian. Many have started well, and have even been baptised, but later fall away because of persecution. Pray for perseverance and growth of individual Turkish believers.

   c) **With so few believers, young converts cannot find suitable life partners.** There are only about 3–4 couples united in both faith and matrimony. Most converts are men. Many marry Muslim girls and fall away; a few marry foreign girls. Pray for more Christian homes to be established.

   d) **Many of the converts eventually leave the country** because of the difficulties. Pray that more may be willing to suffer for Jesus and be a witness in this land.

8) **Missionaries are not officially permitted,** but God has raised up a dedicated force of Christian professionals in universities, teaching and medicine who are contributing much to the establishment of a nucleus of the Turkish Church in the major cities. Pray for their continued, fervent but tactful witness, despite much opposition and even eviction from the country. Pray for all involved.

9) **There are 1,500,000 Turks now working in Western Europe** due to the high unemployment and rapidly growing population in Turkey. Here they are much more accessible to Christian workers. There are now over 15 missionaries of **OM, WEC** and others working full time among these migrant labourers – especially among the 1,000,000 in Germany. There are now about 60 converted Turks in European countries as a result. Pray for all involved in this witness and also for the multiplication of Turkish fellowships.

10) **Christian radio** – a rapidly developing ministry. **TWR** has 6 weekly programmes and IBRA 2. Pray for favourable listening conditions and wide outreach through this.

YEMEN ARAB REPUBLIC (North Yemen)

BACKGROUND

Area: 195,000 sq. km. – a very mountainous country in S.W. Arabia.
Population: 6,900,000. Growth rate 2.9%. Population density – 35.
Peoples: Various tribes of Yemeni Arabs, but mixed with Africans on the coast.
Capital: Sana's 90,000. Urbanisation only 7%.
Economy: Very poor and undeveloped and only now beginning to enter the modern world after centuries of isolation. The country has better rains than other parts of Arabia. There is also good mineral potential.
Politics: The 1962 revolution brought in a republican military government that receives much development aid from Russia, China and the U.S.A.
Religion: **Attitude of the Government** – strongly Muslim and against the proselytisation of Muslims by Christian missions.
Muslims 99% – split up into 5 rival sects.
Jews – a few thousand.
Christians – just a handful of Yemeni believers.

Points for Prayer

1) **Praise God that this land has recently opened up** for a limited Christian presence. At the government's request several missions opened up a medical work in 1964 and later. There is constant danger that this door may suddenly close again.

2) **Medical missions** are the only means open for missionaries to minister in this land. There are 4 missions working through 7–8 centres. There are now about 40 Christian

workers in the land who use medicine as a means to show the love of the Lord and to gain opportunities for personal witness. Pray that this ministry may lead to the conversion of potential Christian leaders and the planting of churches.

3) **The spiritual and physical health of the missionaries** is constantly threatened. Temptation to discouragement in the loneliness of being without much Christian fellowship in a hostile Muslim environment and diseases (especially hepatitis) have been acute problems. Pray for these courageous servants of the Lord. Pray for the entry of the right reinforcements.

4) **The Yemeni staff in the hospitals and clinics** are rarely Christians and there are problems at times. Satanic opposition to this ministry takes many forms and must be resisted in prayer.

5) **The original agreement between the government and the missions** expressly permitted personal witness to patients and the handing out of literature. This has now been virtually withdrawn and the missions issued with a directive not to engage in proselytisation. Pray that the missionaries may know how to handle this difficult and delicate situation.

6) **The Yemeni believers** do not have an easy time. Police threats stopped the first and only little fellowship of believers in 1974. Pray for these isolated and lonely believers and for their testimony. May their lives always recommend the Gospel.

7) **Pray for the tactful ministry** of Christian literature and Gospel records that these may bear fruit as people carry them all over the country and beyond.

8) **The people are remarkably interested in hearing the Gospel,** but the cost of discipleship in this staunchly Muslim land is high. Pray that there may be that longed-for harvest in this needy land.

SOUTHERN YEMEN

BACKGROUND

Area: 160,000 sq. km. – occupying the strategic southern tip of the Arabian Peninsula.
Population: 1,700,000. Growth rate 2.9%. People per sq. km. – 11.
Peoples: Mainly Arab, but small minorities of Pakistanis, Indians and Somalis.
Capital: Aden 250,000. Urbanisation 26%.
Economy: The 8-year closure of the Suez Canal and the radical Marxist policies of the government have impoverished the country.
Politics: Soon after Britain had granted independence to Aden in 1967, a coup brought in a hardline Communist regime.
Religion: **Attitude of Government – gradual erosion of the strong position of Islam in favour of atheism.**
               Muslims 98%
               Christians – probably around 240 believers in 3 groups in Aden.

Points for Prayer

1) **All mission work in the country was terminated in 1972** with the nationalisation of all mission and church property by the government. For years a few brave missionaries suffered and witnessed in this land but with very little fruit. Pray that the land may again be opened for the Gospel.

2) **Pray for literature and remembered messages** to bear fruit in the hearts of Muslims who did not repent when the door was open.

3) **The few national believers** still meet where and when they can, though lack of a legal place in which to gather makes it hard to maintain fellowship. They are under considerable pressure from both atheists and Muslims. Pray that they may not give way and compromise their faith or testimony. Pray that they may be used to win others to the Lord.

4) Almost all evangelistic work was done in Aden. **Most of the country has never been evangelised**. Pray for the Hadhramaut in the centre and north east, and for the island of Socotra – for no known Christians live in these areas.

5) **Pray for the Christian radio broadcasts from Seychelles (FEBA)**. There has been a little response from the Hadhramaut.

VI. AFRICA

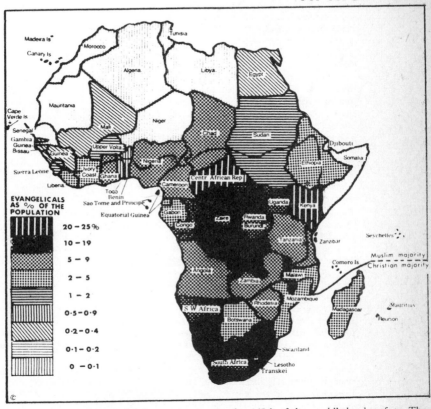

EVANGELICALS AS % OF THE POPULATION	
	20 – 25%
	10 – 19
	5 – 9
	2 – 5
	1 – 2
	0·5 – 0·9
	0·2 – 0·4
	0·1 – 0·2
	0 – 0·1

Area: The whole of the continent occupies 1/5th of the world's land surface. The Sahara Desert separates the Arab North from the African South. (We have therefore included North Africa in the Middle East to which it culturally belongs).
Africa south of the Sahara has an area of 20,865,000 sq. km. (14.6% of land surface of the world). In this region are 49 states or territories, including the 7 Indian Ocean island states and territories.

Population: 313,000,000. Annual growth 2.6%. People per sq. km. – 15
Although 7.7% of the world's population lives in this region, it has 24% of the world's states and territories.

Peoples: Over 1,700 languages are spoken in Sub-Saharan Africa!
Indigenous Peoples – almost entirely Negroid peoples of three major

157

types – West African, Sundanic and Bantu (latter from Cameroon and Kenya southwards). Also the remnants of the pre-Negroid peoples: Pygmies approx. 250,000 in Central Africa.
Bushmen approx. 150,000 in East and Southern Africa.

Immigrant peoples
Europeans 2% (6,000,000) – diminishing and largely found in South Africa and Rhodesia. 1,500,000 living in Black Africa.
Asians 0.5% (1,600,000) – predominantly in South Africa, Kenya and Tanzania. Almost entirely Indians and Pakistanis. Also possibly 70,000 Chinese – mostly from Communist China.
Arab/Berber peoples 950,000 – East African coast and Sahel region. This figure also includes the non-immigrant Sahara Desert Tuareg (750,000).
Urbanisation – 18%. Only 7 of the world's 163 cities of over one million are here.

Economy: Underdeveloped and generally poor. Most people still live on the land, but there is an accelerated drift to the urban areas where there is often high unemployment. Only 2% of the world's industrial production comes from Africa – and most of this from White ruled Rhodesia and South Africa. Some areas (especially nations with large oil reserves) have good prospects for economic growth (Nigeria, Gabon, etc.), while others are doomed to permanent poverty due to their lack of natural resources, distance from the sea and periodic devastating droughts. This latter is expecially true of the Sahel lands, (Mali, Niger, Chad, Upper Volta) and the Horn of Africa (Ethiopia and Somalia) where up to 300,000 people have died in the famines of the last 10 years.

Politics: Black Africa's isolation from the rest of the world ended in the "Scramble for Africa" by the European colonial powers in the last century. For all its faults, the 100 years of colonial rule brought peace, education, better health services and some economic development. In the short space of 20 years since 1957, independence under Black African government has come to all but South West Africa, Rhodesia, South Africa, Mayotte (Comoros) and Reunion, but probably by the end of 1978 South West Africa will become Namibia and Rhodesia will become Zimbabwe.
Independence has brought many problems – let us bear these in mind as we pray for the evangelisation of this great continent.

1)   **Colonially drawn frontiers** cut across racial, cultural and tribal boundaries, making some countries ungovernable or economically unviable. Many of the tensions in the continent today are due to this fact – Somali belligerence; Zairan instability; Sudanese, Nigerian and Ethiopian civil wars; the fighting over the former Spanish Sahara, etc. Tribalism is a curse in Africa.

2)   **Economic weaknesses** lead to "neo-colonialism" (economic dominance and exploitation by industrial nations), and also to resentments against foreign trading interests of Greeks, Lebanese and Indians, etc. The very unequal distribution of wealth in independent countries leads to social unrest and dictatorial regimes, as well as giving ideologies such as Communism opportunities to interfere.

3)   **Nationalism** is leading to the rejection of much of Western culture and a search for African identity. This has led to the rejection of Christianity by some governments and the persecution of believers, such as has occurred in Zaire, Chad and Equatorial Guinea.

4)   **The political importance of Africa.** The massive African vote in the United Nations (out of all proportion to its population size or economic power) leads to the wooing of these states by the contending power blocs of the world. This is also leading to increasing interference by the Communist powers militarily and economically – especially evidenced in the Russo-Cuban subjugation of Angola, etc. This interference is aided by the many tensions in Africa today – the intensifying confrontation between Black and White in Southern Africa, the Arab-African tensions in East Africa, etc. Africa is now of strategic importance in the world.

Religion: **African Traditionalists** 22.6% – in decline before advances of Islam and Christianity, but often the new religion is a thin veneer over the old fears of witchcraft and spirits and the worship of ancestors.

Muslims 25.6% – 81,000,000 south of the Sahara, and a further 100,000,000 in North Africa (included in the Middle East in this survey). The Islamic faith is strongly held in parts of the Horn of Africa (Somalia, Ethiopia), and in parts of West Africa, but generally rather weakened by heathen customs and nominalism. Islam has shown little expansion in East Africa, but in the West there have been considerable advances. The slowdown of this advance after the 1960 rush for independence has ended with the 1974 Oil Crisis, with dramatic gains in the winning of leading politicians (the presidents of Gabon and Central African Republic), and whole communities right across the Sahel belt from Senegal to N. Zaire. This presents a great challenge to Christians that they both pray for and seek to win the uncommitted peoples across Africa.

Hindus 0.4% – largely in the Indian communities of East and South Africa.

Christians 52% – over half the region is now, at least nominally, Christian, with the percentage rising steadily. There were about 9,000,000 Christians of all types in 1900, but now there are 161,000,000 (though only possibly 10% of this number would have experienced the new birth!). These Christians are divided thus:–

Roman Catholics 21% – rapid growth through massive infusion of money and manpower and use of institutions. Generally very weak and lacking in African leadership.

Orthodox 4% – almost entirely in Ethiopia. Largely corrupt and decadent, and many "Christians" giving considerable support to the Communist leaders of the country. There is a small evangelical wing. There are some Orthodox in East and South Africa.

African Independent Churches 7% – a bewildering assortment of nearly 6,000 denominations found predominantly in East Africa, South Africa, Rhodesia, Zaire, Nigeria and Ghana. Some have an evangelical theology, but the majority are more or less syncretic, with very little knowledge of the way of salvation. Some are breakaways from mission-founded denominations, others have risen in protest against the breakdown of African customs before Western Christianity. The growth of these churches is significantly large.

Protestants 20% – with rapid growth over the last decade – especially in Nigeria, Kenya and Central Africa.

Evangelicals 8.5%.

Missionaries to Africa 14,100.

Missionaries from Black Africa 1,830.

i.e. one missionary for every 20,200 people.

Some of the Major Problems the Protestant Church faces

1) **Theology** – the traditional theological liberalism that has so plagued the Western World has had little direct impact on Africa, though about one third of all missionaries are of this persuasion, but their overall influence has speeded the growth of a nominally orthodox Protestantism that lends itself to political action and non Biblical theologies such as:– **Black Theology** – the humanistic theology of the Black Power movement that equates political liberation with salvation. **African Theology** – the attempts to find God in the pre-Christian religions of Africa rather than in the Bible. This leads to syncretism and universalism (i.e., mixing heathenism with Christianity and also saying that all will ultimately be saved).

   There is a great need for strong Evangelical theologians in Africa who are able to express the eternal and universal Bible truths in a way that meets Africa's need.

2) **The impact of politics in Africa** with the tendency to totalitarian governments (Marxist or nationalist dictatorships) has brought many crises to the churches – to compromise, or to be sidetracked from the real task of preaching the Gospel and building up the believers. The increasing amount of persecution endured by believers

makes it imperative that the churches be more adequately prepared for such. In the last 15 years, Christians have been martyred for their faith in at least 12 countries.

3) **The lack of maturity** – too few leaders of calibre, and a great lack of stable lay leadership. This has led to limited results from **New Life For All** (EiD) in all but a few areas. This has also led to tensions between missions and the churches (among other things), and also serious administrative and financial problems in many areas.

4) **Nominalism** – partly due to the huge numbers coming into the churches with inadequate counselling and discipling, and partly due to the past over-emphasis on education, health and social programmes at the expense of careful church planting and leadership training. Few denominations are free from this problem – including good evangelical denominations. Much must be done in helping the churches overcome these problems and build a solid base of strong congregations for future expansion under all circumstances.

5) **Divisions** – one of the tragedies in Africa is the extreme denominational confusion in most countries. Not only have all the national and doctrinal divisions of the West been imported, but also frequent African divisions over personality and tribal differences have further confused the situation. Denominational barriers are often high and there is little understanding of the spiritual unity of all true believers based on the Scriptures.

The Challenge of Africa Today

In the midst of revolutionary change, insurmountable problems and great insecurity, there is an unparalleled spiritual hunger that will need far greater material and manpower resources from African and other Christians to satisfy it. The Church has consistently grown at about 3.8% every year over the last 77 years, but this growth has not always been healthy, and the Church will need much external encouragement in order to finish the task of evangelising the continent and to gain a real missionary vision. The talk of a "moratorium of missions" (the total withdrawal of all missions from the continent in order to help the Church to a true independence) is neither Scriptural nor wise. There is therefore a continuing need for missionaries of a high calibre for all forms of Christian witness and there are many unfilled opportunities despite some closing doors.

Needy Areas and Peoples

There is now no country in Sub-Sahara Africa without a witness for the Lord – though the witness is very small in 10 lands – Comoros, Djibouti, Gambia, Guinea, Mauritius, Niger, Reunion, Senegal, Seychelles and Somakar – all have less than 0.5% Evangelicals and must be considered as pioneer fields. Large parts of another 11 countries have areas that must also be pioneered for Christ – Benin, Angola, N. Chad, Ethiopia, N. Gabon, N. Ivory Coast, Madagascar, N. Mozambique, Togo, Upper Volta, Mali and Guinea Bissau.

There are now 4 of these lands closed for all missionary work – Equatorial Guinea, Mozambique, Somalia and Sao Tomé. There are another 11 that are now very difficult to enter and where the doors may soon be totally shut for missionaries. The other 35 lands are more or less open for missionaries, though governments are increasingly selective in the qualifications they require for new missionaries.

Much has yet to be done in translation of the Bible – only 190 of the 1,700 languages in these lands have even a New Testament. Many languages may not warrant the effort of translation, but at least 200 languages definitely need translators and a further 200 are now being translated.

The Urgency of the Hour

The dramatic penetration of Communism into Africa over the last decade picked up momentum with the sudden collapse of the Portuguese Empire in 1975. There are now 4 openly Communist regimes in Africa – Congo (since 1970), Mozambique and Angola (1975), Ethiopia (1976) with a total population of 45,700,000. There are a further 6 lands, at least, who are committed to a Marxist form of government (Somalia, Benin, Sao Tomé, Guinea, Guinea-Bissau, Madagascar and Zanzibar) with a further 19,700,000 people. The spectre of Communism hangs over such lands as Rhodesia, Malawi, South West Africa, etc. This must determine our strategy as we seek to pray and work for the evangelisation of this continent. The situation is dark, but not discouraging, for the Gospel has been rooted in Africa and all the forces of hell will not be able to blot out the Church of the Lord Jesus Christ! We must seize the opportunities that we have – and these are many!

The Missionary Vision of the Church in Africa

It is not recognised by many believers that much of the pioneering of new fields in Africa over the last 100 years has been done by humble and dedicated African missionaries who have crossed tribal and national boundaries to evangelise tribes not their own. It is impossible to measure their number – possibly 1,830, but may be up to 3,000 are now serving as missionaries (if we include part time missionaries such as are common in Ethiopia). The largest missionary outreach is found in Nigeria, Ethiopia and Cameroon. This vision could be increased but more teaching is needed (most regard missionary work as the work of Europeans). There are also, as yet, few facilities for the training of potential missionaries, though a start is being made in Ghana by **WEC**, Liberia by others and so on.

ANGOLA

BACKGROUND

Area: 1,250,000 sq. km. – Atlantic coastal state that dominates Zaire's and Zambia's trade routes to the Atlantic.
Population: 6,400,000. Annual growth 1.6%. People per sq. km. – 5. Literacy – 30%.
Peoples: **African tribes** – 30 – the largest: Ovimbundu 2,000,000; Kimbundu 1,800,000; Kongo 1,000,000; Chokwe-Lunda 700,000; Ovambo 125,000. **Minorities** – Cubans 20,000. Virtually all the 500,000 Portuguese and Mixed race have left the country.
Capital: Luanda 400,000. Urbanisation 15%.
Economy: Potentially rich in agriculture and minerals and underpopulated, yet economy in ruins, with little prospect of early recovery.
Politics: A Portuguese colony for 400 years; independent in 1975. Nationalist movements fought the Portuguese for 15 years before independence and then each other in a bitter civil war that still continues (March 1977). Communist arms and Cuban troops have ensured the installation of a Marxist minority regime in Luanda.
Religion: **Attitude of Government** – increasingly hostile to Christianity. All religious statistics are only estimations due to national confusion.
             Roman Catholics 60%. African Traditionals 22%.
             Protestants 18%. Community 800,000. Denominations 9; the largest:– Evang. Church of C. Angola (United Church of Canada) 300,000; Methodists 80,000; Baptists (3) 150,000 (?); Christian Brethren 40,000; Evang. Church of S. Angola (**AEF**) 20,000; Filafrican Mission (Swiss) 20,000. Evangelicals 7%.

Prayer Targets

1) **This unhappy land, conquered by Communist arms,** faces the prospects of a long-drawn-out guerrilla war, famine and suffering. Great brutality has been shown by Communist soldiers on all who oppose them, with reports of massacres, etc. Pray for the unfortunate people of this land – that they may find comfort in the Gospel.

2) **Missions** – there are now only a handful of missionaries holding on in the country. The entry of missionaries during Portuguese rule was becoming increasingly difficult, and in 1970 there were only 70 missionaries. Only a minority of the missions have been completely Evangelical – the best known being the Christian Brethren in the centre and north east and **AEF** in the south. Hence much missionary work remains undone – both in pioneer work and in church planting and Bible training. Pray for the complete evangelisation of this land.

3) **Christian work was gravely interrupted** and hindered by the war of independence. The Baptist work in the north collapsed with the withdrawal of missionaries and the destruction of life and property. Many of the Christians fled to Zaire. Both the Brethren and **AEF** work was greatly restricted. Yet in 1975 there was a dramatic period of consolidation and church growth, with a great hunger for spiritual things. Pray for the many young Christians and little churches with few trained leaders who may now face the full onslaught of atheistic persecution.

4) **The persecution of believers** seems to be confined to some areas – a number of Methodist and Brethren leaders have been killed and congregations intimidated. Many Christians have lost their lives because of belonging to tribes considered hostile to the Luanda regime. Yet in other areas there is still much freedom to meet together for worship and to evangelise. Yet these believers need prayer as they face a future without outside help – whether Bible teaching, availability of Bibles, etc. Few leaders in the churches have had much education.

5) **Many of the churches were rather nominal** – especially in the Luanda area and to the south and north. Pray that the present sufferings may bring many to a living faith.

6) **Unreached peoples** –
  a) Many pockets of people have never been evangelised due to the extraordinary difficulties missionaries have experienced all through the years in moving around the country.
  b) Several tribes are both unreached and without a witness – the Bushmen (14,000); Kwangale (30,000) and Mbukushu (10,000) in the south east corner of Angola. Others are only partially evangelised – Mbwela (140,000) in the south (**AEF**) and Chokwe (450,000) in the east (Brethren).

7) **The Portuguese** have fled to Portugal, Brazil and South Africa for refuge. Few were born again believers. Pray that their tragic experiences may open many hearts to the Lord. Pray also for the many Africans, who have sought refuge in S.W.A. (Namibia), Zambia and Zaire from the massacres, that they also may turn to the Lord.

Footnote: June, 1977. There have been some relaxations on the entry and activities of missionaries, and considerable freedom for believers in the west of the country of late.

<u>BENIN</u> (formerly Dahomey)

BACKGROUND

Area:	113,000 sq. km. – a long, narrow country wedged between Nigeria and Togo.
Population:	3,200,000. Annual growth 2.7%. People per sq. km. – 28, denser at the coast.
Peoples:	African Tribes – 19. In south – Fon 1,200,000; Gun-Tofi 220,000; centre – Egba (Yoruba) 400,000; north – Bariba 550,000; Somba 100,000; Fulani 80,000; Dendi 35,000; Gurma 30,000; Dompago 20,000.
Capital:	Porto Novo 100,000 and Cotonou 250,000. Urbanisation 15%. Literacy 5%.
Economy:	Poor and underdeveloped with most people engaged in subsistence farming.
Politics:	Independent from France in 1960. The 5th coup since independence brought the present military government to power. Government recently espoused Marxism-Leninism as country's guide. Marxist policies being implemented.
Religion:	**Attitude of Government** – increasing pressures on churches and missions with limitation on some activities, nationalisation threats and pressures for ideological conformity, despite claims to support religious freedom.
	African Traditionals 64%. **Muslims** 14%.
	Roman Catholics 17%.
	Protestants 4%. Community 67,000.
	Denominations 5 – Methodists 40,000 community; Evangelical Ch. (**SIM**) 12,000; also Assemblies of God and Southern Baptists.
	Evangelicals 1%.

Points for Prayer

1) **This land is another tragic case of a missed opportunity** for the Gospel. The door to

missions is being gradually closed, but the witness has only recently begun and most of the tribes in the land are in need of pioneer evangelism and church planting. Pray that the way may be fully opened for a new evangelistic initiative.

2) **Missions.** For years the Methodists have had a localised witness in several tribes in the south, but this work is rather stagnant and little was done to reach out to other tribes. Since 1946 the **SIM** and Assemblies of God have made a great effort in the north and centre of the country. **SIM** has 40 missionaries in 11 centres. The missionaries need much prayer for they face many pressures – lack of personnel for institutions and ministry, pressures from the authorities and also a ban on all visits to the villages. There are now about 70 missionaries in the land.

3) **Unreached people** – only a small proportion of the population has been evangelised –
   a) **Southern animistic tribes**, especially the large Fon people in their bondage to a powerful form of witchcraft, were neglected for many years, but now the Assemblies of God have begun to witness among them. There are only a few hundred believers. Pray also for the A.o.G. work among the Tofi* (35,000).
   b) **The many tribes in the centre and north** now beginning to be influenced by Islam. The **SIM** and A.o.G. seek to reach the following: Bariba*, Busa*, 25,000, Dompago Somba*, Egba, Nyantruki 5,000, Mokole 8,000 and Soruba* 6,000.
   c) **The Islamised tribes** – Fulani (there are several hundred believers now among them), Dendi, Gbzantche 10,000 and Winji Winji 5,000.

4) **The churches** are strongest among the Dompago, Bariba and Kilinga and growing fast among the Busa. Pray for wisdom for the leaders in these days of difficult decisions of principle when facing an atheistic system. Pray for the raising up of more leaders well versed in the Scriptures – little has yet been done in training full time workers. There are two small Bible Schools. Pray for a greater evangelistic concern and outreach to other tribes. Believers have a good testimony through the economic, agricultural and family betterment the Gospel gives. Pray for the important ministry of **SIM** in improving agricultural methods and introducing better crops and livestock.

5) **There is a growing work in the cities and towns** – especially among young people. The **SIM**, A.o.G. and Baptists all have work in the growing metropolis of Cotonou and elsewhere. Young people are open to the Word, but are coming under increasing ideological pressure and conflict.

6) **Bible translation** is a very great need. Linguists are needed for more than 5 tribes. Work is in progress in 8 – there are 4 **SIM** translation teams operating. Three languages have the whole Bible, two the N.T. and four have portions only. There are acute difficulties being placed in the way of this ministry. Pray that all projects for translation may soon be brought to completion and the Word of God to be placed in the hands of the people while there is opportunity.

BOTSWANA

BACKGROUND

Area:	600,000 sq. km. – very dry; Kalahari Desert occupies centre east and south.
Population:	750,000. Annual growth 2.3%. People per sq. km. – 1.
Peoples:	**Tswana** 71%.
	Minority tribes 21%. Kalanga 150,000; Subia 4,000; Yeyi 8,000; Mbukushu 3,400; Herero 11,000 – all in the less developed northern half.
	Bushmen 35,000 – 5 different tribes speaking different languages.
Capital:	Gaberone 35,000. Urbanisation 13%. Literacy 30%.
Economy:	Very poor due to lack of water and development, though great potential as valuable minerals begin to be exploited – diamonds and copper, etc..
Politics:	Independent of Britain in 1966. Seretse Khama's government one of Africa's most stable and working hard to lessen country's dependence on S. Africa for trade and employment of a large proportion of the work force.
Religion:	**Attitude of Government** – freedom of religion, though local chiefs have a powerful voice in all religious activities in their own areas.
	African Traditionals 60%.

African Indep. Churches (16) 5%.
Roman Catholics 6%.
Protestants 26%. Community 172,000. Denominations 16. Largest – Congregational (LMS) 20,000. Lutheran 50,000; Dutch Reformed Church in Africa (DRC) 21,000; Assemblies of God 3,000; Baptists 800. Evangelicals 3%.

Points for Prayer

1) **The Tswana people** were the first African tribe in Southern Africa to hear the Gospel and a great turning to God occurred in the last century through the LMS from England. Modern theology among later missionaries stunted further development of the Church and little real spiritual life remains in the daughter Church; only 11 ageing pastors remain and many congregations have seriously declined in numbers. The Tswana are Christian in name, but actually given over to immorality and drunkenness that is accentuated by the breakdown of family life and poverty. Other missions followed late in the last century, but nominalism is also a problem with these churches because each became virtually the "state church" of the tribe that welcomed that particular group. Pray for revival and a reversal of the moral collapse.

2) **Unreached peoples** – many of the Tswana of this generation have never heard the Gospel. Pray also for the following:–
   a) **The Bushmen** – now many efforts are being made to evangelise these elusive desert nomads. Pray for the work of the DRC, **AEF** and Lutheran missionaries seeking to win them for the Lord. Unlike neighbouring South West Africa, there is not yet an emerging church among them.
   b) **The Kalanga** resent the cultural domination of the Tswana. There is no Kalanga speaking congregation of believers in the country, apart from some African Independent Churches.
   c) **The northern tribes** have never been evangelised – Yeyi, Mbukushu and Subia.

3) **The last 10 years has been a time of a new evangelical penetration** – pray for the small but growing work of the Assemblies of God (with one Bible School – the only one in the land), Baptists, Swedish Holiness and **AEF** (each with 2 – 8 missionaries). Pray for their evangelistic outreach and church planting ministries. Pray also for the older work of the DRC from two stations in the Mochudi area. Pray for the spreading of the Gospel through these Missions and their institutions. Pray for the development of a strong national Church that is based on the Bible.

4) **Young people** – a most needy section of the population. Immorality, even among the very young, is so prevalent that it is very hard for a young person to follow the Lord. Pray for the witness of SU, newly started by a Rhodesian African staff worker. There are 23 secondary schools, some very atheistic indeed.

5) **There is a critical lack of full time workers** due to the poverty of the congregations, lack of training facilities and the enormous difficulties for those who seek to evangelise this semi-nomadic and scattered people. Pray for the calling of national and missionary workers (latter numbering about 45) to reach this land for Christ.

<u>BURUNDI</u>

BACKGROUND

Area: 27,600 sq. km. – a mountainous country very similar to Rwanda to the north.
Population: 4,000,000 – Growing at 2.4% per year. People per sq. km. – 145 – very overpopulated.
Peoples: **Tutsi** 15% – unlike Rwanda, this minority tribe is politically dominant.
Hutu 84% – it is reckoned that 200,000 died in the 1972 revolt and following reprisals.
Twa 1% – a small pygmy tribe.
Capital: Bujumbura 150,000.
Economy: Probably the poorest country in the world with few natural resources and so overpopulated that there is little chance for improvement.

Politics: The land gained independence from Belgium in 1962. The King was replaced in a coup by a military government. An abortive Hutu revolt in 1972 was followed by massive reprisals so that very few Hutu intellectuals or leaders remain in the country. The army is totally Tutsi.

Religion: **Attitude of Government** – there is freedom of religion.

African Traditionals 33%.

Roman Catholics 60% – mostly nominal, but there are signs of real spiritual life in some sections of this Church.

Protestants 7%. Community 270,000. Denominations 9 – Pentecostals (Swedish) 180,000; Anglicans (Rwanda Mission) 48,000; Free Methodists (U.S.A.) 6,000; Baptists (Danish) 8,000; Friends 5,000; World Gospel Church 2,000. The SDAs are strong. Evangelicals 6%.

Points for prayer

1) **The political situation** greatly affects the churches. The country is quiet now but the scars of the terrible events of 1972 remain. Widows and orphans are many and are in need of the love and help of the believers and missionaries. Pray for the various help programmes of AID, **WV** and **TEAR Fund** channelled through the churches.

2) **The Christians need to be a channel of reconciliation** between the Hutu and Tutsi. Pray for a spirit of love and forgiveness between the believers of both tribes. Pray that the church may be delivered from fear so that it may exercise a prophetic ministry in the land.

3) **The church needs to be stirred** again with revival, for the East African Revival exerted a powerful influence on many over the last 30 years. As the country grows relatively poorer, the churches are often crippled by poverty; of those who could give more for the work of the churches, few give as they should.

4) **The leadership in the churches** – there are a few outstanding men of God, but the majority are still deeply affected by the troubles and are fearful (some of the denominations lost nearly all their pastors in 1972). There is also need for a deeper love and trust between the church leaders and the missionaries.

5) **Praise God for the freedom to preach the Gospel** throughout Burundi. A church leader, recently appointed to a position of great responsibility, was at the 1974 Lausanne Conference and he has a great vision for evangelism. Pray that he may be able to communicate this vision to other leaders and ordinary church members.

6) **Unreached peoples** – there is only one small tribe in this category – the Pygmy Twa. Pray for the outreach of the Anglicans and others to this elusive people among whom are yet very few believers. There are also a few areas in the country that have not yet a settled evangelical witness.

7) **There is a wonderful degree of love** and fellowship between the 170 missionaries in 8 societies serving the different churches, all of whom are evangelical. There are great needs for more personnel – especially in medical work – only 2 of the 7 mission hospitals in the country are manned by doctors. There is a need for more Bible teachers and youth workers.

8) **The World Gospel Mission** run a Bible School that is used by four churches for the training of men for the ministry. The Rwanda Mission also run a Theological School.

9) **Praise God that the Christian Radio station** in Bujumbura, Radio CORDAC, is free to broadcast the Gospel. It is widely heard in East Africa and Zaire with an increasing audience. Pray for the follow-up work, and that the churches may become more aware of their privilege and responsibility to help and share in this ministry.

CAMEROON

BACKGROUND

Area: 474,000 sq. km. – north semi-arid, centre dry grasslands, rain-forest in south.

Population: 6,500,000. Growing at 1.8% per year. People per sq. km. – 14.

Peoples: **African** – 183 tribes, most very small.

Major groups – in south:– Ewondo (200,000), Bulu (220,000); in west:–
Bamileke (920,000); and in the north:– the largely Muslim Fulani (400,000).

Capital: Yaounde 180,000. Urbanisation 22%. Also Dovola 260,000.
Economy: Considerable efforts are being made to develop land with foreign aid.
Politics: Independent of France and Britain in 1960–61. Stable government under
President Ahidjo since 1958. He and many in the government are Muslims.
Religion: **Attitude of Government** – freedom of religion, but some pressures on Chris-
tians from the government and harassment by local authorities and Muslims in
the north.
African Traditionals 30%.
Muslims 18% – mostly in the centre and north.
Roman Catholics 27%.
Protestants 25%. Community 1,000,000. Membership 450,000. Major
denominations:– in west (English speaking) Presbyterians 90,000 members;
Baptists 30,000; and in east (French speaking) Ev. Miss Soc. 140,000: Pres-
byterians 85,000; Ev. Lutheran 40,000; Baptists 16,000.
Evangelicals 8%.

Points for Prayer

1) **There is an open door for the Gospel** in this strategically important land. Pray that the
Church worldwide may make full use of it to win the undecided for Christ.

2) **Islam is politically powerful.** It is socially expedient and its tolerance of polygamy
convenient for many to accept Islam as a veneer over their witchcraft and spirit
worship. There are 8 Muslim tribes in the north and others rapidly becoming
so – notably the Fulani (40% Muslim), Mbum 20,000 (60% Muslim) and Fali 50,000
(80%Muslim). Pray for missions working among these difficult tribes (**SUM** and
several evangelical denominational missions) that their ministry may lead to strong
churches being planted – especially among those not yet committed to Islam. Pray
for a greater concern among Cameroon Christians for the winning of Muslims.

3) **The Fulani are an important people** numbering about 5,000,000 across West Africa.
They once conquered the whole Sahel region from Senegal to Cameroon, and are
now a strongly Muslim ruling class in some areas, or weakly Muslim nomadic
pastoralists. If these influential people could be won for Christ, all of West Africa
would hear of it. There are very few Christians among them (in Benin, Nigeria,
Upper Volta and Cameroon). Pray for their evangelisation in Cameroon, where
many are still animist. Pray for the work of **SUM** and the Lutherans (the latter
through excellent daily Fulani broadcasts) among them. These broadcasts are opening the Fulani to the Gospel. Pray for successful follow-up, and integration of
contacts into witnessing churches.

4) **Unreached animist tribes** – more than 25 in this category and totalling 1,000,000
people. Pray for the effective evangelisation of these uncommitted people – mostly
in the centre of the country. Nearly all have now a resident evangelical witness (**SUM**
+ denominations). Pray especially for the Gude* 110,000; Kapsiki 40,000;
Makatam 150,000; Mambila* 45,000 who are still resistant to the Gospel.

5) **The believers in N. Cameroon** are an occasionally persecuted minority. Pray for their
deliverance from fear to testify and claim their rights as citizens. Pray that they may
influence their Muslim neighbours and lead them to salvation.

6) **Bible translation** is in progress in 20 tribes (**WBT** in 14). Five languages have the
Bible, 18 the N.T. and 25 have Gospels, etc. Pray for those engaged in this arduous
task. Pray for wisdom as to which languages ought to be translated – there are so
many small tribes. Pray that more nationals may be raised up for this ministry.

7) **The majority of the people in the south are "Christian"**, but many churches are
formal, clerical and increasingly non-Biblical in theology and too few preachers
preach repentance. The churches need to be brought to true repentance and then
mobilised for evangelism. The two main cities of Yaounde and Douala need to be
evangelised. The latter has virtually no evangelical witness.

8) **The churches need revival.** Pray for the raising up of spiritual men to preach and teach
the whole counsel of God in the churches. Pray for the newly started National Centre

for Evangelism (1977) – a permanent training centre for the training of evangelists – that this may fill the real need. **New Life For All** was useful in areas where there were good men to follow up contacts.

a) **Missionary personnel** (around 300 in 14 societies; two being interdenominational – **SUM**, Norwegian and Swiss Branch, and **WBT**). Many more workers are needed while the doors remain open – especially in the teaching ministry, training of pastors, medical work, Bible translation, etc. There are only a few African missionaries serving in Cameroon – several from Nigeria.

CENTRAL AFRICAN EMPIRE

BACKGROUND

Area: 625,000 sq. km. – a hot, dry, remote and inaccessible country.

Population: 2,370,000 – growing at 2.1%. Population density per sq. km. – 4.

Peoples: **African tribes** – 24, with most speaking the trade language Sango. Major groups – Mandja and Baya in west, Banda in centre, Zande in east.

Capital: Bangui 320,000. Urbanisation 29%.

Economy: Very poor and undeveloped due to lack of communications with distant sea.

Politics: A republic that is ruled as a personal empire by the life-President, Bokassa, since the military coup of 1966. Declared an Empire in 1977.

Religion: **Attitude of Government** – there is complete freedom of religion, though the conversion of the President to Islam may lead to changes.

African Traditionals 7%.

Muslim 6% – two small Muslim tribes and a sprinkling of Muslims in most other tribes.

Roman Catholics 36%. **African Independent Churches** 1%.

Protestants 46%. Community 680,000. Denominations 10. Almost entirely evangelical. Largest groups:– Evangelical Brethren 120,000 community (in the centre of country): Baptists (Mid-Missions – U.S.A.) 90,000 (centre and east); Baptists (Swedish Orebro) 79,000 (west; Evangelical C.A. (**AIM**) 9,000 (east).

Evangelicals 27%.

Points for Prayer

1) **Few countries have been better evangelised** by evangelical missions. There is an evangelical witness in nearly every tribe and district. The major task is now to consolidate the work, train leaders and translate the Scriptures.

2) **The churches have been growing fast** and the **New Life for All** campaign was very effective in getting the Gospel into unreached and hard areas and many new churches were planted. Pray that the Church may retain the evangelistic fire and grow to spiritual maturity. There are not enough mature, trained leaders for the churches.

3) **The missions** have played a very important role in developing schools, hospitals, vocational and agricultural schools as well as in planting churches, translating the Scriptures, etc. There are now about 190 missionaries. Pray for their health and spiritual keenness in an enervating climate. There are many opportunities for more missionary Bible teachers and those with special skills.

4) **Leadership training** – there are a number of Bible Schools run by the various churches for which there is the constant need for adequate national and expatriate staff. Pray that the right students may be called and that those trained may go out as spiritual and effective Christian workers. The large, underpopulated land makes TEE an essential tool for training local leaders, but much work must still be done to launch this programme all over the country.

5) **The Bangui Evangelical School** of Theology opens in 1977. This worthy project is supported by the AEAM (Association of Evangelicals in Africa and Madagascar) to cater for the need of a degree-level training for all the churches in French speaking Africa. Pray for the staff as they launch this. Pray for the calling of the right students

from all over Africa. It is planned to have 50 resident students eventually, and also to run an advanced TEE course by post.

6) **Bible translation** – only one language (Sango) has the whole Bible, a further 7 have the N.T., and a further 9 have some Gospels. Very much remains to be done. Pray for those engaged in this ministry and pray for the raising up of national and expatriate translators for the work yet to be tackled.

7) **The development of secondary and university education** means that more must be done to meet the spiritual needs of students. Pray for the GBU **(IVF)** group in Bangui, and also for the development of a strong interdenominational witness in the schools.

8) **Several African sects are causing trouble** to the churches with their mixture of Christianity, Islam and witchcraft. Many Christians are still not delivered from the fear of witchcraft, and can be led astray. Pray for wisdom among the church leaders and a Bible-based stability among the believers.

9) **Islam has not been influential**, but with the conversion of the President to Islam and the influx of many Fulani from West Africa over the last few years, this could change. Pray that the believers may be ready and able to handle the new situation, and have a concern for the salvation of the Muslims.

10) **There is a growing missionary vision** among the believers. Some Christian workers have been sent out by the **AIM**-related national Church to work among the Sudan Zande who live an 800 km. bicycle ride from their section of the tribe in the C.A.R.. Pray for development of this vision.

COMORO ISLANDS

BACKGROUND

Area:	2,200 sq. km. – 4 volcanic islands between Madagascar and Mozambique.
Population:	355,000. Growth rate 2.4%. People per sq. km. – 148.
Peoples:	**Comorians** 94% of mixed Arab, Malagasy and African blood, speaking a distinct dialect of Swahili.
Capital:	Moroni 12,000
Economy:	Poor and dependent on the export of perfume oils and vanilla.
Politics:	Three of the islands declared unilateral independence from France in 1975. The island of Mayotte retained links with France. France immediately withdrew all French technical and professional workers from the new republic, leaving the country's administration and economy in ruins. A short-lived leftist revolutionary regime in 1977 and 1978 brought further disasters to the land.
Religion:	**Independent Comoros** (pop. 310,000). All missionaries expelled in 1978 after just two years of freedom for Christian work. The new government may reverse this. **Muslims** 98% **Christians** about 500 Malagasy and 20 Comorians. **Mayotte** (pop. 45,000). Freedom of religion under French rule. **Muslims** 80%, **Roman Catholics** 15%, **Protestants** 2% Most of the Protestants are Malagasy people, and largely nominal. There are about 10 Comorians converted out of Islam.

Prayer Targets

1) **These islands were totally unevangelised until 1973.** In that year the first Comorian was converted. This man is the only national believer with Bible School training. Pray for him.

2) **The revolutionary regime expelled the 20 AIM missionaries in 1978.** Pray that the new government may allow their re-entry.

3) **A few very small groups of believers were left behind.** Pray for their continued growth in the Lord, and their witness at a time when Muslim opposition to them is increasing.

4)   **There is still a team of AIM missionaries on Mayotte.** Pray for the planting of a strong Comorian church which may provide a jumping off point for the evangelisation of the other islands when the door opens again.

DJIBOUTI (French Territory of Afars and Issas)

BACKGROUND

Area: 23,000 sq. km. – a hot, dry desert enclave in Ethiopia and Somalia.
Population: 200,000 with half living in the capital, Djibouti.
Peoples: **Issa Somalis** 45% and **Afars** (Danakil) 40% are related to one another, but there is considerable political tension between them.
            Minorities 15% – French 6%, Arabs 6%, etc.
Economy: Almost entirely dependent on trade revenues from the Red Sea port of Djibouti, which is now Ethiopia's only effective link with the world.
Politics: Became independent in 1977. The economy was shattered by the Somali-Ethiopian war, and is now dependent on Saudi Arabian aid. Communist Ethiopia will dominate or even absorb its diminutive neighbour.
Religion: **Muslims 94%**
            Roman Catholics 5% – almost all French expatriates.
            Protestants – a single French Reformed expatriate group and a handful of backsliding Afar, Somali and Arab believers.

Points for Prayer

1)   **The way opened for the first evangelical witness** in the territory in January, 1975. Praise God for this new opening. Pray for the land to remain open long enough to plant a strong local church.
2)   **The RSMT have started a ministry** through a small Christian bookshop and language school. Pray that this may give contacts with those who will later give their lives to Jesus. The conversion of Muslims in this land, so long totally under the power of the evil one, cannot occur without a hard fight in the heavenlies.
3)   **Pray for the health of the several RSMT missionaries** who live in not very comfortable quarters in a place reputed to be the hottest in the world.
4)   **There has been considerable interest** in Somali and Afar Gospels, and Muslims constantly come to the shop to buy them. Pray that the Word may bring light to them.

CONGO

BACKGROUND

Area: 342,000 sq. km. – north of Zaire and not to be confused with it.
Population: 1,400,000. Annual growth 2.4%. People per sq. km. – 4. Literacy 20%.
Peoples: **African tribes** – 16 – Major groups:– Bakongo, Bateke, Bakwele and Sanga.
Capital: Brazzaville 300,000. Other city – Pointe Noire 150,000. Urbanisation 37%.
Economy: Very underdeveloped in interior but rich mineral deposits bringing some wealth to country.
Politics: Marxist revolutionary government now in power, with much aid from Cuba and China. Independent of France in 1960.
Religion: **Attitude of Government** – Marxism pushed, but church and mission work carries on quietly.
            African Traditionals 20%.
            Roman Catholics 50% – many animists at heart among them.
            Protestants 15%. Community approx. 200,000. Membership 110,000. Denominations 5. Larger groups:– Evangelical Church of Congo (Norwegian and Swedish Covenant Ch.) 100,000 members; Baptists (Orebro) 2,000. Evangelicals 12%.

Points for Prayer

1) **The fragile freedom to preach the Gospel** could suddenly end. Pray that believers may make the full use of present opportunities and be ready for possible persecution.

2) **Communist pressures** have mainly been directed at young people and all mission and church schools have been nationalised. Much of the pressure is talk only and no harsh restrictions have been placed on the churches. There is also some pressure exerted to glorify old heathen customs within the churches.

3) **The churches have grown** dramatically over the past 50 years. Two periods of revival (in the 1920s and 1940s) have helped to make this Church almost entirely Evangelical, strong and evangelistic. There are some outstanding and mature leaders in the churches. Pray that they may have real discernment in these difficult days and help their people to stand against pressures to compromise.

4) **Outreach by these believers** is growing and there is a burden to do something about evangelising the unreached Bateke in the centre of the country. They have also extended an invitation to Billy Graham to preach in Brazzaville. Pray that this latter may become a possibility and that evangelistic outreach may not be forbidden by the authorities.

5) **Young people need prayer,** for schools have been nationalised, and atheism must now be taught to all children. All young people must belong to the Communist Young Pioneer movement. It is hard for young people to live out and out for the Lord. Youth groups in the churches have had to be disbanded. Pray that believers among them may stand firm and live for the Lord.

6) **Missions** – there are 5 mission groups working in the country – most of them from Scandinavia (Sweden and Norway) and it is through these missionaries that the largest groups of believers have come into being. Pray also for the ministry of United World Mission and the Orebro Mission among the largely unreached peoples in the north of the country. Pray for the wisdom and tact for the 100 or so missionaries in their rather delicate situation.

7) **Bible translation** – much remains to be done, but many of the tribes are small, poor and illiterate. There are two languages with the whole Bible, two with the N.T. and a further four with portions.

CHAD

BACKGROUND

Area: 1,284,000 sq. km. – desert in the north, dry grasslands in centre, thick bush in the south.

Population: 4,100,000. Growth rate 2%. People per sq. km. – 3, very few people in the north.

Peoples: **Chad Arabs** 3-5%. 3 nomadic desert tribes in the north, all Muslim.
                 Nilo-Sudanic tribes in centre (over 40) 35%. Most are Muslim.
                 African tribes in south (over 40) 60%, Animist, some Muslims and Christians. There are about 97 languages in Chad. Trade language – Chad Arabic.

Capital: N'djamena 200,000. Urbanisation 12%.

Economy: Previous regime made this country bankrupt. Poor soil, lack of water and natural resources and distance from the sea make economic future bleak.

Politics: Army coup of 1975 removed corrupt and cruel former regime. The great racial, religious and cultural differences between the north and south dominate the political life of the country. The dominance of the southerners over the Muslim north is resented and much of the north and east of the country is now subject to guerrilla warfare instigated by two rebel groups supported by Libya.

Religion: **Attitude of Government** – complete freedom of religion after two years of intense persecution of Christians in south (1973-75).

                 Muslims 42%, African Traditionals 14%, **Roman Catholics 30% Protestants** 14%. Community 459,000.
                 The following figures are very approximate:– Denominations 10; most are

evangelical in theology. Largest:– Evangelical Ch. (**SUM, TEAM, WEC**) approx. 200,000 adherents; Baptists approx. 80,000; Brethren Church approx. 80,000; Brethren (**CMML**) approx. 60,000; Lutheran Brethren approx. 20,000. Evangelicals 8%.

Points for Prayer

1) **Praise God for the ending of persecution,** but pray for peace in this troubled land. The war situation hinders the spreading of the Gospel in the needy north and east where there are scarcely any believers. Two French **SUM** missionaries were captured by rebel groups in 1975, creating an international incident. Pray for freedom to evangelise and safety for missionaries in troubled areas.

2) **The north of the country** has never been evangelised – pray for the opening of this harsh desert land for the Gospel and the calling of missionaries to enter.

3) **The Muslim tribes of the Lake Chad area** are very resistant to the Gospel. Pray for the handful of Nigerian and expatriate missionaries seeking to reach them.

4) **The Ouaddai* in east central Chad** has 800,000 people in 17 tribes and are largely Muslim. They are unwilling to receive the Gospel when preached, but are slowly responding to the loving care of medical and agricultural missionaries who seek to alleviate their sufferings in this semi-desert, drought-prone area. The work of **SUM-WEC** missionaries is hindered by war conditions, climate, lack of supplies, labourers, illiteracy and lack of any Scriptures in local languages. Pray for the Zaghawa 60,000; Maba* 170,000; Dadjo 65,000; Massalit 48,000; Assougou 36,000. There is only a handful of believers in the area.

5) **There are 10 mission groups** with over 190 missionaries working in Chad. The door is open for missionaries of all kinds in pioneer and support ministries. Most work is in the south, where the largest number of believers is found. The martyrdom of many of the finest pastors in 1975 makes the task of training leaders even more imperative. Missionaries from other parts of Africa would be very valuable for this ministry. Pray for the missionaries, for this is a hard country in which to work, and pray too for the valuable ministry of the **MAF** plane without which much work would be impossible.

6) **The severe persecution of the believers** in which many were forced to take part in disgusting initiation ceremonies or be killed was strictly enforced by the government in many areas in the south. Several hundred Christian leaders were brutally murdered, but others compromised. This brief period of suffering has shaken the Church out of its complacency and increasing nominalism. Pray for revival and a greater evangelistic outreach as a result. There are many believers in the area as a result of the fine work of many missions (including **SUM, TEAM,** Brethren, Baptist Mid-Missions, etc.).

7) **The believers who compromised** give an immense problem to the churches. Pray that the remaining leaders may handle them with both justice and love, so as to uphold discipline yet not cause church splits or divisions. Praise God for many who have repented, but pray for those who do not humble themselves.

8) **There is now a critical lack of church leaders.** Pray for Chad pastors in Nigeria to return in this time of need. Pray for all means of training new leaders – Bible Schools, TEE, cassettes for the lonely believers and the manpower to teach them.

9) **Bible translation is an immense, uncompleted task** – two languages have the Bible, 10 the N.T. and 4 more have portions only. Translation work is in progress in 10 but a further 27, at least, need translators immediately. Government plans to standardise the orthography of the tribal languages will mean much Bible revision work.

10) **There are still many tribes in the south that remain only partially evangelised.** Pray that the Chad believers may gain a vision for their evangelisation, especially the following:– Bua 20,000; Gaberi 30,000; Masa 80,000; Mbai 60,000.

EQUATORIAL GUINEA

BACKGROUND

Area:	28,000 sq. km. – a small enclave, Rio Muni, on African mainland and a 2,000 sq. km. island, Fernando Po (now called Macias Nguema) in the Gulf of Guinea.
Population:	300,000 (25% on Fernando Po). A further 100,000, at least, have fled for refuge in surrounding Gabon and Cameroon.
Peoples:	**African tribes** – 6. The mainland Fang-Okak people are politically dominant and number 214,000; also Puku 25,000; Bubi 20,000, the latter on Fernando Po.
Economy:	Almost total collapse with the flight of all Europeans and murder of virtually all the educated and skilled people.
Politics:	Independent of Spain in 1968. A coup in 1969 brought the present President, Macias Nguema, to power. This dictator has turned his country into a virtual concentration camp, murdered all the educated and all likely to oppose him, and imposed a Marxist style government.
Religion:	**Attitude of Government** – militant atheism and all religions ruthlessly suppressed. The only worship permitted is that given to the President.
	African Traditionals 8%.
	Roman Catholics 88% – due to the assiduous efforts of R.C. missionaries to baptise as many as possible. Now all R.C. churches are closed or converted to other uses and the last priests believed to be in prison.
	Protestants 3.5% – though now probably less. 2 denominations. Presbyterians 9,000 community (Rio Muni), Methodists 800 (Fernando Po). **Evangelicals** 2%.

Points for Prayer

1) **The unfortunate people have suffered intensely.** May this turn many to the Lord Jesus for comfort. Pray for an end to this terrible regime.

2) **The persecution of these believers** has rarely been exceeded elsewhere in Africa. Many believers have lost their lives, others are forced into slavery. It is now illegal to hold church meetings, give money to a church or minister, associate with a pastor, conduct Christian funerals or be baptised without government permission. How many would dare to apply? Pray for the believers. There are some reports that the believers still continue to witness where possible.

3) **It is reported that the Presbyterians and Methodists were ordered to worship the President** at the beginning of every service. Pray that the believers may not compromise. Many of the believers in the south of the country are fruit of the years of work of **WEC** – these believers joined up with the Presbyterians when all missionaries were expelled in 1968.

SAO TOMÉ AND PRINCIPE

BACKGROUND

Area:	964 sq. km. – two larger and several smaller islands in the Gulf of Guinea.
Population:	80,000 – mainly **Africans** brought to the islands as slave labour, also some Creoles and Portuguese.
Economy:	Very poor and undeveloped.
Politics:	One of the smallest fragments of the Portuguese Empire that became independent in 1975. It is uncertain what line the new government will take – probably Marxist.
Religion:	There was freedom of religion after the Portuguese Revolution in 1974. **Roman Catholics** 94%, **African Traditionals** 4%, **Protestants** 1%.

Points for prayer

1) **It seems that the only significant Protestant witness is that of the Assemblies of God**, with a large and expanding work in the Capital and suburbs. They have a large church that can seat 800 people and many preaching points. Pray for the growth numerically and spiritually of this work.

2) **Pray that all parts of these islands** may be effectively evangelised and that there may also be the freedom to do so.

ETHIOPIA

BACKGROUND

Area:	1,184,000 sq. km. – fertile mountain plateau surrounded by the deserts of the Red Sea coast, and the Somali, Kenya and Sudan borders.
Population:	28,000,000. Annual growth 2.6%. People per sq. km. – 24, but very unevenly distributed, with high densities in the highland valleys.
Peoples:	There are 89 languages and 200 major dialects spoken.

Semitic 34% Amhara, Tigre, Gurage, etc. who originally came from Arabia, conquering and mixing with the local Hamitic peoples. Amharic is spoken by 60% of the people. The Amharas live in the central and northern highlands.
Hamitic 46% – many Oromo (Galla) tribes in the east, centre and south.
Afars 3% (Danakil) – a semi-nomadic people in the eastern lowlands.
Somalis 5% – a semi-nomadic people in the Ogaden in the south east.
Sudanic 10% – numerous small tribes along the western border.
Falasha Jews 30,000 black Jews who still practice Old Testament animal sacrifices.

Capital:	Addis Ababa 1,050,000. Other cities – Asmara 300,000. Urbanisation 11%
Economy:	Gravely disrupted by the great upheavals following the Communist revolution, because of massive nationalisations of businesses, banks, housing and lands, and also the wars and famines now afflicting the land.
Politics:	The government of Haile Selassie overthrown in 1974 by the army. Only massive Russo-Cuban military intervention has preserved the military government, and prevented the disintegration of the Ethiopian state. There have been about 6 separatist wars in progress in different areas of the country; the worst being those of Eritrea and the Somalis.
Religion:	**Attitude of Government** – strong emphasis on atheism despite promises of religious freedom. Much propaganda against "religionists" and increasing pressures on the Christians. Many Christians and Muslims have perished in the massacres initiated by opposing factions in the ruling military council.

Ethiopian Orthodox Church 46% – one of the ancient Eastern Churches. Its powerful political position is being rapidly eroded.
Islam 35% – now placed on an equal footing with the Christians. Muslims are strong in the north, east and south east.
Roman Catholics 0.6%
African Traditionals 14% – mainly in the south and west.
Protestants 4% – Community 800,000. Membership 450,000. Denominations 28. Largest: Mekane Jesu Church (6 Lutheran missions) 600,000, Word of Life Church (SIM) 500,000, Bethel Evangelical Church (Presbyterian) 20,000 community. Evangelicals 3.5%

Points for Prayer

1) **The Ethiopian people are now going through a period of terrible suffering.** Faminies, war and the vindictive Marxist government have brought death to every part of the country. It is estimated that over one million people have been killed in the government's efforts to eliminate all real or potential opposition. Pray for peace and a God-fearing government.

2) **Between 1975 and 1978 nearly all 900 missionaries serving in the country have been withdrawn.** All mission properties and institutions have been nationalised, including the Lutheran Radio Voice of the Gospel. God has used this missionary effort to plant a strong and live Church. Yet vast areas and millions of people remain virtually unevangelised. Pray for the completion of the evangelisation of this land.

3) **Unreached peoples** – we mention some: –

  a) **The northern provinces** of Gojjam, Wallo, Begemidr, Tigre, and the north eastern provinces of Harar and Bale, were only just beginning to open up for the Gospel when this outreach had to be stopped (**SIM**).

  b) **The Muslim Afars** – only a handful of these people had believed after 20 years of hard work by the **RSMT**. Some RSMT workers still reach the Afars in Djibouti.

  c) **The Muslim Somalis.** Many of the one million Ogaden Somalis died in the 1978 war, and 300,000 fled to Somalia. **SIM**'s witness to these people had shown little visible fruit. Pray for SIM's continuing outreach to these people in N. Kenya, and also for the FEBA Somali broadcasts from the Seychelles.

  d) **The tribes of the south west.** There are over 12 resistant or unreached tribes in this area. SIM and the Presbyterians worked in this area. Related tribes over the border in Sudan are opening up for the Gospel once more.

  e) **The Muslim tribes of Eritrea** – the Beni Amer, Bilayn, Barya, and largely Muslim Tigre, have never been effectively evangelised. 300,000 Eritreans are now refugees in Sudan. Pray for RSMT and MECO as they seek openings to reach these tragic refugees.

  f) **The Falasha Jews** – the Anglican Church Mission to the Jews has sought to evangelise these people, and about 7% are now Christian.

4) **The Orthodox Church is in turmoil.** This ancient, superstitious, tradition-bound Church is being torn by divisions between the traditionalists and those who want to work with the Communists. Pray that the sufferings in the land may bring many to a Bible-based faith. There is a small, but vigorous evangelical wing of this Church; the result of the witness of an Anglican Mission. Most of the Amhara people belong to this Church.

5) **The Protestant Church has grown dramatically since World War II.** Revivals, people movements and missionary outreach have characterised this Church; all in the midst of famines, war and persecutions. Pray that the present sufferings may not impede this expansion. The last word concerning these believers is that they are suffering acute hardships, but face the future with optimism.

6) **The Word of Life Church,** the fruit of the large and successful **SIM** work, is strongest in the 7 large tribes in the south west. There are fine spiritual leaders, and there has been much missionary outreach to unevangelised areas from this Church. Yet there are many difficulties – the lack of sufficient, well trained leaders able to stand up to Communist propaganda; lack of Scriptures in the local languages; and the illiteracy of most believers. Pray for these believers, and for the continuation of their missionary programme, for they have been supporting around 200 missionaries.

7) **Leadership Training.** Pray that the many Bible Schools may be able to continue to function unhindered. The W.O.L. churches had 20 Bible Schools in 1976, and a further 93 rural Bible Schools. Pray for the Christian leaders in this time of intense pressure. They need wisdom and tact, and also firmness not to compromise on essentials

8) **Bible translation** into other languages than Amharic was not allowed until 1972. Much work remains to be done. **SIM**, WBT and others worked on a crash programme to print essential Scriptures in 15 languages, and also to record these Scriptures on cassette tapes. Pray that these may be of great value to the believers now that few missionaries remain in the country. There are at least 39 languages that urgently need translation work.

9) **Students.** There was a strong and growing work in the University before the Communist takeover. Many of the students were killed or scattered in the subsequent upheavals. Yet there were reports of very large numbers of students finding the Lord in 1977 and 1978 despite continual Marxist propaganda.

10) **Preparation of believers for persecution.** There are fears of all-out persecution of

believers, which hitherto has been more limited and localised. Pray that this time of relative freedom may be well used to teach and disciple the Christians in preparation for such times.

11) **Eritrea is a land of tragedy.** The increasingly bitter war between the secessionists and the Government has led to widespread loss of life and property. Now Cuban forces are helping to crush this movement. Pray for a just peace and freedom for the Gospel in this only partially evangelised territory.

12) **Many Eritrean believers have died or are now in prison** because of the war. Pray that the Christians may not lose their glow and desire to witness through bitterness under great provocation. Pray that the Church may be refined through these sufferings. The evangelicals are largely the fruit of the Swedish Evangelical Mission and **MECO**.

GABON

BACKGROUND

Area: 267,000 sq. km. – largely tropical rain forest. People per sq. km. – 3.5.
Population: 950,000. Natural increase – 1%, but high rate of immigration.
Peoples: **African tribes** – 40. The largest: Fang 175,000; Eshira 105,000; Duma 70,000.
Immigrants approx. 40% – refugees from Equatorial Guinea and work seekers from surrounding lands (many of same tribes as those of Gabon). **French** 1.3%.
Capital: Libreville 251,000. Urbanisation 34%.
Economy: Relatively wealthy and rich in natural resources.
Politics: Retains close links with France since independence in 1960.
Religion: **Attitude of Government** – freedom of religion and entry of missionaries.
African Traditionals 12% – actually very much higher and still strong.
Muslims 1% – the dramatic conversion of the President to Islam could give this religion a great impetus – especially among those seeking social position.
African Independent Churches 12%.
Roman Catholics 60% – very dominant with their many schools and services, but most R.C.s very nominal and basically still animists.
Protestants 17%. Community 177,000. Denominations 3. Evangelical (rather nominal) (French Ref.) 130,000; Evangelical Ch. of S. Gabon (**CMA**) 36,000 adherents. Evangelicals 4.2%.

Points for Prayer

1) **Pray that the present religious freedom may be maintained** even though the country's leaders are aligning their land with the Muslim world.

2) **Unreached peoples.** Over half the country has no resident evangelical witness (the centre and north). About 24 tribes have yet to be evangelised (most small).

3) **Most of the Protestants are very nominal** and have little chance to hear the Gospel. Sadly the majority of the French missionaries (including the famous Dr. Albert Schweitzer) were liberal in theology. All missionaries have now been withdrawn from the centre and north of the country and the Church is independent. Pray for a move of the Spirit of God in their many churches.

4) **The CMA is the only evangelical mission operating** in the country. The early missionaries sacrificially opened up the south of the country in the '30s. There are now about 33 missionaries assisting the Church through evangelism, teaching, schools and health programmes, etc. In recent years the Mission has sought to extend the witness to the many growing towns and mines in other parts of the land, but is crippled by the lack of workers. Pray for the raising up of new workers to evangelise and disciple the many unreached. Pray especially for the new outreach to the Capital, Libreville.

5) **The Church in the south** is growing fast. There was a period of revival in 1968. The New Life for All Campaign was beneficial in this area to mobilise the believers in evangelism and many new churches were planted. There is a critical lack of pastors and mature lay leaders to consolidate and extend the work to new areas. Pray for the one Bible School with 11 students, and pray for more men to be called into God's service. Illiteracy is a problem.

6) **There are many opportunities to teach Scripture in schools**, but there are not the workers to seize them. There is a great need for a ministry such as that of SU for work in schools and among young people.

7) **Bible translation** – 2 languages have the Bible, 7 the N.T. and another 14 have portions. National believers are doing much of the work in three languages, hoping to complete the N.T. in their languages soon. Very much work remains for the Bible translator.

THE GAMBIA

BACKGROUND

Area: 11,300 sq. km. – Mainland Africa's smallest state – an enclave within Senegal consisting of the banks of the Gambia River and stretching 400 km. inland.
Population: 510,000. Annual growth 1.9%. People per sq. km. – 46.
Peoples: **African tribes** – 9. The largest: Mandingo 250,000; Woloff 63,000; Fula 100,000; Jolah 31,000; Sarahuli 28,000.
               Descendants of freed slaves 4,500 around Banjul and nominally Christian.
Capital: Banjul 40,000. Urbanisation 14%.
Economy: Poor, but developing with foreign aid.
Politics: Parliamentary democracy independent of Britain in 1965. Increasing cooperation with Senegal, but great cultural differences preclude union between them.
Religion: **Attitude of Government** – freedom of religion despite dominance of Islam.
               African Traditionals 10% – largely among the Jolah and Sarahuli, but these animist pockets are gradually turning to Islam.
               Muslims 85%.
               Roman Catholics 2%.
               Protestants 0.8%. Community 4,500. Denominations 3:– Methodists 2,100 adherents; Anglicans 2,000; Evangelical Fellowship (**WEC**). Evangelicals 0.4%.

Points for Prayer

1) **This Muslim land is open for the Gospel.** There is, however, a lack of expatriate and national Christian workers to evangelise this largely unreached country. Nearly all the Christians and Christian work is near the coast and most of the interior has scarcely been touched with the Gospel.

2) **Islam is gradually gaining** in the few areas where there are still uncommitted animist people. Pray for the evangelisation of these people before the great barrier of Islam is erected around them. Pray also for decisive conversions from among the Muslimised tribes as well.

3) **The churches are largely traditional and nominal,** but in both older denominational groups there are Evangelicals who are increasingly active for the Lord. Pray for revival and also straight preaching of repentance. There are not enough deep conversions and Christian teaching is woefully inadequate. A greater vision is needed among the converted people for the evangelisation of the Muslim majority – most believe that it is impossible for a Muslim to be saved. Pray for the bridging of the great cultural and tribal differences.

4) **There are a few expatriate Christian teachers** in the secondary schools who seek to run **SU** groups. Pray for the deepening and developing of this witness, that these converted through **SU** may really have an impact for the Gospel all over the land. There are also some Christian nurses in the hospitals.

5) **The only evangelical mission in the country is WEC,** who now operate from 4 centres inland in a medical, agricultural and literacy outreach. These ministries are well thought of by the government and there are many more openings for technical missionaries to augment the 16 missionaries now there. These ministries are valuable to open people's hearts to the Gospel and some are being converted. There are now three little churches and several groups of believers along the river. Pray for the growth of this work in a rather difficult and resistant area.

6) **Bible translation** – three languages just have small portions of the Word of God. Five languages urgently need translators – especially the dominant Mandingo people. These Mandingo people number about 4 million in this and surrounding lands and are a strategic, but resistant people, upon which prayer must be focussed.

GHANA

BACKGROUND

Area: 239,000 sq. km. – grasslands in north and thick forest and farming land in south.

Population: 10,100,000. Growing annually at 2.7%. People per sq. km. – 42, though two thirds of the people live in the better watered south.

Peoples: **Tribes** – 57. Major language groups – Akan 40% (Fanti, Ashanti, etc.), Ewe 13%, Ga-aDangme 7%, Togo group (13 tribes) 1% in southern half. Dagbani 3%, Gurene-Kusal 3.5%, Wali-Dagari 3%, etc. (26 tribes) in the north.

Capital: Accra 800,000. Urbanisation 29%. Other cities – Kumasi 400,000.

Economy: Government making strenuous efforts to restore order to economy after the profligacy of previous regimes. Potentially very wealthy.

Politics: Independent of Britain in 1957. Alternating civilian and military rule since then. The present military government is preparing the country for civilian rule once order is fully established.

Religion: **Attitude of Government** – helpful to churches and missions; many leading men are Christian – some very actively so.

African Traditionals 45% in south, 75% in north.

Muslims 5% in south, 14% in north – growing in latter region.

Roman Catholics 16% in south, 2% in north.

African Independent Churches 8% – there are around 300 denominations – pentecostally inclined, with considerable admixture of superstition and animism in most.

Protestants 28% in south, 5% in north. Community 1,110,000. Denominations 40+. Major denominations: Presbyterians (2 groups) 450,000 adherents; Methodists (3) 302,000; Anglicans 222,000; Pentecostals (many) 300,000. Evangelicals 8%.

Points for Prayer

1) **The south is, to a large extent, Christianised.** Sacrificial missionary work by the mainline denominations over the last 150 years has resulted in a large Christian community, yet much of this is nominal. Revival is needed.

2) **The mainline denominations in the south** are all-too-often formal with little life, though orthodox. Yet there are also many fine and very lively congregations with a warm spiritual fellowship that has been stimulated by the many converted through SU work, the NLFA Campaign and also the charismatic movement. Pray for more definite preaching on repentance that will lead nominal Christians into a living

relationship with the Lord. Pray for more pastors to be raised up who can provide a teaching ministry for those who are converted.

3)   **The rapid growth of the Pentecostal and Independent Churches** is a revolt against the deadness and formality of much of the worship in the mainline churches. Pray for both of these groups to be more based on the Scriptures than on emotion or heathen superstitions.

4)   **The New Life For All Campaign** (launched in 1970) was beneficial in some areas, but indifference, denominational isolationism and lack of truly converted leaders limited its impact. Nevertheless a good beginning was made, some pastors were converted or brought to a place of clear testimony and some congregations revived. Pray for the continued outworking of the principles of NLFA in mobilising believers to reach out to the lost.

5)   **The need for converted and called Christian leaders** was never greater. There are many middle level Bible Schools in the south, but only one degree level seminary. Many come for training without a real call to the ministry. Pray for the raising up of a new generation of well educated, spiritual men of God that may set high standards of Christian living, teaching and evangelising. This need is especially acute in the less evangelised north where poverty and low educational standards drive the better educated potential Christian leaders to the comforts of the south. Pray also for the **SIM** run Maranatha Evening Bible School in Accra that provides a valuable training to over 140 earnest believers of various denominations.

6)   **The Church in Ghana has great potential for sending out missionaries,** but the vision is small. The new Christian Outreach Fellowship is developing into an inter-denominational sending agency – pray for it. The Christian Service College in Kumasi (**WEC**) trains some for missionary service from all over Africa. There are now (1976) 12 students from 5 lands, but prayer is needed that the desired expansion may be carried out. There are several Ghanaian missionary workers with **WBT**, **CEF** and **SU**.

7)   **Scripture Union and GHAFES (IVF)** have made a deep impact on the 149 secondary schools, 61 teacher training colleges and 3 universities. It is entirely run by Ghanaian leaders and many are being converted through the school groups, camps, etc.. Many converts of this ministry are now in positions of importance in every sphere of the life of the country. Many school leavers (who often cannot find jobs) are helped by the school leavers' town fellowships. There is a need that these young Christians become involved in church life.

8)   **Literature** is an essential tool for the Gospel in this very literate country. Yet high printing costs and small import quotas allowed by the government greatly cripple this ministry. The **SIM** African Challenge magazine had to close down in 1975, and a very effective full page advertisement in a popular newspaper every month now replaces it; the response has been excellent – pray for this ministry. Both this and the extensive BCC ministry is now run by the Ghanaian **Challenge Enterprises**. The **Africa Christian Press** is now well known all over Africa for the excellent Christian literature by African authors they produce (now over 80 book titles) – pray for this widespread and useful ministry and also for dissemination of this literature. There is a dearth of suitable vernacular literature and writers able to produce it.

9)   **Missions** are welcome and much needed for all aspects of ministry – pioneer work, assisting churches, teaching, Bible translation, as well as for the still extensive mission hospitals and schools system. The need is especially great for the far less evangelised and more resistant northern half of the country. Pray for the issue of visas to those needed, for the government is limiting the number of missionaries by a quota given to each mission. There are now about 30 missions with about 280 missionaries serving in the land.

10) **Unreached peoples** are almost entirely in the north. In only 3-4 of the 26 tribes has there been a significant response to the Gospel. There are only about 3 small tribes without a resident missionary presence, but 20 tribes must still be classed as "unreached" through the lack of response to the Gospel. The reasons for this hardness are:– very strong heathenism, the advances of Islam and lack of the Word of God in the languages. Especial mention could be made of:– Nawuri (14,000), Nchumuru (7,000 – 1% Muslim), Gonja (70,000 – largely Muslim), Hanga (5,000),

Vagala (6,000), Birifor (40,000), Wali (60,000) in the **WEC** area; and Sissala (73,000), Kasena (85,000), Builsa (68,000), Frafra (306,000), Mamprussi (95,000), Kusasi (147,000), Moba (51,000), Dagari (240,000), Dagomba (348,000), Konkomba (175,000), Nafara (26,000) among whom the Assemblies of God and two Baptist groups are doing a heroic work.

11) **Islam is growing**, with influence in the population centres and in tribes with a strong system of chiefs (what the chief says, all do). There have been very few real conversions from among Muslims, though their religion is only a thin veneer of customs over a basic heathenism.

12) **Bible translation** – 5 languages have the whole Bible, eleven the N.T. and 18 have portions only. Much valuable work has and is being done by **WBT** who have teams working in 14 tribes in the north. Pray for this ministry and also for the raising up of more nationals able to take on much of this translation work.

GUINEA

BACKGROUND

Area:	246,000 sq. km. – on west coast between Sierra Leone and Guinea-Bissau.
Population:	5,000,000. Annual growth 2.4%. People per sq. km. – 20.
Peoples:	**Tribes** – 18. The largest:– Fula 1,667,000; Malinke 731,000; Soussou 400,000; Kissi 366,000; Toma 73,000.
Capital:	Conakry 520,000. Urbanisation 16%.
Economy:	Potentially rich, with large deposits of bauxite, etc., but government policies have not helped the economy.
Politics:	Independent of France in 1958. Much aid and technical assistance from Communist lands with which Sekou Toure's government has close links. 27 attempted coups since independence and consequent strict security measures have brought much suffering to the people.
Religion:	**Attitude of government** – secular state, but with Islam dominant. Great freedom for national believers to evangelise despite strict control on entry and activity of missionaries.
	Muslims 70% – strong among the Fula, Malinke, etc., and slowly growing.
	African Traditional 29% – stronger in the southern forests.
	Roman Catholics 1% – unpopular with government due to involvement with politics, and now with few priests. They are decreasing in numbers.
	Protestants 0.3%. Believers 15,000 – membership 2,600, all of the Evangelical Protestant Church (**CMA1**). Evangelicals 0.3%.

Points for prayer

1) **All Protestant and Roman Catholic missionaries were expelled** in 1967 when the government enforced indigenisation on the churches. The **CMA** missionaries were, however, allowed to retain some missionaries in the land because the national Church was already independent. There are now 14 **CMA** missionaries on two stations. Pray that more visas may be issued to needed missionary staff now that the government is becoming more sympathetic.

2) **Most of the country is unevangelised** and 15 of the 18 tribes must be considered unreached. Pray for the animistic tribes in the south and south west among whom there are very few Christians, if any – Konyanke, Bassari, Soussou, Gbaga, Lele, Koranko and Yalunka. These tribes are coming under the influence of Islam. Pray that the Guinean believers may have a burden and opportunities to evangelise these tribes.

3) **Islam is very strong among the Fula and Malinke**, who together make up nearly half the population. There are very few believers among them – 5 among the Malinke. They are not open to the Gospel, but Radio ELWA's daily Fula broadcasts and also

frequent broadcasts in 4 other languages are listened to by Muslims. These programmes make good opening for visiting evangelists. There are 8 Muslim tribes in
Guinea – all without a single church planted among them. There are 3 national
pastors working among Muslims.

4) **The Church** has developed and matured greatly since the expulsion of most missionaries. They were forced to take over, at short notice, the work of the missionaries.
There are now over 60 church groups and 70 Christian workers – mostly among the
Guerze, Toma and Kissi tribes. In these three tribes there is a mighty work of the
Spirit in progress and many hundreds are being converted each year, and the tempo is
quickening. Pray for the establishment of strong, missionary minded churches that
will reach out boldly to surrounding heathen tribes and beyond, to the hard Muslim
people. There is no limit on the work of national believers – pray that they may use
the opportunities they have.

5) **The one Bible School** in the country at Telekoro is run by nationals but has missionary
staff as well (it needs reinforcements). There are 33 students from three tribes. Pray
for the calling of more students from these tribes and also from those tribes now just
beginning to be affected by the Gospel. All teaching is done in French, so this sets a
high standard for would-be students in a land where education facilities are not
extensive.

6) **There are many opportunities for witness** in Conakry for the few missionaries there.
This is a hard, largely Muslim city, but many southern Christians come there for study
or work. Pray for the witness to the international community and university students,
as well as all contacts with officialdom in the capital.

7) **There is only one Christian bookshop** in the country. A considerable amount of
literature and Bibles is sold to Muslims and diplomats and technicians from Communist lands. Stocks are limited because of import troubles. Pray for this strategic
witness.

8) **Many Guinean students** go to Iron Curtain universities – some Christians as well.
Pray that the latter may remain strong in the faith and also witness boldly.

9) **Bible translation** – 6 languages have the N.T., 4 others have portions. There are 4
others that urgently need translators – pray that these may be provided.

GUINEA-BISSAU

BACKGROUND

Area: 36,000 sq. km. – marshy coastal lowlands between Senegal and Guinea.
Population: 550,000. Annual growth 1.5%. People per sq. km. – 15.
Peoples: **African tribes** – 22. The largest: the animist Balante 33%, Mandjako 13% and •
                Muslim Fula 20%, Mandingo 12%.
Capital: Bissau 20,000. Urbanisation 20%. Literacy 5%.
Economy: Ruined during the long independence war. Government making strenuous
                efforts to rectify the situation.
Politics: Independent of Portugal in 1974. Socialist government seeking aid from east
                and west for the development of the country.

Religion: **Attitude of Government** – Christians have been free to preach and witness
                since Independence, though no new mission groups have yet been allowed to
                enter.

                African Traditionals 58% – more among the coastal tribes.

                Muslims 33% – slowly extending influence towards coast from inland tribes.

                Roman Catholics 8%.

                Protestants 0.6% – about 2,000, mostly among the Balante, Bijago (25,000)
                and Mandjako (71,000) tribes. All of Evangelical Church (**WEC**). Evangel-
                icals 0.6%.

Points for Prayer

1) **There are unprecedented opportunities for evangelism**, Christian literature work and church planting. Pray that the door might remain open for complete evangelisation of this land.

2) **Unreached peoples** – all 22 tribes must still be considered unreached – only 4 have a resident evangelical witness of local believers. Pray especially for the evangelisation of the animist Banyun (15,000), Biafada (15,000) and other smaller groups. Pray also for the unoccupied Muslim tribes inland – especially the Fula (100,000), Mandingo (71,000), Mankanya (26,000), etc.

3) **The only Protestant mission** until recently was **WEC** – now with 24 missionaries in 4 centres. Pray for the calling and sending out of new missionaries to open up unoccupied tribes for the Gospel. Pioneer workers, teachers, Bible translators and technical missionaries are urgently required.

4) **The Church** is strongest among the Balanta, among whom there are now 1,000 believers and 14 churches. Pray for the training of more leaders through the agricultural Bible School, short term Bible Schools and the new residential Bible School (1976) with 9 students. Some believers have volunteered to go to the interior tribes to evangelise them; other believers have been sent into the less developed interior by the government because of their technical skills. Pray that this witness may lead to the planting of churches in new areas. Believers have suffered persecution from their heathen relatives in the past – loss of family rights and the denial of girls in marriage. Pray for the growth and witness of these believers.

5) **Literature** is eagerly sought after as the literate population begins to increase. Pray for the witness of the Christian bookshop in Bissau to both nationals and also to the many aid personnel from Communist countries (quite a number of Bibles, etc., are going back to Iron Curtain countries by these means). Pray for the effective use of cassette tapes and Gospel Records in this multilingual and largely illiterate nation.

6) **Bible translation is an urgent necessity.** Two languages have the N.T. and another two have Gospels. **WEC** workers are translating in 4 more, but 3 other languages need translators.

CAPE VERDE ISLANDS

BACKGROUND

Area:	4,000 sq. km. – 10 dry volcanic islands 600 km. from West African coast.
Population:	300,000 of Portuguese/African descent. Annual growth 2.3%.
Economy:	Very poor and subject to severe and prolonged droughts.
Politics:	Seeking to prepare for union with Guinea-Bissau since independence from Portugal in 1975.
Religion:	**Roman Catholics** 96%.
	Protestants 2.5% (all are of the Nazarene Church). Evangelicals 2.5%.

Points for Prayer

The Nazarene Church has planted churches on most of the little islands. Pray for the growth of this witness among the many Roman Catholics and that these believers may also make a contribution to the evangelisation of Guinea-Bissau. These believers suffer from great poverty.

IVORY COAST

BACKGROUND

Area: 332,000 sq. km. – between Liberia and Ghana.
Population: 6,800,000. Annual growth 2.5%. People per sq. km. – 20.
Peoples: **African tribes** – 58. The largest:– Baoule 1,300,000; Senoufo 560,000; Bete
                 360,000; Dan 300,000; Gouro 260,000; Anyi 242,000; Attie 210,000.
                 Others – up to 1,000,000 from Upper Volta, mostly Mossi.
                 French 50,000.
Capital: Abidjan 1,000,000. Urbanisation 30%. Literacy 25%.
Economy: Most prosperous state in Francophone Africa because of wise economic
                 policies of government. Based on agriculture and growing industries.
Politics: Close links retained with France after independence in 1960. Government is
                 stable and progressive under leadership of Houphouet Boigny.
Religion: **Attitude of Government** – very sympathetic and helpful to missions.
                 African Traditionals 51%.
                 Muslims 24%.
                 Afr. Ind Churches (40) 3%.
                 Roman Catholics 19%.
                 Protestants – 4%. Community 251,000. Denominations 14. The largest:–
                 Methodists 51,000 adherents; Ev. Prot. **(CMA)** 60,000; Ev. Ch. of W. Africa
                 (WEC) 3,000; Ev. Ch. of S.W.I. 60,000; Baptists (3) 8,000; Assemblies of
                 God 30,000. Evangelicals 3%.

Points for Prayer

1) **This is one of the most responsive and open countries** for the Gospel in W. Africa.
   There are unlimited opportunities for evangelism among young people, in schools,
   cities and many of the tribes. The 1973 Giraud campaign helped to open up the
   country in a new way for the Gospel, with many being converted.

2) **The Muslim people are especially needy**, but little has yet been done for them. Pray for
   the Malinke (250,000), Diola (80,000) and Ngan (10,000) who have no resident
   evangelical witness and are largely Muslim. Several missions are concerned for this
   outreach to begin (**WEC**, Cons. Baptists, **CMA**). There are several other partially
   Muslim tribes that are resistant among whom two Baptist groups work – Senoufo
   (580,000), Ligbi (25,000). There have been a few conversions from Islam – pray for
   more.

3) **Unreached animist tribes** – nearly all the peoples of the country should be included in
   this category, though many tribes are responsible and turning to the Lord. Note:–
   a) **The South West** where the French-Swiss Mission Biblique has a good and growing
      work among the Bete, Nyabwa (28,000), Wobe (65,000), Guere, Dan, etc. Also
      together with the MB works the British **UFM** (among the Godie' (25,000) and Bete.)
   b) **The East Centre** – WEC among the Gouro*, Gagou (28,000), Tura (25,000), Wan
      (13,000).
   c) **The Centre** – CMA among the responsive Baoule and Anyi.
   d) **The North** – Conservative Baptists among the rather difficult Senoufo and Free Will
      Baptists among the resistant Lorhon* (7,000), Kulango (80,000) and Lobi (60,000).

4) **The Church** is experiencing rapid growth – about 25–30% per year – especially
   among the Baoule, Godie and Gouro. Pray that this growth may also be in spiritual
   depth – too many are satisfied with a deliverance from the old life only. There is,
   generally, very happy fellowship and cooperation between the national churches and
   missions in outreach. Pray that this burden for the lost may grow and that there may
   be a development of a real missionary concern for other tribes – especially in the
   more resistant north.

5) **The Christians in the south** are mostly Methodists and all too often nominal. They are
   the descendants of the 100,000 converted at the beginning of the century through the
   preaching of the Liberian, Prophet Harris. There are many small tribes in the coastal

region that are largely Christianised, but few have anything of the Word of God and growth is minimal. The Assemblies of God and Southern Baptists are seeing many converted in this area. The help of the **WBT** translation teams is bringing blessing to some Methodist groups. There are also some strong churches in the south among the immigrant Mossi people.

6) **Leadership** is, as usual, the big bottleneck. Congregational support is still too small and not enough men are going into full time service. There is a lack of pastors – especially those with the ability to teach the Word. Pray for the few Bible Schools in the country – especially for the **CMA** Yamoussoukrou higher level Bible School and the Mission Biblique B. School at Man. Pray for the provision of national and expatriate staff of high calibre.

7) **Missions** have made a great effort over the last decade, but more workers are urgently needed for the many openings in institutional, literacy and church work. There are now about 300 missionaries in the land in 10 agencies – largest: Cons. Bapt. (84), Miss. Bib. (50), **WEC** 35, **CMA** 31. Nearly all are evangelical.

8) **Young people** are responsive and church youth teams are being greatly used of the Lord. Pray for the extensive, but inadequate, Scripture teaching programme in church and state schools; also for the small but growing witness of **SU**. There is a keen GBU (**IVF**) group at the university.

9) **Literature** – pray for the ministry of **CLC** through several well used bookstores. Pray also for the inter-mission/church Evangelical Publications Centre in Abidjan which co-ordinates much of the production of evangelical literature for all Francophone Africa – publishing books and 2 evangelistic magazines. Pray for this valuable ministry and for solutions to many problems – lack of qualified staff (especially French speaking), financial pressures and lack of good distribution outlets.

10) **Bible translation** in progress in 25 languages (15 by **WBT** and others by other missions and nationals). At least 7 other languages wait for translators. Only one language has the whole Bible, 4 the N.T. and 15 have just portions.

11) **Radio work** – the ELWA (**SIM**) Francophone Africa programme and follow-up work is now based on Abidjan. Pray for the provision of staff, cooperating churches willing to help with programmes and also for fruitfulness in these under-evangelised lands. It is hoped that an inter-mission **cassette ministry** may soon be started.

KENYA

BACKGROUND

Area: 576,000 sq. km. – much of north and east is desert, most people living in the better watered south and west.

Population: 13,800,000. Annual growth 3.4%. People per sq. km. – 24 (400 in the highlands).

Peoples: **African tribes** – 35, speaking 50 languages. Three major racial groups. Largest tribes: Kikuyu 2,800,000; Luo 1,900,000; Luyia 1,800,000; Kamba 1,500,000; Gusii 900,000; Meru 700,000. Literacy 45%.
Minorities 3% – Asians (Indo-Pakistani) 180,000; Whites 45,000; Arabs 35,000.

Capital: Nairobi 630,000. Other cities: Mombasa 300,000. Urbanisation 10%.

Economy: Hampered by lack of natural resources, overpopulation and unemployment, but considerable development through tourism, agriculture and industry.

Politics: Independent of Britain in 1963 and stable under leadership of ageing President Kenyatta. Tribal divisions and hostile, well-armed, adjoining nations threaten future stability.

Religion: **Attitude of Government** – complete religious freedom.
African Traditionals 23% in rapid decline.
Muslims 6% – largely on coast and among the north eastern tribes.
Roman Catholics 26%. **Orthodox** 2%.
African Independents (156 groups) 15%.

Protestants 26%. Community 2,500,000. Denominations 49. The largest: Anglicans (Evangelical – CMS 600,000; Pentecostals (12 groups) 700,000; Africa Inland Church (AIM) 300,000; Methodists 110,000; Presbyterians 100,000; Salvation Army 100,000; Friends (Quaker) 1,000,000. Evangelicals 20%.

Prayer Targets

1) **There is more freedom for the preaching of the Gospel** than ever before – pray that these opportunities may be well used. Pray also for continued peace and harmony in the future.

2) **The Church in Kenya** has grown dramatically since the sacrificial missionary pioneers of the 1890's, etc. Over 70% of the population now claims to be Christian. Most of the Protestant Churches are Evangelical and evangelistic with mature Christian leaders. The East African Revival has greatly influenced the Anglicans, Presbyterians and the Methodists over the last 40 years and 90% of the leaders in these churches have close links with these Revival groups. Sadly, the Revival Movement (largely a lay movement) is now riven with bitter divisions. Pray for real spiritual unity among the Lord's people, and for spiritual growth.

3) **The problems faced by the Church in Kenya:–**
   a) **Nominalism** is a growing problem with many 2nd and 3rd generation Christians.
   b) **Tribalism** – most churches started out on a tribal base, and divisions are common – both for this reason and also disputes over personalities and customs.
   c) **Lack of good Bible teaching.** Pray for the 12 or so Bible Schools and the two major Seminaries – Scott Theol. (AIM) with 55 students and St. Paul's United Theol. (Presbyterian, Anglican and Methodist) and thier contribution to the training of leaders.
   d) **The need for a greater missionary vision** and concern for the less privileged tribes needing the Gospel, the largely unevangelised Muslims and for other lands. Some Africa Inland Church pastors are interested in missionary outreach to Sudan.

4) **Missions** – 70 agencies with about 1,150 missionaries; the largest being the AIM with 370 workers. There are many opportunities for missionary service of all kinds – in institutions, church work, Bible teaching and also pioneer work.

5) **Young people** are very open to the Gospel and a number of youth organisations have made a significant impact in the cities and in the schools. Pray for the encouraging work of SU and the live IVF group in the university. Integration of such young people into active church life is not easy, but their contribution is essential.

6) **Unreached peoples** – probably about 12% of the peoples of Kenya belong to tribes or peoples little affected by the Gospel, though few are totally without a witness.
   a) **The Muslim tribes in the N.E.** – 4 Somali tribes* totalling 312,000; Boran 42,000 and the Galla tribes 90,000. The BCMS have a good work among these hard peoples, but the converts are few.
   b) **The Muslim coastal strip and Tana River area** where 1,000,000 people live. Pray for the new outreach of AIM to the Pokomo 44,000; Segeju 35,000; Somalis and the coastal Swahili and Arab peoples; also for the older work among the largely Muslimised Mijikenda tribes 600,000.
   c) **The pagan Turkana** 260,000; **Suk** 200,000 **and Massai** 200,000. The AIC-AIM work among these peoples (among others), but the churches are yet few and small.

7) **The AEAM** (Assoc. of Evangelicals of Africa and Madagascar) is based in Nairobi. Pray that spiritual unity in love of Evangelical Christians may be enhanced and the Gospel more clearly proclaimed in Africa through the ministries of AEAM.

LESOTHO

BACKGROUND

Area: 30,000 sq. km. – a mountainous enclave within South Africa.
Population: 1,100,000. Annual growth 2.1%. People per sq. km. – 40.

Peoples:	**Sotho**, with minority of **Xhosa** in south.
Capital:	Maseru 15,000. Urbanisation 5%. Literacy 70%.
Economy:	Only 11% of country fit for agriculture. There is gross overpopulation, severe soil erosion and very few natural resources. Over 25% of the labour force is forced, through poverty, to seek jobs in South Africa.
Politics:	Independent of Britain in 1966. A constitutional monarchy. Political unrest has caused the government to maintain a State of Emergency since 1970. Land torn between the O.A.U. anti-South Africa line and need for friendly relations with South Africa.
Religion:	**African Traditionals** 10%.
	African Independent Churches (210) 11%.
	Roman Catholics 40% – dominant in all spheres of national life.
	Protestants 39%. Community 336,000. Denominations 8. The largest: Evangelical Church (the French PEMS) 190,000; Anglicans 90,000; Methodists 6,000; Pentecostals (4) 8,000 community. Evangelicals 4% of population.

Points for Prayer

1) **Lesotho is tragically poor spiritually and physically.** The great work of the French missionaries in the last century is in decline, with much nominalism in national Church. Pray for its revival.

2) **The Roman Catholics have invested vast sums of money and manpower in the country.** The entire cabinet, the Prime Minister and also the King are R.C.s, and most of the schools and hospitals are run by the R.C.s. There is therefore considerable intolerance of Protestant work by some chiefs and officials, and Protestants sometimes suffer discrimination in schools and the health services. Pray for many R.C.s to turn to a Biblical faith.

3 **The evangelical witness is very weak.** The more live denominations are small – though growth is occurring in the Pentecostal groups, and also in the Dutch Reformed Church (all 5 groups having about 20–30 little church groups). The Mahon Mission (Baptist) after years of witness is in decline through lack of national and missionary personnel. There are only about 16 missionaries of these denominations in the country.

4) **The churches are very weak.** Congregations are almost entirely made up of women – the few men usually being illiterate. The absence of so many men for most of the year in South Africa makes it almost impossible to build up lay leadership, adequate family life and giving for the Lord's work. Pray for the conversion of more men and the planting of strong churches all over the land.

5) **Evangelistic work** is now hindered by the ban on evening meetings, yet carries on in a small way. Pray for peace in the land and for freedom to preach in all areas. Especially needy are the little evangelised mountain villages – often only reached by horseback or terrible roads. Pray for these Mountain Sotho*. Pray also for the raising up of more preachers willing to make the great sacrifices essential if this difficult land is to be won for Jesus.

LIBERIA

BACKGROUND

Area:	112,000 sq. km. – coastal state between Ivory Coast and Sierra Leone.
Population:	1,600,000. Annual growth 2.9%. People per sq. km. – 14.
Peoples:	**African tribes** 90% (24) – largest:– Kpelle 262,000; Kru 120,000; Bassa

200,000; Gio 120,000; Mano 105,000; Grebo 100,000.

English speaking Africans 10% – descendants of liberated American slaves settled on coast in 1822, and detribalised Africans.

Capital: Monrovia 150,000. Urbanisation 28%. Literacy – a low 10%.

Economy: Considerable development with rubber plantations, iron ore and large "flag of convenience" shipping fleet.

Politics: Black Africa's first independent country (1847), and one of the world's most stable politically.

Religion: **Attitude of Government** – A Christian state – President Tolbert a committed Christian.

        African Traditionals 40%.

        Muslim 18% (Vai and Mandingo tribes).

        Roman Catholics 2%. **African Independents** 8%. **Protestants** 40%. Community 139,000. Denominations 24. The largest: Methodists (3) 36,000; Baptists 25,000; Pentecostal Assemblies 20,000; Assemblies of God 26,000. Evangelicals 5%.

Points for Prayer

1) **Unreached peoples** – only about 5 tribes have no effective resident evangelical witness (mostly small sections of tribes found in surrounding countries). Yet a number of tribes have yet to make a significant response to the Gospel – notably the Gio; Dey 8,000; Mano; Krahn 33,000; also the unoccupied and resistant Muslim tribes – the Vai 40,000 and Mandingo 45,000.

2) **Islam is slowly advancing again** and the international Muslim missionary movement considers Liberia the most strategic base for their big new West Africa missionary effort.

3) **The older, coastal churches need revival**, for in the midst of orthodoxy there is much nominalism, lack of depth in spiritual life; immorality and alcohol are real problems among church members. They need to have a greater concern for the evangelisation of the less privileged sections of the country.

4) **The inland churches have grown slowly until recently**, but there is now encouragement. The main problems:– the diversity of tribes, lack of the Scriptures, low literacy and the difficult climate; the latter having greatly hindered the missionaries. Much work has been done to rectify these problems. Pray for the development of strong, well taught, well led churches. Also pray for the drawing together of evangelicals from all the peoples of the country in a supra-tribal fellowship. Pray for the newly started Liberia Evangelical Fellowship.

5) **The training of leaders for the churches** is hard for the above reasons. Pray for the **WEC** agricultural Bible School at Gaypeter, and also for ELWA **(SIM)** programme of radio TEE in Bassa and Gola – both proving valuable tools for training of actual leaders in the churches. The cassette ministry is being successfully launched in a number of languages and is valuable where literacy is so low.

6) **The West Africa Bible College** – for more advanced students from all over West Africa will soon be built at Yekepa (1977-79). A radio Bible School will be launched in English (with ELWA) in 1977 and resident students will be taken in in 1979. Pray for the launching of this project and the supplying of all needs and staff.

7) **Missions** have opened up the interior tribes over the last few years. There are now about 450 missionaries in the country. The most notable work has been that of WEC (Bassa, Gio, Mano, Kissi), Baptists and Pentecostal Assemblies. The major emphasis of missionary work is on teaching believers, training leaders and Bible translation.

8) **Bible translation** – one language has the whole Bible, 6 the N.T., 11 have portions. Work is in progress in 6 and at least 7 urgently need translators – especially the Dey and Kissi.

9) **The Missionary vision of the Liberian Church is growing.** Some pastors are showing concern for Muslims. At a 1975 pastors' conference 80 pastors volunteered to give a few weeks each year to pioneer evangelism – this programme has now been launched as W. African Movement for Advancement of Missions (WAMAM), and results have been dramatic. Follow-up work is being done by visitation and cassettes of

Scripture on tape. Some young people are doing more and more evangelism over the border in poorly evangelised Guinea. Pray for this vision to increase.

10) **Radio ELWA (SIM)** is Africa's best known Christian broadcasting station. Pray for the staff of 50 expatriates and 150 Africans. The impact through their hospital, school, T.V. and many radio programmes on Liberia is immense (average 6,000 letters per month from Liberia). Broadcasts in 46 languages are also prepared in studios in 3 other countries. Pray especially for the outreach to the Arab and African Muslim lands to the north and east. Pray also for the many follow-up ministries.

MADAGASCAR

BACKGROUND

Area: 594,000 sq. km. – a 1,600 km. long island off the coast of Mozambique.
Population: 7,700,000. Annual growth 2.7%. People per sq. km. – 13. Literacy 30%.
Peoples: The 18 tribes of Malagasy people all speak the same language, which is related to Malay. These people came originally from Borneo, Indonesia. Some admixture with both Arabs and Africans – especially on the coast.
Capital: Tananarive 382,000. Urbanisation 14%.
Economy: Largely agricultural and relatively poor.
Politics: Independent of France in 1960. Military government since 1972 that has become increasingly Marxist. There is considerable unrest in the land.
Religion: **Attitude of Government** – increasingly anti-Christian. **Traditional Religions** 44% – great resurgence of former heathen practices, astrology, etc., since independence, and which has official approval.
Muslims 9% – largely found in the northern coastal belt and among Comorian immigrants in the north east, though the latter are decreasing through forced repatriation.
Roman Catholics 25% – came with French colonial rule in 1885 and stronger in the lowlands.
Protestants 22% – largely among the more sophisticated highlanders – fruit of the early L.M.S. missionary work. Community 1,200,000. Denominations 7. The largest: The Church of Jesus Christ in Madagascar (LMS, Paris Miss. Soc.) 800,000; Lutherans 300,000. There is very much nominalism. Evangelicals 3%.

Prayer Targets

1) **The strongly leftward trend in the government** could close the door for the preaching of the Gospel and even bring persecution to the Christians again. Pray for God's overruling in the affairs of men for the good of the Gospel.

2) **The Lord worked with power in the last century**, with a great turning to the Lord in the midst of persecution from the heathen rulers and then by the Roman Catholics after the French took over the country. There have been more localised movements of revival in the southern parts of the country in the Lutheran Church in this century, but now the great need of the land is a revival that will strike at the roots of the prevailing nominalism.

3) **The deadness in the larger churches** is partly due to the influx of many into the churches without adequate discipling and partly due to the generally liberalistic views of the later missionaries. Many national pastors today are seeking to accommodate Christianity with astrology, heathen customs and Marxism. Pray that these churches may return to a Biblical theology and warm personal faith – even if it does have to be by way of suffering.

4) **The evangelical witness is very small indeed.** This is confined to sections of the Lutheran Church, several small Pentecostal groups totalling 10,000 and a small Baptist fellowship of several thousand. As a result, very few people are aware of what the true Gospel really is and large areas of the country are nominally Christian, but without any evangelical witness – about 5,000,000 people in the north of the country are in such a position.

5) **Young people's work is limited but encouraging. SU** has a small work, but its witness is extending, with many young people being touched by the Lord. There is a lively GBU **(IVF)** group in the university. Young people's evangelistic teams formed in the last few years are seeing much fruit. Pray that all opportunities to evangelise and plant churches may be used while there is time.

6) **Missions** – there are now less than 100 missionaries in the land. There is a great need for evangelical missionaries for church planting, church support literature and Bible training ministries, but the present situation makes entry hard – even miracles would be needed! Pray for the winning of this neglected land.

7) **Training of evangelical leaders** – little is now being done. Pray for the possible commencing of an Evangelical Seminary and also for the development of a TEE programme.

MALAWI

BACKGROUND

Area: 117,000 sq. km. – a long narrow country extending down Lake Malawi and its outflow river, the Shire. Virtually an enclave in Mozambique.

Population: 5,100,000. Annual growth 2.4%. People per sq. km. – 44. Literacy 10%.

Peoples: **African tribes** – 10. In north: Tonga 58,000; Tumbuka 400,000. In centre: Chewa (Nyanja) 3,320,000. In south: Yao 700,000; Sena and Lomwe.

Capital: Lilongwe 25,000. Also Blantyre-Limbe 170,000. Urbanisation 6%.

Economy: Poor, lacking in enough land and natural resources. Many Malawians leave to seek work in other countries – Zambia, Rhodesia and South Africa.

Politics: Independent of Britain in 1964. One party state, under rule of President Banda. Isolated from southern Africa by unfriendly Mozambique government.

Religion: **Attitude of Government** – freedom of religion, though J.W.s are banned.
African Traditionals 26%.
Muslims 15% – largely of the Yao tribe.
Roman Catholics 26% – overdependent on foreign priests; very nominal.
Protestants 29%. Community 1,300,000. Denominations 10. The largest: Church of Central Africa, Presbyterian or CCAP 900,000; Anglican 80,000; Evangelical Church (**AEF**, Nyasa Mission, Zambesi Mission) 61,000. Evangelicals 14%.

Prayer Targets

1) **There is, at present, peace and freedom to preach the Gospel.** Pray that this may continue despite the ominous turn of events in surrounding lands.

2) **There is great interest and hunger for the things of God** with many coming to the Lord whenever the Gospel is preached. There are, however, far too few trained and spiritual Christian workers available to lead the many coming into the churches into a living relationship with the Lord and then to disciple them.

3) **By far the largest church is the CCAP** which has been formed out of the work of the Evangelical NGK (Dutch Ref. Ch. of S. Africa) and the more liberal Free Church of Scotland in the north and the Church of Scotland in the south. There are some fine leaders in the Nhkoma Synod, but there are few evangelical pastors in the north and south of the country. Pray for the Theological School at Nhkoma. Revival is needed to root the Gospel deep in the hearts of the people.

4) **The Evangelical Church** has a strong witness in the south of the country, but there are too few full time workers and a lack of the funds to support them. Pray for the Likubula Bible Institute run by the **AEF**-Nyasa Mission – Zambesi Mission. The witness of the Baptists, Nazarenes and Assemblies of God is growing.

5) **New Life for All** has proved a blessing in some areas, but the impact was not as great as it could have been due to the lack of converted and spiritual lay leaders able to make the programme effective.

6) **Missions** – there are now about 200 missionaries in the country. Many are involved in institutional work. Pray for these brethren labouring for the Lord – that their ministry may be a blessing to the national believers and help the churches to maturity and effective outreach.

7) **Young people's work** is expanding and effective. Pray for the growing ministry of SU in the schools. Pray also for the large group of believers at the university.

8) **Unreached peoples**
   a) Some tribes in the north have no evangelical witness – all are small.
   b) The largely Muslim Yao are fairly resistant to the Gospel, though some churches have been planted by several groups – especially of the Nhkoma Synod of the CCAP.
   c) Many tribes overlap into poorly evangelised Mozambique. Pray for the witness of Malawi Christians in villages over the border, which still continues despite the open opposition of the Marxist government to any Christian evangelism.

MALI

BACKGROUND

Area: 1,204,000 sq. km. – dry southern grasslands merge into the advancing Sahara desert in the north.

Population: 5,800,000. Annual growth 2.4%. Population density – 5 people per sq. km.

Peoples: **Arab-Berber** (Mauritanians and Tuareg nomads) 5% in north.
African tribes – 29. The largest: Bambara 1,740,000 – though language spoen by 80% of Malians; Fula 500,000; Songhai 350,000; Dogon 335,000; Senoufo 260,000; Malinke 250,000; Mianka 330,000; Kita 174,000; Bobo 116,000; Kasonke 110,000.

Capital: Bamako 240,000. Urbanisation 12%. Literacy 5–10%.

Economy: The 1968–73 drought and subsequent famine devastated this already very poor land. Economy totally disrupted and only slowly recovering.

Politics: Independent of France in 1960. Military government since 1968 seeking to restore economy and prepare for civilian rule.

Religion: **Attitude of Government** – great freedom for Gospel despite Muslim majority.
African Traditionals 21%.
Muslims 77% and increasing.
Roman Catholics 1%.
Protestants 0.5% now rapidly increasing. Community 25,000; Members 6,000. Denominations 4 – all evangelical. Evangelical Chr. Ch. (**CMA**) 4,600 members; Evangelical Protestant Church (**GMU**) 1,260 members. Evangelicals 0.5%.

Points for Prayer

1) **This land is open for the Gospel and is still very much a pioneer field**, yet there are only 4 missions with about 100 missionaries (**GMU** in centre, **CMA** in east, United World Mission in west and Evangelical Baptists in north). Pray for the entry of more missionaries able to contribute to the development of the Church and pioneering new areas. There are openings for every form of missionary outreach.

2) **The Sahel Famine** affected the whole country, with great movements of Muslim northern peoples to the south. Much aid was administered by the missions and **W.V.** through the local churches. The honesty, hard work and love of the believers has given an unprecedented opening for the Gospel among heathen and Muslims. Pray that continuing more long term aid may further help others to believe and churches to planted in hitherto unevangelised areas.

3) **Unreached peoples** – it is estimated that 3 million Muslims in the centre and north have never really clearly heard the Gospel. A number of tribes have no Christian witness – the Fulas, Bozos, Marakas. Pray for the Baptist witness among the Muslim Tuareg, Songhai and Masina – where very few have believed and no church has yet been planted.

4) **In the west the U.W.M.** is beginning to see churches formed among the heavily

Muslimised Malinke and Kasonke, but the unoccupied Kagoro and Kita peoples need to be evangelised (now only having R.C missionaries).

5) **The dominant Bambara people are largely Muslim** and not very open for the Gospel. Nevertheless **GMU** has developed a work with a strong national Church and supported by a fine range of ministries in the Capital – especially valuable is the literature produced in the widely used Bambara language for the many newly literate people. Pray for the new **GMU** Ev. Lit. Centre and the production of locally written literature.

6) **In the east the CMA have seen a remarkable work of God** among the heathen Dogon among whom many churches have been planted. This turning to the Lord has now started among the Bobo and Mianka, and even in several Muslim tribes. There are now Christian groups in 327 towns and villages. The work is extending to many new areas and tribes. Pray for labourers.

7) **The churches are growing and enthusiastically evangelising.** Teams of evangelists are being used of God to establish new churches. About 10% of the believers come from a Muslim background. They face considerable opposition from Muslims at times. The Church is increasingly supra-tribal, with large and blessed conferences. There are great weaknesses – $\frac{3}{4}$ of the believers are illiterate and too few of the pastors are able to give much pastoral teaching. There are, however, some fine spiritual leaders in the two major denominations.

8) **Leadership training** – pray for the **CMA** and **GMU** Bible Schools – more truly God-called students are needed, for there is a paucity of trained leaders to pastor the new churches being planted. A more advanced training in French for pastors is needed -- pray for the raising up of such a training institution.

9) **Young people** – there are many opportunities to witness to school children, run camps and start Christian groups, but the lack of workers hinders this. The young people are very open now. There is also a small GBU (**IVF**) group at the university – some of these students are former Muslims, but now live for the Lord.

10) **Technical aids** – the cassette ministry is now being used extensively to help the illiterate and lonely believers to obtain good teaching and to hear the Scriptures. **Radio ELWA** also is a profitable means of outreach with the three programmes a week in Mali languages.

MAURITIUS

BACKGROUND

Area:	1,942 sq. km. – an island 800 km. east of Madagascar in the Indian Ocean.
Population:	900,000. Annual growth 1.2% (with considerable emigration). Grossly over-populated with 463 people per sq. km.
Peoples:	**Europeans** 1.6% – largely French, who dominate the big businesses and the sugar estates.
	Creoles 27% – mixed African and European; largely Roman Catholic.
	Indians 68% – politically dominant; 25% Muslim, 75% Hindu.
	Chinese 3% – who control the retail trade.
Capital:	Port Louis 140,000 – but with 46% of the people living in its environs.
Economy:	Over-dependence on the sugar industry and limited land space makes diversification of the economy essential.
Politics:	Independent of Britain in 1968. Unemployment and tensions between racial and religious groups fuelling rapid rise to power of pro-Marxist political party. There is serious trouble ahead for this island state.
Religion:	**Attitude of Government** – at the moment there is religious freedom. **Hindus** 51%, **Muslims** 17%, **Buddhists** 2%, **Roman Catholics** 30%. **Protestants** 1%. Community 8,000. Largest groups:– Anglo-Catholic Anglicans, Seventh Day Adventists. Evangelicals – Assemblies of God 1,800 members, Evangelical Church (AEF). Evangelicals 0.05%. Rate of growth of Protestants – negligible.

Points for Prayer

1) **Mauritius is one of the forgotten mission fields of the world.** The evangelisation of this island has scarcely begun. Although there is religious freedom, the darkening political clouds could bring radical changes in 1978. Pray for the evangelisation of the diverse racial groups of the land.

2) **Most of the island and its population groups remain unreached** – pray for:–
   a) The socially isolated French in their Roman Catholic faith.
   b) The Muslims and Hindus.
   c) The poor Creole population of Rodriguez Island (30,000) – 500 km. east of Mauritius.

3) **Evangelical missionaries are few** – 2 couples of the **AEF**, an independent couple among the Chinese, and a Chinese Presbyterian pastor from Taiwan. More workers, local and expatriate, are urgently needed for developing youth work and church planting. Pray for the ministry of the overworked few who labour for the Master.

4) **The national believers** are largely Pentecostal, but these assemblies are led by untrained pastors and are prone to doctrinal extremes. Pray for the two little Evangelical Church congregations and the raising up of mature leaders from among them. Pray for a unity of believers that reaches across racial divisions, and pray for an effective outreach from them to people of all racial and religious groups.

5) **Young people** – many have been touched by the Gospel, but have not committed their lives to the Lord because of pressure from parents, other young people and also dead and liberal churches. Pray for the raising up of youth workers who are able to build up good youth groups and develop musical groups to witness to young people in the schools and teacher training college.

6) **There is a great need for a good Christian bookshop ministry** among this largely literate people. The Roman Catholics are now more interested in reading the Bible.

7) **Pray for the ministry of the radio broadcasts from FEBA Seychelles** to Mauritius in both French and the major Indian languages.

MOZAMBIQUE

BACKGROUND

Area: 785,000 sq. km. – occupying a strategic 2,800 sq. km. stretch of coast of S.E. Africa.

Population: 9,300,000. Annual growth 2.3%. People per sq. km. – 12.

Peoples: **African tribes** – 21 larger tribes and unknown number of smaller. Larger tribes – in **north**: Macua 1,300,000; Lomwe 1,000,000; Maconde 350,000; Yao* 250,000; in **centre**: Sena 1,000,000; Shona 250,000; Ndau 600,000; Nyanja 300,000; in **south**: Tsonga (Shangaan) 800,000; Tswa (Ronga) 550,000; Chopi 300,000.
Portuguese – several thousand – all that remain of the 200,000 in 1974.

Capital: Maputo (Lourenco Marques) 500,000. Urbanisation 12%. Literacy 6%.

Economy: The neglected and underdeveloped economy in ruins with the flight of the Portuguese, independence and the immediate application of Marxist policies of nationalisation of all lands, businesses and property.

Politics: A 10 year guerrilla war ended with the sudden handover of power by the Portuguese to the Communist Frelimo forces in 1975 after 470 years of colonial rule. The hard-line Marxist regime is very unpopular, but retained in power by Russian arms and aid, the artificial stimulation of confrontation with Rhodesia and the presence of Tanzanian troops.

Religion: **Attitude of Government** – committed to the destruction of all religious "superstitions", with considerable degree of harassment of churches.
African Traditionals 54%.
Muslims 12% – mostly among Macua, Yao and Maconde.
Roman Catholics 27% – very nominal and rather discredited by association with the colonial power – numbers falling rapidly under persecution.
Protestants 7%. Community 418,000. Denominations 22 – Methodists (4)

70,000 adherents; Anglicans 30,000; Presbyterians (Swiss Mission) 28,000; Baptists (AEF) 60,000; Nazarenes 20,000; Pentecostals (5+) 35,000. Evangelicals 4%.

Points for Prayer

1) **The Communist government that replaced the Portuguese is even more hostile** to the true Gospel. Pray that the door may be opened to evangelise the whole land.

2) **Mozambique contains the largest unreached population in the Southern Hemisphere.** In only two areas in the central provinces were Protestant evangelical missionaries ever allowed to operate (Beira – several groups, N. E. Tete – Nazarenes) and in the north one SAGM-AEF station among the Lomwe. This means that the Macua, Maconde, Yao (mostly Muslim, but also many High Anglican), Sena and most of the Shona tribes have no more than a handful of Christians. Many other peoples such as the Chopi and Ndau are under-evangelised. Many of these tribes are without the Scriptures – Chopi, Sena, Kunda, Macua, Maconde, etc.

3) **God has been raising up a witness in the centre and north over the last 5 years.** The Lomwe Church (AEF related, but without missionaries since 1959) has grown dramatically in this period to a church of 25,000 members with missionary outreach to the Yao, Macua and Maconde. Brethren missionaries in south Tanzania have seen many Mozambique Maconde refugees turning to the Lord; these have now returned to evangelise their home areas in Mozambique. There still continues a considerable witness from the strong churches in Malawi to areas around the borders with Mozambique. Pray for the growth and extension of the witness from these three sources. Several indigenous African Pentecostal Churches were beginning to show dramatic growth among the Sena and Shona peoples in the Beira-Tete areas.

4) **The Protestant Church is strongest in the southern provinces**, where most of the missionaries operated. Now there are no more missionaries in the country. Growth was marked during the last few years with many new churches being planted – especially of the Nazarenes and Pentecostals. Many of the believers are illiterate, and there are very few trained pastors – pray for the believers all over the country in this time of increasing persecution.

5) **The Communists very quickly imposed strict controls** on the activities of believers. No form of evangelism is allowed, no children may be baptised or "influenced religiously", and Christian literature cannot any longer be imported or printed or even distributed or read in public. The number of meetings has had to be reduced and all known believers are closely watched. There are a considerable number of believers now in prison or harsh and primitive labour camps euphemistically called "re-education centres". Persecution has been exceptionally severe for the Watchtower sect with 35,000 in these camps. There are persistent rumours that all children over the age of 5 will soon be removed from parents and sent to training camps. The initial fear of the believers seems to be wearing off and witnessing continues, with many young people seeking the Lord. Pray for our persecuted brethren. In December 1976 there were still 150 pastors in prison for their witness.

6) **Literature** is now in short supply and the only Christian bookshop may have to close. Pray for the preservation of the Bibles now in the land, and also for those brought in by mine workers returning from South Africa (confiscation is usual). For Radio outreach to Mozambique see Swaziland (p. 210) and Seychelles (p. 202)."

**Footnote: June 1977 – an easing of pressures on believers is reported, with fewer in prison and more freedom for meetings.

<u>NIGER</u>

BACKGROUND

Area: 1,187,000 sq. km. – all but a narrow strip of country along Nigerian border in south and Niger River in south west is semi-desert or desert.

Population: 4,700,000. Population growth 2.7%. People per sq. km. – 4.
Peoples: **African tribes** – 14. The largest: Hausa 2,200,000; Zerma-Songhai 1,000,000; Beriberi-Manga 400,000; Fulani 400,000.
Tuaregs 420,000 – a nomadic Berber people living in Sahara.
Capital: Niamey 120,000. Urbanisation 8%. Literacy 5%.
Economy: The country most affected by 1967-74 Sahel Famine, which has re-appeared again in 1976. Very poor and undeveloped.
Politics: Independent of France in 1960. Military coup in 1974.
Religion: **Attitude of Government** – Islam is the national religion and is actively encouraged. The work of Christian Missions in helping the country through institutional work is much appreciated.
Muslims 86%.
African Traditionals 13% – only two small tribes are predominantly such.
Roman Catholics 0.4%.
Protestants 0.05%. Community 2,600. Denominations 2. Evangelical Church (SIM) 750 members, Baptists. Evangelicals 0.05%.

Points for Prayer

1)   **This Muslim land is open for the Gospel**. Pray that this may remain so and that believers from other lands may be called to serve the Lord.
2)   **There are only about 160 missionaries serving the Lord** with three Missions. The lack of development makes the contribution of technical skill by missionaries extremely valuable. There is a need for personnel to seize the many opportunities that exist in rural development schemes, health (**SIM** runs one of the three hospitals in the country) and education. Pray for both tact and usefulness as the missionaries seek to witness to the Muslim majority.
3)   **Islam is strong** and a new School of Islamic Studies is now being built in Niamey. Yet, paradoxically, the Muslims are more open than ever before to listen to the Good News – the excellent witness of the missionary institutions playing no small part in this. Pray for the many unreached Muslim peoples and tribes.
4)   **Unreached peoples** –
  a) There are two Traditionalist tribes (with whom **SIM** is in contact – the **Kurfei** 60,000 and **Mauri** 120,000. Pray for the planting of churches among these people.
  b) The **Zerma** are still 25% animist. Pray for the work of the Evangelical Baptists among these and other tribes.
  c) **The Fulani** are coming increasingly under the sound of the Gospel – in Nigeria to where many travel in search of pasture for their cattle, and by means of the Radio ELWA Fulani broadcasts. Pray for conversions.
  d) **The Tuareg**, once rich, have been impoverished by the famine, and many reduced to the state of begging refugees. The remarkable and selfless ministry of the missionaries and national believers in aiding and rehabilitating refugees has opened many to the Word. Pray for the **SIM** evangelistic, medical and Bible translation work among them. Only a handful have believed.
5)   **The Protestant Church** is growing in maturity and numbers. There are 10 pastors and 27 evangelists serving in the Evangelical Church. There is a new and welcome interest in evangelism that bodes well for the future. Pray for this small body of believers that their testimony may be pure and bold. Pray for courage and wisdom as they seek to witness to Muslims – a number of Muslims have sought the Lord.
6)   **Leadership training**. There is one high level Bible School using French in Niamey that is run by **SIM** and serves Upper Volta and Benin as well as Niger. Pray for the staff and also for the 30 students (1976). There is a great need for well trained Christian leaders. Pray also for the **SIM** TEE programme run in 9 widely separated places – there are now over 100 students.
7)   **There is a very small GBU (IVF) group in the university** – none are of Niger. Pray for the witness of these students to the Nigerians.
8)   **Bible translation** – at least 2 languages need translators and work is in progress in 3 languages. 2 languages have the Bible, 3 the N.T. and a further 2 have portions. The lack of literacy hinders the progress of literature work.

NIGERIA

BACKGROUND

Area: 924,000 sq. km. – divided into 19 states to minimise the influence of tribal loyalties in national politics.

Population: 64,700,000 (estimate). Annual growth 2.7%. People per sq. km. – 70.

Peoples: **African tribes** – over 500, most very small, some very large (seebelow).

Capital: Lagos 1,500,000. Other major cities: Ibadan 1,000,000; Kano 500,000; Port Harcourt 400,000. Urbanisation 21%. Literacy 25% (rapidly increasing).

Economy: Oil wealth being used to improve medical and educational services, communications, etc., and economic benefits spreading over the whole country.

Politics: Independence from Britain in 1960. A Federal Republic at present ruled by a progressive military government that plans to hand over power to a civilian government in 1979. The tragic 2½ year Civil War ended in 1970; enlightened policies have led to a rapid healing of the economic and social wounds caused thereby.

Religion: **Attitude of Government** – great freedom with the government strongly in favour of religious activity – both of Muslims and Christians.

              African Traditionals 22% – still strong among some tribes in central Nigeria, but also very influential within the Muslim tribes in the north and Christian communities in the south.

              Muslims 50% – very strong in the north and in some areas in centre and west, with considerable missionary activity in centre among animist tribes.

              Roman Catholics 11%.

              African Independent Churches (over 600) 8%.

              Protestants 27%. Community 15,980,000. Denominations 35+, see below for statistics of churches. Evangelicals 8%.

Points for Prayer – General for whole land

1)   **Nigeria returns to civilian rule in 1979**. Pray for wisdom and statesmanship for the land's present and future rulers and for continued freedom for the Gospel.

2)   **Nigerianisation of the economic and religious life of the country continues.** This is bringing a healthy development of national leadership and initiative to the churches, with work once handled by missionaries being turned over to Nigerian believers. Missionaries work more and more as part of the national Church and under its leadership. Pray for a continued harmonious relationship between expatriates and national believers. Pray that mission leaders may know the mind of the Lord as to strategic aims they must follow in these days of rapid change.

3)   **Missions are much needed and desired by the churches.** There are very many openings for expatriates in this time of dramatic growth – especially in the training of national leaders, TEE programmes and those with technical skills. Many state governments are pleading with missions to provide them with qualified staff to train religious knowledge teachers in Nigeria's rapidly expanding educational system. Pray for the calling and entry of needed expatriates (visas are not easy to obtain – and only issued to those which have technical or professional qualifications). There are now about 1,300 missionaries in Nigeria.

4)   **Institutional Work** has played a great part in opening up Nigeria for the Gospel, but now the government is gradually taking over mission schools and hospitals. Pray that these changes may be smooth and beneficial for the Gospel. Pray for Christian teachers and nurses and their witness within these government schools and hospitals. Many schools are still run by the churches, placing a big burden on overworked pastors.

5)   **The training of leaders for the Church is a priority.** Much is being done through theological training in the 40+ Seminaries and Bible Schools and the rapidly expanding TEE programmes in many languages throughout Nigeria. Pray for the raising up of more Nigerian and expatriate staff for this ministry – the need is so great that the present supply of workers cannot meet it. The level of education of pastors must be raised to meet the needs of better educated congregations.

6) **Young people** do not receive enough attention in many churches and are a needy field. SU has a good work in the southern part of the country in the secondary schools and the Fellowship of Christian Students in the centre and north. Many young people are finding the Lord in the school groups and in camps run by these worthy organisations. Pray for the staff and Christian teachers who make this ministry a success. NIFES **(IVF)** has a very successful witness on the campuses of all 17 universities and other post-secondary educational institutions. Pray for the winning of many of these students and their upbuilding in the faith, and also for the integration of these young Christians into local churches.

7) **Universal primary education**, recently made government policy, is causing an explosive growth of teacher training colleges. Bible teaching or Islamic teaching is compulsory in all schools. All children will have to decide between Christianity and Islam. Both Christians and Muslims are making a great effort to train teachers to take advantage of this opportunity. Pray for the calling of those able to train Christian teachers for this ministry. Pray that the believers may make full use of this chance to win young people.

8) **Literature** is more needed than ever before. Pray for the valuable publishing ministry of **SU**, **Africa Christian Press**, etc., who are producing good, locally written books. Pray for the ministry of the evangelistic "Today's Challenge" magazine (ECWA Publications – **SIM**) and also the 38 Challenge bookstores all over Nigeria.

9) **Gospel Recordings** with records in 419 of the country's languages, has a useful ministry for reaching people in this multi-lingual land where many smaller tribes still remain unreached.

10) **Bible translation** – 9 languages have the whole Bible, 20 the N.T. and a further 62 have portions. Work is in progress in 52, but at least 48 still await translators. **WBT**'s extensive ministry in the land has now been handed over to the Nigerian Bible Translation Trust. Pray for the latter, for the handover in 1976 had to be very sudden. A few **WBT** workers are allowed to spend a limited period training Nigerians both to translate and also to teach other nationals how to do the same. There are, at present, 8 N.T.s ready for publication that have been translated by nationals, and other teams are working in a further 20. Pray for these brethren as they tackle this complex and painstaking task.

Prayer Points for different areas of the country

NIGERIA – The South-West

The Yoruba (10 million) are in the great majority – 47% are Protestant or of African Ind. Churches, 5% are Roman Catholic and about 15% are Muslim.

1) **The region was pioneered** by the Anglicans, Methodists and Southern Baptists and each denomination has large independent Churches. It is repectable to be a Christian, but among professing Christians sin, worldliness and witchcraft are common. Revival that affects the whole of society is an urgent necessity.

2) **The many growing cities are insufficiently evangelised.** Praise God that there are now a number of young and enthusiastic evangelists who are beginning to make a significant impact in these cities. This work needs to be better co-ordinated and related to local churches that can conserve the fruit of this ministry.

3) **There is a notable lack of concern for outreach** in many churches and among individual believers – especially to the Muslims and also other areas in the land.

4) **There are many little Pentecostal groups** mushrooming all over the south of the country. Pray for stability and freedom from personality clashes and divisions.

NIGERIA – The South-East and South

Main tribes:– Ibo 9,000,000; Ibibio-Efik 2,000,000; Ijaw 500,000; Edo-Isoko 800,000 – the great majority Christianised but some animists remain.

1) **Pioneered** by Presbyterians and **QIM** – now there are large and growing daughter churches. The harrowing experiences of the Civil War brought revival and a great spiritual deepening. The Qua Iboe Church doubled its membership in 5 years to

240,00 adherents. Pray that the rapid economic improvements since 1970 may not dampen the fervour of these believers.

2) **Evangelistic outreach** to the local non-Protestants has increased. Pray for the conversion of many R.C.s, who are very strong in the area; there is a new openness to the Gospel as a result of greater interest in the Scriptures.

3) **There is a missionary vision** with the QIC-QIM reaching out to less well evangelised tribes to the north, such as the Igala (600,000) and Basa (70,000). Pray for the calling of more into full time service as pastors or missionaries.

NIGERIA – The Middle Belt

This area stretches right across the country from east to west. Many tribes live in this area – some well evangelised and with strong churches, such as the Tiv (1,200,000). Yet others are still animist and unreached or Muslim.

1) **Pioneered at great cost** by SIM in the west and centre, and SUM in the centre and east. Denominational societies have also played a vital role such as the S. African DRC among the Tiv (now part of the SUM field). These missions are merged into the daughter churches (Evangelical Churches of W. Africa or ECWA **(SIM)**, and Fell. of Churches of Christ in Nigeria – TEKAN **(SUM)**) but still have a large investment of personnel in the country. Most of the institutions have now been taken over by the government or the national churches. ECWA has a community of 600,000 and TEKAN 750,000. Pray for the work of these missions in their self-effacing ministry of helping the national churches to maturity.

2) **The churches have grown dramatically** over the last 30 years. Many denominations have experienced 400% growth in the last 10 years. The churches are almost entirely evangelical with a vigorous evangelistic outreach. New Life For All proved most successful in this area and many believers were mobilised for profitable outreach. Pray for the continued (though in a lower key) NLFA outreach through witness teams in the centre and north of the country. Pray also for the continued spiritual growth of believers and also for the conversion of the younger generation – nominalism could become a problem. The Anglicans and the Baptists are making a significant contribution to the evangelisation of the area.

3) **Unreached peoples.** There are probably about 50 ethnic groups totalling 2,500,000 people in this area that are unreached or resistant. A recent Evangelical Fell. of Nigeria survey has analysed the needs of some 30 animist groups. Pray for the right strategy for winning these people, and pray for the raising up of more Nigerian missionaries to work among them. We mention a few:– The Muslim Nupe 600,000; Animist Kamuku 50,000; Gbari* 600,000; Bunu 150,000; Igbira 500,000; Jerawa 100,000; Kadara 50,000; Koro 40,000 in the SIM-ECWA area; and the Afo 30,000; Jarawa 150,000; Jukun 20,000; Mada 100,000; Mbula 30,000; Mumuye 140,000; Vere 25,000 in the SUM-EKAN area. There are also about 10 Muslimised tribes in the area that are unreached.

4) **Muslim missionary advances** have increased since the Oil Crisis with large investments in vehicles, schools, dispensaries, hospitals and literature in the Middle Belt. There are considerable efforts being made to win backsliding Christians. The Ammadiya Muslim sect is very active. Pray for the conversion of Muslims.

NIGERIA – The North

Peoples – largely Hausa (25 million speak this language as a language of wider communication), Sokoto-Fulani (up to 5,000,000), Kanuri (2,500,000) who are nearly all Muslim, but with strong underlay of animism.

1) **There have been great Gospel advances into this Muslim area** over the last 15 years. There is a slow but steady trickle of Muslims being converted and churches planted in both the Muslim centres of Sokoto and Kano as well as in the rural areas. Pray for a greater harvest in coming days. Converts out of Islam face considerable opposition and hostility from relatives. Pray for these believers.

2) **Unreached peoples** – the Kanuri have proved very resistant, and after years of

witness by Nigerian missionaries there is only a handful of believers. Pray for outreach to the animist Hausa, called the Maguzawa* (500,000) who are now receptive, but largely unreached.

3) **The need for missionaries.** SIM and SUM have sought to evangelise in this area for many years, but the work has been hard. Praise God for the increasing missionary concern of the Nigerian Church for the evangelisation of the north. ECWA now has 129 and Tekan 50 missionary couples in cross-cultural mission work (many in the north). The Nigeria Congress on Evangelism in 1975 has proved a great boost to the missionary vision. The Nigerian Church is also beginning to show interest in missionary work in other lands – several Nigerians have gone to Ghana, Benin, Chad and Niger and invitations from Sudan are being considered. Pray for the development of this vision. There are now over 900 Nigerian missionaries serving the Lord.

4) **Pray for the calling of ex-Muslims into full time service,** and also for their training as missionaries to Muslim peoples.

5) **The well known Muslim Fulani** form both the northern upper class and also a large body of nomadic cattle raisers that wander all over sub-Saharan Africa. They number about 5 million. Believers in Nigeria have become concerned for the evangelisation of this strategic people. There are evidences that increased efforts to win these people are bearing fruit. There are now several hundred believers among them in Nigeria – many very isolated and often persecuted. Pray for the planting of strong witnessing churches among them which could mean so much for the spreading of the Gospel in West Africa.

REUNION

BACKGROUND

Area: 2,510 sq. km. island 900 km. east of Madagascar.
Population: 510,000. Annual growth 2.1%. People per sq. km. – 204.
Peoples: Great variety, with **French** 10%, **Chinese** 8%, **Creole**, **Indians**, **Vietnamese**, etc.
Capital: St. Denis 104,000. Urbanisation 43%. Literacy 70%.
Economy: Unhealthy overdependence on sugar with much unemployment.
Politics: Overseas Department of France, but growing autonomist movement may become powerful in 1978 elections.
Religion: **Roman Catholics** 94% – very strong and dominant.
             Muslims 2%.
             Protestants 0.5%. Community 3,000. Denominations 3 – Assemblies of God, S.D.A.s and Evangelical (**AEF**). Evangelical 0.4%.

Points for Prayer

1) **This little island is a pioneer field for missions.** The spiritual need is great with poverty (especially in the highlands), alcoholism (much rum made), loose morals (25% illegitimacy) and witchcraft. Many areas have no settled evangelical witness.

2) **The evangelical witness** began with the Assemblies of God, who now have a number of meeting places around the island. **AEF** entered in 1970 in response to an appeal by a group of believers coverted through the Back to the Bible radio broadcasts. **AEF** now has several couples ministering in church planting, evangelism and Bible teaching. Reinforcements are needed. **AEF** works in cooperation with the South African **Islands Mission**.

3) **The Protestant Church is growing.** There are now 4 churches with 125 baptised believers associated with the **AEF** witness. The great need is for the many young believers to be built up in their faith – through Bible study groups and short term Bible Schools. Pray for the fostering of the evangelistic concern of these believers. Pray that they may effectively reach out to every population group on the island.

4) **Young people face many problems** with the poor prospects for employment, and little has yet been done to reach them and provide camps for them. This ministry could be greatly expanded.

5)   **Literature** is rather scarce and has hitherto been little used among this largely literate population. Plans are afoot to visit every home with Gospel literature. Pray for the saving of some thereby. A little bookshop has now been selling much Christian literature for the last few years.

6)   **The improved signal from Seychelles** is making the **FEBA** French broadcasts much more useful as an evangelistic tool.

RHODESIA (Zimbabwe)

BACKGROUND

Area: 389,000 sq. km. – landlocked state surrounded by Mozambique, Zambia, Botswana and South Africa.

Population: 6,500,000. Annual growth 3.4%. People per sq. km. – 17. Literacy 40%.

Peoples: **Europeans** 4.5% – dominant in government and economy.
               Indians 15,000. **Coloureds** (mixed race) 0.5%.
               Africans 16 tribes – Shona (5 groups) 71%, Ndebele 15%, Nyanja 6% (mostly immigrants from Malawi and Zambia), others 8%.

Capital: Salisbury 600,000. Other cities – Bulawayo 400,000. Urbanisation 22%.

Economy: Growth slowed by sanctions since 1965, but greatly diversified thereby. Very rich in agricultural land, minerals and growing sophistication in industry. One of the world's highest birthrates hinders rise in living standards.

Politics: European minority government declared independence from Britain in 1965. Political and economic isolation as well as increased Communist inspired terrorist incursions from Zambia, Botswana and Communist Mozambique speeded a settlement between whites and internally based black leaders in 1978. The plan was for Independence at the end of 1978, but the increased level of warfare and economic strains prevented this. A Marxist regime imposed by war is not impossible in 1979.

Religion: **Attitude of Government** – there is freedom of religion outside the war zones, but in many of the rural areas the Marxist trained insurgents have stopped church meetings, and killed some Christians.
               African Traditionals 38% – but still strong among "Christians".
               Muslims 1.5% – largely immigrant Yao from Malawi.
               African Indigenous Churches 7% – strong in rural area.
               Roman Catholics 17% – growing, but weak and often syncretic.
               Protestants 35% Community 1,300,000. Denominations 60 + Largest: Methodists (3 groups) 220,000 adherants, Anglicans 140,000, African Reformed (NGK-South Africa) 87,000, Salvation Army 157,000, All Pentecostals est. 180,000 (40+ groups), Evangelicals 9%

Points for Prayer

1)   **The brutality and horror of guerilla warfare** according to Marxist tactics has greatly intensified since 1976. Pray for a just peace and the setting up of a God-fearing government.

2)   **An imminent Communist takeover is possible.** About half the rural population is now dominated by one or other faction of guerillas. Civil war between these factions is likely once white control ends. Pray for the believers and the churches that they may be adequately prepared for possible persecution by a hostile government. Persecution has already begun, with incidents of killing of Christian workers and burning of Bibles.

3)   **Needy areas and peoples.** Although the land is relatively well evangelised, many areas need a fresh wave of evangelism. Other areas and peoples have been neglected.

  a) **The rural areas** – very little true Christianity remains in most areas. There is a great declension from the older churches to the sects or to heathenism that has been speeded up by the tensions and fear pervading the country. Many "Christians" even pray to their ancestors in the church.

b) **The farming areas.** About 1,000,000 labourers and their dependents live on white owned farms – about half of these come from Mozambique or Malawi. Only the CCAP (NGK-South Africa) maintains an extensive witness to these people – and that largely among the Malawians.

c) **The protected villages** – about 200 of these villages, with about 450,000 people, have been built by the government for the protection of the rural population and denial of support to the insurgents. Scattered rural peoples are now concentrated in small areas which make for easier evangelism. Pray that this may occur. **TEAM** with **MAF** help maintain a good witness in some of these villages.

d) **Unreached tribes** – Tonga (80,000), Nambya (45,000), and Kalanga (113,000) in the north west and west, and the Kunda in the north east need pioneer evangelism.

4) **The African Church** is very large, but largely nominal. Too little emphasis was placed on Bible teaching, and really ensuring that church leaders had a really vital living faith in the Lord Jesus. Truly liberated and rejoicing Christians are not so common in the older churches. Missionary-national tensions, and the racial overtones to the present ideological war, have sadly embittered and side-tracked many church leaders. Pray for a spiritual unity that transcends race, tribe and denomination in this sad land. The country has never had a deep moving of the Holy Spirit in revival. Pray for this.

5) **The evangelical witness** is strongest among the fast-growing, but often divisive, Pentecostal Churches. There are fine evangelical leaders in most denominations, though these are often in a small minority. The more evangelical groups are the Brethren in Christ, Baptists, TEAM, AEF, and their daughter Churches. Much that has been built up over the years is now being destroyed. Pray for eternal fruit from the Word that has been sown.

6) **The need of the urban areas** has never been greater. There is a vast influx of work seekers and refugees from the rural areas. There are many churches, but few are able to really go out to evangelise them. Pray for the evangelistic work of the **DM**, youth work of TEAM and AEF etc.

7) **Missions** – There has been a rapid reduction of the missionary force from about 800 in 1975 to about 250 in 1978. Most rural mission stations have been closed, and those that remain are potentially dangerous. About 40 missionaries (R. C. and Protestant) and their families have been martyred. Pray for those who remain – for safety, and also clear guidance. Pray for the right strategy in times that could now be very short. Pray that they may help the national believers to be strong in coming days of trouble

8) **The European Churches** also need revival. Many whites have shown increased concern for spiritual things, but others remain materialistic and complacent. The evangelical witness is strongest among the Baptists and Pentecostals.

9) **The Indian community** is 60% Hindu and 40% Muslim, and is very resistant. Pray that God may give the breakthrough in these close knit communities of Gujarathis and Marathis. There are very few Christians among them.

10) **Scripture Union** has had a decisive impact on the 300 secondary schools in the country. Even in a time when many schools have been closed, there are growing groups in most of them. This is probably the most open section of the population at this time. Pray for the extension of this work to primary schools. There is a Christian Union at the University, but this group needs prayer in the present complex tensions in this multiracial institution.

11) **The missionary vision of the Church is limited.** There are about 20 white and 7 black believers now serving in other lands as missionaries.

RWANDA

BACKGROUND

Area: 26,000 sq. km. – a mountainous country similar to its southern neighbour, Burundi.

Population: 4,400,000. Growth rate 2.8%. People per sq. km. – 169 – Africa's most densely populated country.

Peoples:	**Hutu** (89%) overthrew their erstwhile overlords the **Tutsi** (10%) in 1959. **Minorities** – Twa (Pygmy) 1%.
Capital:	Kigali 7,000 – probably the world's smallest and poorest capital city.
Economy:	Very poor and overpopulated agricultural land with few natural resources.
Politics:	Benign military government that emphasises peace and national unity after years of intertribal mistrust and warfare. Independent in 1962.
Religion:	**Attitude of Government** – complete religious freedom.

African Traditionals 30%.

Roman Catholics 52% have a very powerful influence on national life.

Protestants 18%. Community 660,000. Denominations 6 – almost all evangelical in theology, though the largest is the S.D.A. Church. Anglican (Rwanda Mission) 210,000 adherents; Pentecostal (Swed.) approx. 30,000; Presbyterian (Belgian) 18,000; Free Methodist (U.S.A.) approx. 15,000; Baptist (Danish) 13,000. Evangelicals 13%.

Points for Prayer

1) **Praise God for the open door for the Gospel**, for there was a time when the Communist powers had a big influence in the land.

2) **There is a spontaneous movement of the Spirit** in the Roman Catholic Church. Many prayer meetings are springing up all over the country that are nourished by the Scriptures and centred on Jesus. There are spiritual conflicts in the hearts of many nationals and expatriates because of the division of loyalty between tradition and the truth they have experienced.

3) **The Rwanda Revival** spread from the Anglican mission stations in the '30s to all of East Africa, parts of Zaire and beyond. The inter-tribal violence of the '60s left its marks on the churches with a resulting drying up of spiritual blessing. Pray for the removal of all hatred and bitterness among believers and also for a fresh visitation from God. There are reports of a move of the Spirit among young people over the last few years.

4) **The Church** needs to be brought back to a love for the Scriptures and a greater earnestness for God. There is a tendency to worldliness among the older believers and also a growing generation gap.

5) **Christian leaders** – need discernment at this time when compromise is easy. Pray for the calling of better educated men for the ministry. Pray for the continued out-workings of a large conference for pastors and theological students in 1976, that churches throughout the land may have a deeper spiritual life and greater outreach to the lost.

6) **Scripture Union** has an expanding and blessed ministry among young people in the schools. Pray that this ministry of literature, school groups and camps may lead to the saving of many who will later play an important role in this underdeveloped country.

SENEGAL

BACKGROUND

Area:	198,000 sq. km. – a largely arid land with few natural resources.
Population:	4,500,000. Annual growth 2.4%. People per sq. km. – 23.
Peoples:	**Tribes** – approx. 22 – largest:– Wolof* 1,600,000; Serere 800,000; Toucouleur 520,000; Fula 320,000; Malinke 250,000; Diola 250,000. **Minorities** – French 70,000; Mauretanians 20,000.
Capital:	Dakar 800,000. Urbanisation 30%. Literacy only 5%.
Economy:	Poor, susceptible to terrible droughts and dependent on French aid. About 80% of all wage earners live in the capital with its many industries. Most of the people live off the land at subsistence level.
Politics:	Independent of France in 1960, but retains close ties with France. Stable democratic government under leadership of President Senghor.
Religion:	**Attitude of Government** – complete freedom of religion.

African Traditionals 4%.

Muslim 89% and increasing among the Diola, Serere and other smaller animistic tribes.
Roman Catholics 6.5% – largely among the Serere.
Protestants 0.1%. Community 2,400. Membership 450. Most of believers in Assemblies of God, some in **WEC** related Evangelical Church and a few in several other groups. Evangelicals 0.05%.

Points for Prayer

1) **West Africa's most needy country is wide open for the Gospel,** though the people are largely Muslim and very resistant. Pray for a continued open door and also for the calling of Christian workers from other lands.

2) **The first permanent mission work** was that of **WEC** in 1936, who entered the Casamance region between the Gambia and Guinea-Bissau to evangelise the less Islamised tribes of that region. There are now 10 missions with about 110 expatriate workers: **NTM** among the Balante (heathen), Finnish Mission among the partially Islamised Serere, **WEC** among the Dioia and Malinke, Assemblies of God in three centres and a number of groups in Dakar. Pray for fruit for these servants of God in a very unresponsive field, and where discouragement and a hot climate can take some out of God's will for their lives.

3) **The little pockets of animist peoples** are rapidly being Islamised – pray for the raising up of strong national churches among the Balante, Diola, Serere and Malinke peoples before Islam takes over completely.

4) **Most of the Muslim east, centre, west and the northern Senegal River Valley is unevangelised** and unoccupied by evangelical Christians. WEC is burdened to place workers in the north to reach the Toucouleur, Fula and also the Mauritanians who have settled in the area. The latter are not able to be evangelised in their own land to the north. Pray also for the small beginnings of national churches coming into being in the City of Dakar – also a pioneer field. Pray that the humble and useful aid given by missionaries through various secular ministries such as health, education and agriculture may soften the hard and fearful hearts of Muslims. Pray for a great harvest in this seemingly unpromising land.

5) **The Church** is so small and the believers outside Dakar so isolated that it is very difficult for them to be effectively taught and find sufficient fellowship. Few of the believers can read and there are, as yet, no Bibles in any national language. Pray for the very valuable cassette ministry run by **WEC** and others for these believers. The believers suffer much pressure from both heathen and Muslim relatives. Many young men backslide through marrying unbelieving girls or falling into immorality because there are so few converted girls.

6) **There are very few Christian leaders** – there are probably no more than 28 full time national Christian workers – and most of these are of the Assemblies of God. It is only the latter that maintains a Bible School. WEC runs an agricultural Bible School for the training of lay leaders. Pray that God may raise up other national pastors and leaders as well as those dedicated to the evangelisation of the many Muslims.

7) **There is a small GBU (IVF) group at the Dakar University,** but all are non-Senegalese. Pray for the witness of this group to the local students.

8) **Bible translation** is one of the greatest needs for this land. One language (Wolof) now has the N.T. and another 2 have a few Gospels. Work is in progress in Toucouleur and Diola, but another 5 languages need translators. Much literacy work will also have to be done. Pray also for the Bible bookshop in Dakar, and also for the projected **CLC** book centre – that useful literature may reach those who so need it.

SEYCHELLES

BACKGROUND

Area: 277 sq. km. – 92 islands spread across 400,000 sq. km. of the Indian Ocean.
Population: 60,000. People per sq. km. – 216.
Peoples: Largely **Creoles** – descendants of French and English colonists and African slaves. Both French and English are spoken.

Capital:	Victoria 15,000. Urbanisation 28%. Literacy 70%.
Economy:	Poor, and dependent on British aid. Tourism increasingly important.
Politics:	Independent of Britain in 1976 as a neutral republic.
Religion:	**Roman Catholics 80%.**
	Anglo-Catholic Anglicans 19%.
	Evangelicals 0.5% (mostly expatriates).

Points for Prayer

1) **The Seychellois all claim to be Christian**, but they are steeped in superstition and dependent on the outward rites of baptism and confirmation; immorality is a real problem. **FEBA** has asked **AIM** to come to help evangelise these people from within the Anglican Church. There is a need for Bible loving evangelical Anglican missionaries for this outreach, also for youth work and running a Christian Bookstore. Pray for the evangelisation of these needy islands.

2) **There is one small evangelical fellowship** that meets regularly on an inter-denominational basis. A number of young people have been converted as a result. Pray for this outreach and also that this may be useful for building up a strong nucleus of witnessing believers.

3) **The Far East Broadcasting Association** began transmissions from Mahe in 1970. These islands are strategically placed for this ministry to S. Asia, the Middle East, the Indian Ocean Islands and Southern and East Africa. Most of these lands are very dark spiritually and some closed to the Gospel (Mozambique, Somalia, South Yemen, Saudi Arabia, Afghanistan, etc.). Pray for the following:–

    a) The preparation of programmes in receiving areas in India, Middle East and Africa.
    b) Continued permission to broadcast and for the good working of expensive equipment.
    c) The staff – expatriate and national – needed to run the equipment, for their physical health in a hot, humid climate and for their spiritual health.
    d) The growing response from Muslims and Hindus in India-Pakistan and for follow-up work among these enquirers.
    e) The broadcasts in Arabic to the needy Middle East and also for a settled studio in the area (the Lebanese Civil War put the Beirut studio out of action).
    f) For the newly begun African outreach and news service in English which draws many listeners.
    June 1977: Leftist coup. Implications for spiritual and political future uncertain, but possibly very serious.

SIERRA LEONE

BACKGROUND

Area:	73,000 sq. km. – a small coastal state between Guinea and Liberia.
Population:	3,100,000. Annual Growth 3.1%. People per sq. km. – 42. Literacy 42%.
Peoples:	**Creoles** 2.5% – descendants of freed slaves settled on the coast by the British in 1807. They speak Krio – a perverted form of English.
	Tribal peoples – 16. Largest: Mende 950,000; Temne 920,000; Limba 275,000.
Capital:	Freetown 215,000. Urbanisation 14%.
Economy:	Fairly poor and dependent on agriculture, diamonds and some mining.
Politics:	Independent of Britain in 1961, followed by considerable political instability. The President, Siaka Stevens, is left wing and depends on Guinean troops to retain power. Communist influence grows steadily.
Religion:	**Attitude of Government** – freedom of religion, but with increasing restrictions on Christian work in some areas. If the vice-president, a strong Muslim, were to gain power, there could be more difficulty.
	African Traditionals 52%.
	Muslims 38% – some advances inland in recent years.
	Roman Catholics 2%.

Protestants 5%. Community 150,000. Denominations 16. Largest:– Anglicans, Methodists, Evangelical United Brethren, Assemblies of God. Evangelicals 1.5%.

Prayer Targets

1) **Pray that this land may remain open for the Gospel** and also that present opportunities may be used to the full.
2) **There are over 100 churches in Freetown**, but there is much nominalism, worldliness and sin among professing Christians. Almost the entire Creole population professes to be Christian, but their pride and lack of consistent Christian living is one of the major factors hindering the spread of the Gospel to the "inferior" tribal people.
3) **The evangelical witness is small and weak.** Believers among the tribes are often hindered by feelings of inferiority. The evangelical witness is rather divided. There is also little encouragement for young people to go into the Lord's work and hence a dearth of leadership with intiative.
4) **Missions** have worked in the land for 170 years, but there have been many discouragements. There are now about 19 agencies with around 200 missionaries. This has proved a hard and unresponsive field – Islam has proved a great hindrance to Gospel advances in the interior. The many tribes with differing languages together with the fact that few missionaries serve long enough to master these languages has also been a limiting factor. Pray for the witness of those now serving and for the blessing of God to rest on their labours. A greater effort is now being made in the tribes. More could be done if the coastal churches were revived and began to send missionaries to these areas.
5) **Islam has been making gains in some tribes** – pray for the following:– Mende (40% Muslim), Temne (60%), Yalunka (22,000–60%), Koranko (120,000–30%), Kissi (80,000–7%), Loko (100,000–39%), etc. Pray that God may raise up missionaries and nationals with a burden for Muslim evangelisation. Pray for the evangelisation of the 3,000 or so Fulani immigrants who are all Muslims. Pray for the winning of the pagan Kono people who number 160,000.
6) **The lack of trained and spiritual leadership is serious.** Pray for students in the few Bible Schools run by several churches and missions.
7) **Christian Radio** – Radio ELWA (**SIM**, Liberia) has had a considerable impact with many conversions and even churches planted in both remote and Muslim areas. Pray for this ministry, and also for those who prepare programmes.
8) **Literature** – CLC has a strategic and well-used bookstore in Freetown. Pray for the ministry of the written page. Pray also for the granting of permits for the importation of literature – these are often hard to obtain.
9) **Young people's work** has proved to be the most fruitful field in recent years. Both Scripture Union and Youth for Christ have been used of God for the winning of many young people. These young people are beginning to make an impact for God in the churches and in evangelistic outreach.
10) **Bible translation** is still a major need. At least 4 languages need translators. Only one language has the whole Bible, 4 the N.T. and 7 just portions of the N.T.

SOMALIA

BACKGROUND

Area: 700,000 sq. km. The Horn of Africa – a dry and barren land.
Population: 3,200,000. Annual growth 2.5%. People per sq. km. – 5.
Peoples: **Somalis** 94% – 7 tribes all speaking one language. A mixed Arab-Hamitic people.
            African tribes approx. 10 small tribes along rivers in south 4%.
            Minorities of Arabs (35,000)
Capital: Mogadisho 200,000. Urbanisation 26%. Literacy 10%.
Economy: Over 70% of population are nomadic pastoralists. The severe famine of 1973–76 has brought many Somalis to utter destitution and many now live in

big refugee camps. A further 300,000 Ogaden Somalis fled to Somalia in 1978. The land is very dependent on foreign aid.

Politics.   Revolution of 1969 brought a leftist regime to power. Russian support was rejected when Russia wooed Ethiopia. Somalia's invasion of Ethiopia's Ogaden ended with Somalia's crushing defeat by Russian arms and Cuban forces. The regime is unpopular and the future uncertain.

Religion: **Attitude of Government** – vigorous suppression of Islam and other religions since 1975 and seeking to replace "superstitions" with scientific atheism.
Muslims: 99.7% – Somalis have been very devout Muslims for centuries.
Roman Catholics 0.2% – a few around Mogadisho.
Protestants 0.006% – about 200 believers, but few of these are baptised.

Points for Prayer

1)   **This closed land** needs to be prayed open for the Gospel. Only a few areas were ever exposed to the Gospel, and this was just for a limited period of 20 years.

2)   **The witness of missions** ended in 1973–74 after some very difficult years of seeking to win Somalis under almost impossible restrictions. Yet the courageous witness of **SIM** and the Mennonites led to the conversion of a number of Somalis and also the translation of the Somali Bible.

3)   **The national believers** continue to live for the Lord under very difficult conditions. Many are isolated and it is hard to meet for fellowship. Most of the believers are young men; they find much difficulty in obtaining employment, or girls whom they can marry. They face much opposition from both the authorities and their own families. Some believers have now taken refuge in Kenya. Pray that God may preserve His own and bless their witness.

4)   **The minority tribes** and also the whole of the former British Somaliland in the north have never been evangelised. Pray for this needy land and its peoples.

5)   **Over 1,000,000 Somalis live in the surrounding lands** of Ethiopia, Djibouti (p. 169) and Kenya (80,000). It is only in the latter two countries that any Christian witness can be made. Pray for the new **RSMT** witness in Djibouti, that this may lead to the conversion of Somalis and planting of strong churches among them that can later become a witness to Somalia itself.

6)   **The Somali Bible** was published in 1977. Many N.T.s were handed out just before the expulsion of missionaries in 1974. Pray for Bible distribution through the post in Somalia and to Somalis in surrounding lands. The government sponsored crash literacy programme should raise the literacy level and help others to read the Word.

7)   **Radio broadcasts** are prepared by **SIM** in Ethiopia and transmitted daily from Thursday to Sunday by **FEBA** Seychelles. Somalis are listening in.

<u>SOUTH AFRICA</u>

BACKGROUND

Area: 1,221,000 sq. km. – the strategic southern point of Africa, well watered in the north and along the east and south coasts, drier inland and to the west.
Population: 26,100,000. Annual growth 2.7%. People per sq. km. – 21. Literacy 80%.
Peoples: **White** 16.5% – **Afrikaans** 2,412,000; English 1,636,000; Portuguese 260,000.
Other European immigrant minorities merging into the major language groups.
Coloured 9.3% – predominantly Hottentot mixed with European, Asian and African blood. 90% live in the Western Cape Province.
Asians 3% – descendants of labourers brought from India to work on the Natal sugar plantations. There are also about 8,000 Chinese.
Black Africans 71.3% – 9 tribes: Zulu 5,020,000; Xhosa 2,800,000 (with a further 2,000,000 in the independent Transkei); Tswana 2,100,000; Pedi 2,010,000; Sotho 1,690,000; Venda 469,000; Shangaan 967,000; Ndebele 543,000; and Swazi 618,000.
Capital: Pretoria 575,000 and Cape Town 1,125,000. Other major cities:–

Johannesburg (incl. adjoining Rand cities) 2,550,000; Durban 1,040,000. Urbanisation 51%.

Economy: The richest and most developed country in Africa with much industrialisation. Well endowed with natural resources of all types but oil and water.

Politics: White minority democracy. Government seeking to implement policy of the separate development of each racial group to economic and political maturity. A satisfactory solution to the complex racial problems is urgent in the light of world hostility, Black urban unrest and the Communist seizure of neighbouring Angola and Mozambique in 1975. Russia's deep commitment in the region is ultimately aimed at the control of S. Africa's wealth, industrial power and strategic geographical position.

Religion: **Attitude of Government** – freedom of religion. Sympathetic to genuine spiritual missionary work.
African Traditionals 26%.
Hindus 2% – Indians.
Muslims 1.3% – Indians and Malays.
Jews 0.6%.
Roman Catholics 8.6%.
African Independent Churches 20% (approx. 4,500).
Protestants 43% – 80% of the Coloureds, 73% of the Whites, 32% of the Blacks. Community approx. 7,800,000. Denominations 70+. Largest:– Nederduits Geref. Kerk (NGK) 3,374,000 adherents (50% White, 30% Black, 19% Coloured); Methodists 2,410,000 (20% White); Anglicans 1,928,000 (31% White); Lutherans (5% White) 964,000; Presbyterians 506,000 (35% White); Congregationals 361,000 (mainly Coloured); Apostolic Faith Mission 337,000 (33% White), Baptists 240,000 (30% White). Conservative Evangelicals 14%.

Prayer Targets – General

1) **The Government needs prayer** – that policies may be both fair to all peoples and helpful to the cause of the Gospel.

2) **A spiritual awakening** is needed – one that deeply affects every race and tribe in the country.

3) **Pray for peace**, harmony and mutual respect between the diverse peoples who must live together. There are no longer any workable solutions that man can devise; only prayer can decisively affect the situation. Pray that these crisis times may stir Christians to earnest prayer.

4) **The missionary vision** continues to be strong despite South Africa's political isolation. There are now about 1905 South Africans in cross-cultural missionary work, of which only 4% have moved further afield than Southern Africa. For special mention in prayer:–

   a) The major contribution of the NGK (DRC) to the evangelisation of Southern Africa and beyond. There are now 1,078 missionaries serving in 15 home and 9 foreign mission fields in many institutions and in church planting and developing ministries.

   b) South Africa is the birth place of a number of famous missions that have made an impact on the world:– South Africa General Mission (**AEF**) with work in 10 lands, IHCF among medical workers and now ministering in 100 lands, JMHE with a growing work in Japan and also the Africa Evangelistic Band, Dorothea Mission, etc.

   c) The first Coloured missionary has now left S. Africa for the Philippines with **OMF**. Pray for an increase of interest among the Coloured believers in missions. Pray also for the Indian Christians to gain a vision for the evangelisation of India, Mauritius, etc.
   Pray for South Africa's Christians that they may become a blessing to the world through a greater missionary outreach.

Prayer Targets – The Whites

1) **The Southern Africa dilemma** can be used of God to shake people out of their

complacency, selfishness, materialism and sin. The moral slide of the Western World is affecting the land – though not yet so radically as elsewhere.

2) **The Afrikaans people** – most are adherents of one of the three Dutch Reformed Churches. By far the largest of these is the theologically conservative Nederduits Geref. Kerk (NGK). There are many outstanding ministers and theologians as well as fine people of prayer in this Church; though there is also much orthodox nominalism. Pray for revival, the calling of more into the ministry and an increased concern for the evangelisation of the world. Pray also for the two Theological Seminaries – in Stellenbosch and Pretoria. Pray that this church, with a large membership in all 4 major population groups, may become a catalyst for peaceful change and future harmony.

3) **The English speaking people** tend to be less religious than the Afrikaans. There is more liberal theology in the major denominations, yet remarkable changes are occurring in the Anglican Church through the charismatic movement, with a significant return to a more Biblical theology and personal faith. The Evangelical denominations such as the Baptists, Church of England in S.A., Assemblies of God, etc., are growing steadily.

4) **The need for evangelism** is especially great among the many nominal and unchurched English speaking people in the growing cities and in the large Portuguese and Greek communities. Increasing efforts are being made to win the Portuguese by the Pentecostals and the NGK.

5) **Young people** – there are many denominational and inter-denominational groups seeking to witness among them – Youth for Christ, SU, Student Christian Assoc., YWAM, etc. Pray for young people to be won for Christ and hear God's call into Christian service.

Prayer Targets – The Coloureds

1) **The Coloureds**, with their mixed racial origins, uncertain social status and lack of real national identity are increasingly vocal in expressing their resentment at being treated as second class citizens. Centuries of feelings of inferiority, loose morals and a high rate of alcoholism can only be remedied by the power of the Gospel.

2) **The Coloureds** are about 80% Protestant, but religion and daily life are not closely related. The number of truly converted people among them is growing, although most of the churches are weak, inward looking and dependent on missionary leadership and funds. The most effective evangelical work among them is that of **TEAM**, NG Mission Church and some Pentecostal groups. Pray also for the Bethel evangelists of the AEB and their evangelistic campaigns, for through them many have come to the Lord. There are few outstanding Christian leaders among the Coloureds – pray for gifted young people to be called into the Lord's work.

3) **The Cape Malays** (100,000) still cling tenaciously to their customs and their religion of Islam. Little has been done to evangelise these resistant people and very few have ever believed on the Lord Jesus.

Prayer Targets – The Asians

1) **The vast majority** of the 763,000 Indians are in Natal where they form large communities. The great and traumatic social and economic changes over the last 70 years have speeded the westernisation of the people, and with it has come a dramatic openness to the Gospel among the Hindu people who form 70% of the Indian community. Yet many Hindus remain in the bondage of idolatry and demons. Pray for the many groups, both denominational and interdenominational who are seeking to evangelise these people – including several Pentecostal groups, **TEAM, AEF** and the **DM**.

2) **The Muslims** are very resistant to the Gospel despite being often ignorant of their own religion. Little Christian work has been done among these people and there are probably less than 10 converts to Christ out of Islam from this group.

3) **The growth of the Church among the Indians** has been dramatic and now about 13% of this community is Christian, and this is almost entirely Evangelical. There are

more than 15 denominations working among the Indians – some of the more significant being the Indian Evangelical Church (**AEF**), Evangelical Bible Church (**TEAM**), Indian Reformed Church (**NGK**) and especially the Bethesda Temple (Full Gospel). The latter now has 38,000 members and 62% of all Indian Christians. There are weaknesses evident in some churches – increasing nominalism, Hindu thought patterns and practices still prevailing, and an often weak and divided leadership.

4) **There are three good Bible Schools** – pray for the calling and equipping of believers for both pastoral and missionary work. Over one fifth of Christian converts out of Hinduism in the world live in South Africa. Pray that there may be a growth of concern for the evangelisation of needy India, Mauritius, etc.

Prayer Targets – Black Africans

1) **Missionary work is 260 years old in South Africa.** Nearly every major denomination in Europe and North America has played some part in its evangelisation. Heroic effort and tragic mistakes have marked its progress, leaving a legacy of a fragmented and spiritually weak Church. Pray for an outpouring of the Holy Spirit.

2) **Missions today** – over 2,800 missionaries in nearly 100 agencies. A relatively large proportion of these are in institutional work. Although there are very few pioneer areas, missionary work is needed – especially in disciple making, leadership training, youth, literature and radio work. Missionaries need prayer in the rather unusual South African situation:–
   a) Single-mindedness in proclaiming the Gospel in the tense political scene.
   b) Grace and ability to bridge the barriers of race and culture to communicate effectively the message of the Gospel.
   c) Eternal fruit in a difficult field and vision as how best to use present opportunities.

3) **The churches are poor and weak.** Few churches show healthy growth, though a good work is being done by such groups as **TEAM**, **AEF**, the Nazarene Church and the large work of the NGK and Assemblies of God. Pray for:–
   a) The enlivening of orthodox, but nominal, churches in theologically conservative denominations. Sin and pagan practices are common among professing Christians.
   b) Harmonious relationships between churches and missions and their daughter churches.
   c) Spiritual leaders who are prepared to stand firm on the truths of the Bible. Many pastors are influenced by Black theology with its doctrines of social change and political liberation.

4) **Black African protest** has harmed the development of the churches:–
   a) In a considerable reversion by nominal Christians to old heathen ways.
   b) In a multiplication of breakaways from mission-founded denominations over leadership, money, African customs, etc.
   c) In the medley of African Independent Churches that frequently emphasise Pentecostal gifts, emotion and incorporation of customs contrary to the Word of God. Some are theologically sound, but others are more pagan than Christian. There are now reputed to be over 4,500 of these groups.
   Pray for revival of the churches throughout the country so that they may demonstrate the power of the Gospel to all and bring spiritual unity to believers.

5) **The 10 Homelands** set aside by the government for each of the tribal units. One is independent as the nation of Transkei (see p. 214). Bophuthatswana is likely to become so in 1977. The other 8 are also being prepared for nationhood. Most of these are fragmented and not politically or economically viable without enlargement, consolidation and investment. In some, the evangelical witness is very limited and a fresh evangelistic initiative is needed; especially in Lebowa (Pedi people), Qwa-Qwa (Sotho), Venda and S. Ndebele. There are reports of revival in one area of Kwa Zulu.

6) **The urban areas** in which 6 million Black Africans live. Black satellite townships ring most South African cities. These are strategic for the Gospel and for the forces that would bring chaos to the country. This is a very hard field for the Gospel, with rampant materialism, a breakdown of tribal and parental authority, violence, social insecurity and immorality. There are a few really committed, witnessing Christians.

Pray for Gospel victories in this critical hour. Pray for Soweto with its 1,200,000 people (in Johannesburg), now world famous for the tragic riots of 1976 that also spread to other cities.

7) **The believers in the urban areas** suffered in the 1976 rioting with intimidation and even loss of life. An anti-Christian spirit was demonstrated by the leaders of this unrest. Pray that the believers may stand firm in persecution. Pray also for the evangelistic work of the **DM**, Assemblies of God and others in the urban area, and for the youth work of **AEF** in the Rand area – there was some disruption in 1976. Pray for the right strategy to win these townships of today.

8) **Christian literature** takes on a new importance as other avenues of witness become more difficult. Much is done in producing evangelistic and Christian growth literature by such as **All Nations Gospel Publishers** (who send large quantities of Gospel literature all over the world), **NGK Press**, **AEF** and many others. Pray also for **SU** work in the cities and homelands – this extensive work has brought many young people to the Lord, but they need leaders for the developing work in the Homelands.

9) **Christian Radio**. Many Christian programmes are produced by the S.A. Broadcasting Corporation and also by the new **TWR** station in Swaziland. Pray for all who produce programmes in the **TWR** studios in South Africa and for eternal fruit from this ministry in South Africa and in surrounding lands.

10) **The mines** draw many from all over S. Africa and beyond for longer or shorter periods. At any one time there are 400,000 living in the large mine compounds of the Transvaal and Orange Free State. Pray for the workers of **AEF**, **NGK**, **DM** and others who evangelise and disciple these migrant mine workers in transit camps and compounds. Some still come from the closed land of Mozambique and many others from Lesotho, Transkei, Botswana, Rhodesia and beyond.

SOUTH WEST AFRICA (Namibia)

BACKGROUND

Area: 824,000 sq. km. Much of the land is desert; most people live in the better watered northern regions adjoining Angola and the central plateau.

Population: 900,000. Annual growth 2.2%. People per sq. km. – 1.

Peoples: Racially Africa's most complex with 5 races and 23 distinct tribes.
Bushmen 21,000 – the original inhabitants who are nomads in the N.E. deserts.
Nama and **Damara** (38,000 and 78,000). The Nama are a Hottentot people and the Damara an African people that has absorbed Nama culture.
African tribes – in north: **Ovambo** (6 tribes) 408,000; **Kavango** 60,000; and east **Caprivi** tribes (3) 30,000. In centre – **Herero-Himba** 66,000.
Europeans 107,000 (Afrikaans 60%, German 30%, English 10%).
Coloureds (Mixed Race) 33,000 and Rehoboth Basters 19,000.

Capital: Windhoek 60,000. Urbanisation 25%. Literacy 70%.

Economy: Vast mineral resources, but limited by lack of water.

Politics: This former German colony has been ruled by South Africa since 1915, but this rule was contested by the United Nations. The land is heading for independence in 1978, but the manner in which it is attained is a subject of international dispute. Communist guerrillas seek to conquer the land by subversion and infiltration from Angola.

Religion: **African traditional and Christo-pagan sects** 16%.
Roman Catholics 15%.
Protestants 66% – 80% of these being Lutheran. Other significant denominations:– Dutch Reformed Church (DRC) and Anglicans. Evangelicals 18% of population (especially among the Ovambos and Whites).

Points for Prayer

1) **The political future of the country is uncertain.** The promising constitutional conference was overshadowed by the intransigence of the Communist SWAPO move-

ment that continues to disrupt the country's life through terrorist incursions from Angola. Pray for a peaceful transition to a multiracial government that will uphold Christian values.

2) **In the northern border area** Christian work is increasingly hindered by the hostilities. Pray that Christians may remain true to the Lord in the face of intimidation. Pray that the local believers may become more active in winning the unconverted in these days when evangelism is difficult. Pray that many of the thousands of Angolan refugees fleeing the brutal oppression of Communist forces may hear the Gospel.

3) **Much of the land is Christianised,** yet few understand about the new birth. The evangelical voice has been greatly weakened over the last few years by the drift away from Biblical theology in the Lutheran Church founded by the Rhenish Mission from Germany. The one Theological Seminary is turning out politically leftist pastors, few of whom preach the Gospel. Pray for revival. Pray also for the witness of the **DM** team that seeks to bring people to a saving knowledge of the Lord.

4) **The Church among the Ovambo,** a tribe which forms one half the population, is the fruit of the Finnish Mission (Lutheran) and was blessed with revival in 1952, so there is more of an evangelical witness among the older people. Pray also for the relatively new and widespread witness of the DRC to many of the racial groups and for the smaller **AEF** witness recently begun. There are very few evangelical believers among the Herero, Nama and Damara.

5) **Christian leaders** who are uncompromising for the Gospel are few. Pray for the raising up of many more who love the Lord and His Word.

6) **The Church among the Europeans** needs revival, yet there are many fine Christians and some really earnest prayer groups in various denominations.

7) **Needy areas and peoples:–**
   a) **The Bushmen** – many people thought that these people could never believe, but the first significant turning to the Lord occurred at a DRC mission station in 1973; the work, however, is in its infancy. Pray for the planting of a strong, evangelistic church.
   b) **The Herero** have been very resistant to the Gospel, most adhering to several Christo-pagan sects. 80% of this tribe died in the uprising against German colonial rule in 1905. There is a new openness among them now. Pray for their evangelisation and also for that of the closely related, but backward, Himba in the Kaokoveld.

8) **Bible translation** continues in a number of the languages, but only small groups do not, as yet, have the N.T. – 3 Bushmen languages and the Caprivi tribes.

SWAZILAND

BACKGROUND

Area: 17,400 sq. km. – a small enclave between Mozambique and South Africa.
Population: 500,000. Annual growth 3.2%. Population density – 29 per sq. km.
Peoples: Almost entire population is **Swazi** – minorities of **Shangaan** 2% and **European** 2%.
Capital: Mbabane 18,000. Urbanisation 10%. Literacy 30%.
Economy: Favoured with abundant water, mineral resources and not overpopulated. Expanding economy with bright prospects for the future.
Politics: Independent of Britain in 1968. A monarchy with the King exercising supreme power. Maintains a difficult neutrality between White South Africa and Communist Mozambique.
Religion: **Attitude of Government** – African traditional religion and Christo-pagan sects more favoured by government. Christians tolerated, but watched.
              African Traditionals 33%. **African Sects** (approx. 40) 27%.
              Roman Catholics 10%.
              Protestants 30%. Community 98,000. Denominations 15. Largest:– Methodist 20,000; Anglicans 15,000; Nazarenes 12,000; Africa Evangelical Church (**AEF**) 7,000. Evangelicals 11%.

Points for Prayer

1) **Pray for a continued open door for the Gospel.** Christianity faces attack on two fronts – Communist ideology filtering over the border from Mozambique and traditionalists within the leadership of the country.

2) **The national believers** face many pressures if they want to live close to the Lord, for compromise is easy and materialism in the rapidly advancing economy has a great attraction. As a result there are few believers who are willing to pay the price of going into full time service for the Lord. There are not many mature spiritual leaders in the ministry, though there are fine Christians witnessing in all walks of life.

3) **The churches are growing** slowly in numbers and spiritual depth, but there is a lack of good Bible teaching, real evangelistic concern and a missionary vision for other lands. Pray also for fruit from the increasing cooperation between the Evangelical Churches.

4) The evangelical witness is strong with almost all the missions being Evangelical. There are about 160 missionaries working in the land, the largest mission being **TEAM**, Nazarenes and **AEF** who run a number of hospitals and schools as well as supporting the national churches they have planted. Pray for a happy and close relationship between the expatriates and nationals.

5) **Pray for the growth of the Christian Union** in the new University College and also for the work of **SU** in secondary schools. Pray that many young people may be converted and contribute much for the Gospel in the land.

6) **Trans World Radio** started a powerful new radio station in Swaziland, with an outreach to all of Southern Africa. Pray for the cooperation of churches and pastors in preparation of programmes and also for the staff working in the Johannesburg studios in South Africa. Pray for broadcasts to the needy lands of Angola and Mozambique, now closed to all other normal means of witness, and for the raising up of believers able to prepare programmes in the languages of tribes that have scarcely been touched with the Gospel.

TANZANIA

BACKGROUND

Area: 940,000 sq. km. Mainland Tanganyika and Zanzibar (2 offshore islands 2,650 sq. km.).

Population: 15,600,000. Annual growth 2.7%. People per sq. km. – 17.

Peoples: **African tribes** – 122. Only one tribe of over one million. Tribalism is not a divisive force and most tribal languages are being replaced by Swahili.
Minorities – Asians 90,000; Burundi refugees 52,000; Chinese 30,000 (?); Arabs 26,000; Europeans 17,000.

Capital: Dar-es-Salaam 400,000 – but soon to be Dodoma. Urbanisation 8%.

Economy: Poor and adversely affected by drought, inefficient government planning, over-zealous application of nationalisation and collectivisation of rural areas into ujamaa villages.

Politics: Strongly socialist and receiving much aid from Communist lands – especially China. Zanzibar has hitherto been far more Marxist, with much aid from East European Communist lands. Tanganyika independent of Britain in 1961. Union with Zanzibar in 1964, but union more theoretical than real.

Religion: **Attitude of Government** – churches accepted as part of national life, but expected to cooperate with government in applying socialist policies.
African Traditionals 28%; **Muslims** 26%; **Roman Catholics** 31%. **Protestants** 14%. Community 1,800,000. Denominations 18. Most significant:– Lutherans 580,000 adherents; Anglicans 570,000; Moravians 100,000; Africa Inland Church **(AIM)** 180,000. Evangelicals 9%.

Points for Prayer

1) **There is freedom for Christians to witness** despite the growing influence of Marxist thought. Pray that this freedom may be well used and also maintained.

2) **The compulsory gathering** of the majority of the rural (and some town!) people into the ujamaa villages has greatly disrupted tribal society and is of doubtful economic value. Yet, for the first time, nearly the whole population can be relatively easily and freely evangelised. The hearts of the people are open for the Gospel as never before and provision has been made in each village for the building of a church. Pray for labourers to be thrust forth into this ripe harvest while the people are receptive.

3) **Unreached peoples** – the evangelisation of Tanzania has been patchy.

   a) **Muslim coastal tribes** such as the Zaramo* (320,000), the three tribes on Zanzibar-Pemba, and the Rangi, Luguru and Digo peoples are basically animist with a veneer of Islam. Few believers have been won from among them and a greater evangelistic effort is needed.

   b) **The Muslim tribes on the Mozambique border.** The Brethren have done a fine work among the Maconde (600,000) and Yao and some have been saved, but the greater harvest was among the erstwhile refugees of these tribes from Mozambique.

   c) **Animist tribes** with no settled evangelical witness – Matumbi (80,000), Sandawe (95,000) and Dorobo (3,000).

   d) **Resistant animist tribes** – Sukuma (2,000,000), Zinza (100,000) – **AIM**, also the Arusha* (130,000), Barabaig (56,000), Iraqw (250,000), Maasai (110,000), Sonjo* (7,400), Turu (350,000) – Lutherans and Pentecostals, also Burungi (20,000) CMS (Anglican), Kwere (70,000), Nyamwezi (650,000), Safwa (102,000), Wajita* (70,000).

4) **The churches are growing**; the town churches are overflowing and there is a marked hunger for the Word of God in these days. Yet there are weaknesses – lack of well trained pastors able to teach the believers, much formalism and adherence to European traditions in some churches, plus too little effective outreach and church planting in these days of opportunity.

5) **The evangelical witness** is strongest in the north west, – (**AIM**) in the central province (Evangelical Anglicans), in the south (Brethren) and also in the areas touched by the East African Revival. Yet there are many large areas that need pioneer evangelism. The 800 strong missionary force needs to be augmented by others untied by institutional work (which still forms an important aspect of the work) for evangelism, literature work, church planting, etc. There are now about 22 societies working in the land. Pray for wisdom and tact for the missionaries in these days. Pray also that they may make the best strategic use of the time that the Lord gives them.

6) **Bible training** is very important for the supply of needed manpower. Pray for the two AIC* AIM Bible Schools and others. Pray also for the TEE programme which is now extensively used.

7) **Young people** can be reached through the schools where R.E. is taught – there are many opportunities for this ministry for both nationals and expatriates, but too few use it. **SU** is, as yet, small and not able to cover the whole field. There are too few Christian teachers to use the existing opportunities. Pray for the raising up of other SU workers and the development of the work. The CU groups (**IVF**) are also small and weak. Pray for the evangelisation of this strategic and needy section of the population.

8) **Bible translation and literature**. Four languages have the whole Bible, 24 the N.T. and 34 have portions. Swahili is increasingly used, so the need for further translation is not so great as in other lands. There is too little good evangelical literature to feed the minds of many now becoming literate in the government literacy campaign.

9) **Among the Burundi refugees** in the north east there is a move of the Spirit in progress with many thousands seeking the Lord in their sorrow and need. See Burundi (p.164).

10) **Pray for evangelisation of Chinese** Communist technicians and aid officials. A tactful witness by African believers goes on and some literature is passed on to them, but this is not easy with the strict regimentation by ever-watchful leaders.

11) **Zanzibar** has a population of 420,000 Africans and Arabs and 18,000 Asians. Almost the entire population is Muslim. The bloody coup of 1964 overthrew the

Arab sultanate and brought in a Marxist-oriented revolutionary government. Persecution of the minority groups and religions was severe at first, but things have
considerably eased now. The believers are very few and need prayer that they remain
strong and be an effective witness for the Lord. There are some Anglicans and
Quakers. There are a few Christian workers now operating – several Church Army
workers on Pemba and a Swedish Pentecostal missionary in Zanzibar. Occasionally,
Tanzanian believers come over to preach, witness and hand out literature. Pray for
the evangelisation of these largely unreached people.

TOGO

BACKGROUND

Area: 56,000 sq. km. – a 56 km. coastline, but stretching inland for 540 km.
Population: 2,300,000. Annual growth 2.7%. People per sq. km. – 41.
Peoples: **African tribes** – 36; most tribes also found in surrounding territories.
               Largest:– Ewe-Mina 500,000; Watchi (Fon) 430,000 in south, and further
               north the Kabre 300,000; Losso 140,000; Kotokoli 120,000 and Bassari
               110,000.
Capital: Lomé 200,000. Urbanisation 15%. Literacy 7%.
Economy: Great improvements over the last few years.
Politics: Independent of France in 1960. Military government since 1967.
Religion: **Attitude of Government** – Emphasis on African "authenticity" beginning to
               limit activities of "foreign" religions.
               African Traditionals 50% – some very resistant to the Gospel.
               Muslims 25% – Islam on the increase of late.
               Roman Catholics 20%.
               Protestants 6%. Community 105,000. Denominations 5 – Église Evangélique
               (French Ref. and Bremen Miss.) 56,000; Methodists 30,000; Assemblies of
               God 8,000; Baptists (S. Bapt. U.S.A.) 2,000. Evangelicals 0.9%.

Points for Prayer

1)   **Togo is the most needy non-Muslim country in Africa.** For years the door was open for
     Protestant missionaries, but the opportunity was not taken. The government cam-
     paign for African "authenticity" is now making it very hard for African and Western
     missionaries to enter and could, in future, stop all foreign missionary activity. Pray
     for a continued open door and also for the speedy issue of residence and work permits
     for new and re-entering missionaries.
2)   **The older Église Evangélique and Methodist Churches** are rather nominal and in
     decline. Evangelistic and missionary outreach to other tribes has been mini-
     mal – hence the tragic poverty and localisation of the Protestant witness.
3)   **Evangelicals** have only fairly recently begun to make an impact through the
     Assemblies of God among some of the northern tribes, the Apostolic Church among
     the Ewe and the Southern Baptists in Lomé. There is no tribe in Togo that has a
     strong and outgoing witness for the Lord. Pray for a new surge of spiritual life and
     vigour among the few believers, the raising up of strong Togolese leaders and an
     outreach to the many needy tribes. The lack of Christian workers is so great that the
     speedy evangelisation of this land is difficult without a large infusion of expatriate
     help. There are only about 70 missionaries in the country.
4)   **Unreached peoples.** There has been a considerable outreach to the tribes mentioned
     below by the Roman Catholics, but the Protestant effort has not been able to match
     it. We mention for prayer the following:– the Adele 5,000; Bassari 110,000;
     Chakossi 33,000; Kabre* 300,000; Moba 100,000; Naudeba (Losso) 140,000; the
     Muslim Kotokoli 120,000; Wachi* 430,000; Konkomba* 30,000; Lamba* 32,000.
     Some, such as the Wachi, Konkomba and Lamba are very resistant – the powers of
     darkness in the very strong and respected spirit world must be bound in prayer.
5)   **Young people are largely unreached.** The few Christians are subjected to much

pressure to compromise in the godless atmosphere of the schools. **SU** has made a small beginning in the south, but the lack of staff and Christian teachers limits the growth of the work. There are some Christians in the Lomé University, but all are from surrounding lands; there is no organised GBU **(IVF)** group, and hence little effective outreach to Togolese students.

6) **Bible translation is major need.** There is work in progress in 10 of the languages of Togo (some being done in other lands), but at least 11 languages need translation teams. **WBT** now has work in three tribes, but seeks at least 13 more workers for other groups. Two of the languages have the whole Bible, 2 more the N.T. and 5 have portions only.

TRANSKEI

BACKGROUND

Area:	43,000 sq. km. – S.E. coastline of South Africa between Natal and Cape Province.
Population:	2,000,000. Annual growth 2.8%. People per sq. km. – 47.
Peoples:	**African tribes** – 2– Xhosa 94%, Sotho 5%.
	Minorities – Europeans 10,000; Coloured 8,000.
Capital:	Umtata 35,000. Urbanisation 3%. Literacy 80%.
Economy:	Heavily dependent on economic links with South Africa and income from migrant labour. About 44% of Transkeians live in South Africa.
Politics:	Independent of South Africa in 1976. Independence not recognised by other governments for fear of implying approval for S. African policy of separate development. Stable semi-democratic government.
Religion:	**Attitude of Government** – complete freedom for the churches promised, provided they remain non-political.
	African Traditionals 33–50%.
	Roman Catholics 5%. **African Independents** 12% – 25%.
	Protestants 35%. Community 950,000. Membership 400,000. Older significant denominations – Methodists 150,000 members; Anglicans 140,000; Presbyterians 18,000. Younger denominations – Pentecostals (various) approx. 60,000; Dutch Reformed Church in Africa approx. 6,000; Baptists 4,000. Evangelicals 11% of population.

Points for Prayer

1) **Pray for stability and progress** for this newly independent country and a continued open door for the Gospel.

2) **Unevangelised and needy areas** remain (despite the fact that the Transkei has had continuous missionary activity for over 150 years) especially some of the more isolated valleys and the coastal area.

3) **The larger and older churches** are more formal and the general picture is one of discouragement and decline. though there are some bright and spiritual believers among them. Pray for revival.

4) **There have been some important post-1945 advances** by more evangelical groups. The DRC has made a large investment in institutions, manpower and evangelism, especially in the less evangelised areas, and there is now an independent national Church as a result of this outreach. The Baptists also have a growing network of churches. There is a smaller and older **AEF** work that gave birth to the Evangelical Church. There are still quite a number of missionaries in the Transkei – the largest group being that of the 29 DRC missionaries and a further 59 affiliated mission workers in institutional work.

5) **The Protestant Church** needs prayer that it may be Bible based in doctrine and Christian living and that it may have a real spiritual impact on the newly independent nation. Pray for the right strategy as many churches plan post-independence evangelistic outreaches. Spiritual growth is hindered by the high proportion of the

population that works in South Africa in the mines, Natal sugar farms and in industry in the Western Cape. Scarely a home does not have at least one of its number away for work. This adversely affects leadership, family life and witnessing.

6) **There are too few church leaders with an evangelical training.** Pray for the Union Bible Institute and Johannesburg Bible Institute (the former run by various evangelical missions in S. Africa, and the latter by **AEF**) where many Transkeians are trained. Pray also for the Decoligny Theol. Seminary of the DRC in Umtata. There is a Theological faculty at Fort Hare University, but this is more liberal in theology. Pray for the raising up of national and non-Transkeian staff who love the Lord and the Word of God for these institutions.

7) **Institutional work** has been extensive in the past and played an important role in the development of the country. Now most schools and all mission hospitals have been taken over by the government (of the 22 hospitals 11 were of the DRC). Many of these institutions still have missionary doctors and nurses on the staff. Pray for the witness of these and Christian national staff to the patients in the general and T.B. hospitals. Pray for the witness of the IHCF groups in many of these hospitals.

8) **Young people.** There are over 500,000 children in the Transkei schools in a rapidly expanding education system. There are 732 secondary schools alone. Pray for the witness of the evangelical SCM school groups and the staff of SCM (many more workers needed!). There are also many opportunities for Christian teachers – pray for them and pray that their numbers may increase. Pray for the Christian groups in the strategic Teacher Training Colleges.

9) **Literature** is produced by M.E.M.A. (DRC) and others for the increasingly literate population. Pray for the printing and distribution of the right materials. M.E.M.A. also produces radio programmes.

UGANDA

BACKGROUND

Area:	233,000 sq. km. – a fertile, well watered land.
Population:	11,900,000. Annual growth 3.3%. People per sq. km. – 51. Literacy 40%.
Peoples:	**Africans** (51 tribes) Nilotic and Nilo-Hamitic peoples 55%, Bantu 40%. Largest tribes:– Baganda 2,600,000; Teso 900,000; Nyankole 900,000; Nyoro 700,000; Lango 600,000; Acholi 500,000. Amin is a Kakwa (30,000). **Minorities** – only a few thousand Asians and Europeans remain after the expulsion of 50,000 Asian businessmen, professionals and industrialists.
Capital:	Kampala 331,000. Urbanisation 8%.
Economy:	Virtually a subsistence barter economy since Amin's Ugandanisation of all industry, trade and education.
Politics:	Independent of Britain in 1962. General Amin seized power in 1971 and, despite his international clowning, has retained power by ruthlessly murdering all likely to oppose him. About 300,000 people are thought to have been killed (mostly the wealthy, Christian professionals and members of tribes that supported the former President). There are about 150,000 refugees in other lands.
Religion:	**Attitude of Government** – Amin is a Muslim and actively seeks to promote the advance of Islam in Uganda. Muslims are favoured in the army and civil service. **African Traditionals** 21%. **Muslims** 6% – growing slightly and temporarily. **Roman Catholics** 47%. **African Independent Churches** 5%. **Protestants** 26%. Community 1,800,000. Denominations 12, but all Anglicans made illegal in 1977. Evangelicals 18%.

Prayer Targets

1) **The reign of terror** of the army and secret police (many being Sudanese and Pales-

tinians) and economic collapse have brought great fear and suffering to the land. Pray for the peace of this unhappy nation and the raising up of a government that loves righteousness.

2) **A new wave of persecution of Christians** began towards the end of 1976. The godly Anglican Archbishop Luwum and many others were martyred. Pray for the believers, that they may maintain a Christ-like spirit and continue to testify boldly. Many of the Christian leaders have had to flee the country. Pray for lay and ordained leaders seeking to maintain stability in the churches in this time of fear and persecution.

3) **The Protestants are almost entirely Evangelical.** The remarkable work of CMS missionaries over the last 100 years as well as that of the **AIM** in the north west (working within the Anglican fellowship) has borne fruit in a mature Church that has known persecution and revival. The East African Revival has had a deeper and more lasting impact than in any other land and almost the entire leadership of the Church have their spiritual roots in that revival. The increasing nominal adherence to the forms of the revival and petty legalisms that were creeping in have been partially swept away by the harsh times now being experienced. There are reports of full churches and renewed outbreaks of revival in some areas. Pray for these brethren. Pray for the raising up of other leaders for the churches.

4) **There are probably no more than 60 missionaries left in the country.** A number of Pentecostal and interdenominational missions were expelled by Amin in 1974 and continual threats against Europeans since then have further whittled down their numbers. Pray for those who remain – that their ministry may be of value to the hard-pressed believers. Pray for their safety and health.

5) **Unreached peoples** – these are few and largely confined to the dry north east where the Karamojong (250,000), Suk (30,000) and Jie (35,000) live, among whom are few believers. Most Ugandans are now nominally Christian, but many have low moral standards – bribery and corruption being common.

6) **Young people** are being effectively reached through the witness of **SU** in the schools and the strong **IVF** group in Makerere University. Pray for the young people who believe. Pray also for a willingness to remain in the country (where possible) as a witness when they complete their studies. There is the usual problem of the generation gap between the young, well educated and the older believers.

7) **The missionary vision of the Ugandan believers** is greatly limited by the strict restrictions on sending out funds and personnel. This Church could contribute much to the world – and indeed has done so. Sudan is a potentially promising field for Ugandan missionaries.

UPPER VOLTA

BACKGROUND

Area:	274,000 sq. km. – one of the Sahel lands – prone to drought and famine.
Population:	6,200,000. Annual growth 2.2%. People per sq. km. – 23. Literacy 7%.
Peoples:	**Tribes** – 60. The largest and most dominant:– Mossi 3,000,000. Other important tribes:– Fulani 600,000; Mandingo 380,000; Bobo 367,000; Senoufo 300,000; Gourma 300,000; Gourounsi 290,000: Lobi and Birifor 200,000.
Capital:	Ougadougou 150,000. Urbanisation 7%.
Economy:	One of world's poorest and least developed nations. The Sahel drought continues to play havoc with the economy and the lives of the people. There is little chance of much for the land. Many men seek for work in Ghana and the Ivory Coast.
Politics:	Independent of France in 1960. A military government preparing for the return of power to civilian rule.
Religion:	**Attitude of Government** – freedom of religion and entry of missionaries. **African Traditionals** 56%. Many of the tribes have long resisted Islam. **Muslims** 35% – majority in Fulani, Mandingo and several other tribes in north. Also significant minority in most other tribes.

Roman Catholics 8%.
Protestants 2.1%. Community 126,000. Denominations 7 (all evangelical).
Largest:– Assemblies of God 80,000; ECWA (**SIM**) 9,500; Evang. Chr. Ch.
(**CMA**) 5,500; **WEC** 2,000. Evangelicals 2.1%.

Points for Prayer

1) **This land is open for the Gospel**, but has been long neglected. This is one of the few lands where no restrictions on the type of missionary are made. Pray for the present small force of about 140 missionaries in 7 missions to be increased by others prepared for the hardships of a pioneer field in a difficult climate.

2) **Mission agencies** have done much through the years through medical and educational work, and this has opened many hearts to the Gospel in a field that has proved exceptionally resistant. The Sahel famine brought many relief agencies such as **WV** to the scene and the Federation of Evangelical Churches and Missions came into being to co-ordinate this relief and development work. This type of ministry has its dangers for church growth, yet there has been a much greater receptivity in tribes that have received help.

3) **The churches are now experiencing rapid growth** among the Mossi (Ass. of God), Gourma (**SIM**), Bobo (**CMA**), and some good men are coming to the fore in leadership of the churches; also, there are Christians in positions of importance in the country. There have been hindrances to the development of strong churches – the strongly entrenched, idolatrous heathenism in many tribes (especially among the Lobi and Birifor in the **WEC** area), the lack of converted, and spiritual, Christian girls for the men and especially for the pastors and evangelists, the difficult heathen customs relating to marriage, illiteracy and the lack of well trained, spiritual men for the ministry.

4) **Leadership training**. All missions run small Bible Schools in the tribal languages but the illiteracy of many of the believers means that few are able to make use of this training. Pray for the students that they may be formed by the Holy Spirit to be mighty instruments for God in this needy land. Pray also for the French language, higher level Bible Schools recently started by **SIM** and **CMA**.

5) **Little has been done to meet the need of the young people**. The secondary school system is still very small, but there is a need for an **SU** type ministry. Several missions are now running small youth centres and camps, but this large field has yet to be covered. Youth workers are needed.

6) **Unreached peoples** – this really includes every tribe in the country! We mention:–
   a) **The Muslims** – relatively little has yet been done to reach these people. The Assemblies of God have seen about 300 Fulani Muslims believe, but they are somewhat persecuted. **WEC** have now two missionaries assigned to this ministry among Muslims. Pray for the witness of national believers to Muslims within their own tribe.
   b) **The animist tribes** – **WEC** among the Lobi, Birifor and Gan; **CMA** among the Bobo, Dafi 50,000, Guin 80,000, Samo 150,000 and Karaboro 50,000; the Canadian Pentecostals among the Dagari 150,000, Dian 15,000, Gourency 250,000, etc., and also many other smaller unoccupied tribes still need to be evangelised. In all, the Church is small, if there is a church.

7) **Bible translation** – only one language has the whole Bible, 6 the N.T., and 8 have portions. All missions are seeking to reduce languages to writing and do translation work, but much must still be done. **WBT** have now entered 5 tribes. The government is trying to standardise the alphabet for all tribal languages, which will mean a total revision of Bible translations done hitherto. Literacy work is also being slowed by government red tape. Pray for all involved, who face so many frustrations.

ZAIRE

BACKGROUND

Area: 2,346,000 sq. km. – a vast land of great rivers and tropical forests.
Population: 25,600,000. Annual growth 2.8%. People per sq. km. – 11. Literacy 18%.
Peoples: **African tribes** – 200 (only 14 of over 200,000). The four trade languages are increasingly important – Swahili in east, Luba in south, Kongo in west and Lingala in Kinshasa and north.
             Pygmies – various tribes totalling about 150,000.
             Europeans 50,000.
Capital: Kinshasa 1,800,000. Urbanisation 22%.
Economy: Huge agricultural, mineral and hydro-electric power potential, yet crippled by effects of post-independence wars and too speedy Zairisation of administration, commerce and institutions leading to large scale corruption, maladministration, grave shortages and severe inflation
Politics: Hasty granting of independence by Belgium in 1960 led to 8 years of chaos and bloodshed. Stability restored by Gen Mobutu's autocratic military government since 1965, though recent emphasis on "African authenticity", etc., has proved a severe setback to progress and stability.
Religion: **Attitude of Government** – many restricting laws on Christian activities, largely aimed at the powerful Roman Catholic Church which sought to interfere in politics. Protestants seriously affected also – but now, for the first time, treated impartially by the authorities.
             African Traditionals 12%–30%.
             Muslims 1%.
             Roman Catholics 50%.
             African Independent Church (orig. 500) 6% – now only Kimbanguist Church recognised by Government.
             Protestants 29%. Community 5,700,000. The 1972 Presidential decree permits only one Christian body in the place of the 50+ denominations previously existing. Known as the Church of Christ in Zaire (CCZ) – each denomination now being recognised as a "Community" of the CCZ. Dissenting Churches had to dissolve. Many of the Communities are Evangelical, but some are sectarian or affected by liberal theology. Evangelicals 16%.

Points for Prayer

1) **God has moved mightily in this troubled land.** There have been powerful revivals in many areas both before independence and after the sufferings of the 1960–64 wars. These prepared the believers for persecution by Communists and pressures from the present regime. Many thousands of Zairois believed and 32 Protestant missionaries were killed in 1964. Pray for a continued mighty working of the Spirit of God in these days.

2) **The Mobutu campaign for "Authenticity"**, compulsory unification of Protestants, the laws banning youth organisations, Bible teaching in schools and institutions, and the printing of Christian periodicals, sent shock waves all over the country. Many feared more persecution, but this has not developed and some of these legal limitations have actually resulted in more effective outreach and spiritual deepening in the churches. Pray that there may not be further encroachments on the freedoms of believers. In fact, in 1976, the government has asked the churches to resume control of mission schools nationalised in 1974, and permission has also been granted to teach the Scriptures in them!

3) **The unification of the Protestants** under one central organisation has potential dangers. Pray for wisdom and discernment for Christian leaders to know where to say "no". Pressure is exerted on the leaders to increase conformity among the different communities. Some CCZ leaders seek absolute authority over doctrine, funds from abroad, placing of missionaries and interchangeability of pastors. Pray for firmness among believers and a love for the Truth amidst pressures to compromise.

4) **The Church has grown** much in spirituality and numbers over the last 10 years and there is considerable evangelistic activity – open air meetings, tent and mass evangelism which continues unhindered. The Church is financially poor due to the harsh economic conditions, therefore the emerging missionary vision is somewhat stunted. Pray for openness to the movings of the Spirit of God and deliverance from traditionalism. There is the ever-present danger of nominalism and allowance of heathen practices among professing Christians. There are some outstanding national pastors and evangelists whom God is using, but they are too few for the many opportunities.

5) **The training of leaders.** There are many Bible Schools that use one of the trade languages as a teaching medium. Increasing use is being made of TEE by such as the **CMA** and **AIM** in the trade languages; but lack of teaching materials and their expense, and the enormous distances between groups with poor roads, hinders the expansion of this, though the **MAF** planes do, to an extent, help to overcome the latter. Pray especially for the key French medium seminaries that are now seeking to train better educated pastors – to mention some:– the **UFM** Bunia Seminary, the École de Théology de Kinshasa (the former university Faculty of Theology), and the planned Evangelical Inter-Community Seminary which will start in 1977.

6) **Young people** are subjected to many pressures by the authorties, but in some areas the turning to the Lord of young people is almost of revival proportions. The nationalisation and subsequent banning of all religious instruction in schools led to a mushrooming of Bible clubs, fellowships, camps after school hours which are run by the churches and **SU** (which has been given full permission to operate despite ban on youth organisations). **CEF** also has a work among children in a few areas. Since these activities are voluntary, there has been a great rise in fervour and earnestness in such youth groups. Pray for the integration of young people into the churches. Pray for wisdom for the churches who again have to take responsibility for the former mission schools, with all its demands on scarce manpower and funds.

7) **Missions** – there are fewer missionaries in the country than for many years (approx. 1,000), but the churches are pleading for more expatriate help in medical ministries, Bible teaching and Bible training. Missionaries are now concentrating more on evangelism and church growth ministries. We mention just a few societies of significance of the many:– in the north east **WEC, AIM** and **UFM**; in the west **RBMU, CMA**; in the south the Brethren (**CMML**) and the Assemblies of God. Pray for missionaries in these days of many frustrations through limitations on activities and lack of equipment and supplies, yet there are so many opportunities. Pray for the work of **MAF** with 7 well used planes in a land without efficient land communications. Pray also for the medical work still done by missions – pray for the big medical centre in the N.E. at Nyankunde run by three of the above missions.

8) **Unreached peoples** are now not so many. Pray for resistant peoples such as the Zande (300,000), Bira (70,000), Budu (80,000) and Hunde (300,000) in the north and east, and the Kela, Songo and Kuba peoples in the south east. There are few true believers among the Pygmy forest dwellers.

9) **Bible translation** – much work has been done; 20 languages have the whole Bible, 30 the N.T. and another 26 have portions. Some work remains, but the increasing use of the trade languages will lessen the need for translation into some of the smaller languages. The poverty of the people and the very high expense of paper and literature in Zaire is hindering Bible and Christian literature distribution.

ZAMBIA

BACKGROUND

Area: 752,000 sq. km. – a landlocked and underpopulated land.
Population: 5,100,000. Annual Growth 3.1%. People per sq. km. – 7.
Peoples: **African tribes** 32 – Nyanja group 1,000,000; Bemba group 850,000; Tonga 450,000; Lozi 300,000; Lamba-Bisa 370,000; Kaonde 200,000.
                 Europeans – largely on Copper Belt 70,000. **Asians** 12,000.

Capital: Lusaka 500,000, with further 1,000,000 in Copper Belt towns. Urbanisation 30%. Literacy 25%.

Economy: Overdependent on large copper mining industry. Economy hard hit by fall in copper price and unreliable communications with the distant sea (due to border closure with Rhodesia, Angolan Civil War and port congestion, etc. in Tanzania).

Politics: Independent of Britain in 1964. Political life dominated by confrontation with Rhodesia and South Africa and the growing power of Marxism in Angola to the west and Mozambique to the east.

Religion: **Attitude of Government** – complete freedom of religion with the churches accorded many privileges, such as use of State broadcasting system.

African Traditionals 40%.

African Independent Churches 7%.

Roman Catholics 30% numerically strong, but spiritually weak.

Watchtower 8% – probably the land with the second highest percentage of JWs in the world. Unpopular with the government due to their anarchistic doctrines.

Protestants 15%. Community 460,000. Denominations 24. Largest:– United Church of Zambia (6 miss. socs. – Presbyterian, Methodist and Congregational) 50,000 community; Anglicans 90,000; Reformed Church (S. African DRC) 90,000+; Baptists (3 groups) 16,000; Brethren (CMML) 50,000; Evangelical (AEF) 20,000: Brethren in Christ 6,000. Evangelicals 4% of population.

Points for Prayer

1) **Pray for the peace of the land.** The government of Pres. Kaunda strives to develop the country in the face of enormous odds – externally with the unrest and extreme political ideologies in surrounding lands and internally with serious economic problems, unemployment, inefficiencies and tribal loyalties that threaten unity. In some areas there are serious problems with armed gangs roving the countryside.

2) **The evangelisation of this generation** of Zambians is patchy. There is a strong evangelical witness in the N.W. (through the Brethren, AEF and Baptists) among the Luvale, Kaonde and Lamba; in the south (Brethren in Christ, Pilgrim Holiness) among the Tonga; the cities (various); and in the east (through work of DRC) among Nyanja. Yet the N.E. among the Bemba, etc., and most of Lozi in S.W. have very little of a true evangelical witness. There are several tribes that are **unreached** – mostly in S.W – a portion of the Tonga* (80,000), Mashi (5,000) and Subia (20,000). The Lumpa sect grew up in the N.E. in an area largely devoid of an evangelical witness.

3) **The influential United Church** has only a very small, but live, evangelical witness. There is much nominalism. There is much pressure from some quarters to re-introduce dangerous heathen customs into the churches. Pray for a move of the Spirit of God.

4) **There is nominalism in all denominations** due to most having a tribal base. Too many consider themselves "Christian" because of contacts with the Church and its institutions in their tribal area. The NLFA programme has therefore met with limited successes due to the lack of believers with a real personal experience of salvation. The churches in the cities are therefore generally rather weak and ineffective in outreach.

5) **There is a paucity of outstanding Christian leaders** of maturity and very few pastors have a real teaching ministry. The ministry is not attractive to believers with a better education due to the low level congregational support. Pray for all engaged in training men for the ministry – the two AEF Bible Schools, also that of the Brethren in Christ and Reformed Church. Pray also for the developing TEE programme and the preparation of programmed instruction materials by the Brethren in Christ and the AEF workers.

6) **The young people** are the most open section of the community, but in the permissive society, the rate of backsliding is high due to lack of teaching, fellowship and the lack of Christian girls as marriage partners. Pray for the many AEF missionaries who

teach the Scriptures in government and mission schools. Pray for the growing work of SU and for the keen Christian Union (**IVF**) group in the university.

7) **The urban areas** are rapidly growing, often through the mushrooming of squalid satellite shanty towns where the Christian witness is minimal. Pray for the churches and also for the **DM** seeking to evangelise these rather materialistic and needy people. The English medium, multi-racial Baptist churches in Kitwe and Lusaka are making a significant impact on the better educated with sound Bible teaching.

8) **Missions** are still welcome in Zambia, but the emphasis is on working within the structure of the national churches or in preparing Zambians for leadership. There are about 480 missionaries in the land, the majority being Evangelical – largest **AEF** (115) and Brethren (130). Pray for both wisdom, tact and humility for these brethren as they seek to help the Zambian Church. There are many opportunities for service in Bible teaching in schools, leadership training and in technical skills, such as radio, literature, etc. The government is gradually taking over the missions schools and hospitals, though there are still a number of secondary schools entirely mission run.

9) **The European community is drawn from many nations.** Many have come on short term government contracts or to work in the mines and are there just for the riches they can gain. Pray for the evangelisation of this resistant group. Pray also for the evangelisation of such groups as the Communist Yugoslavs and Chinese who are engaged in various development projects. There are some Zambian believers deeply concerned to witness to those from Communist lands – in fact, some Christians are courageously witnessing in universities behind the Iron Curtain!

10) **Bible translation** – work is in progress in 9 languages, 12 languages have the Bible, 9 the N.T. and a further 4 have portions. Some of the smaller languages still await translators.

VII. CARIBBEAN AREA

THE CARIBBEAN & CENTRAL AMERICA 1978

Note: Please see Map on p. 234 for Guiana.

BACKGROUND

We are defining the Caribbean area as all the islands of the Caribbean Sea, as well as the non-Spanish speaking territories of Guyana, Surinam, French Guiana and Belize on the Latin American mainland.

Area: 730,000 sq. km. – the 4 mainland territories 491,000 sq. km. Greater Antilles (Cuba, Hispaniola, Puerto Rico, Jamaica) 211,000 sq. km. Lesser Antilles (the many smaller islands) 27,000 sq. km.

Population: 29,666,000. Annual growth 2.1%. Average population density – 41 per sq. km.
Mainland territories 1,406,000. People per sq. km. – 3.
Greater Antilles 25,000,000. People per sq. km. – 118.
Lesser Antilles 3,260,000. People per sq. km. – 120.

Peoples: **Amerindians** 0.33% – the original inhabitants – virtually wiped out through disease and ill treatment. 51,000 in 10 tribes in the Guianas and 48,000 in three tribes in Belize.
Europeans 30% – largely Spanish (96%), some British, French, Dutch, etc. They originally came as sugar planters. Majority in Cuba.
Negroes 35% – introduced as slave labour for the sugar plantations. These, together with the mixed blood **Creoles** or **Mulattos** 28%, form the majority in all territories but Cuba, Guyana and Surinam.

222

Asians 3.7% – brought in by the British and Dutch from India and Java (Indonesia) to Trinidad, Guyana and Surinam. There are about 60,000 Chinese in these three lands and Cuba. Asians are in the majority in Guyana and Surinam. Urbanisation 44%. Havana (Cuba) is the only city in the region with over one million inhabitants.

Economy: Mainland states underdeveloped and underpopulated, with great economic potential. Most islands over-populated, with limited possibilities for development. Hence much poverty and emigration to North America and Europe. Overdependence on sugar growing and tourism. Economy further held back by poor communications between the many and scattered islands.

Politics: But for Puerto Rico, all the larger territories are independent. Britain, United States, France and the Netherlands still rule a number of the smaller and less viable islands and territories. Hopes of greater political unity are doomed by:–
Language divisions – due to the haphazard acquisition of colonial possessions by the European powers. The Caribbean population is linguistically divided thus: Spanish 59%, French 21%, English 17%, Dutch 3%.
The insularity of the island peoples – each island has its own character and is resentful of outside influence and control. There are 22 political entities in the region.
Communism from the running sore of the Caribbean – Cuba. Since the Communist conquest of Cuba in 1959, a steady stream of propaganda and subversion has flowed out to the surrounding lands and latterly to Africa. This activity has not borne much fruit of permanence in Latin America or the Caribbean, but now Jamaica, Guyana and possibly Surinam are toying with Marxist policies for their own lands.

Religion: **Roman Catholicism** 57% – brought by the original Spanish conquerors. All the Spanish speaking lands, Netherlands Antilles, Trinidad, Dominica, St. Lucia and the French speaking territories are Roman Catholic – though now with a growing Protestant minority.
Muslims 1%.
Hindus 1.9% – largely Asians.
Animists 0.13%.
Voodooism is the Caribbean version of the original African witchcraft and spiritism which was never completely eradicated by the Negro slaves' nominal adherence to Roman Catholicism. This religion could be termed the national religion of Haiti.
Protestants 16% – most of the English speaking territories are predominantly Protestant, but there is very much nominalism. Evangelicals 6% – strongest in Jamaica, Puerto Rico and Haiti. Missionaries to Caribbean lands – 1865 (missionaries to people ratio 1–15,906). Missionaries from the Caribbean – less than 90 – once far greater and significant in the last century's evangelisation of West Africa.

The English Speaking Territories of the Caribbean

Independent states in the British Commonwealth
Jamaica, Guyana, Trinidad, Barbados, Grenada and Bermuda.

Dependent Territories of Britain
Belize, West Indies Associated States, Montserrat, British Virgin Is. and the Caymans.

Dependent Territories of the United States
U.S. Virgin Islands (see p. 230 for Puerto Rico).

Please note that there is much in common between the English speaking peoples of all these areas and much of what we say of Jamaica applies to all.

JAMAICA

BACKGROUND

Area: 11,500 sq. km. – a medium sized island south of Cuba.
Population: 2,100,000. Annual growth 1.9%. People per sq. km. – 190.
Peoples: **Negro 77%.**
               Mulatto 20%.
               European and **Chinese** 3%.
Capital: Kingston 614,000. Urbanisation 37%.
Economy: Recession since 1974 has halted growth and increased unemployment.
Politics: Independent of Britain in 1962. Left leaning government flirting with Cuba's
               Communist government.
Religion: **Attitude of Government** – freedom of religion now, but many fearful of
               Marxist tendencies and possible future limitations.
               Roman Catholics 7%.
               Protestants 75%. Community 903,000. Denominations 70. Largest groups:–
               Anglicans 350,000 adherents; Baptists (3) 160,000; all Pentecostals (6+)
               150,000; Methodists 55,000; Brethren 10,000. Evangelicals 20%.

Prayer Targets

1)   **Pray for continued political and religious freedom**. Many are in need of the Gospel
     message – especially in the violent and vice-ridden shanty towns, where there is so
     much immorality. Confused marriage relationships and illegitimacy make it difficult
     for the lives of new converts to be put right. Pray for more holy, Christ-like living
     among the Christians that will commend the Gospel.

2)   **The Protestant Church is very large**. A majority of the Protestants are nominal but
     the Evangelicals are strong. Few countries in the world have been better evangelised.
     There are the stirrings of revival, but pray that this may be fanned by prayer into a
     blaze for God. The Baptists and Pentecostals are the strongest groups. Yet there is
     much superficiality, lack of deep Bible teaching and a loss of young people from the
     fellowships. The missionary vision is very limited. There are a few expatriate mis-
     sionaries left, but there are sufficient qualified Jamaicans to replace them.

3)   **Leadership training**. There are 43 Theological and Bible Schools in the Carib-
     bean – 14 of them in Jamaica, from which come a stream of potential workers. Pray
     that God may raise up Spirit filled pastors, evangelists and missionaries from these.
     We mention the **WIM** Bible College with students coming from all over the Carib-
     bean as worthy of much prayer. **WIM** also run an extensive TEE programme all over
     the West Indies from their Caribbean Bible School. Independence has brought a new
     responsibility and maturity to the leadership of many churches, yet the need for more
     men of real calibre, drive and spirituality is insatiable. It is in this field of leadership
     training alone that there is a need for some expatriate workers.

4)   **Literature**. The **CLC** maintains a chain of Christian bookstores (5 in Jamaica) in
     many of these territories that contribute much to evangelism and building up the
     Christians. Over 26 workers are committed to this ministry – but the great need is for
     more West Indian workers who have a real vision for the literature ministry and the
     ability to administer it. **CLC** print and distribute a Christian magazine entitled
     Caribbean Challenge that has quite a wide distribution all over the region, but high
     printing costs and great difficulties with distribution throughout the scattered islands
     hinders a more widespread effectiveness – pray about this.

5)   **Missionary vision of the Caribbean churches** has waned. In the last century believers
     from Jamaica and other islands played a significant part in planting the Church in
     West Africa. This decline has been due to a failure to teach missions to believers, and
     also to the relative poverty of the churches. Only one of the 43 Bible Schools in the
     region even offers a course on Missions. There are now about 15 Jamaican mis-
     sionaries serving the Lord among peoples of other races. Pray for the **International
     Missionary Fellowship**, a West Indian interdenominational group that seeks to
     actively promote the cause of missions in schools and churches, and that also runs an

excellent School of Mission Training through which over 27 graduates have gone out into pastoral and missionary ministries.

GUYANA

BACKGROUND

Area:	215,000 sq. km. – a narrow, developed, coastal strip with large under-developed and forest covered hinterland.
Population:	800,000. Annual growth 2.2%. People per sq. km. – 3.
Peoples:	**Negro** and **Mulatto** 41%. **East Indians** 50%. **Amerindians** 4% (3 tribes).
Capital:	Georgetown 180,000. Urbanisation 40%.
Economy:	Great potential as the interior is opened up.
Politics:	Independent of Britain in 1965. The government is becoming increasingly Marxist and radical in every sphere – very atheistic.
Religion:	**Hindus** 30%. **Muslims** 8%. **Roman Catholics** 12%. **Protestants** 40%. Community 282,000. Denominations 20. Major groups:– Anglicans 130,000 adherents; Lutherans 14,000; Moravians 2,000. Evangelicals 6%.

Prayer Targets

1) **The rapidly increasing secular-atheist line** of the government is hindering some Christian activities. Pray for the believers that they may become more fervent for the Lord and not waste present opportunities to evangelise and to prepare believers for hard times ahead.

2) **There is much nominalism in the churches**, though younger, more evangelical groups are growing. Very little work is now done by missionaries and Guyanan believers are in all positions of leadership. Pray for these brethren and for the wisdon they need as they seek to stand true to the Scriptures in all the pressures they are now experiencing. Pray for the ministry of the Guyana Bible School which is now sending out a number of new Christian workers every year.

3) **Unreached peoples** – very little has been done to evangelise the **Hindu** and **Muslim** population (descendants of labour imported by the British earlier in the century). Christians among the Indian people are very few.

4) **Work among the Amerindian tribes** of the interior has resulted in churches being planted among the Macushi (5,000), Wapishana (6,000) and Wai Wai (200) by the **UFM**. There are now only 2 workers on the field, thus much limiting the work of translation and building up the believers. Pray for the raising up of a strong, well led Church among these people that will be able to adapt to the materialistic coastal culture of Guyana.

TRINIDAD and TOBAGO

BACKGROUND

Area:	5,100 sq. km. – two islands off the coast of Venezuela.
Population:	1,100,000. Annual growth 1.5%. People per sq. km. – 215.
Peoples:	**Negro** 43%, **East Indian** 40%, **Mixed race** 14%, **European** 2%, **Chinese** 1%.
Capital:	Port of Spain 100,000. The land is relatively wealthy.
Politics:	A republic independent of Britain in 1962.
Religion:	**Hindus** 23%, **Muslims** 8%, **Roman Catholics** 38%. **Protestants** 30%. Com-

munity 253,000. Denominations 16. Largest groups: Anglicans 120,000 adherents, Methodists 50,000; Presbyterians 32,000; Nazarenes 8,000; Open Bible Standard Churches 3,000; Pentecostal. Assemblies 30,000. Evangelicals 6%.

Prayer Targets

1) **Pray for God's guidance for the leaders in the government.** Pray also that they may be sympathetic to the preaching of the Gospel.
2) **The Protestants are strong,** though nominal. The evangelical witness is strongest on Tobago, where there are many churches. Pray that the Christians may live lives that influence every aspect of the country and its diverse peoples. The few missionaries are in an advisory role and seek to help in leadership training.
3) **Some churches do have contacts with the Muslims and Hindus,** but the impact has been relatively small. Pray for an effective ministry of the churches to these people.

THE SMALLER ISLANDS

BACKGROUND

Area: Densely populated little islands in the East Caribbean and West Atlantic.
Population: **Bahamas** 216,000 – Independent 1973. Negro 75%, Mulatto and White 25%.
            Barbados 256,000 – Independent 1966. Negro 77%, Mulatto 18%, White 5%.
            Bermuda 60,000 – Independent 1976. Negro 50%, Mulatto 15%, White 35%.
            Grenada 110,000 – Independent 1974. Negro 80%, Mulatto 17%, White 3%.
            Virgins 82,000 – British Crown Colony. Negro and Mulatto 95%, White 5%.
            Montserrat 14,000 – British Crown Colony. Negro and Mulatto 97%, White 3%.
            Caymans 12,000 – British Crown Colony. Negro 26%, Mulatto 54%, White 19%.
            West Indies Associated States – in voluntary association with Britain: St. Lucia 126,000; St. Vincent 120,000; Dominica 77,000; Antigua 70,000; St. Kitts, Nevis and Anguilla 60,000. Total population 1,203,000.
Economy: Most are overpopulated, poor and dependent on foreign aid and tourism.
Religion: **Roman Catholics** 31% – only a majority in Dominica, St. Lucia and Grenada.
            Protestants 57% – nearly all islands are at least nominally Protestant. Largely Anglicans (Anglo-Catholic) and Methodist. Evangelicals 8%.

Prayer Targets

1) **The main line churches** are largely nominal. The most evangelistic and growing groups on most islands are those of the Brethren and Pentecostals. There are now many keen evangelists and pastors who are doing a good job and the churches are seeking to recruit and train more Christian workers – may this lead to a greater missionary outreach!
2) **The problems in the churches** are partially due to poverty which leads to the emigration of the believers with the greatest potential for leadership and also partially due to the lack of teaching, resulting in losses to the many active sects. There is much evangelism, but little good Bible teaching and understanding of the deeper life. Pray for a moving of the Spirit in the churches. Pray also for the application of TEE by **WIM** to many of these islands.
3) **Unreached peoples**
  a) **The smaller islands** are difficult to reach and have been neglected – pray for the interdenominational group of believers now seeking to reach the Grenadines (between Grenada and Trinidad) by means of a Gospel boat.
  b) **The Roman Catholic island of Dominica** – though there are live churches witnessing there – including **WEC**, Pentecostals and the Christian Union, the evangelical witness is very small.

BELIZE (British Honduras)

BACKGROUND

Area: 23,000 sq. km – an enclave in the east of Guatemala on Central American Mainland.
Population: 146,000.
Capital: Belmopan 4,000. Largest town – Belize 45,000.
Peoples: **Mulatto and Mestizo 50%, Amerindian 25%, Carib 10%, European 10%.**
Economy: Underdeveloped and prosperous
Politics: British ruled self governing colony that is vociferously claimed by Guatemala.
Religion: **Roman Catholics 55%.**
Protestants 40%. Community 38,000. Denominations 9. Major groups: Anglicans 15,000; Methodists 14,000; Nazarenes 3,000; Pentecostals (3) 3,000 adherents. Evangelicals 6%.

Prayer Targets

1) **This tiny land has quite a strong evangelical witness** through the Baptists, Brethren, Mennonites, Nazarenes and Pentecostals as well as the **GMU.** There are growing churches with evangelistic vision that use both Spanish and English. The Anglicans and Methodists have done more educational work and are rather nominal.
2) **The Nazarene Church** works among the isolated Indian tribes of Mayan descent. The work is slow and hard. Pray for the breakthrough.
3) **The Carib* people** form rather insular communities in both the urban and rural areas. They are neglected, and a concerted evangelistic effot must be made to reach them. There are some Brethren and Mennonite believers among them, but they are only 1% of the group.

SURINAME

BACKGROUND

Area: 162,000 sq. km. – underdeveloped country in north-east South America.
Population: 400,000. Annual growth 3.2%. People per sq. km. – 3.
Peoples: **Mulatto 35%, East Indians 35%, Javanese 15%, Bush Negroes 10%, Amerindians 3%, Chinese 2%, Dutch 1%.**
Capital: Paramaribo 135,000. Urbanisation 49%.
Economy: Rich in natural resources, but much unemployment (30%).
Politics: Independent of Netherlands in 1975 amid great fears of racial violence between the majority Mulattos and Hindustanis (E. Indians), but peace since. The potential for serious trouble hangs over the land.
Religion: **Attitude of Government** – freedom of religion
Animists 6–15%, Muslims 22%, Hindus 32%, **Roman Catholics 21%.**
Protestants 20%. Community 72,000. Denominations 11. Major groups: Moravians 52,000. Community; Reformed 9,700; Lutherans 4,000; Pentecostals 900; other evangelical groups (7) 400 Community. Evangelicals 2.5%.

Prayer Targets

1) **Pray for political peace and religious freedom** in this land with an astonishingly complex racial mixture. The ruling coalition government has much Communist influence. Religious freedom is leading to a rapid resurgence of witchcraft and spirit worship and also much openness to the Gospel. Pray that this land may be won for the Lord Jesus.
2) **The Protestant Church** is very nominal and very little is known of the new birth or holiness in the Moravian or Reformed Churches. The smaller evangelical groups are showing a slow but steady growth, but the number of Bible believing Christians in all denominations is reckoned to be only 3,000. Pray for revival, an experience of true

unity among believers and a more aggressive and prayer backed outreach to the many unreached racial groups.

3) **Missions** – there are now only about 80 missionaries in the country. Evangelical missionaries labour under big disadvantages in that only the larger and more nominal groups are recognised by the government – the smaller groups being just tolerated. There is a need for more expatriate workers for Bible School and TEE work as well as for pioneer work among the unreached.

4) **The Amerindian work** has progressed well in the interior, where the **WIM** missionaries have seen many of the three tribes there turning to the Lord and some even going out as missionaries to other tribes across the border in Brazil. Pray for continued growth among these churches and faithfulness to the Lord. Pray also for the valuable work of the two **MAF** planes that makes this ministry possible. The coastal Caribs and Arawakans are more needy and relatively ignored, though there are several churches among them. The former total 1,000 and the latter 9,000.

5) **Needy peoples**
   a) **The Mestizos or Creoles** are nominally Christian, but need a personal faith in the Lord.
   b) **The Hindu** are unreached, there being just a handful of Christians among them. International Missions and **WIM** each have one couple in this ministry.
   c) **Javanese** – are mostly Muslim and also some Indians. Pray for the Indonesian missionary couple from Timor seeking to begin a work among these resistant people.
   d) **Bush Negroes,** the descendants of escaped slaves who live in the underdeveloped interior and speak several languages of their own. Very little has been done to evangelise them. They are bound by the fear of demons. Several groups have a small witness to these people, including **WIM.**

6) **Bible translation** is an essential uncompleted task. **WBT** is working in 5 languages. The greatest need is for a Bible translation in **Sranen** which is the strange mixed language that has become the main language of communication in the country and is spoken by 80% of the population.

NETHERLANDS ANTILLES

BACKGROUND

Area:	1,000 sq. km. – 3 islands off coast of Venezuela – Curacao, Bonaire and Aruba, and three islands in the north west Caribbean.
Population:	237,000. Annual growth 1.8%. People per sq. km. – 240.
Peoples:	**Negro** 50%, **Spanish-Indian,** etc. Mixture 40%. **Europeans** 10%.
Economy:	Dependent on refining of Venezuelan oil and therefore relatively wealthy.
Politics:	Internal autonomy, but associated with the Netherlands.
Religion:	**Roman Catholics** 82%. **Protestants** 8%. Community 9,000. Denominations 3. Largest: Evangelical Churches **(TEAM)** 1,000 members (Curacao, Bonaire and Aruba), Baptists (St. Eustatius and St. Maarten). Evangelicals 1.5%.

Prayer Targets

1) **These islands are only partially evangelised** and the believers few. There are only about 6 pastors of the National Assoc. of Evangelicals. The work is still in its infancy. Pray for the planting of more churches and for a burden among believers to win the lost around them.

2) **Missions are still needed.** Pray for the witness of the 25 **TEAM** missionaries – the largest evangelical witness. Pray for their church planting and radio ministries.

3) **Christian Radio. TEAM** has a local station broadcasting in Dutch, English, Spanish and Papiamento. **TWR** has a very powerful international transmitter on Bonaire which beams programmes out all over South and Central America. There is a large number of listeners. Pray for the smooth running of equipment in the harsh climatic

conditions and for the large technical staff. Pray for the production, broadcasting and follow-up departments.

CUBA

BACKGROUND

Area: 115,000 sq. km. – the largest Island in the Caribbean.
Population: 9,400,000. Annual growth 1.8%. People per sq. km. – 82. Literacy 92%.
Peoples: **Europeans** 73% – largely of Spanish origin.
Negro and **Mulatto** 26%. **Chinese** 1%.
Capital: Havana 1,755,000. Urbanisation 60%.
Economy: Increasing poverty and lowering of living standards since the Communist takeover. Great dependence on the sugar harvest which now largely goes to the Communist Bloc. Communist military and economic aid is essential for the country to survive.
Politics: Castro's revolution brought Communism to power in 1959. Since then Cuba has sought to export revolution to Latin American countries and in the last two years also to Africa, where Cuban troops helped to install a minority Communist government for Russia in Angola.
Religion: **Attitude of Government** – the strict surveillance of all religious activities and the gradual elimination of religious influence.
Roman Catholics 35% – a marked decline in adherents (80% in 1960) and priests (from 723 in 1960 to 228 in 1971).
Protestants 1% (It was 6% in 1957, but most have emigrated to U.S.A.). Community 85,000. Denominations 24, Largest:– Baptists, Pentecostals and Methodists. Evangelicals 0.9% – though many secret believers also.

Prayer Targets

1) **The believers are subject to harassment and discrimination** at the hands of the Communist regime. Pastors and believers suffered much in the early days of Communist rule and many were imprisoned, but there are not known to be any in prison today for their faith. Much economic and social pressure is brought to bear on pastors and young believers. Pray for the leaders of the churches, that their faith may not fail under the many stresses and that they may be a strength to the believers.

2) **The churches continue under many restrictions.** All home meetings and any activities outside the walls of a church are illegal and the government must be informed of all meetings and conferences and lists of church members. In spite of all these limitations the Christians are becoming more confident and the churches are beginning to grow slowly again. Many churches lost a majority of their membership through emigration after the Communist takeover. The trials of the last 15 years have purified the believers and made them more earnest for God. Witnessing is illegal – pray for the believers who continue to do so.

3) **Leadership training** continues on a low key at two Baptist Colleges and the **WIM** and Nazarene Bible Schools, but the number of students is small and insufficient to meet the need. Pray for these courageous students and the staff that instruct them – for to serve the Lord costs much.

4) **Many of the young people are keen believers** in spite of the fact that this endangers their prospects for a good education and employment. There is now a little more freedom for the churches to legally hold Vacation Bible Schools and camps. Pray that these ministries may bless and build up the faith of these young people. Pray for their witness to other young people.

5) **Missions** – there is still a handful of missionaries serving in the land, but their activities are restricted to little more than being available to offer help and advice to those who request it. Pray for their ministry – that this may be useful to the national believers and that they may have the freedom to minister for as long as the Lord needs them there.

6) **There is a severe shortage of all Christian literature.** All Christian bookstores are now closed and Bibles are hard to obtain. Pray that this literature may somehow enter the country.

7) **Christian Radio** is one of the most important means of strengthening the believers – a high proportion of whom listen in to Spanish broadcasts from the States and from **TWR** Bonaire, etc. Pray for this ministry.

8) **There are now about 1,000,000 Cuban refugees living in the U.S.A.** Pray for these uprooted people – that they may have good opportunities to trust in the Lord. Pray that peace may come to their land again and permit their return.

DOMINICAN REPUBLIC

BACKGROUND

Area: 49,000 sq. km. – the eastern two thirds of the island of Hispaniola, shared with Haiti.
Population: 4,800,000. Annual growth 3.5%. People per sq. km. – 98. Literacy 65%.
Peoples: **Spanish descent** 15%, **Mulatto** (mixed race) 70%, **Negro** 15%.
Capital: Santo Domingo 925,000. Urbanisation 40%.
Economy: Fairly poor and high unemployment.
Politics: Military-civilian rule after some years of unrest and civil war. There has been military and economic support from the U.S.A. in the face of leftist opposition to the government.
Religion: **Attitude of Government** – Roman Catholicism the state religion, though freedom for other religions.
               Roman Catholics 96%.
               Protestants 2.3%. Community 110,000. Membership 33,000. Denominations 19. Largest:– Free Methodists 6,600; Assemblies of God 9,000; Brethren 3,000; **WIM** 1,500. Evangelicals 2% of population.

Prayer Targets

1) **Protestant growth** has not matched other countries of Latin America. There is not much enthusiasm for evangelism in most local churches, but efforts are fruitful when made. The city population is receptive.

2) **There have been many leadership problems in the churches** – immaturity, mission-church relationships and lack of money to support pastors locally. Pray for the emergence of a strong and mature leadership. Pray for the Bible School ministry of many missions – such as **WIM** and **UFM.**

3) Missions – there are about 150 missionaries in the land. Pray for church planting, evangelistic and technical ministries of such interdenominational societies as **WIM** and **UFM.** Reinforcements are needed – especially those already at home in a Latin American culture. This is a good potential field for Latin American missionaries.

PUERTO RICO

BACKGROUND

Area: 9,200 sq. km. – the smallest island of the Greater Antilles.
Population: 3,200,000. Annual growth 2.4%. People per sq. km. – 348. Literacy 90%.
Peoples: **Mulattos** and **Europeans** 80%, **Negroes** 19%.
Capital: San Juan 937,000. Urbanisation 58%.
Economy: Rapid industrialisation and economic growth with much U.S. aid.
Politics: A self-governing commonwealth associated with the U.S.A. Growing support for moves to make P.R. the 51st U.S. State. Small radical minority supported and armed by Cuba aims at complete independence.
Religion: **Roman Catholics** 87%.

Protestants 12%. Community 400,000. Membership 168,000. Denominations 26. Largest:– Pentecostals (7) 67,000 members; United Methodists 14,000; Baptists (2) 15,000; Disciples of Christ 11,000; **CMA 5,000. Evangelicals** 8% of population.

Prayer Targets

1) **There has been a great turning to the Lord** in this century that has accelerated over the last few years. There are now many Pentecostal and Evangelical churches with mature leaders who are well able to handle the evangelisation of the land. Pray for a consolidation of the work and a growth of the yet small missionary vision. Fastest growth is taking place in the Assemblies of God and Baptist Churches.

2) **There are about 37 missions** with around 270 workers working largely with the younger post-war churches in church planting and Bible teaching. There is no longer much need for reinforcements.

3) **Over population and unemployment** has forced many Puerto Ricans to emigrate to New York where they have drifted into the poorest areas of the city and been exposed to the very worst sins and crime. Pray for those who witness among these people.

HAITI

BACKGROUND

Area: 28,000 sq. km. – the western third of Hispaniola Island, shared with Dominican Republic.
Population: 5,500,000. Annual growth 1.6%. People per sq. km. – 194. Literacy 15%.
Peoples: **Negroes** 95%, **Mulattos** 4%, **Whites** 1%.
Capital: Port-au-Prince 500,000. Urbanisation 20%.
Economy: The poorest state in the Western Hemisphere, plagued with overpopulation, poverty, soil erosion, illiteracy and disease.
Politics: Slaves revolted against French rule in 1804 to form the first black republic in the world. Dictatorship that is less harsh since 1971, with greater stability and progress under Jean Claude Duvalier.
Religion: **Roman Catholicism** 70%, the state religion, but considerably compromised by close contacts with Voodooism. There is freedom of religion.
Voodooism is really the national religion – an outgrowth of African spiritism and witchcraft. Its satanic influence is everywhere apparent.
Protestants 18%. Community 880,000. Membership 290,000. Denominations – over 20 (also many hundreds of indigenous groups). Largest:– Baptists 80,000 members; Evang. Bapt. of S. Haiti **(WIM)** 58,000; all Pentecostals 50,000; MEBSH **(UFM)** 15,000. Evangelicals 13% of the population.

Prayer Targets

1) **The poverty of the country** gives great opportunity for demonstrating Christian social concern. Pray for the many medical services run by mission and church groups that these may alleviate the need and bring many to the Lord Jesus. Pray also for many other relief and help programmes to improve the unhappy lot of the people.

2) **Very many are bound by fear** of the spirit world and need deliverance. Pray that many may find complete liberation in Christ. Voodooism hinders Christian workers in their efforts to bring people to the light, but most of the converts in Haiti are from among Voodoo worshippers. Voodooism is not so much of a problem within the Protestant Churches as it is in the Roman Catholic Church.

3) **The Protestant Churches are growing** fairly fast and the people are very receptive. Pray that this time of opportunity may be used to the full by the national believers. Weaknesses found in the national churches are due to poverty, illiteracy of believers and overdependence on overseas funds and initiative. Pray for the small, but growing

vision for missionary work. Several Haitien Churches support missionary work in neighbouring Dominican Republic.

4) **The MEBSH Church (WIM)** has shown rapid growth through a continuing programme of saturation evangelism under the title of "Christ for all". There are about 6,000 prayer cells operating and many believers are now actively witnessing to the unconverted. The MEBSH and other churches have an active outreach programme. Pray for the discipling of the many new converts coming into the churches and also for literacy programmes being run to enable these believers to read the Bible.

5) **Missions** – there are about 84 agencies with about 360 missionaries serving in the land. Some missions are merging with their daughter church organisation (**WIM, UFM** and the Baptists) with a marked improvement in missionary-national relationships. Some missionaries have tended to retain leadership and have failed to develop a strong and well trained Haitien leadership with tragic results in bitterness, lack of spiritual and numerical growth in the churches. Pray for love and trust as well as good cooperation between expatriate and national Christian workers.

6) **Leadership training** – there are about 12 Bible Schools operating in the country. Pray for the 60 or so who graduate annually as they go into the Lord's service – there is a great lack of spiritual and well trained Christian workers. There are also about 1,000 TEE students following various courses in different parts of the country. Pray for these and also the pastors and missionaries who run this programme.

7) **Bible translation** – the national language is French, but most of the people speak a dialect called Creole. The N.T. has been translated into Creole and it is now available on cassette tapes and will soon be printed. Pray that this translation may have a deep impact on the churches and also pray for literacy programmes to encourage people to read in Creole.

8) **Christian Radio. WIM** runs five stations under the title "Radio Lumiere" in south and central Haiti and **OMS** runs a station in the north. These programmes are well patronised. Pray for all engaged in the production and transmission of them. Pray also for a higher degree of co-ordination between the churches and missions running the stations for their more effective use in evangelism and Christian education.

GUADELOUPE

BACKGROUND

Area: 1,702 sq. km. – two large and five smaller islands in the Leeward Islands.
Population: 370,000. Annual growth 1.4%. People per sq. km. – 217. Literacy 78%.
Peoples: Largely **Negroes** and **Mulattos** and some **French**. Much emigration to France.
Capital: Basse Terre 18,000.
Economy: Overpopulated; dependent on tourism and export of rum and sugar.
Politics: Overseas department of France. Considerable Communist influence.
Religion: **Roman Catholics 94%.**
             Protestants 3.5%. Community 115,000. Significant groups – **WIM** and Baptists. Evangelicals 1.5%.

Prayer Targets

1) **There were few, if any, born again believers until 1947.** God has blessed the witness of **WIM** and others since then and there are a number of growing churches. Pray for the ministry of the missionaries in helping the churches to maturity. Pray that the believers may be effectively mobilised for evangelism, which some areas still lack.

2) **The churches are now pastored by nationals** and there are encouraging signs of growth among the young people. Inflation, poverty, materialism and the permissive society are the chief hindrances to spiritual growth.

3) **Pray for the entire ministry of leadership training.** Some believers go to other lands for Bible training, another 45 are following TEE courses run by **WIM**.

MARTINIQUE

BACKGROUND

Area: 1,100 sq. km. – an island in the Windward Islands.
Population: 350,000. Annual growth 0.5%. People per sq. km. – 318. Literacy 85%.
Peoples: Economy and Politics – as for Guadeloupe.
Capital: Fort de France 100,000.
Religion: **Roman Catholics** 96%. **Protestants** 3%. Community 105,000. Denominations 4. Evangelicals 0.5%.

Prayer Targets

1) **Many communities on this island are without an evangelical witness.** Pray for the reaching of these people.

2) **The most significant Protestant churches** are the Baptist and Pentecostal. Pray for the believers and their witness in the rather permissive society of Martinique.

3) **There are over 200,000 emigrants in France** from Martinique and Guadeloupe, where they are proving to be very open for the Gospel. Pray for their evangelisation.

FRENCH GUIANA

BACKGROUND

Area: 91,000 sq. km. – largely uninhabited jungle territory in north east South America.
Population: 60,000 – **Negro** and **Mulatto** and some **French. Amerindians** 4,000. People per sq. km. – less than 1.
Capital: Cayenne 26,000.
Economy: For years infamous as a French penal colony. Very undeveloped and dependent on French economic aid.
Politics: Overseas Department of France.
Religion: **Roman Catholics** 88%
           Protestants 5% – Community 2,200. Denominations 4. Brethren 250 members, Assemblies of God 200 members. Evangelicals 2%.

Targets for Prayer

1) **The most effective evangelisation** has been done by the Brethren with a witness in many settlements along the coast and also in Cayenne. The churches are growing. Pray for the complete evangelisation of this little land.

2) **The Amerindians** of the coast have had some contact with the Gospel, but those living inland remain unreached but for occasional contacts with believers from Amerindian tribes in Suriname who are desirous to start a permanent work among them. Pray for these jungle tribes – that they may prove receptive to the Gospel.

VIII.   LATIN AMERICA

For this survey, we exclude the Caribbean Islands, Belize and the Guianas.

SOUTH AMERICA 1978

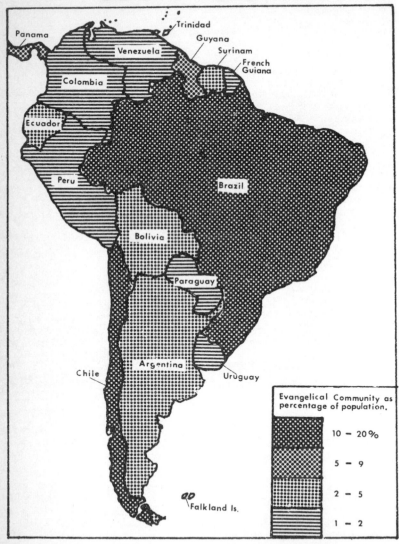

Evangelical Community as percentage of population.

10 – 20%

5 – 9

2 – 5

1 – 2

Note – please refer to map on p. 222 for Central American Republics.

BACKGROUND

Area:	19,841,000 sq. km. – 14% of the land surface of the world.
Population:	297,900,000 – this is 7.4% of the world's population. Annual growth 2.8%. Average no. people per sq. km. – 15.
Peoples:	**Amerindians** 11% – the original inhabitants. A majority in Guatemala and Bolivia, and nearly one half the population in Peru and Ecuador. Two distinct groups:– **the large nations of the highlands** whose empires were crushed by the Spanish in the 16th Century – the Aztecs of Mexico, the 13 million Quechuas and Aymaras of the Andes, etc. **The many small primitive tribes** of the jungle lowlands – 5,000,000 of these people in over 600 tribes. **Europeans** 41.4% – 56% of these are Spanish speaking, 44% Portuguese. Large minorities of Italians, Germans, Poles, etc. being absorbed into these two national languages. Europeans in the majority in Argentina, Brazil, Chile, Costa Rica and Uruguay. **Negroes** 6.9% – descendants of slaves brought from Africa. Most live in Brazil; many along Caribbean coast of Latin America and also Ecuador. **Asians** 0.80% – largely Japanese in Brazil; colonies of Japanese and Chinese in many other lands also. **Mixed Blood – Mestizos** (European-Amerindian) called **Ladinos** in C. America. **Mulattos** (European-Negro) 39.8%. These people are in the majority in 8 lands. It is hard to draw a distinct boundary between the races, for there is more class than colour consciousness. Urbanisation 60% – there are 19 cities of over one million inhabitants in this region.
Economy:	A period of rapid change, mushrooming cities, industrialisation and severe inflation in many countries. Many factors cause instability – the great gap between the wealthy and the many poor, the exploitation of the Amerindian rural population (though this is changing) and resentment at the economic domination of the U.S.A.
Politics:	Social inequalities and economic hardships make these lands very susceptible to Communist subversion and revolution. Some lands have dictatorships or minority governments determined to maintain the status quo, while others have nationalistic leftist governments dedicated to sweeping reforms.
Religion:	**Animists** 5% – largely among the Amerindians. Much animism found among many nominal Roman Catholics, both of Amerindian and African origin. **Jews** 0.26% – most living in Argentina, Brazil and Uruguay. **Roman Catholics** 87% in 1900, almost the entire population was, at least in name, Roman Catholic. The forcible conversion of the Amerindian population by the invading Spanish led to a weak and corrupt Church that was very dependent on foreign personnel. The last 25 years have brought dramatic changes to the R.C Church – the rise of a revolutionary leftist faction in the Church, the growth of theological liberalism, the emphasis on reading the Bible and above all, the astonishing development of the charismatic movement within the Church The charismatic movement is growing even faster than the Evangelical Church and its overall impact on Latin America will be large in coming years. **Protestants** 7.5% – of which about 70% are Pentecostal. There are now about 22,000,000 Protestants (or as they are known in Latin America – Evangelicos), of which about 8,437,000 are church members. In 1900 there were about 70,000 Protestants in Latin America, so there has been an **average growth rate of 8% a year** this century. Evangelicals 6%. Missionaries to Latin America – 10,800. Missionaries from within Latin America – approx. 960.

The Growth of the Evangelicals

One of the great success stories of modern missions – though much of this growth has not been directly connected with Western missions, but rather in indigenous Pentecostal Churches. The growth rate has accelerated over the last 15 years due to:–

1)   The ending of Roman Catholic persecution of Evangelicals.
2)   The immense changes within the Roman Catholic Church, together with the radical change in attitudes towards the Bible and Evangelicals since the Vatican II Council.
3)   The rapid socio-political changes in the continent.
4)   The increasing confidence and aggressive witnessing of Evangelicals. Ordinary church members have been better mobilised than in any other area of the world for personal witnessing and the starting of house churches.
5)   The very great impact of mass evangelism. This is especially true of the Luis Palau campaigns of the past few years – some being of continental proportions with mass media.

This growth is not uniform, but most marked in Brazil, Chile and Bolivia and now in Guatemala and Ecuador. In Paraguay, Uruguay and Venezuela the picture has been less rosy. This growth is likely to be adversely affected by:–

1)   Increasing nominalism in second and third generation Evangelicals, and greater inroads of liberal theology (which is relatively limited at present).
2)   The rapid development of the renewal movements within the Roman Catholic Church – many converts now tend to go to charismatic and Bible study groups within the Roman Catholic Church.
3)   The ever present possibility of Marxist revolutions leading to persecution of Christians.
4)   The dearth of mature Bible-teaching church leaders is leading to spiritually immature congregations. Generally Bible truths are not related to the very real problems in Latin America. There are some fine Latin American theologians of note, who are beginning to give the Gospel a Latin American dress.

THE TYPES OF PROTESTANT CHURCHES

1)   **The older mainline denominations** – often more strong among the immigrant European communities and with little impact on the Spanish and Portuguese speaking majority. Of such are the Waldensians, some Lutherans, Methodists and Reformed Churches. These churches are often liberal in theology and declining in numbers as they fail to retain many of their young people.
2)   **Evangelical denominations** – related to Western denominations and Faith Missions. Their impact has been more to the lower middle class sections of the population. They tend to have a limited Bible School-trained pastorate, but are often poor in theology, Bible exposition and mobilisation of church members. Growth rates have been slow in the past, but there are marked signs of improvement over the last decade.
3)   **Pentecostals and some of the Faith Mission-related Churches** – there has been fast growth through vigorous evangelism by most of the church membership. Leadership is often in the hands of young Christians with little education and limited knowledge of the Scriptures. Their greatest appeal is to the lower classes in the cities. Among the Pentecostals there is an over-emphasis on emotion and experience and a tendency to isolate themselves from political and religious developments around them. The various sects therefore find Latin America fertile ground for their doctrines.
4)   **The Amerindian Churches** – many good evangelical missions have made a great effort to evangelise the many Indian tribes with considerable success. A disproportionately large effort has been made to reach the 600 odd Indian tribes in the lowlands (most with a population of only several hundred). Yet the sacrificial labours of **WBT** and others in Bible translation, and **UFM**, **NTM**, etc. in church planting has brought the light of the Gospel to many of these tribes. This work is far from complete, but is under attack from many quarters – from anthropologists (because the missionaries "spoil" the cultures of these people), from leftist governments (because the missionaries are "C.I.A. agents") and yet other governments (because the missionaries hinder the integration of these tribes into the national life). Only in the last decade have the larger and more neglected Andean Indian peoples begun to respond in large numbers to the Gospel through the good work of **GMU**, **CMA**, **AEM**, **EUSA**, etc. Much remains to be done to disciple these people and help them integrate into the national life of their countries.

The Areas of Unmet Need

1)   Less well evangelised sections of the population:– **the upper and upper middle**

classes – there have been few converts from among these people – more missionary effort is needed in this area: **the university students** in the very Marxist oriented universities – the **IVF**, Minamundo (**LAM**) and **CCC** are beginning to make good progress, but in many universities the evangelical voice is scarcely heard; **some Indian tribes** remain unreached – some because of government prohibitions.

2) **Bible teaching and training of leaders** will be one of the main targets of missions and the churches they serve during the coming decade.

3) **The need for the Latin American Church to gain a missionary vision.** This is coming, but rather slowly, for many problems have to be overcome – the lack of teaching regarding missions in the churches, lack of knowledge and vision of the need, and lack of funds and organisations through which to channel missionaries to other lands. It is only in Brazil that there have been significant advances. 500 Brazilian missionaries are now serving the Lord in Brazil, Latin America and in other continents in both international, denominational and now even Brazilian missions. Latin America could become a source of many missionaries. At present there are probably no more than 960 Latin American missionaries.

COSTA RICA (Central America)

BACKGROUND

Area: 51,000 sq. km. – good agricultural potential.
Population: 2,000,000. Annual growth 2.3%. People per sq. km. – 39. Literacy 90%.
Peoples: **European 81%, Ladino** (Mestizo) 14%, **Negro 4%, Amerindians** 2,000.
Capital: San José 250,000. Urbanisation 41%.
Politics: A stable presidential democracy.
Religion: **Attitude of Government** – Roman Catholicism is the state religion, but there is freedom for other faiths.
Roman Catholics 94%.
Protestants 4.5%. Community 91,000. Membership 26,000. Denominations 30. Largest: SDAs 3,000 members; Pentecostals (3) 3,000; Bible Churches (**LAM**) 2,700; Evangelical Churches (**CAM**) 1,400. Annual rate of growth 7%. Evangelicals 3%.

Prayer Targets

1) **Roman Catholic opposition to the Gospel has waned**, and in its place has risen a very evangelical charismatic movement. The evangelistic work of these charismatics has won more people to the Lord in 5 years than the Protestants in 50. These believers are very open to work with and be helped by evangelicals. Pray that this movement may become more and more Biblically based.

2) **Evangelical church growth has been patchy. CAM** related churches have stagnated and urgently request prayer for a work of the Spirit to get the believers in a position to reach out to others in a receptive population. The Pentecostals and the **LAM** related churches are growing – the latter with a great emphasis on discipleship training. Pray also for the raising up of leaders for the churches through both the **TEE** and residential Bible Schools. **LAM** has a seminary.

3) **Needy areas and groups:**
 a) Alcoholism, spiritism and immorality are rife and many need the message of the Gospel. Pray for converts out of this background.
 b) **Students are not responsive.** Christian students are not very willing to take on responsibility for the evangelisation of their fellow students. Pray for the ministry of MINAMUNDO (**LAM** student outreach).
 c) There are two small Indian tribes – **CAM** has a couple working in one. Pray for the planting of churches among them and also for their integration into national life.

4) **Missions** – 32 groups with 240 missionaries, all Evangelical. Most needed is cooperation and fellowship between them, for there is much frustrating duplication of work. Noteworthy is **LAM** which has pioneered many of the advances for the Gospel in the continent. Now the US mission has submerged itself into the international Community of Latin American Ministries (CLAME) with valuable ministries in promoting the more streamlined and low-profile EiD, radio programming, as well as

the more localised ministries within Costa Rica of evangelism, church planting and Bible teaching.

5) **Evangelism in Depth**, pioneered by **LAM** in Guatemala in 1960 later spread round the world (with local modifications) as a new and revolutionary concept of mobilising all believers to totally evangelise a country. There were wonderful success stories, but weaknesses in the programme have brought radical changes to this timely idea. Pray for **LAM** missionaries working in many countries in Latin America who seek to help local churches in discipleship training in preparation for more localised EiD outreaches.

6) **Christian Radio**. DIA, the radio arm of **CLAME**, acts as a co-ordinating body for the production of radio programmes for all of the Spanish speaking world. 5,000 programmes are now sent out by DIA to 500 radio stations in 21 countries. Pray for this ministry, that it may lead to conversions and church growth.

EL SALVADOR

BACKGROUND

Area: 21,000 sq. km. – the only republic in region with only a Pacific coast.
Population: 4,200,000. Annual growth 3.2%. People per sq. km.–200 – very dense.
Peoples: **Europeans** 14%, **Mestizos** 85%. There are only about 30 **Amerindians**.
Capital: San Salvador 400,000. Urbanisation 39%.
Economy: Poor and dependent on agriculture.
Politics: Presidential democracy.
Religion: **Attitude of Government** – Roman Catholicism is the state religion, but other churches free to operate (though sometimes with official obstruction).
               Roman Catholics 95%.
               Protestants 4.5%. Community 200,000. Membership 58,000. Denominations 14. Largest: Assemblies of God 14,000 members; SDAs 8,000; Evangelical Churches **(CAM)** 4,600; Baptists 4,000. Annual growth rate 5.5% and increasing now. Evangelicals 4%.

Prayer Targets

1) **There is an increasing openness among the people**. Growth is rapid in the Assemblies of God, SDAs and now in the Baptist and **CAM** related churches. The **CAM** asks for prayer, that their aim of doubling membership between 1974 and 1984 may be realised.

2) **Leadership training** is one of the weak spots in Christian outreach. The **CAM** runs a short term Bible School for pastors and most of the pastors in the work have had this training. There is a need for a higher level Bible School.

3) **Missions** – there are not so many missionaries in this land as in the other 5 Central American republics. There are 17 agencies and about 65 missionaries.

GUATEMALA (Central America)

BACKGROUND

Area: 109,000 sq. km.
Population: 5,700,000. Annual growth 2.8%. People per sq. km. – 26. Literacy 40%.
Peoples: **Europeans** 14%, **Ladinos** 26%, **Negroes** 1%.
               Amerindians 59% – 42 tribes descended from the ancient Maya peoples. Largest: **Quiche** 500,000; **Cakchiquel** 300,000; **Kekchi** 250,000; **Mam** 250,000.
Capital: Guatemala City 750,000 – devastated by 1976 earthquake. Urbanisation 34%.
Economy: Poor, but growing through association with the Central American Common

Market which is stimulating industry, trade and communications development.

Politics: Military dictatorship with occasional Communist subversion.

Religion: **Attitude of Government** – Roman Catholicism the preferred religion, but freedom for evangelicals.

Roman Catholics officially about 85%, but though many of the Indians are superficially Roman Catholic, most still adhere to their old religion of worshipping the sun and moon, and fear of spirits and witchcraft.

Protestants 10%. Community 580,000. Membership 168,000. Denominations 15. Largest: All Pentecostals (4) 80,000 members; Presbyterians 15,000; Evangelical Churches (**CAM**) 23,000; SDAs 11,000; Baptists 5,000. Annual rate of growth 9%. Evangelicals 5%.

Prayer Targets

1) **The devastating earthquake of 1976** left 26,000 dead, 76,000 seriously injured and 2 million homeless (35% of population of the country). Many Christian missions and relief organisations (**WV** and **TEAR** Fund etc.) did much to alleviate the immediate needs of the afflicted people. Reconstruction will take years. This disaster has made the people even more receptive to the Gospel, and many churches report large increases in membership despite the many believers who lost their lives and the hundreds of churches that were destroyed.

2) **The churches among the Spanish speaking people** are very divided and there is much interdenominational rivalry and bitterness (sadly much imported from North America). Pray for a spititual unity and power among believers and a greater mobilisation for outreach to the responsive people.

3) **Leadership training** – much is being done in residential Bible Schools by most church planting missions and denominations. The **CAM** have a well known and useful Seminary and **CAM**, Presbyterians and Nazarenes each have 2 Bible Schools for the training of pastors and lay workers for the Indian churches. The Presbyterians pioneered the famous TEE programme (see page 32) in this land in order to meet the very urgent need for leadership training in the poor rural areas. This concept has now become one of the great new weapons for church growth round the world. Pray for the development of a strong national leadership for the Church in the land.

4) **Missions** – 36 agencies with 370 missionaries. Much of the work of these missions is now concentrated on the evangelising and discipling of the **Indian majority**. **WBT** is doing translation work in 20 languages. 9 languages have the N.T. and a further 10 have portions. The Presbyterians have a large and growing work among the Quiche and Mam peoples, **CAM** have a very good work in 11 tribes with growing churches under national pastors. The Nazarene Church also has work in 7 tribes. Pray that the barriers of fear of change, language, illiteracy, etc., may be removed by the light of the Gospel.

HONDURAS (Central America)

BACKGROUND

Area: 112,000 sq. km. – the most mountainous and least developed of Republics.

Population: 3,200,000. Annual growth 3.5%. People per sq.km. – 29. Literacy 50%.

Peoples: **European** 14%, **Ladino** 77%, **Amerindian** 5% (6 tribes), **Negro** 5%.

Capital: Tegucigalpa 300,000. Urbanisation 28%.

Economy: One of the poorest of the Republics.

Politics: Military government, freedom of religion.

Religion: **Roman Catholics** 90%.

Protestants 4.3%. Community 137,000. Membership 39,000. Denominations 22. Largest: All Pentecostals 8,000 members; SDAs 6,000; Evangelical Churches (**CAM**) 3,690. Almost half the Protestants are among the English speaking West Indians on the east coast, who are only 5% of the population. Annual growth rate 8.5%. Evangelicals 2%.

Prayer Targets

1) **The 1975 hurricane that devastated much of the country** has brought a new recep-
tiveness to this nation. Pray for the reaping of the potential harvest and for the
national and expatriate labourers to harvest it. There are now 260 missionaries in 35
agencies.
2) **The nominally Protestant West Indians** are isolated from the rest of the population by
geography and language. They need to experience the moving of the Holy Spirit
convicting of sin and bringing them to a living faith in the Lord Jesus.
3) **The Spanish speaking Church is small, young and still very dependent on outside help.**
Pray that this Church may grow spiritually and in maturity, and reach the point of
takeoff in evangelism. The **CAM** Church is now growing at 27% per year.
4) **The Brethren have a good ministry among the Black Caribs** on the coast in both
Honduras and Nicaragua. These people are descendants of both Indians and Negroes
and speak their own language. There are now a number of assemblies among them.
WBT is translating the Bible for one small tribe.

NICARAGUA (Central America)

BACKGROUND

Area: 148,000 sq. km. – the largest of the Central American Republics.
Population: 2,300,000. Annual growth 3.3%. People per sq. km. – 15. Literacy 50%.
People: **European 14%, Ladino** and **Mulatto 71%, Amerindian 4%, Negroes** 8%.
Capital: Managua 300,000. City almost totally destroyed in 1972 earthquake.
Economy: Poor and greatly set back by the earthquake. Gap between rich and poor is
               very great.
Politics: Military-civilian dictatorship.
Religion: **Attitude of Government** – Roman Catholicism officially recognised, but free-
               dom for other faiths to operate.
               Roman Catholics 92%.
               Protestants 7%. Community 91,000. Membership 26,000. Denominations
               12. Largest: Moravians 13,000 members; Baptists 2,000; SDAs 3,200;
               Evangelical Churches (**CAM**) 1,210. Evangelicals 1.5%. Growth per
               year – 3%, and this largely among the Negroes.

Prayer Targets

1) **Nicaragua is one of the most needy countries in Latin America today.** Very few of the
people have heard the Gospel and many churches were stagnant and even in decline
until recently.
2) **There are signs of a coming harvest.** The 1972 earthquake brought about an unprecedented openness and many began to seek the Lord. The **CAM** churches have
grown in numbers – 87% between 1972 and 1976. The 1976 Managua Campaign has
had a dramatic impact on the capital and much fruit is expected as a result. This
campaign was televised and seen by 100 million people all over Latin America, and
over 200,000 letters were received as a result. The day for mass evangelism is not
over – so long as the follow-up leads to conservation of the fruit! There is also a great
openness among young people now. The Catholic charismatics now number 7,000
and are growing rapidly.
3) **The Church among the Negroes** has grown and now makes up nearly half the
Chrisitan community. There is some life in the large Moravian Church, but also much
nominalism. The Negro people are very poor and isolated from the main stream of
the life of the country; for they live on the unhealthy east coast where they are
labourers on large plantations. Most of these people are nominally Protestant and
most speak English, though the younger people are starting to use Spanish. **Africa
Enterprise** conducted a most encouraging and fruitful campaign among these people
in 1976. Pray that these churches may begin to play an important part in the
evangelisation of this needy land.

4) **Missions** – about 24 groups with 118 missionaries. Pray for harmonious and profitable relationships between the missionaries and nationals – unfortunately, these have often not been good in these Republics – especially in Nicaragua.

5) **The Indian people** are few and there is only one significant tribe – the Miskito (40,000). The Moravians work among them.

PANAMA (Central America)

BACKGROUND

Area: 29,000 sq. km. – bisected by the U.S. Panama Canal Zone.
Population: 1,700,000. Annual growth 2.6%. People per sq. km. – 90. Literacy 80%.
Peoples: **European** 12%, **Ladino** 69%, **United States Citizens** 40,000, **Negro** 14%, **Amerindian** 5% (8 tribes).
Capital: Panama City 500,000. Urbanisation 49%.
Economy: The Canal has brought the land more wealth than that enjoyed by the other 5 Republics.
Politics: Resentment against U.S.A. for continued retention of sovereignty and many privileges in the 16 km wide and 80 km long Canal Zone is giving opportunities for Communists to exploit.
Religion: **Attitude of Government** – there is freedom of religion.
                Roman Catholics 86%.
                Protestants 9% (only one half among the Spanish speaking majority). Community 154,000. Membership 61,000. Denominations 22. Largest groups: Pentecostals (5) 35,000 members; Baptists 11,000; Churches 47% Spanish speaking, 35% English and 18% Indian languages. Annual rate of growth – 5%. Evangelicals 6%.

Prayer Targets

1) **The Panamanian people are indifferent to the Gospel** and the breakthrough must yet come. Church growth in all but the Pentecostals among the Spanish speaking people has been very disappointing. Pray for the opening up of these people for the Lord.

2) **Many of the churches cater for the needs of the English speaking West Indians and large U.S. Canal Zone community.** Among these people there is much nominalism and contact with the other language groups is minimal. Pray for revival.

3) **Literature work** is now carried on by **CLC** through two large bookstores at either end of the Canal. Pray that this ministry may be used of God to get evangelistic literature into the hands of the many not yet reached with the Gospel, and pray that the Christians may be built up in their faith thereby.

4) **Missions** – 24 agencies with 200 missionaries and pastors. More pioneer work is needed in the poor and indifferent rural areas.

5) **Work among the Indian tribes.** All the 10 tribes are now occupied by missionaries. Two have the N.T., **WBT** is working in the 8 other languages. **NTM** with 47 missionaries is planting churches in 4 tribes and the Brethren in a further 2. The largest tribes are the Guaymi 45,000 (**NTM**) and Cuna 24,000 (**NTM**).

MEXICO

BACKGROUND

Area: 1,973,000 sq. km. – Latin America's 4th largest country.
Population: 62,300,000. Annual growth 3.5% (highest growth rate in the world). People per sq. km. – 32 (2nd most populous Lat. Am. nation). Literacy 76%.
Peoples: **Spanish descent** 20%, **Mestizos** 59%, **Negroes** 1% – all speaking Spanish.
           Amerindians 20% – speaking 56 major languages, and further subdivided into 200 dialects that are divergent enough to need separate Bibles.

Capital: Mexico City 10,000,000. Other large cities: Guadalajara 1,500,000. Urban-
                isation 61% and rapidly increasing.
Economy: Rapid growth in agricultural, mining, oil and industrial production. Economic
                hardship for many due to recession since 1974, rural poverty, urban unem-
                ployment, political tensions and explosive population growth.
Politics: Federal republic with much stability since bloody 1910–24 civil war with a one
                party democracy. Increasing unrest now due to unsolved socio-economic
                problems.
Religion: **Attitude of Government** – secular state with some restrictions on both Roman
                Catholics and Protestants, but otherwise religious freedom.
                Roman Catholics 85% – 15% actually practising their religion – much
                Romano-paganism among the Indians and Mestizos.
                Protestants 2.8%. Community 1,700,000. Membership 700,000. Denomi-
                nations 66. Largest groups: All Pentecostals (8+) 400,000 members; All
                Methodists (2) 45,000; Presbyterians 50,000; SDAs 80,000; All Baptists (2)
                45,000. Annual rate of growth 11%. Evangelicals 2%.

Prayer Targets

1) **The present unsettled conditions and hardships for many** are helping to break down
    the barriers of prejudice against the Gospel and make the people more open to hear
    the Lord's voice. Pray that believers may be ready and willing to seize the oppor-
    tunities and keep a balance between preaching the Gospel and social concern.

2) **The Roman Catholic Church** has retained the loyalties of the people more than in
    most Latin American countries despite the loss of political and economic power in
    1910. There has been much opposition in some areas to Protestant work, but this has
    now waned considerably. Yet many remain in bondage to the dogmas of the Church
    and also to the underlying and powerful spiritism. Pray for the liberation of the
    Mexican people through the preaching of the Gospel.

3) **The evangelical witness has grown dramatically** among the lower classes, the urban
    immigrants and the Indian tribes of the south east. There are now more churches in
    the north and south, but relatively less in the centre of the country, yet there is
    scarcely a town or village that does not have a group of believers. Pray for a
    consolidation of this outreach through the growth of strong, nationally led and
    supported congregations. Pray also for bold plans for outreach. The **Overseas
    Crusades** mass evangelism preaching by Luis Palau has had a decisive influence in
    increasing evangelical cooperation and church growth. Billy Graham will, God
    willing, hold a campaign in 1977, though there is considerable opposition in the press
    against such a North American outreach. The ministry of **LAM** has done much to
    strengthen the churches through promoting EiD methods and new initiatives in
    literature evangelism (newspaper articles, comic magazines, etc.) and radio prog-
    rammes.

4) **Some churches are growing fast**, especially the Pentecostal groups. Other denomi-
    nations have shown less growth through lack of outreach, pessimism in the face of
    Roman Catholic bigotry and a lack of the power of the Holy Spirit. Pray for revival
    and also for the raising up of more who are willing to forsake all to go into the Lord's
    service. There is a need for outreach to the rapidly growing urban areas – especially
    in the huge capital city.

5) **Missions** – there are over 125 agencies with about 1,300 missionaries currently in the
    country – 11 Baptist groups, 14 Pentecostal, 7 Mennonite and 20 inter-
    denominational missions (nearly all from the U.S.A.). The best known of the latter
    are largely involved in Indian work (see below), though the **CMA, GMU** and **CAM**
    have a small Spanish speaking church planting ministry. Pray for these brethren and
    their acceptability among the people in a day when anything from North America is
    suspect culturally and politically. Pray for their strategic deployment for the
    speediest maturing of the national churches. There are many openings for the right
    kind of missionary, though the national believers are doing more and more of the
    outreach.

6) **Migrant Mexican labour in the U.S.A.** has long been a feature of national life. Pray
    for the very many Mexicans in the U.S. States of California and Texas – for in these

areas they have many opportunities to hear the Gospel. Pray that the believers in the U.S.A. may use these opportunities to demonstrate the love of God and win many to the Lord.

7) **Work among the Amerindians** has been immensely advanced by the outstanding ministry of **WBT** – with an aim to complete the N.T. in 130 languages within 20 years. **WBT** has now 506 workers in 80 languages; 37 tribes now have a N.T. and a further 48 have portions. 37 languages still await translators. Pray for other denominational and interdenominational missions who work to plant churches among these tribes – about 73 have now at least one group of believers and some have seen powerful movings of the Spirit of God and strong evangelistic churches formed as a result. Yet other tribes remain resistant, such as the Chamula* (50,000), Yaqui* (14,000) Zinacantecos* (10,000) and Mizteco* (15,000).

8) **Leadership training** is a major part of the ministry of many missions now. There are over 90 Bible Colleges and Seminaries in Mexico – for all levels from tribal language to degree awarding schools. Pray for the sending out of many Spirit filled workers into the white harvest fields.

9) **Christian Radio work** has only been permitted since 1964, but this ministry has expanded enormously. Many programmes are broadcast daily with encouraging results, though it is hard to get good listening times on some stations due to their opposition to the Gospel. There has also been a more limited TV outreach.

ARGENTINA

BACKGROUND

Area: 2,808,000 sq. km. – Latin America's second largest country.

Population: 25,700,000. Annual growth 1.4%. People per sq. km. – 9. Literacy 92%.

Peoples: **Europeans** 89%. Largely Spanish with many Italians, also many other national minorities that have tended to retain their national identity.
Mestizos 10%, **Amerindians** 65,000 – mostly in the Chaco in the far north, and Patagonia in the far south.

Capital: Buenos Aires 9,200,000. Also Rosario 1,000,000, a major city. Urbanisation 81%.

Economy: Largely based on agriculture, but increasingly industrialised. Although having the highest Latin American living standards, runaway inflation has played havoc with the economy.

Politics: Peronist misrule, inflation and increasing leftist urban terrorism provoked the 1976 military takeover. There has been a considerable improvement in the stability and economy of the country since.

Religion: **Attitude of Government** – Roman Catholicism is the official religion and compulsorily taught in the state schools. There is freedom of religion.
Roman Catholics 88% – a waning influence in face of Marxism, materialism and Protestant activity.
Jews 2%.
Protestants 5%. Community 1,335,000. Membership 387,000. Denominations – largest groups: Pentecostals (30) 190,000; Lutherans (7 immigrant minorities) 45,000; Brethren 34,000; Baptists 26,000; SDAs 30,000 members. Evangelicals 3.5%. Annual growth rate 5%.

Prayer Targets

1) **The political turmoil since 1974 has opened the hearts of the people in a new way.** There was a large increase in the number of conversions during 1976 after years of stagnation and slow growth in most Protestant Churches. Pray for a large harvest.

2) **The need of the people** is seen in the turning to drugs among the youth, immorality, and widespread superstition and witchcraft. Yet there is still much prejudice against Protestants. The major cults such as the Watchtower and the Mormons are growing.

3) **The Roman Catholic Church** is in turmoil with polarisation between the leftist radical

priests and the traditional conservatives. Vatican II and the Roman Catholic charismatics have brought a new willingness among Roman Catholics to read the Word and listen to the Gospel. Pray that believers may use these opportunities to the full and be delivered from their self-satisfaction and unwillingness to witness to the R.C. majority.

4) **The Church** is growing fastest among the Pentecostals (who are prone to superficiality in conversion, and to many divisions) and also the Brethren and Baptists. The Luis Palau **Rosario campaign** of 1976 set a new standard for the use of mass evangelism for church growth. There is now a greater unity among the Evangelicals than ever before (denominational barriers being high) – pray for the Fellowship of Evang. Churches (41 groups affiliated) that this may provide for more effective evangelism and use of resources.

5) **Pray for some of these problems to be resolved that plague the churches** – inadequate local leadership, the weakness of the rural churches, divisions caused by the strong charismatic movement within the non-Pentecostal churches.

6) **The immigrant minority Churches** make up 30% of the national Church. They have attended to the spiritual needs of the Italian, Danish, Dutch, Welsh, etc. communities and have not evangelised the Spanish speaking majority, though some, such as the Italian, Russian and Chilean believers, have evangelised their own groups. They are in decline, partly because their Spanish speaking children do not feel at home in the churches.

7) **Leadership training** – there is a great need for the raising up of Godly national theologians and pastors who will be able to stand for the truth in the Argentinian context, for there is a trend in many theological colleges to emphasise humanism, Marxism and social action rather than the preaching of the Word. The Protestant Church is largely Evangelical, but liable to be influenced by such teaching. There is a great lack of pastors who are able to mobilise their members for evangelism.

8) **Missions** – now about 48 groups with 46 missionaries. Many are needed for pioneer evangelism, church planting and Bible teaching, especially by those who can master Spanish. Pray for the church planting and support work of such missions as the **CMA**, **EUSA** and **GMU**.

9) **Needy peoples** – those living in the vast and sparsely inhabited Patagonia, the north and west. Also needing evangelising are the 500,000 Jews in the cities, and the many slum dwellers newly moved to the cities.

10) **The Amerindians** in the northern Chaco have been evangelised by the Evangelical Anglican South American Miss. Soc. and Baptists, and a strong church is emerging but it needs to be integrated into national life. There are about 14 tribes in the region, some unreached. The largest – the Chiriguano (20,000) is 5% Protestant.

BOLIVIA

BACKGROUND

Area:	1,099,000 sq. km. – a landlocked and mountainous country.
Population:	5,200,000. Annual growth 2.6%. People per sq. km. – 5. Literacy 60%.
Peoples:	**Spanish speaking Whites** 13% and **Mestizos** 25% dominate politics and economy.
	Amerindians – Quechuas 34%, Aymaras 25% in the Andes and valleys. Lowland tribes (43) 3%. All totalling 62%.
Capital:	La Paz 800,000. Urbanisation 35%.
Economy:	The poorest country in South America, dependent on tin and oil exports.
Politics:	Unstable with 180 revolutions in 160 years. Present right wing military government has given 5 years of stability and some progress.
Religion:	**Attitude of Government** – Roman Catholicism is the state religion, though there is freedom for other faiths.
	Roman Catholics 75% – actually 25% practising Roman Catholics among Spanish, and 5% among Indians. Much animism mixed with nominal Roman Catholicism among the latter.

Protestants 6%. Community 208,000. Membership 94,000 (though one third of this is of the SDAs). Largest denominations: Evangelical Christian Union (**AEM** and **UFM**) 12,000 members; All Pentecostals (5) 11,000; Friends Churches (3) 8,000; Baptists (3) 6,000; Brethren 3,000. Evangelicals 4%. Annual rate of growth of Protestant Church 6% (10% among the Aymaras).

Prayer Targets

1) **There is greater receptivity in all groups than ever before.** The long resistant middle class and the growing student population are now open to the Gospel. The Aymaras, lowland Indians and the migrant populations in the mines and cities are turning to the Lord. The Luis Palau campaign in 1975 has had a significant impact on church growth. Yet the explosive political situation in South America could suddenly change all this. Pray that expatriate and national brethren may use the present opportunites.

2) **The Roman Catholic Church** is in decline through the lack of priests (90% of the 800 priests are foreign), nominalism, revolt of the educated and polarisation between radicals, traditionals and charismatics. Roman Catholics are open to the Bible as never before, and willingly receive and study it. Pray that believers may use this openness to run home Bible study groups – one of the best means of winning Roman Catholics.

3) **The Church is growing**, but apathy and worldliness among many Evangelicals is hindering more rapid Gospel advances. Pray for revival and the mobilisation of Spirit filled believers for evangelism. Lack of trained pastors and sound Bible teaching limit believers in their outreach and lay them open to the many very active sects that abound. There are some outstanding Spanish, Aymara and Quechua speaking Christian leaders which augurs well for the future.

4) **The rapidly growing Church needs well trained leaders.** There are about 14 Bible Schools and Seminaries with nearly 400 residential students, with yet others studying through the expanding TEE courses. Pray for all involved in this leadership training ministry and also for the spiritual growth of all students.

5) **The missions working in Bolivia** number about 36 with some 650 missionaries. The AEM is the largest evangelical mission with a widespread and blessed ministry to all peoples and areas. AEM has pioneered most of the major Gospel advances in the country, with workers in almost every Christian ministry. The NTM has had a significant breakthrough in combining a vital church planting ministry in 8 tribes with a similar ministry to the lowland Spanish speakers, and seeing small tribal churches well integrated into the national Church. Pray for more labourers, both for pioneers work and also to serve the growing Church with its many needs. Pray also for a happy and fruitful fellowship between national and expatriate workers.

6) **The Amerindian Quechua and Aymara** in the Andes are turning to the Lord in large numbers – pray especially for the development of strong churches with well taught believers – many are illiterate and find it hard to fully grasp the basics of the Gospel. There is a growing literature programme being developed in their languages.

7) **The many Amerindian tribes** of the lowlands and forests are being reached by more than 5 missions – **WBT** with 57 workers in 16 tribes, **NTM** in 8 tribes with 104 workers and also the South American Mission, AEM and UFM in others. Some smaller and more inaccessible tribes still need to be contacted with the Gospel, but many are now occupied and Bible translation is in progress in at least 16 of the 40 tribes. Pray for the planting of churches among these peoples and also for their wise integration into the life of the country.

8) **Unreached peoples** – the elite upper class remains virtually untouched by the Gospel. The student population is now more open, despite Marxist leanings, but so far there has been little effective work done and the outreach of both the CCC and IVF related groups has not yet made much impact.

BRAZIL

BACKGROUND

Area:	8,512,000 sq. km. – one half of the land surface and population of South America. The world's 5th largest country (36 times size of United Kingdom!).
Population:	110,000,000. Annual growth 2.8%. People per sq. km. – 13. Literacy 67%.
Peoples:	Brazil is a melting pot of the nations, with much intermarriage.

Europeans 60% – mainly of Portugese origin, also many German and Italians.
Negroes 15% – descendants of slaves brought from West Africa and Angola.
Mixed race (Mestizos and Mulattos) 25%.
Asians 1.5% – Japanese (1,000,000), Chinese (200,000) and Arabs, etc.
Amerindians 0.1% – probably number 100,000 and decreasing through the encroachments of civilisation and disease. About 160 tribes.

Capital:	Brasilia 600,000. Other major cities: Sao Paulo 7,200,000; Rio de Janeiro 5,000,000; Belo Horizonte 1,600,000. Urbanisation 58%.
Economy:	Rapid growth until 1974 and rising standard of living for many, but severe balance of payments difficulties and economic hardship since. Great economic potential with vast untapped reserves of raw materials and hydro-electric power in the underdeveloped hinterland. Much industrial growth.
Politics:	A Communist takeover forestalled in 1964 by military intervention. The strong military government since then has brought much stability and some progress and there is a gradual return to more democratic rule.
Religion:	**Attitude of Government** – complete freedom of religion.

Roman Catholics 83%, but only about 10% reckoned to be practising Roman Catholics. There is a general disillusionment with the Roman Catholic Church and the priesthood is discouraged. Roman Catholics are seeking to prevent erosion of position by reforms, infusion of foreign priests and the use of Protestant methods and vocabulary. The Charismatic movement is growing.
Spiritism 15–30% estimate – a major, but rather underground force in the land, and has even been called the "national" religion. Roman Catholics and some Protestants are corrupted thereby. Every stratum of society influenced by the various forms – of European, African and the old Amerindian spiritism and witchcraft, together with a veneer of Roman Catholicism.
Protestants 13%. Community 13,000,000. Membership 4,980,000. Two thirds of South American Protestants in Brazil. Annual growth approx. 6% now. Denominations – over 100 (one half Pentecostal). Largest: Assemblies of God 2,000,000 members: Other Pentecostals 1,200,000 (Pentecostals being 70% of all Protestants); Lutherans 480,000; Baptists 435,000; Presbyterians 230,000. Evangelicals 11%.

Prayer Targets

1) **Brazil is one of the most exciting areas for church growth in the world.** The land is wide open for the Gospel, the people are receptive and the national churches are vigorously multiplying through personal evangelism, forming satellite house churches. One in nine Brazilians is now Protestant, yet at the turn of the century there were only a few thousand believers in the land. Pray for the continued growth and maturing of the Church in Brazil.

2) **The Pentecostal Churches have shown the most dramatic growth** through their aggressive evangelism, use of lay workers and believers and their enthusiasm. Yet there are serious weaknesses – superficiality in conversions and spiritual life, lack of Bible reading and teaching, There are therefore many divisions over personalities and over-emphasised doctrines and also openness to heresies such as unitarianism. Most of the pastors are untrained. Pray for a deepening of the work and a greater love and concern for the teachings of the Word of God, and also for the growing interest in stimulating systematic Bible School training.

3) **The growth rate in non-Pentecostal Churches has not been so great** due to formalism, lack of evangelistic concern, missionary-national tensions and the unfortunate ten-

dency of some evangelical missions of keeping "captive" national congregations under their supervision. Yet the evangelical churches are increasingly mature and well led, and several promising denominations have come into being as a result of cooperation between various interdenominational missions. Pray for the believers in these days of opportunity, that their energies may be used for extending the Kingdom of Christ and not in lesser things.

4) **The greatest need of the Brazilian Church is revival** – the great growth and expansion of the Church with all its evangelism is not revival such as Western lands knew in 1859-60, with deep repentance, breaking down of denominational barriers and jealousies, deepening spirituality and rooting believers in the Scriptures. The charismatic movement has brought an increase in evangelism in some denominations, but also a greater divisiveness in others.

5) **The present training of leadership for the churches cannot supply the needed manpower**. Much is being done, but the multiplication of churches is such that other means apart from Bible Schools and Seminaries must be used. Pray for the 82 or more residential schools – but there are the problems due to the lack of national staff, spirit of nationalism, lack of students of the right calibre and lack of local funds. Pray for the increasing use made of TEE by many of the above; there are more extension students than residential. More must be done for the training of lay leadership in the churches – for on these fall the main burden of the work and preaching, so pray for missionaries and national pastors engaged in this ministry.

6) **Liberal theology** with its emphasis on social problems, and even encouraging leftist revolution is gaining an entrance through some seminaries and also the clever use of literature. Although the Brazilian Church is almost entirely conservative evangelical, few leaders are equipped to contend with this error. Pray for the strategic ministry of the ABU (IVF) in Brazil in publishing more literature that emphasises the authority of the Scriptures.

7) **Missions in Brazil** are still needed to pioneer unreached areas and groups, as well as to stand alongside the national believers. There are now about 3,100 missionaries in 155 agencies (80% from North America). There are about 50 interdenominational societies with about 1,050 missionaries, but nearly half of these work among the isolated Indian tribes in Amazonia. Pray for these servants of the Lord – that they may also be servants of the Church and not its masters! Unhelpful missionary attitudes and methods have not always been absent, but God gives grace in answer to prayer.

8) **Christian literature is in great demand** with the rising literacy rate. Many publishing and distributing agencies are ministering in this field – most under the umbrella of the co-ordinating Evangelical Literature Committee of Brazil – we mention the ministries of **EUSA, CLC** and **IVF** in particular. There is a need for more Brazilian writers. Pray for the distribution of evangelistic literature – mentioning in particular the ministry of **WEC** through "CEDO" – an evangelistic broadsheet with a large circulation and significant impact.

9) **Young people** are, generally, not well catered for in the churches and there is a need for more missionary and national youth workers – especially among students. There are about 700,000 university students in over 44 universities. The **CCC** is active and the ABU (IVF) is having a big impact with groups in most universities, helping students to come to the Lord, be built up in the Word and also to get a missionary vision. This is stimulating the missionary concern of young people and also the churches. The ABU is also pioneering a ministry to Christian graduates.

10) For years over 300 **WBT** missionaries (in 41 tribes), **NTM** (20), **UFM** (5) have been seeking to evangelise **the many small Amerindian tribes in the Amazon jungles.** Most of these tribes are very isolated, and small (around 100–600 people). The government terminated this work in 1978. Pray for wisdom for the missionaries as they seek to minimise the damage to the work built up over the years. Pray for the completion of the evangelisation and Bible translation work that has been begun. Pray for the believers among these people, and that they may gain a missionary vision for the unreached tribes.

11)   **Areas of need:–**
   a) **The slum dwellers** in the cities – averaging about one third of the city inhabitants. These people are needy and open to the Gospel.
   b) **The little settlements** along the many rivers in the vast Amazon jungle are poor and needy physically and spiritually. The believers are few and often isolated. **UFM** is doing a good pioneer work in the Upper Amazon region in planting little churches. These churches need prayer – they constantly suffer losses to the more wealthy towns and cities of those most able to support the ministries of the fellowships. Pray for those engaged in pioneer evangelism by means of river launches – a hard and dangerous ministry.
   c) **The pioneer colonies** along the new roads being driven through the virgin jungles of the west and north – the Brazilian Church is seeking to reach out to these rough settlements and plant churches.
   d) **The one million Japanese** with very few Protestants among them.
12)   **The missionary vision of the Brazilian Church is growing.** There are now about 500 Brazilians in cross-cultural mission work – mostly within Brazil, but also in Europe and Africa (especially the Portuguese speaking lands), and to Latin America and Asia. A number of Brazilian organisations seek to prepare missionaries for overseas service – notably the Bethel Fellowship Bible School and the **WEC** Missionary Orientation Institute. Pray also for the development of Brazilian sending structures and societies to support them. A number of Brazilians now serve with **NTM, WEC, TEAM** and also with denominational missions. Brazil has great potential as a missionary sending land.

CHILE

BACKGROUND

Area: 757,000 sq. km. – a 4,200 km. long country wedged between the mountains of the Andes and the Pacific Ocean and averaging only 150 km. in width.
Population: 10,800,000. Annual growth 1.7%. People per sq. km. – 14.
Peoples: **European** and **Mestizo** Spanish speaking people 95%. **Amerindians** 5% – Mapuche (400,000) in south, Aymara and Quechua immigrants in the north.
Capital: Santiago 3,700,000. Urbanisation 76%. 40% of people live near the capital and 85% in the temperate central provinces. The northern desert and wet, cold, mountainous south have few inhabitants.
Economy: Severe droughts, social injustices and runaway inflation, as well as the disastrous policies of the former minority Communist government brought the land to the brink of disaster. Inflation has been curbed and recovery is coming, though with much suffering and poverty.
Politics: The 1970 election resulted in a Communist minority government. A military coup forestalled a violent Communist takeover. The internationally unpopular military government is seeking to eliminate Communist influence and build a more fair and democratic society.
Religion: **Attitude of Government** – freedom for both Roman Catholics and Protestants to carry on all religious activities.
                Roman Catholics 80%.
                Protestants 17%. Community 1,728,000. Membership 920,000. Pentecostals 125 groups and 85% of Protestants. Almost entirely indigenous denominations with no affiliation with missions or denominations in other lands. Other Evangelical groups – Baptists 14,000; CMA Churches 5,100. Evangelicals 16%.

Prayer Targets

1)   **Pray that this unhappy and divided land may have peace**, justice and freedom. Since the military coup there have been unparalleled opportunities for the winning of souls among a people more receptive than ever before.

2) **The Roman Catholic Church is going through a dramatic transformation** from a nominal and traditional upper class-supporting edifice to an outgoing evangelistic body. The charismatic movement seems to have had a great evangelical impact on many, with an emphasis on repentance, faith and total surrender. Pray for a full return to Biblical standards.

3) **The Protestant Church has grown dramatically over the last 60 years**, and the troubles of the land since 1970 have caused this rate to accelerate. Yet there is a great lack of unity among believers, and denominational rivalry based on strong leadership personalities. There is also a lack of nationally known evangelical leaders of the calibre found in other S. American lands. The missionary vision for other cultural groups and countries is small.

4) **The Pentecostal Churches** have great evangelistic zeal, but are often very shallow spiritually and ill-taught. The pastors need prayer, for there is the common scorn for those who value Bible School training, or careful preparation of sermons beforehand as being "unspiritual". The importance of dominant personalities and neglect of the teaching of the Scriptures lead to frequent divisions. The Pentecostals have made a deep impact on the working class.

5) **The other Evangelical Churches** have been more effective among the middle classes. They often lack the power and cultural adaptability to reach all sections of the community. The **CMA** and Baptist Churches are making good progress. The Methodists and Presbyterians are more inclined to liberal theology.

6) **Missions** – there are about 400 missionaries in some 27 agencies in the land. There is a need for pioneer missionaries in some areas – especially among the Mapuche Indians, and in the many large slums around the main cities. Yet the major task for missionaries is to serve the Chilean Church in youth work, literature, teaching and discipling the believers and the training of Christian workers. Pray for them in these disturbed days – that they may be effective and fruitful and not be sidetracked by minor, but seemingly important issues.

7) **Literature work** is hampered by the grave economic crisis and the rise in printing costs. Many cannot afford to buy literature now. Importing literature is very hard with the present restrictions. Pray for the writing and publication of more literature within the country. Pray for the excellent literature ministries of **CMA** and CLC.

8) **The work among the resistant Mapuche (Araucans)** has been slow and hard due to their bondage to the power of the witch doctors and spirits. Pray for the binding of the evil one. There are several missions (the Anglican S. American Missionary Society and also **CMA**) seeking to plant churches among them, but only about 1% of these people have believed on the Lord Jesus Christ.

COLOMBIA

BACKGROUND

Area: 1,139,000 sq. km. – mountainous in west, and plains and forests in east.

Population: 24,000,000. Annual growth 3.2%. People per sq. km. – 21.

Peoples: **Europeans 20%, Mestizos 48%, Mulattos 18%, Negroes 5%, Amerindians** 6% – 70 tribes; largest: Guajiro 100,000.

Capital: Bogota 3,000,000. Other cities Medellin 1,300,000; Cali 1,000,000. Urbanisation 64%.

Economy: Relatively poor, but with great agricultural and mineral potential.

Politics: A democratic country, but marred by virtual civil war between the two largest political parties between 1948–60 – a time known as "La Violencia". Over 200,000 people died in that time. Now increasing Communist activity.

Religion: **Attitude of Government** – state support for the Roman Catholic Church. Great limitations on Protestant work now replaced by unprecedented liberty, but this may be changing again to a period of restrictions.
Roman Catholics 96% – "La Violencia" was used as an opportunity to persecute the Protestants, but all is rapidly changing within the Church.
Protestants 1.8%. Community 432,000. Membership 205,000. Denomi-

nations 38. Largest groups: All Pentecostals 38%, Churches related to faith missions 14%, SDAs 29%. Growing at 10% a year. Evangelicals 1.1%.

Prayer Targets

1) **The persecution of believers was severe**, 57 churches were destroyed and 100 believers lost their lives. Others suffered robbery and rape, yet in the last 15 years all this has disappeared. There is now liberty for believers to hold open air meetings, evangelistic campaigns, street parades and to broadcast. Pray that believers may use these opportunities to the full.

2) **There is an unprecedented openness to the Gospel.** The good testimony of believers in the terrible time of persecution, the new openness among Roman Catholics and the 1968 Evangelism in Depth campaign all helped to bring people to Christ and to the churches. Membership in the churches increased sevenfold between 1950 and 1967 and the growth is still being maintained. Pray for a continued harvest among peoples of all classes and groups.

3) **The Protestant Church** has matured and now carries the main burden of leadership and evangelism. Many missions are now working under the direction of the national leaders. Yet there is a dearth of trained leaders to disciple the many new converts. Pray for the 19 Bible Schools and Seminaries – **CMA** having 2, **WEC** 1 (40 students), and **GMU** 1, etc. Pray for the calling and equipping of men truly called of God. Pray also for the many TEE courses run by a number of churches and missions, for this is beginning to make a significant impact on local leadership.

4) **The Roman Catholic Church** has moved from bigotry to indifference and now to an embracing of the charismatic movement. This has had a dual effect – some groups have clung even more closely to church dogma, and others have become evangelical in experience and doctrine. There are over 100 such groups in Bogota alone. The upper and middle classes seem to be more affected – groups largely untouched by Evangelicals.

5) **Missions** number over 50, with about 850 missionaries. More and more the role of missionaries has become one of support for the national Church in every field – pray for a happy, profitable and blessed partnership between missionaries and nationals. Much work still awaits both the pioneer and church-support missionary.

6) **Missions have come under pressure from the government** since 1976. It looks as if there will now be a quota system applied to the number of missionaries each society may have. Also missions working among the tribal Indians have come under severe attack by anthropologists and government officials, and all is in a state of flux at time of writing (Dec. 1976). Pray that no hindrances will be placed on the ministries of the Lord's servants.

7) **Work among the Indians was forbidden in 1953**, but this later fell away in answer to prayer. Pray that the threatened banning may not occur again. Only 25 of the 70 tribes have groups of believers and translation work is far from complete. **WBT** (225 missionaries) is working in 43 tribes, **NTM** (68 miss.) in 5, **CMA** in 3, **WEC** in 2 and **TEAM** and **OMS** in 1. Only 3 languages have the N.T. and a further 17 have portions. There are still tribes unreached with whom missionaries are seeking to make their first contacts in their inaccessible forests.

8) **Student work** has been slow and hard until recently. 90% of the lecturers are Marxists. Yet God has been working and Bible study groups are now growing fast. Pray that many of these key intellectuals may be won for Christ – even those poisoned by the bitter teachings of Marx and Mao.

ECUADOR

BACKGROUND

Area: 292,000 sq. km. – dry coastal strip, central high mountains, jungle in east.
Population: 6,900,000. Annual growth 3.2%. People per sq. km. – 11. Literacy 70%.
Peoples: **Europeans** 10%, **Mestizos** 41%, **Negroes** 10%, **Chinese** 10,000. **Amerindians**

40% – the Quechua (largely in Andes) 3,000,000; and the 8 jungle tribes of the east 50,000.

Capital: Quito 650,000. Other major city: Guayaquil 840,000. Urbanisation 39%.

Economy: Great inequality between rich landowning upper class and the poor majority – especially the Quechua. Oil revenue bringing rapid development.

Politics: Military government rather unstable and unable to handle the land's grave social and economic problems. A return to civilian rule is planned.

Religion: **Attitude of Government** – there is freedom of religion.

      Roman Catholics 95% – weaker on the coast, but dominant in Sierra (Andes). Opposition to evangelicals formerly severe, but now slowly disappearing, due to the liberalising influences in the Church.

      Protestants 2.5%. Community 158,000. Membership 44,000. Denominations 40. Largest: Pentecostals (5) 9,000 members; **GMU** related Churches 7,500; Alliance Church **(CMA)** 4,000; SDAs 8,000. Evangelicals 2%. Present Protestant growth rate 15%.

Prayer Targets

1) **Ecuador long held the record for the smallest percentage of evangelical believers in Latin America**. This was due to the strong opposition of the Roman Catholic Church, divisions among believers and inefficient methods of outreach. This is now rapidly changing, though many areas of need remain – the rural areas, the upper and middle classes and the school and university students. There are open doors for Christian work and sections of the population are now receptive.

2) **The Protestant Church** has been both small and divided. Pray for a real spiritual unity among believers and a new evangelistic thrust with resulting church growth. There is now dramatic growth among the many Quechua (see below) and also good progress in the cities through the witness of several Pentecostal groups, the **GMU and CMA**. Yet the real breakthrough among the Spanish speaking Mestizos and Whites has not yet come.

3) **There is a mighty move of the Spirit among the long oppressed Quechua people**, resulting in rapid church growth, moral uplift and the development of the latent talent and leadership gifts of these descendants of the ancient Incas. In 1967 there were but 120 believers among nearly 3,000,000 people, but now there are over 10,000 baptised believers and a community of 25,000+! Pray for the **GMU** and **CMA** missionaries who have worked for years for this harvest, and pray that they may know the mind of the Lord as how best to help this growing work.

4) **The Quechua Church** has some fine leaders, but most lack training. **GMU** now have a remarkable TEE programme with over 900 Quechua leaders studying the Word. Pray for the maturing of this Church and its growing outreach to other provinces, the cities and even to Quechua in Colombia. The Church urgently needs literature, and also the believers await the completion of the Old Testament. Pray for the integration of the Quechua Church into national life and for the Spanish speaking peoples to be blessed by this fellowship.

5) **Missions** – there are more than 37 agencies with 710 missionaries (about one third with the international ministries of HCJB – see below). The largest interdenominational groups are **GMU, CMA** and **OMS**. Missionaries are needed in all population groups for pioneer and church-support ministries, as well as in technical fields such as Bible translation and radio. Especially needed are workers for the unreached middle and upper classes and also school and university students for which very little is being done. Pray for the new evangelistic thrust by workers of **GMU** and HCJB to high schools planned for 1977.

6) **The radio ministry of HCJB is known and appreciated both in Ecuador and world wide.** The **World Radio Missionary Fell.**, with 270 expatriates, prepares and transmits 50 programmes a day in 19 languages internationally, as well as running a very valuable coverage of Ecuador through both radio and television. Pray for this ministry and the extensive follow-up work that the large response necessitates.

7) **The pioneer work among the small jungle tribes** attracted worldwide attention in 1956 when 5 missionaries were killed by the primitive 500 strong Aucas. Nearly the

whole tribe has subsequently been converted to Christ. **WBT, CMA and GMU** work among these tribes (numbering about 8). The work has been slow and hard, but the larger Jivaro tribe (25,000) is now beginning to turn to the Lord **(GMU)**. Pray for the continuing work of Bible translation and church planting. There are probably only one or two small unreached tribes yet to be contacted by missionaries.

PARAGUAY

BACKGROUND

Area:	407,000 sq. km. Paraguay River divides the more developed west from the Gran Chaco – an undeveloped region of marshes, forests and ranches.
Population:	2,600,000. Annual growth 2.7%. People per sq. km. – 7. Literacy 68%.
Peoples:	Some **Europeans**, mostly **Mestizos** of Guarani Indian and Spanish descent. **Indian tribes** 2% – 14 small groups totalling 45,000 – most in Chaco.
Capital:	Asuncion 400,000. Urbanisation 38%.
Economy:	Landlocked, underdeveloped and poor, with much exploitation of the Guarani and other Indian tribes.
Politics:	Virtually one party government.
Religion:	**Attitude of Government** – Roman Catholic Church is the official Church. There is religious freedom for other groups, but with some harassment of church groups working for the betterment of the Indians. **Roman Catholics** 95%. **Protestants** 2%. Community 52,000. Membership 31,000. Denominations 15 – largest: Mennonites 3,000; Anglicans 1,500; New Testament Churches 3,000; Pentecostals 4,000; Baptists 2,000. Evangelicals 1.6%. Growth rate 11%.

Prayer Targets

1) **The work of the Lord in Paraguay is generally discouraging**. The growth of the churches has not always been healthy and there is considerable evangelical nominalism due to an overemphasis on institutional work in the past. Pray for the effective evangelisation of this needy and troubled land.

2) **The Protestant Church is generally weak**, dependent on missionary funds and lacking in dynamic leadership and outreach. The 1976 Luis Palau Campaign in Asuncion was a real shot in the arm for the local denominations. There was much cooperation between the different denominations and many people were added to the churches. The Mennonities, Assemblies of God and the Baptists are doing a good work of evangelism. Pray that believers may have a burden to win the lost.

3) **Missions** – there are about 200 missionaries serving in the land. Many are tied to administrative and institutional work. More workers are needed for evangelism, church planting and leadership training. Pray for happy and harmonious relationships between missionaries and national workers – for there have been tensions in recent years. The largest missions are those of the South American Miss. Soc. (Anglican) with 21 workers and **NTM** with 67 workers – both majoring in work among the Indian peoples.

4) **Work among the Indians** has been fruitful in the west and south west, where God has used the witness of SAMS missionaries to bring a strong national Church into being. There have been significant people movements and now most of the tribes in the area are Christian, with national leaders of good calibre. The **NTM** missionaries have been sowing the Word in 7 tribes in the west and north west for some years, but the going has been hard and hindered by poverty, illiteracy and the oppression suffered by these peoples. Pray especially for the work among the Guayaki tribe. The **NTM** has come in for much unfair criticism from the press in the country. Bible translation continues in two languages, but three others await translators. Only two tribes have the N.T. and a further two have portions.

PERU

BACKGROUND

Area: 1,285,000 sq. km. Dry coastal strip (most of cities and industries), the Sierra or high plateau of the Andes (agricultural) and the tropical jungles of the upper Amazon in the east.

Population: 16,000,000. Annual growth 2.9%. People per sq. km. – 12.

Peoples: **European** 12%, **Mestizos** 41%, **Amerindians** 47% – two major groups:– Quechuas and Aymaras (7,350,000 people speaking 16 dialects) – since 1975 Quechua has been one of the two national languages.
Smaller tribes (50) – most living in the tropical forests of Amazon.

Economy: Reforms in economy, land tenure and education drastically transforming the land, and lessening serious social injustices due to class and race prejudice.

Politics: Military government in power, having removed leftist military regime in 1976. Reforms continuing, but at a slower pace.

Religion: **Attitude of Government** – freedom of religion, but the official Roman Catholic Church favoured in many fields.
Roman Catholics 97% – still very dominant in the life of the country, though they have lost considerable popular support in recent years.
Protestants 2.4%. Community 382,000. Membership 109,000. Denominations 38. Largest:– SDAs 55,000 members; Assemblies of God 12,000; Other Pentecostals (5) 6,000; Evangelical Church (**EUSA** and **AEM**) 21,000; CMA Church 2,500; Brethren 2,000. Growth rate per year 65%. Evangelicals 1.2%.

Prayer Targets

1) **Peru is a land of great spiritual need** and one of the less well evangelised in S. America. Areas of special need are the great shanty towns that ring the coastal cities, the rural areas and the Quechua and Aymara of the Sierra. The people are more open than ever before – largely because of the lessened power of the Roman Catholic Church and the disturbing social upheavals of recent years. Pray for Peru to be effectively evangelised. Pray that both Peruvians and expatriates may catch a vision for the evangelisation of this land.

2) **The Spanish speaking churches are growing** and many new churches are being planted by different denominations. Yet there is a lack of a spirit of prayer and power because of internal divisions, denominational jealousies and sin in individual members and leaders. Lay leaders in some churches are doing a good work in the churches, but there is a lack of good, spiritual, Bible-loving pastors. Pray for a greater spiritual depth, the calling of men into the service of the Master and, above all, for revival.

3) **The increasing political awareness of the people** and the growth of Marxist thought has led many ministers into political agitation rather than preaching the Gospel. Other evangelical leaders have tended to isolate themselves from the burning issues of the day. Pray for a right balance among Christian leaders and a right relationship with the Lord Jesus.

4) **The Quechua Church** is now more mature than the Spanish speaking Church and is growing. Generally the Quechua work is hard, due to centuries of oppression resulting in prejudice, mistrust of things foreign, malnutrition, lack of medical care and apathy. Pray for the work of **RBMU** and **EUSA** among these people, and pray for the calling of others to join the pitifully small band of missionaries seeking to evangelise these people and train the needed church leaders.

5) **Leadership training** – pray especially for the interdenominational Lima Seminary (**EUSA, RBMU, AEM**, etc.) and other Bible Schools giving a residential training to future pastors. Pray also for the TEE programme, so needed, but hampered by lack of missionary and national staff, the right materials and also the interest of those most needing it.

6) **Missions** – about 46 agencies with 700 missionaries. Many work in the eastern Indian

tribes which make up 1% of the population. Missionaries are now under considerable pressure from the press and the government – especially North Americans. This is partly because of the objectionable activities of the many Watchtower and Mormon missionaries, and partly the suspicions of many for U.S. missionaries that they may be spies for their government (one of the tragic outworkings of the Watergate scandal). The 145 missionaries of **WBT** working in 35 tribes were almost expelled in 1976, and all U.S. missionaries are experiencing serious difficulties in obtaining visas. Pray about this delicate situation. The need for reinforcements for the depleted missionary force has never been greater – pray especially for the critical need of **EUSA** in this respect.

7)   **The tribal Indians of the jungle** – about 41 tribes are now occupied and translation work has been initiated in all these languages. Pray for missions and national workers as they seek to continue evangelisation and translation ministries among these many small tribes. Pray for the emergence of strong churches among them, for as yet there is little visible fruit in more than a few tribes. Pray for the work of **RBMU**, S. American Indian Mission and the Swiss Indian Mission labouring in this field.

8)   **The witness among university students** is vital for the future of the Church in Peru. The 105,000 students are constantly involved in violence and strikes because of their intense political feelings – usually Marxist, but divided between loyalty to Peking and Moscow. The ABU (**IVF**) groups are small and number about 13 in the 35 universities, but are growing due to a greater openness among students. Pray for the two national staff workers and their ministry as they seek to establish groups in universities. Pray that these groups may provide many leaders for the churches in times to come.

URUGUAY

BACKGROUND

Area:	187,000 sq. km. – a small buffer state between Brazil and Argentina.
Population:	3,000,000. Annual growth 1.1%. People per sq. km. – 16. Literacy 80%.
Peoples:	**Europeans** 90% (Spanish and large minority of Italians), **Mestizos** 10%. There are no Amerindians.
Capital:	Montevideo 1,200,000 – but 50% of population live in its environs.
Economy:	Largely agricultural; suffering from severe inflation due to overspending on a very extensive welfare state system and the oil price rises.
Politics:	A long record of democratic government. Present military backed government has finally defeated the troublesome Communist urban terrorist movement.
Religion:	**Attitude of Government** – freedom of religion.
	Roman Catholics 90% – influence waning in face of materialism, disillusionment and anti-Christian ideologies.
	Jews 1.6%.
	Protestants: 2.1%. Community 63,000. Membership 36,000. Denominations 18. Largest: All Pentecostals (3) 8,000; Waldensians 6,000; Methodists 2,800; Baptists 2,200. Evangelicals 1.3%. Annual growth rate – 7%.

Points for Prayer

1)   **Uruguay is a needy land** with a reputation for pleasure loving and loose living. There are more atheists in this land than in any other in Latin America. The welfare state dulls the spiritual concern of the unconverted and the sense of responsibility of the believers. Yet there has been a noticeable increase in interest in spiritual things as a result of the unsettled political situation. Pray for the long awaited harvest of souls in this day of opportunity.

2)   **There are many areas and groups** in the land that have been inadequately reached with the Gospel – the rural areas, many of the city districts, the Jews and the virtually untouched student population. The **CCC** have a small but poorly led group in the universities; its impact is limited.

3) **The Protestant Church** has been more plagued by liberal theology than any other Latin American country – yet some of the churches thus affected have been seeing their mistake and there is a welcome return to more evangelical and Biblical preaching.

4) **The evangelical witness** is strongest among the Pentecostals (the most rapidly growing group), Baptists and the faith missions such as WEC, WEF and the South American General Mission. There is growth, but spiritual depth and enthusiasm is lacking. Pray that prevailing apathy may be swept away by revival. There is also a need for unity among believers of different groups. Pray for the Luis Palau campaign planned for the beginning of 1978 – that this may bring about that needed unity and also a reaping of souls.

5) **Leaders of stature** are woefully few. There are also very few young men willing to pay the cost of following the Lord by going into full time service. There is no interdenominational Bible School where leaders may be trained.

6) **Missions** – about 18 agencies with about 150 missionaries. The great need is for teaching missionaries rather than pioneer evangelists. The Church needs to be both taught and inspired to do the job of reaching out itself.

7) **Pray for the expanding literature ministry** of CLC with two bookstores as these brethren seek to supply Christian literature to this needy, literate nation.

VENEZUELA

BACKGROUND

Area: 912,000 sq. km. – bordering on Colombia, Brazil and Guyana.
Population: 12,300,000. Annual growth 2.9%. People per sq. km. – 13. Literacy 80%.
Peoples: **Europeans** 21%, **Mestizos** 65%, **Negroes** 7%. **Amerindians** 7% – 6 tribes on the coast, and a further 26 in the interior.
Capital: Caracas 2,200,000. Urbanisation 75%.
Economy: Relatively wealthy through export of oil. Oil revenues being used to diversify economy and build up industry.
Politics: Rather unstable, with the Communists becoming more vocal and powerful.
Religion: **Attitude of Government** – Roman Catholicism is the official religion, but all faiths permitted.
                 Roman Catholics 95%.
                 Protestants 2.4%. Community 300,000. Membership 153,000. Denominations 16. Largest groups: All Pentecostals (5) 35,000; Brethren 14,000; Bethel Evangelical 9,000; Baptists 2,800; TEAM 4,500. Annual rate of growth 14%. Evangelicals 1.3%.

Prayer Targets

1) **There is an open door for the Gospel** and after years of little growth the churches are moving ahead. Yet clouds of uncertainty hang over the land. Pray that believers may use present opportunities to the full.

2) **The churches**, although growing, are weakened by prevalent materialism in this relatively wealthy land. In 1975-76 a new surge of growth was discernible. This growth is greatest among the Pentecostals and the Brethren. Pray for a deeper and more humble walk with God among believers – superficiality is all too common.

3) **Leadership in the Church** – there are too few national leaders of high calibre who are really prepared to take on responsibility. There is a continual loss of pastors to secular employment, and many who supplement their income with a part time job. Pray for the calling of more into the Lord's work who are prepared to take up their cross.

4) **Missions** – about 25 agencies with about 490 missionaries are currently serving in the land. The better known church planting interdenominational missions are TEAM (97 missionaries), WEC (13), Orinoco River Mission (80) whose major ministry is to the Spanish speaking majority. Missions still suffer from the legacy of strong anti-foreign

sentiments and violent opposition of the R.C. Church at the turn of the century which forced a greater isolation between missionaries and the people than is usual in Latin America. Only now are the resulting difficulties in missionary-national relationships fading away. Pray for these relationships to become very close and fruitful.

5) **The need for missionary reinforcements** is not easily met, for visas for new and returning missionaries are not readily obtained. Pray for the calling and entry of expatriates. Pray for such who will be able to completely identify with the people and thereby be profitable in the needed ministries of evangelism, church planting, teaching and literature, etc.

6) **Christian literature** is now extensively used in this largely literate country. The need for more evangelistic and teaching literature is immense – both to win and disciple the people. This literature may be crucial for the future development of the Church should persecution come. Pray for the witness of the **CLC** bookstores.

7) **The witness among the Indian tribes** is rather limited, since many of the tribes have been assigned to Roman Catholic missions and are therefore closed to an evangelical witness. The **NTM** have now 80 missionaries serving in 5 tribes in the south, the Orinoco River Mission in 3 tribes in the east, and also **TEAM** in 2 other tribes. The **MAF** plane is an essential part of this programme. Pray for these brethren and their work as they seek to plant strong indigenous churches among them. Pray that these tribal churches may be adequately prepared for the inevitable impact of the encroaching Spanish culture and all the trappings of "civilisation".

IX. PACIFIC (Australia & Oceania)

This area consists of the continent of Australia, the large islands of New Guinea (excluding the western half which is part of Indonesia) and New Zealand, and several thousand small islands in over 30 major island groups.

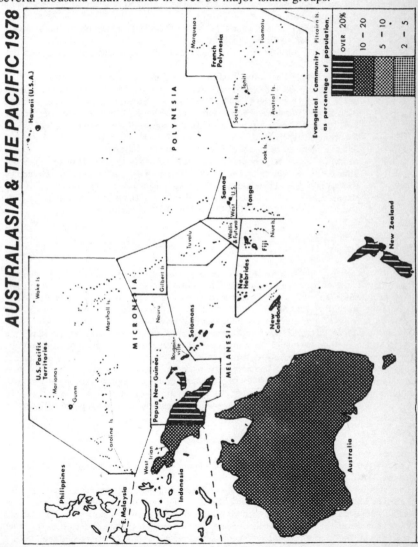

AUSTRALASIA & THE PACIFIC 1978

Evangelical Community as percentage of population.

OVER 20%

10 – 20

5 – 10

2 – 5

BACKGROUND

Area:	8,499,000 sq. km. This is 5.9% of the world's land surface.
Population:	21,555,000. Annual growth 1.8%. People per sq. km. – 2.5 only.
Peoples:	**Europeans** 77% – largely Australia and New Zealand, and mostly of British descent. Totalling 16,685,000 people.
	Melanesians (Melanesia meaning "black islands") 16.3%. New Guinea, Solomons, New Hebrides, New Caledonia and Fiji (3,526,000 people). A further one million Melanesians live in the Indonesian part of N.G.
	Polynesians ("many islands") 3.8% (818,000) – New Zealand and islands of the central Pacific.
	Micronesians ("small islands") 0.91% (196,000) – living on the many small islands on, or north of, the Equator.
	Asians 1.8% – Indians in Australia and Fiji, Chinese scattered throughout the region.
	Urbanisation 71% – only 2 cities with a population over one million.
Economy:	Australia and New Zealand very wealthy and with much development potential in industry and agriculture. New Guinea is underdeveloped. The smaller islands are poor, overpopulated and with very little chance of further development. There is much inter-island migration with many seeking work in the more prosperous areas.
Politics:	All but a few of the smaller island groups are independent.
Religion:	**Animists** 1.1% – largely in New Guinea and the Solomons. **Hindus** 2%, **Muslims** 0.4%, **Buddhists** 0.2%, **Jews** 0.4%. **Roman Catholics** 27%, **Orthodox Churches** 1.9%. **Protestants** 60%. Evangelicals 17%. Missionaries to the Pacific 3,558. Missionaries from the Pacific 4,320. Of these 3,700 are English speaking and approx. 620 Melanesian or Polynesian.

The Coming of the Gospel

The islands of the Pacific were one of the first areas to be evangelised by Protestant missionaries at the beginning of the modern missionary movement. The L.M.S. sent their first missionaries to Tahiti in 1796. Few areas of the world have claimed the lives of so many missionaries through violent death, cannibalism and disease. The task of the missionaries was made no easier by the appalling behaviour of unscrupulous European traders who terrorised and enslaved the islanders right until the end of the 19th century. This generated a very great hatred and mistrust of the European and added to the dangers the missionaries faced. Nevertheless, there were great movements of people to the Lord in which whole islands became Christian. In the last century most of the smaller islands became Christian and this movement has continued in this century in New Guinea and the Solomons. Although Papua-New Guinea was one of the last great primitive pioneer mission fields in the world, this young nation has probably the highest percentage of evangelical believers of any in the world!

The Present Spiritual Situation

The present spiritual state of Australia and New Zealand mirrors that of the rest of the Western World.

The Islands of Melanesia and Polynesia, evangelised in the last century, need rivival, for emigration and nominalism are sapping the spiritual life of the churches. There is a considerable drift away from the churches and the missionary vision that made these churches famous in the last century has waned. These islanders played a very important role in the evangelisation of the Pacific and some still serve the Lord in New Guinea.

The Papua-New Guinea Church is large and is beginning to face the same problem of nominalism among the third generation Christians on the coast. The astonishingly complex linguistic situation could give many troubles in the future. A considerable number of missionaries have gone out from these churches to evangelise the primitive tribes of the interior.

Areas of need

1) **Unevangelised areas** – some tribes in the interior of New Guinea.
2) **Under-evangelised areas** – there are very few evangelical believers in New Caledonia, Tahiti and relatively few in the New Hebrides.
3) **Bible translation** – the huge variety of languages that are spoken by just a handful of people make it problematic as to which languages to translate. Much is now being done, but more translators are needed.
4) **Bible teaching and leadership training** – diversity of languages and lack of the Bible in the local languages makes the instruction of believers harder, and strange sects have arisen as a result.

AUSTRALIA

BACKGROUND

Area: 7,682,000 sq. km. This island-continent is largely grassland and desert in the interior, but well watered in the east, south east and south west coastal regions.

Population: 13,800,000. Annual growth 0.9% natural, 0.6% immigration. People per sq. km. – 2.

Peoples: **British** origin 86%, **other Europeans** 13%, some Indians, Chinese and Turks. **Australian Aborigines** 1% in 200 tribes – but now only 40 languages used.

Capital: Canberra 150,000. Other cities: Sydney 3,000,000; Melbourne 2,700,000. Urbanisation 86%.

Politics: Wealthy and expanding economy with a parliamentary democracy.

Religion: **Roman Catholics** 30%.
            Various Orthodox Churches 3%.
            Protestants 60% – Anglicans 30% of population, Methodists 9%, Presbyterians 8%, Baptists 1.3%, etc. Evangelicals 14%.

Prayer Targets

1) **A national turning to God is needed,** for the same materialism, permissiveness and revolt against all authority characteristic of the whole Western World is just as discernible here. Pray for the Festival of Light as it seeks to mobilise public opinion to prevent many of these excesses from being legalised and practised.
2) **The churches** are losing people and church attendances are gradually falling in all but a few denominations. A union of the Presbyterians, Methodists and Congregationals planned for 1977 is provoking much bitterness and greater divisiveness, and the new United Church will probably have a very small evangelical witness within it. Some of the smaller and more evangelical groups continue to grow and the evangelical voice is becoming more powerful. There is a mood of optimism and there is now an aggressive evangelistic outreach. The Sydney diocese of the Anglicans is a centre of evangelicalism and national and missionary outreach.
3) **The missionary vision of the Australian believers** has been good and there are now about 2,500 Australians serving among the Aborigines in the South Pacific and all over the world. Pray for these brethren who have gone out to serve the Lord.
4) **Unreached peoples**
   a) **Many Australians live in isolated mining and farming communities** in the vast interior and are neglected spiritually and are also hard to reach.
   b) **New Australians** come from many lands such as Italy, Greece, Yugoslavia, Poland, Turkey, etc., where the true Gospel is little known, or even banned. Pray that such may be evangelised and that the churches may become more involved in this ministry. Pray that more believers from among these people may be able to return to their own lands of origin as missionaries, as some have already done.
   c) **The 110,000 aborigines** are a despised people who have sunk into moral and spiritual degradation through contacts with Western culture, or retreated to the more inac-

cessible and inhospitable regions of the country. Only a few have managed to adapt and become fully absorbed into national life. **The Christian witness** among them has not yet brought a strong Church to life, though there are 126 missionaries with 26 mission agencies seeking to witness to them and translate the Scriptures. This work is much hindered by their love for a nomadic life, the adverse effects of the dominant Western culture, poverty and the smallness of the tribes. **Bible translation** is in progress in 12 of these small language groups, 16 languages have at least a portion of the N.T., but 18 still need translators. **Gospel Recordings** have made records in 66 of these languages. There is a newly established **Aborigines Evangelical Fellowship** – pray that this may help Aborigine believers to develop an effective leadership and outreach programme to bring Biblical growth to the little churches among them.

5)   **The student witness.** The **IVF** has a good witness in all of the 18 universities. **The Inter-Schools Christian Fellowship (IVF)** seeks to build up a good evangelical witness in secondary schools, but in some of the states it is legally difficult to run Christian groups in schools. Pray for both wisdom and effectiveness under these conditions. Many young people's organisations maintain an active programme of outreach and fellowship for young people, such as **SU**, etc.

NEW ZEALAND

BACKGROUND

Area:	269,000 sq. km. Two large islands south east of Australia.
Population:	3,200,000. Annual growth 2.2% (1.1% by immigration). People per sq. km. – 12.
Peoples:	**Europeans** 88% – almost entirely from the British Isles.
	Maoris 8% – a Polynesian People, the original inhabitants.
	Polynesians 3% – are mostly immigrants from Pacific Islands to the north.
Capital:	Wellington 350,000. Largest city Auckland 800,000. Urbanisation 81%.
Economy:	Prosperous and largely dependent on the export of agricultural produce.
Politics:	Parliamentary democracy aligned with the Western world.
Religion:	Freedom of religion.
	Roman Catholics 17%. **Mormons** 1%.
	Protestants 65% – Anglicans 33% of population, Presbyterians 22%, Methodists 7%, Baptists 1.8%, Brethren 1%. There is a planned union between Anglicans, Presbyterians, Methodists, Congregationals and Churches of Christ. Evangelicals 22%.

Prayer Targets

1)   The spiritual climate closely parallels that of the British Isles, with similar denominations, para-church organisations, etc. **New Zealand needs a national awakening** to stem the rising tide of permissiveness and decline in many denominations.

2)   Although many of the denominations have a **strong liberal element**, there are significant evangelical groups that are growing, though if the planned United Church becomes a reality, many of these evangelical groups will form their own denominations. There are the same divisions and tensions within the Evangelicals of the various denominations as in Britain – over Calvinism, Arminianism and the charismatic movement. **The charismatic movement** has had a greater impact on nearly all denominations than in any other country in the English speaking world. There is a growing spirit of expectancy and optimism among Evangelicals that God is going to do great things. Pray for these believers.

3)   **The missionary vision of the New Zealand Church** has resulted in one of the highest national average of missionaries to population in the English speaking world. Pray for the continued nurture of this concern.

4)   **The Maori Church** is lacking in spiritual and well educated ministers. There are tensions due to the common Maori confusion between true Christianity and the

Western culture that brought it. This has resulted in a lack of spiritual depth in orthodox Protestant Churches and also the rise of several syncretic sects such as the Ratana (30,000) and Ringatu (6,000). Sadly the Mormons have been very successful in leading many Maoris astray with their doctrines, through their abundant funds and appeal to Maori traditional values. The Maori people need a deep work of the Holy Spirit in their midst.

5) **The immigrant Polynesian people** are nominally Christian, many coming from the New Zealand administered Cook (21,000) and Niue Islands (4,000); these people are mostly Congregationals. Other Polynesians come from other islands. These people need to be evangelised again, but tend to congregate in rather exclusive minority ghettoes. Auckland is the largest Polynesian city in the Pacific with nearly 100,000 Polynesian inhabitants.

PAPUA NEW GUINEA

BACKGROUND

Area: 456,000 sq. km. – the eastern half of New Guinea (866,000 sq. km.), the world's second largest island. Western half is part of Indonesia and now called Irian Jaya.
NOTE – many of the prayer points for PNG also apply to Irian Jaya, so references will also be made to the latter.

Population: 2,800,000. Annual growth 2.6%. People per sq. km. – 6. A further 1,000,000 people live in Irian Jaya (IJ).

Peoples: There are about 800 tribes in PNG and a further 300 in IJ, each with their own languages. Most languages spoken by a few hundred people, a few have more than 5,000 speakers, and only two have over 100,000 – the Highland **Danis** (200,000) in IJ and the **Enga** in PNG (120,000). Pidgin English in PNG and Indonesian in IJ are increasingly used by all.

Capital: Port Moresby 80,000. Urbanisation 11%. Literacy 35%.

Economy: Largey subsistence agricultural economy, but with considerable development.

Politics: Independent of Australia in 1975. Tribal and regional loyalties have raised secessionist groups in Bougainville Is. (One of Solomon Is. and rich in copper), and also in Papua (more developed S. half of PNG).

Religion: Freedom of religion – almost entire government professes to be Christian. **Animist** 7% – though many heathen ideas are still strong among "Christians". **Roman Catholics** 31%, **Protestants** 61% – **total Christian** 92%. Largest Protestant Churches: Lutheran 28% of population, United Church (LMS and Methodists) 15%, Anglicans 5%, Baptists 2%, Evangelical Churches associated with Evangelical Alliance (APCM-**UFM**, SSEM, **NTM**, etc.) 9%. Evangelicals 30%.

Prayer Targets

1) **There has been an amazing mass movement to Christ in New Guinea since 1945,** and now 92% of the people claim to be Christian in PNG, and a little less in IJ. The whole of society has been revolutionised by the Gospel – in earlier years in the coastal areas and more recently in the highland regions. Warring stone age tribes have become modern world citizens in the short space of 30–100 years.

2) **PNG is newly independent and faces immense problems** in keeping the country united and moulding the bewildering variety of tribes into a modern nation. Pray for peace and also for a deepening work of the Word of God in this Christian nation.

3) **Early missionaries suffered much** through disease and martyrdom, but the faithful work of these Western and South Sea Island missionaries has now borne abundant fruit. There are now 33 missions with over 2,100 Protestant missionaries in PNG. Much pioneer work is still being done by such interdenominational missions as **UFM** (Asia Pacific Chr. Miss.) and **WBT** in PNG and IJ; also SSEM and **NTM** in PNG,

CMA; **TEAM** and **RBMU** in IJ; though the main thrust of missionary work is now to train national leaders, help in adult literacy and literature programmes and serve in various help ministries.

4) **The churches** have grown dramatically as a result of a massive investment of manpower and technical skills by missions and resulting in rapid social changes through health and education ministries. Great people movements have brought hundreds of thousands into the churches – with the accompanying dangers of many not truly being converted and bringing heathen thought patterns, fears and superstitions into the churches. The number of trained national workers has grown to around 5–10,000, but this is totally inadequate to meet the need for Bible teaching and discipling these people. A number of strange "cargo" cults have risen and faded in which conversion and material blessings are equated.

5) **The young Church faces many problems** – the large number of languages, illiteracy among believers, a large generation gap between the older people and the better educated youth, rapid urbanisation and resulting loss of people from the churches and the lack of well trained pastors. There is also a growing division between some leaders of denominations espousing the ecumenical cause and the great mass of the people who are basically evangelical and evangelistic in outlook. There is also the above problem of a growing nominalism. There are, however, outstanding spiritual leaders in all denominations.

6) **Leadership training** is a problem in the churches where many of the leaders are often semi-literate. Many small tribal Bible Schools are run by missions, but there is the growing need for a better educated leadership. There are a number of denominational theological colleges (13) and also the fine Christian Leaders' Training College of APCM where leaders are trained for Evangelical Churches all over PNG. There are some good men now in training who should contribute much to the life of the churches, but there are many temptations for such to go into secular work in this land where there are few qualified people to run the country.

7) **The missionary vision of the PNG Church** needs to be enlarged to include other lands. National missionaries have played a decisive role in the evangelisation of most of the tribes of PNG and IJ – especial note must be made of the enthusiastic missionaries of the Dani tribe in IJ reaching out to many of the tribes in C. New Guinea.

8) **Unreached peoples are many**, but most are small and isolated. Many of these tribes still live in the stone age and are still bound by frequent wars, occasional cannibalism and fear of spirits and taboos, and need to be delivered from the tryranny of sin and degradation (in spite of the views of some anti-Christian "enlightened" Western anthropologists!). Pray for missionaries engaged in this difficult work of contacting tribes, seeking to evangelise them, plant a church and reduce the languages to writing for Bible translation, etc., in some of the most trying physical conditions in the world.

9) **The planes of MAF** are vital for the opening up of these unreached tribes. Pray for the **MAF** staff and their flying ministry to many missions. They have 17 planes and a helicopter in PNG (4 on the island of Bougainville). Pray for safety as they fly in cloud-covered, mountainous jungle areas for much of the time.

10) **Bible translation** is one of the most difficult and demanding ministries yet to be completed. There are 111 languages now being worked on in PNG and possibly 30 more in IJ. **WBT** is working in 83 languages in PNG alone, and most other missions also have a translation programme. Three languages now have the Bible, 25 the N.T. and a further 70 have portions – but this is only the beginning! Pray for wisdom for translators as to which languages need to be reduced to writing for Bible translation – for so many have but a few hundred speakers. Pray also for the essential accompanying literacy programmes to help the believers to be able to read that which is translated.

11) **Gospel Recordings** have performed the astonishing feat of making Gospel records in 680 of the languages of PNG and a further 168 of IJ. Pray for the ministry of these records – often the only ministry of evangelism possible to many of these small and illiterate tribes.

FIJI (Melanesia)

BACKGROUND

Area:	18,000 sq. km. – two larger and 104 smaller inhabited islands.
Population:	600,000. Annual growth 1.9%. People per sq. km. – 33.
Peoples:	**Fijians** (Melanesians) 42% and **Polynesians** 2%. Indians 50% – brought in by the British to work on the sugar estates. Now largely Hindi speaking, also Gujarathi, Tamil, Telugu speakers. **Minorities** – Europeans 1.3%, Mixed race 2%, Chinese 1%.
Capital:	Suva 60,000. Urbanisation 33%.
Economy:	Rather dependent on the growing of sugar.
Politics:	Independence from Britain in 1970. The Fijians retain political control, though in the minority. There is a delicate balance of power between the two communities.
Religion:	**Hindus** 35%, **Muslims** 6% – all being from the Indian community. **Christians** 50% (only 3% of the Indian community is Christian). **Roman Catholics** 8%. The Fijian community is almost entirely Christian. **Protestants** 42%. Community 200,000. Largest denominations: Methodists 39,000 members; SDAs 5,000; Anglicans 3,000; Assemblies of God 3,000; Christian Brethren. Evangelicals 20%.

Prayer Targets

1) **There is much potential for inter-communal violence** for the differences between the indigenous Fijians and immigrant Indians are so great. Pray not only for peace, but also for a loving concern among Fijian believers to work for the salvation of the Indians. There is only a little indication of this occurring.

2) **The Church among the Fijians** has been a mighty force for evangelism all over the Pacific area in the past. Pray for the present high degree of nominalism to be dissolved in the fires of revival. The Methodist Church claims 80% of all Fijians. Pray also for the smaller and more aggresively evangelical witness of the Assemblies of God and also for the smaller Brethren witness. The Ambassadors for Christ (Australia) have recently opened a Bible School – pray for this and all other institutions that train national leaders.

3) **The missionary vision of the Fijian Church** was great in the past, and over 270 missionaries have been sent out in the past 120 years to evangeliseother parts of Oceania – especially New Guinea, but there are not many today.

4) **The Indian people remain largely unreached**. For years this community was neglected and a good opportunity to evangelise them was missed. Both the Hindu and Muslim communities are now resistant to the Gospel. Pray that the small Christian Indian community may become an evangelistic force – most of the 5,000 or so Protestants among them belong to the Methodist Church and the Assemblies of God. Many of these believers are young converts. Pray for the evangelisation of these people and pray for the right strategy to be used in this.

SOLOMON ISLANDS

BACKGROUND

Area:	29,000 sq. km. – an island archipelago S.E. of New Guinea.
Population:	200,000. **Melanesians** 92%, **Polynesians** 6% speaking 78 distinct languages.
Capital:	Honiara 12,000.
Economy:	Underdeveloped and dependent on foreign aid, but has agricultural potential.
Politics:	Independent of Britain in 1977.
Religion:	**Animists** – pockets of spirit worshippers on most islands. **Roman Catholics** 18%, also a number of **Christo-Pagan sects**. **Protestants** 70% – Anglicans (East Solomons) 34,000 adherents; Methodists

(now part of United Church of PNG and Solomon Is.) 22,000 adherents; and South Seas Evangelical Church (SSEM) 48,000. Evangelicals 21%.

Points for Prayer

1) **This newly independent little nation** could have acute difficulties with island and tribal loyalties dividing it. Pray for continued peace and freedom for the Gospel.

2) **The Church is strong** and has many believers in all walks of life. There are some good spiritual Christian leaders who have influence far beyond these islands. The Holy Spirit has been working in the hearts of many over the last few years. The work of the South Seas Evangelical Church is expanding fast with 6 Bible Schools and hundreds of pastors and evangelists. There are 40 missionaries of the SSEM serving with this Church. There was revival in 1935 and 1970.

3) **The believers need discernment to know the true from the false** in a time when local and foreign sects are making great inroads among the people. They also need to be continually freed from tribalism and divisions within the churches.

4) **Bible translation** is a colossal problem with so many very small tribal groups. Pray for wisdom as to which languages need translation. Only one tribe has the whole Bible, 9 others have the N.T. and a further 9 have portions only. **WBT** are seeking to enter this field. There is a need for the Bible in Pidgin English.

NEW HEBRIDES

BACKGROUND

Area: 15,000 sq. km. – a group of 12 large islands S.E. of the Solomons.
Population: 90,000 – **Melanesians** 90% speaking over 100 languages. **Minorities** of French, Chinese and Polynesians.
Politics: Jointly administered by France and Britain, but economically dominated by Australia to the S.W. Independence likely in 1978.
Religion: **Roman Catholics** 14%.
                   Protestants 70% – Presbyterians (3) 54,000 community, Anglicans 13,000. Also several newer groups that are growing. Evangelicals 10%.

Points for Prayer

1) At great cost in life and effort, the Gospel was preached on most of these islands in the last century by the Presbyterians of Scotland, Australia and New Zealand. Nominalism is now very common and **an evangelical awakening is needed**.

2) **The Church** faces almost identical problems to the Solomon Islands (see above). The even smaller tribal groups of the New Hebrides make the instruction of believers, translation of the Scriptures and the building up of a strong unified Church very difficult. Two languages have the whole Bible, seven have the N.T. and 19 others have portions. There is translation work being done in two languages.

NEW CALEDONIA

Area: 19,000 sq. km. – a large 400 km. long island and other small ones east of Australia.
Population: 135,000 – **French** 39%, **Melanesians** 53%, **Polynesians** 8%, **Vietnamese** 3%.
Capital: Noumea 60,000.
Economy: Very rich in valuable minerals.
Politics: Overseas Territory of France.
Religion: **Roman Catholics** 63%.
                   Protestants 20%. Few heathen, but many of the Melanesians belong to the Christo-pagan "Cargo" cults. Evangelicals 3%.

Points for Prayer

1) **Many tribal and immigrant groups need to be evangelised.** French speaking missionaries are needed for pioneer work, Bible translation (only 6 of the 28 languages have anything of God's Word) and the planting of vigorous churches.

2) **The Protestant Church has some very keen leaders.** The Evangelical Church is less liberal theologically than its parent Reformed Church in France. The Free Evangelical Church is growing. Both have members among all race groups. There is need for revival, for the general level of spiritual life is low, due to the prevalent materialism. There is much laziness, drunkenness and immorality among the young people and the Christians are often tainted with this.

POLYNESIA

BACKGROUND

Area: 8,000 sq. km. – a large number of rugged volcanic islands or coral atolls covering a vast area of the Pacific.
NOTE: We exclude the U.S. State of Hawaii and the land of New Zealand which rightfully belong to Polynesia.

Peoples: **Polynesians** 850,000 (including 145,000 in Hawaii; 256,000 in N.Z.) speaking 16 languages and dialects. Total in our area 450,000.
Minority groups – 13,000 Asians in French Polynesia, some Europeans.

Politics: 5 political entities:–
West Samoa – Population 150,000; area 2,842 sq. km.; two largish islands. Independent of New Zealand in 1962. Member of British Commonwealth.
Tonga – Population 100,000; area 700 sq. km. Many small islands. Independent of Britain in 1970.
French Polynesia – Population 130,000; area 4,000 sq. km. There are 5 island archipelagoes – Society Is. (Tahiti the most famous) (106,000), Tuamotu Is. (7,000), Gambier Is. (8,000), Austral Is. (5,000) and Marquesas (5,000), an overseas department of France.
U.S.A. Territories – American Samoa – Population 30,000; area 197 sq. km.
British Territories – just a few very small island groups such as Pitcairn Is. with 71 people, etc.

Religion: All these island people are nominally Christian and have been so for over 100 years. There are few significant non-Christian religions.
Roman Catholics 24%.
Protestants 55%. **Evangelicals** 11%.

Prayer Targets

1) **These Polynesian peoples turned to the Lord in great people movements in the last century** – through the LMS (Congregational) in the Society Is. (later handed over to French Presbyterians), and Samoa and the Methodists in Tonga. Nominalism is very common, and revival is needed to stem the rise of materialism and the drift of the young into sin and away from the churches. Unemployment forces many to migrate to other lands where they lose all contact with churches.

2) **There are true believers to be found in these older churches**, but there is more life in some of the newer and smaller groups – especially the Assemblies of God, with about 4,000 adherents in the Samoas.

3) **Most needy areas** – especially the French islands. Although 66% of the people are reckoned to be Protestant and 33% Roman Catholic, sects such as the Mormons, Sanito (indigenous sect), etc., have made many converts. Tahiti has become infamous for immorality, gambling and drunkenness, and marriage as an institution hardly exists any more.

4) **The missionary vision of the Polynesian Church** was very great – the Gospel being carried by brave missionaries in the last century all over the Pacific – many lost their

lives at the hands of warlike cannibal tribes they sought to win for Jesus. This burden
has diminished, but there are still Tongan and Samoan missionaries serving in New
Guinea.

MICRONESIA

Area:	3,200 sq. km. – thousands of small coral islands covering an area of the Pacific Ocean almost as large as the Soviet Union, the world's largest country. There are 5 separate political entities.
Population:	280,000.
Peoples:	**Micronesians** approx. 70% – speaking 15 separate languages. **Polynesians** 3% – Tuvalu (Ellice Is.) and some on Nauru. **Immigrant minorities** 27% – Filipinos, Spanish and Americans on Guam, and Chinese and Europeans on Nauru.
Economy:	Poor and isolated but for the phosphate rich Nauru and military base of Guam.
Politics:	**United States Commonwealth** of Marianas, Marshalls and Carolines added to Guam after plebiscite of 1976. Population 220,000 (Guam 110,000). **British Colonial Rule** Gilbert Is. (55,000) and Tuvalu (Ellice Is.) (7,000). Total land area only 226 sq. km. **Independent Republic** – Nauru 8,000 – the world's smallest state.
Religion:	**Guam** – Roman Catholic with some Baptists (2,000) and Assemblies of God (300). **Marianas, Marshalls** and **Carolines** – United Church and Lutherans with smaller groups of Assemblies of God (1,000) and Liebenzell Mission. **Gilberts** – Congregationals with a few Pentecostals. **Tuvalu** – Anglicans. **Nauru** – majority Congregational. Evangelicals 11% (approx.).

Prayer Targets

1) **These islands have been Christianised** but after a century or more, nominalism is commonplace. All the larger language groups have the N.T or Bible. These islands need a fresh visitation from the Lord. Evangelism is needed but the smallness and isolation of these many islands do not help the evangelist. The most effective evangelistic outreach in the U.S. islands is that of the Assemblies of God.

2) **Many islands have no effective witness for the Lord** – especially the nominal Christians and others of the Gilberts, Tuvalu and Nauru.

3) **The immigrant minorities** of Chinese in Nauru, Filipinos and Vietnamese, etc., in Guam, need to hear the Gospel in a way that is culturally attractive to them.

4) **Christian Radio** – TWR have set up a powerful broadcasting station on Guam for reaching both the local islands and also the lands of East Asia. Pray for this.

Workers and groups in the Western World (N. America and Europe) for whom I will pray:

Workers and groups in the Communist Bloc for whom I will pray:

Workers and groups in Asia for whom I will pray:

Workers and groups in Africa for whom I will pray:

Workers and groups in the Middle East for whom I will pray:

Workers and groups in Latin America for whom I will pray: